Cooperative Flourishing in Plato's 'Republic'

A Theory of Justice

Also available from Bloomsbury

Aristotle and the Ethics of Difference, Friendship, and Equality, by Zoli Filotas
Beyond Hellenistic Epistemology, by Charles E. Snyder
Platonism and the Objects of Science, by Scott Berman
Rewriting Contemporary Political Philosophy with Plato and Aristotle, by Paul Schollmeier
Virtue Ethics and Contemporary Aristotelianism, edited by Andrius Bielskis, Eleni Leontsini and Kelvin Knight

Cooperative Flourishing in Plato's 'Republic'

A Theory of Justice

Carolina Araújo

BLOOMSBURY ACADEMIC
LONDON • NEW YORK • OXFORD • NEW DELHI • SYDNEY

BLOOMSBURY ACADEMIC
Bloomsbury Publishing Plc
50 Bedford Square, London, WC1B 3DP, UK
1385 Broadway, New York, NY 10018, USA
29 Earlsfort Terrace, Dublin 2, Ireland

BLOOMSBURY, BLOOMSBURY ACADEMIC and the Diana logo are trademarks
of Bloomsbury Publishing Plc

First published in Great Britain 2023
This paperback edition published 2024

Copyright © Carolina Araújo, 2023

Carolina Araújo has asserted her right under the Copyright, Designs and
Patents Act, 1988, to be identified as Author of this work.

For legal purposes the Acknowledgements on p. xi constitute an extension
of this copyright page.

Cover image: Meu Limão (detail), Beatriz Milhazes, Acrylic on canvas, 249 x 320 cm
Photo: Manuel Águas & Pepe Schettino (© Beatriz Milhazes Studio)

All rights reserved. No part of this publication may be reproduced or transmitted in any form or by any means, electronic or mechanical, including photocopying, recording, or any information storage or retrieval system, without prior permission in writing from the publishers.

Bloomsbury Publishing Plc does not have any control over, or responsibility for, any third-party websites referred to or in this book. All internet addresses given in this book were correct at the time of going to press. The author and publisher regret any inconvenience caused if addresses have changed or sites have ceased to exist, but can accept no responsibility for any such changes.

A catalogue record for this book is available from the British Library.

A catalog record for this book is available from the Library of Congress.

ISBN: HB: 978-1-3502-5703-0
PB: 978-1-3502-5707-8
ePDF: 978-1-3502-5704-7
eBook: 978-1-3502-5705-4

Typeset by Deanta Global Publishing Services, Chennai, India

To find out more about our authors and books visit www.bloomsbury.com and
sign up for our newsletters.

For Flora and Joaquim
source of joy and light

When a man from Seriphus criticized him by saying
that his reputation was due, not to himself,
but to his city, Themistocles replied that,
indeed, had he been from Seriphus, he wouldn't be famous,
but neither would that man, had he been an Athenian.
(*Rep.*, 329e6-330a1)

Contents

List of tables	x
Acknowledgements	xi
Introduction	1

Part One Interaction

1	Desire and reasoning	19
2	*Thumos*	30
3	Unreasonable belief	37
4	Cognition	48
5	Power	58
6	Personality	68

Part Two *Politeia*

7	Thrasymachus	79
8	Socrates against Thrasymachus	89
9	Evil	99
10	Reasons for a city	109
11	Justice	118

Part Three Citizens

12	Popular virtue	131
13	Community	143
14	The good	153
15	Philosopher-King	163
16	Kallipolis	174
17	Flourishing	187

Conclusion	203
References	207
Index nominorum	224
Index locorum	236

Tables

1	The Principle in *Republic* IV	23
2	The Division of Goods in *Republic* II	189

Acknowledgements

I owe my being a philosopher to the fertile soil of Universidade Federal do Rio de Janeiro, a stronghold of free public education in one of the most violent cities in the world. As I live, I am filled with gratitude to all my colleagues and students. In concluding this book, I had the enormous privilege of being cross-examined by philosophers Alice Haddad, Luisa Buarque, Admar Costa, Nelson Menezes Neto, Daniel Nascimento, Rodolfo Lopes and many other colleagues who took part in the *Sabatina Kallipolis*. I was also given the opportunity of being questioned by senior professors Maria das Graças de Moraes Augusto, Maria Isabel Santa-Cruz, Elena Garcia, Jacyntho Lins Brandão, Ulysses Pinheiro and Luiz Henrique Lopes dos Santos. I am deeply thankful to them.

The research that led to this book benefitted from various kinds of financial support from Capes, Cnpq and Faperj. I am also very thankful to Jade Grogan, who took this project under her care, to Yara Frateschi, who commented on some excerpts of the manuscript, and to Beatriz Milhazes for "Meu Limão".

Whatever I have done, it would not be any good without the love of Elizabeth Bomfim, Alcione Araújo, Flávio Friche, Francisco Gonzalez, Flora Costa and Joaquim Costa.

Introduction

The work of Plato called the *Republic* has the Greek name of *Politeia*, or *Politeiai* in the plural.[1] *Politeia* means the lifestyle of a citizen (the *politēs*), or all that is entailed in the concept of public behaviour for the inhabitant of a city-state (a *polis*). It is used in both a distributive sense, namely to designate the behaviour of each individual, and a holistic sense, namely to denote the characteristics of the entire city as a set of citizens. The term may therefore refer to social practices as well as to the formal institutions of the state, such as the government and constitution.

'Citizenship' is thus a perfectly adequate translation of the Greek title of Plato's dialogue. The first occurrence of the term *politeia* is found in Herodotus' *History*, IX, 34, 536 in the account of Tisamenus of Elis, where it is stated that the Lacedemonians granted him *politeiē* on account of an oracle of the god Apollo. Here, *politeiē* refers to all the rights and duties of a born citizen and thus 'citizenship'. Instead, the standard nomenclature of Plato's dialogue (*Republic*) comes from the title of Cicero's work, *De re publica*, which was formulated as a response to Plato's masterpiece. Cicero's term *Res publica* adequately renders the Greek *politeia* in its holistic and institutional sense, but, in doing so, introduces an inherent assumption that its central theme is the Constitution, the State or the Form of Government. In a Roman context, this rendering is intentional, for the alternative *ciuitas* (citizenship) would have a distributive meaning that would not correspond to Cicero's project. It is this emphasis on the institutional approach, however, which establishes a bias in how Plato's text is interpreted, and which, as I shall argue, causes his approach to be understood as a top-down project enacted by philosophers who aim to control the power of political decision-making.

Plato's *Politeia*, however, builds a theory of *citizenship*: it analyses what it means to live in a city; explains why this is important for human beings and their personal flourishing (*eudaimonia*);[2] argues that justice constitutes the excellence of citizens which, when pursued, engenders cooperative flourishing; and, finally, it identifies the formal institutions necessary to guarantee this kind of common life. In other words, Plato's *Republic* describes the different ways of being a citizen – the diverse *politeiai* – and seeks to determine which of them are the cause of our flourishing and why. A primary purpose of the present book is therefore to demonstrate

---

[1] The title of the *Republic* – *Politeia* – has been established since antiquity (see for instance Plato, *Timaeus*, 17c1-3; Aristotle, *Politics*, 1261a6), but some of the manuscripts record the title in the plural: see Westerink 1981: 112; Boter 1992: 82; Tarrant 2012: 1. For both the distributive and the holistic meaning, see Liddell, Scott, and Jones 1996: 1434; Bordes 1982: 14–18; Dawson 1992: 8; Wolff 2004: 963; Schofield 2006: 33. Most interpreters assume that the title intends the holistic meaning. Even Menn, who is very cautious in this matter, states that the genre of *politeia* is a 'normative study of how a city should be best *governed*' (Menn 2006: 4, my emphasis). For *ciuitas* being an adequate Latin translation for *politeia*, see Benveniste 1969: I, 335–7, 367 and Benveniste 1970: 594–5. For *politeia* as the way of life of the citizen, see Blössner 1997: 190, 2007: 369; Moraes Augusto 2012/3: 104–5.

[2] To understand Socrates' arguments in the *Republic*, it is crucial to realize that they are grounded in a concept of *eudaimonia* understood as flourishing rather than a notion of 'happiness' that may be mistaken for some conative conception of the good (see Anscombe 1958: 18; Foot 2001: 44; Kraut 2007: 156). This is not to deny that there are instances of *eudaimonia* in the latter sense – as 'prosperity' or 'success' – as Thrasymachus, for example, uses it (see Ostenfeld 1998: 74).

that, when Plato's concept of *politeia* is understood in this distributive sense, the text acquires a radically different profile to that presented on the standardly accepted interpretation.

The number of analyses of *politeiai* throughout fifth and fourth centuries BCE Greece was such that these prose treaties, dedicated to presenting and discussing the various mores and social institutions of different cities, came to constitute a literary genre on their own.[3] The approaches of these texts included praise, such as in Xenophon's *Politeia* (or Constitution) *of the Lacedemonians*; reproach as, for instance, in the *Politeia* (or Constitution) *of the Athenians* (a work of uncertain authorship nowadays attributed merely to an 'Old Oligarch'); and scientific interest – most notably in the systematic compilation of at least a hundred *Politeiai* attributed to Aristotle, of which only the *Politeia* (or Constitution) *of the Athenians* now remains. Other pre-Platonic non-extant *Politeiai* include the work of Hipodammus of Miletus, which is said to be the first of its genre; as well as by Phaleas of Chalcedon, Protagoras of Abdera and by Critias of Athens who dedicated his treatise to Sparta.

Across the genre is a persistent focus on the description of human and civic mores. The recurrent themes of these treatises include attitudes regarding sexual intercourse, marriage, the generation of children and their education, legitimate punishments, the societal role of women and the institution of slavery. They also describe details such as how to serve meals, how to care for one's own health and for the elderly, how to perform funerary practices, how to distribute the goods and to institute business contracts, etc. These matters evidently go far beyond mere institutional forms of government; they are details of human interactions – a diverse range of civic mores based on human choices that eventually become the basis of laws.[4]

It seems reasonable to consider Herodotus' writings as the legitimate predecessor to the genre. For in his *History* (III, 80-82, 1299-1370) we find the famous Constitutional Dialogue[5] which distinguishes between oligarchy, democracy and monarchy, not only by the formal criterion of number of rulers but also by the way of life of both rulers and ruled in each regime. As such, the Dialogue exhibits a common feature of the *politeiai* tradition, namely, the account of various peoples' diverse modes of life and their distinct political institutions, including those of the Persians, Egyptians, Scythians, Thracians, etc. (compare with T1 herein). Here, a *politeia* is a form tied to, and emergent from, the citizens themselves and is not restricted to the specific

---

[3] For *politeia* as a literary genre, see Bordes 1982: 126–227; Schofield 2006: 33; Menn 2006: 5–8. For the information on the non-extant *politeiai*, see Aristotle, *Politics*, 1267b22-1268a15; in particular 1267b29-30 for Hipodammus (see Shipley 2005: 335–403); Aristotle, *Politics*, 1266a39-b5, b31-38 for Phaleas; DK 88 B 32-37 for Critias; Diogenes Laertius, *Live of eminent philosophers*, IX, 55, 60 for Protagoras. In 443, in the context of the imperialist expansion by the foundation of new colonies, Protagoras was said have been invited by Pericles to write the constitution of Thurii (see Diogenes Laertius, *Lives of eminent philosophers*, IX, 50, 3–4 and Ehrenberg 1948: 165–70.) Some speculation comes from Diogenes Laertius, based on Aristoxenus, that Plato's *Republic* is a plagiarism of Protagoras, though of a work named *Antilogy* (Diogenes Laertius, *Lives of eminent philosophers*, III, 37, 420–1).

[4] The ambivalence of the term *politeia* reflects that of the term *nomos*, which is both mores (as *ēthos*) and positive law. Every human being has mores – they are intrinsic to the shared life that is natural to us; positive law is a convention and it should be established with our just mores as a primary reference (see Barker 1919: 185; Nettleship 1922: 54–7; Gagarin 1989: 53). For this reason, I sometimes favour the translation of *nomos* as 'mores', and adopt 'law' when context makes the meaning more restricted. On the interconnection of *politeia* and justice, see Proclus, *Commentary to Plato's Republic*, I, 11.5 ff.

[5] Romilly (1959: 81) maintains that the debate (until Plato) classifies regimes exclusively by the 'extension of sovereignty': a single individual, a group or the people as whole. However, the Constitutional Debate in Herodotus is not decided by the number of rulers but by factors such as the character of the ruler, the quality of life of the citizens in the regime, the political status of women, the conduct of trials, the position of citizens before the law, the justification of decisions, the efficiency in executing them and the level of use of force, so much so that the discussion that begins with the ailments of monarchy (in the form of tyranny) ends with the decision in favour of this same regime (Herodotus, *History*, III, 83, 1371–2).

political structure that becomes renowned as a Greek *polis*. It should therefore not come as a surprise that in the *Republic* the word *polis* stands for such different political organizations.

Based on the object of Herodotus' investigations and the extant treatises of the genre (including Plato's *Republic*), we must infer that a *politeia* is neither simply the institutional form of the State, the number or behaviour of rulers when in power, nor the basic framework of law (see Aristotle, *Politics*, 1289a15-18). Though all of these aspects are contributory, the concept of the *politeia* as a whole is significantly more than that: it is the complex result that emerges from the interaction of people living together.

One way to determine how all of these factors interrelate within a single subsumed type is to identify a predominant end of action (see Aristotle, *Politics*, 1289a16-18) that unifies the *politeia* with a single character. Classical understandings of the *politeia* in this sense are those of Isocrates – who identifies it as the 'soul' of the city – and of Aristotle, who terms it the city's 'life'.[6] For the latter, this understanding engenders a method of enquiry which is the equivalent to that of his Ethics (Aristotle, *Politics*, 1295a40-b1), since an enquiry into the *politeia* is also an enquiry on human flourishing, albeit of our life *in common*. Human flourishing is, as the epigraph of this book (329e6-330a1) states, deeply connected to the city we inhabit: humans are not isolated islands, but develop under the influence of the actions of others and of the community.

Aristotle justifies his methodological proposal by arguing that an enquiry into the *politeia* should consider the best way of life for human beings by taking into account people's ordinary manner: as a good *politeia* must have a feasible form in which most people can take part, exceptional circumstances should be disregarded in favour of the ordinary. He is not alone in insisting upon the feasibility, given that the tradition of *politeiai* ultimately had a practical purpose: endeavouring to change cities. Hipodammus, for instance, was a city planner who reformed the Piraeus and designed the new Athenian colony at Thurii. The laws of Thurii were subsequently commissioned by Pericles to a further *politeia* writer, Protagoras.

A related purpose, which, although sometimes implicit, is indicated as integral to the literary genre of *politeia* by Aristotle, is to establish the *best* alternative. Descriptions of *politeiai* are never unbiased: there consistently appears a framework of praise, reproach and normative proposals which are indicative of an evaluation of the best way of living. In attempting to specify which, among a diversity of mores, is the most desirable, a *politeia* describes the evils experienced by the people under certain civic regimes, and, in doing so, undertakes to persuade the reader that something must be done, even where it might leave open the question of *what*. Within these attempts at persuasion, it is the manner in which a particular *politeia* accounts for our human desires and our failures upon which the inferences about which course of action to take are founded. Here lies the affinity of the *politeia* genre with that of the pamphlet.

How might a *politeia* treatise succeed in this persuasion? Evidently there exists a great distance between the thoughts of an intellectual and the ordinary civic life: why, therefore, would people who already live in a certain way – through habits, mores and laws – relinquish their way of life in order to conform to this or that scholar's new proposal? It is in this context that the example offered by real cities – those that had obtained positive results in dealing with some of

---

[6] For Isocrates' definition of *politeia*, see Isocrates, *Areopagiticus* 14, 1–2 and *Panatenaicus*, 138, 9; see also Menn 2006: 10. For Aristotle's definition, see Aristotle, *Politics*, 1295a40-b1. Perhaps it would be more interesting to paraphrase this passage by saying that the *politeia* is the city's personality, for the term *bios* refers to the life of a person and not of a living being, for which Aristotle would certainly use *zoē* (see also Schofield 2006: 33). The prevailing end of a community is, according to Aristotle, what gives a *politeia* its unity and definition rather than its laws (Aristotle, *Politics*, 1289a15-18); I shall argue that this was a point already made in Plato's *Republic*. For the thesis that a *politeia* is defined by its laws, see Lane 2013: 112.

these human challenges – functioned as 'living proof' that it was worthwhile undertaking the Herculean task of changing civic laws and habits.

For this purpose, the 'Sparta case' was very persuasive. The pre-eminence of the Spartan model as a 'living proof' explains the influence of the laconizing approach in some *politeia* treatises. Some interpreters have gone so far as to employ it as evidence that the *politeiai* genre constituted a kind of pamphlet literature. To restrict the entire genre to mere praise of the Lacedemonians, however, would be a rushed conclusion: what we know of Hipodammus' work is difficult to frame in a laconic pattern, and neither the *Politeia of the Athenians* of the Old Oligarch nor the homonymous work by Aristotle expresses a particularly Spartan tone. Indeed, the emphasis on Sparta is more likely explained both by the original and unique character of its way of life and by the political importance the city gained during the Peloponnesian War, rather than a particular characteristic of genre.

This becomes evident in the aftermath of the war: when Sparta's vices became more evident than its virtues, 'living proof' gave way to 'rational proof', where persuading the reader depended on the inferences drawn from the investigation itself. The act of enquiry thus became more important than beliefs that one ought to do as X or Y. Indeed, as we have seen, a treatise on *politeia* differs from a pamphlet by virtue of being a theoretical investigation: it confronts cases, analyses concepts, makes inferences and reaches conclusions about the best way to live. This is, I argue, Plato's purpose in the *Republic*: to persuade by means of a rational proof. Although the dramatic date of the text places it during the war,[7] the work cannot be classed a pamphlet. It is, in fact, distinctly critical towards Sparta.

The strategy for persuasion unfolds, in broad brushstrokes, in four stages across the *Republic*. The first step (369c9-376d8) is to make the readers understand that they live in cities not because they fear injustice, but because life in common allows them to flourish. This stage is indicative of what it means to ground (or found) a city in arguments (a *polis logō*), that is, to justify it as something good for human beings. The second stage (376d9-427e8) is then to raise the readers' awareness that this first conclusion is not self-evident: not every city is necessarily a good one – in fact, the one they inhabit is most likely not. Although some of Socrates' interlocutors claim that it is preferable to occupy certain social positions in unjust cities, they all admit that, when this status is not an option, it is better simply to live in a just city. By exploiting this concession, Socrates demonstrates to the reader that it is always preferable to be just and to dwell among just people. The third stage of persuasion is then the enquiry about the sort of environment that is desirable (427e9-472e5) which constitutes an invitation to formulate a *politeia logō* (473d7-e1; 501e3), the good life of a citizen. In other words, it describes a way of life wherein citizens interact based on the reasons they have to live together. This reasoning implies that each citizen pursues their flourishing without hindering others from doing the same: the result is cooperative flourishing as the excellence of the citizens. The final step, once the reader has come to recognize the good *politeia*, is to investigate how to transform their own city, or better yet, the institutions which are necessary to obtain the best political life (472e6-544a1). Plato concludes that the most

---

[7] For the *Republic* as a laconic pamphlet, see Menn 2006: 10; Schofield 2006: 37–9; for being a general manifesto, see Annas 1981: 1–2. There are two distinct controversies about the dates of the *Republic*. One is about the dramatic date, which varies between 424 and 408 BCE (see the outline of the debate in Nails 1998: 383), and the other about the date of its composition, which varies between 390 and 350 BCE (see the different proposals in Thesleff 1982: 7–17). None of these possibilities deny that the scene is located at a date during the Peloponnesian War, while the composition may be located at a time of a decline in Spartan prestige, reflected in Socrates' criticism of Sparta (544c1-3, 545a3-547c8).

important institution is that which ensures that the *politeia* is constantly discussed, analysed, scrutinized and justified to the citizens at large.

This book thus asserts that the philosophical discussion which introduces the readers to the form of the *politeia,* and subsequently persuades them that it is the rationality intrinsic to this debate that produces the best political life is integral to how the *Republic* is framed. In order to do so, it argues for several theses about the text and its interpretation.

The first of these theses is, as already mentioned, that the dialogue is primarily an analysis of the flourishing of citizens in their diversity rather than an enquiry into the systems of government. In contrast to the standard theory propounded across contemporary interpretations, I propose not that the city in the *Republic* is a whole with normative power over its parts, but that Socrates builds his argument *from individuals* – specifically, from their principles of action – to spell out how cities and their rules subsequently emerge from them.

> [T1] Well then, I asked, is it necessary to agree that in each of us there are the same types (*eidē*) and customs (*ēthē*) that exist in a city? After all, there is nowhere else they would come from to get there. It would be ridiculous for anyone to think that the impetuous type has not arisen in cities from people who actually have such a principle (*aitia*), for example those living in the manner of (*kata*) Thrace, or Scythians or some other region up north; or the love for learning ascribed mainly to our region; or the love for riches[8], that someone would say exists mainly among the Phoenicians or those living in the manner of (*kata*) Egypt.
>
> It is very necessary, he said. (435d9-436a4)

The mention of Thracians, Scythians, Phoenicians, Egyptians and Athenians in T1 aims at contrast. The assertion that Thrace is spirited, Athens loves wisdom and Egypt loves riches is to be understood as the 'cities'[9] themselves that possess certain character traits, a 'soul' or 'personality' derived from the customs of people who inhabit them. Each of these peoples differ in their customs, differences through which it is possible to identify the distinct principles of action which cause them to vary: it is a brute fact that people simply act in contrasting ways (I realize that John did something I would not do in the same circumstance), and we attempt to account for people 'there' acting differently than 'here' through various explanations grounded in character and principles. Identifying that there exists different *politeiai* is a first step to understanding what human beings are, and how they live together.

Aitia is a key term in this context. In passage T1 it is usually translated simply as 'reputation', as 'notoriety for certain acts'; however, this choice simply makes the argument circular. According to this reading, Socrates would be saying that the qualifications of these cities are justified by the reputation of their citizens.[10] An *aitia* is, however, an item that is both prior and explanatory to

---

[8] The translation includes the relative *to* which is conjectural (see Slings, Boter, Ophuijsen 2005: 69). The alternative construction, without the relative, presents some difficulties of syntax and would read something like 'or that someone would say that love for riches exists mainly among . . .'. All exclusively numerical references are of Plato's *Republic*. The translations are my own from the Slings 2003 edition.

[9] The Scythians are nomads and the Egyptian political organization is not that of a *polis*. When Socrates speaks of cities, he has a very broad notion in mind, and thus refers to different ways in which people live together (see Cross and Woozley 1964: vi). He also uses 'citizen' in this broad notion – all those who share life in these territories are citizens of these cities – although, as we shall see, in a just city there is a specific rule for citizenship. Note, however, that T1 in no way suggests something like social classes as intermediating the relation between people and cities (for arguments on social classes, see Cross and Woozley 1964: 109–10; Bobonich 2002: 50; Penner 2005: 57; Sauvé-Meyer 2005: 230, Barnes 2012: 37).

[10] *Aitia* has the meaning of reputation in Plato, *Gorgias*, 503b7; *Theaetetus*, 169a5. The context of T1, however, entails the notion of priority in explanation. The reason for avoiding translating *aitia* as cause is that we tend to

whichever phenomenon it describes – in other words, it is something that grounds something else. It is for this reason that I suggest the alternative translation, 'principle', which foregrounds these internal types in humans as the explanation of our customs (*ēthē*) and the diversity of cultural mores in cities. These differing 'principles' constitute differing personalities, recurrent attitudes. They are the most basic explanatory factor behind action, behaviour and mores, as well as the differences and similarities among human beings.

What is the cause for these identities and their differences? In Williams's notorious definition, T1 commits Socrates with the 'whole-part rule', that is, that 'a city is F if and only if its men are F' (Williams 1973: 256).[11] Although this definition is not precisely attested in T1, the passage also does not explicitly deny it. The crucial problem with it, however, is that, if T1 means to imply that 'to be F' means 'to have parts that are F', the result is almost certainly an infinite regress, unless the rule is restricted purely to people and cities and excludes parts of the soul (anticipating that specific characteristics of these *politeiai* will later correspond to different parts of the soul).[12] Avoiding a regress is necessary to circumvent the problem that the whole-part rule supposes for a citizen to be F, all its parts must be F. But, if all its parts are F, there do not exist different parts of the soul. If there are no different parts of the soul, then it is not possible to preserve the principles that explain the differences in the *politeiai*.

A point worth noting about T1 and the whole-part rule is that Socrates describes a personality by comparing it both with a group of citizens – 'the Scythians' or 'the Phoenicians' – and with a city – 'in the manner of Trace' or 'in the manner of Egypt'. Because personality is explained by the principle of action, the passage suggests that (i) a person does not need to be part of a specific city in order to have a personality similar to it: there can be spirited people in Egypt or in Athens; (ii) this personality can be identified both by grouping together individuals in contrast to others, and by grouping cities (or cities and individuals) in contrast to others. In claiming that the types in the soul are the explanatory principles behind the diversity of human mores, T1 grants that, while there is no way to explain the latter without resorting to the first, other factors may be included in the explanation. As a matter of fact, as I shall argue, explanation requires further information, such as how the soul's diverse principles interact, determining different ends and modes of action.

This sets an explanatory priority about characters of cities that avoids the problems of the 'whole-part rule' by defending a bottom-up approach, wherein the parts and their interrelation design the 'whole'. In arguing that justice is likewise a character trait of human beings which

---

think of a cause both as an agent and as a sufficient reason for its effect (see Vlastos 1969a: 296). The distinction between the agent and the *aitia* appears in the *Phaedo* (99c6-105c6) together with a terminological distinction between *aitia* and *aition*. The latter is an agent accountable for some state of affairs, bearing praise or blame for it (see Frede 1980: 221, 226, reference to the stoics may be traced back to Plato), a role that, in T1, is ascribed to the person. The former is the reason why the agent is accountable – the account or the 'because' that gains a propositional form and refers to something X, present in an agent *a*, that explains why *a* is responsible for an event (see Vlastos 1969a: 305, 324). We should not, however, expect that the general use of the terms *aitia* and *aition* in Plato to be always consistent with this differentiation (see Sedley 1998: 115). On the other hand, our modern notion of sufficient cause seems useless when applied to principles such as *a*, for there may be other factors involved in obtaining a certain state of affairs (see Sedley 1998: 121 against Frede 1980: 227–8). T1, for instance, states that the presence of the principles in people explains why a city has a certain character, but some other factors, as we shall see, such as predominance and power, are also important in giving a reasonable account.

[11] The whole-part rule is adopted for justice, for instance, by Vlastos: 'a moral attribute is predicable of a given polis only when, and *exactly because*, it is predicable of [all] the persons who compose that polis' (1969a: 512, my brackets, my emphasis); see also Vlastos 1995 [1977]: 82–3; Kamtekar 2010: 80; Woodruff 2012: 94. For a critique of this reading of T1, see Taylor 1997: 40–1.

[12] For the regress see also Barnes 2012: 46 and Woodruff 2012: 94.

generates a certain kind of *politeia*, Socrates, I claim, follows the same explanatory priority. This means that justice is a kind of interaction of the parts of the soul that causes certain actions and customs, which, in turn, design a *politeia*. If this is correct, then we should reject what I shall call a top-down holistic concept of justice in the *Republic*, that is, the assumption that justice is a property of the whole in relation to its parts, in particular, the duty of parts normatively imposed by the whole through commands.[13] According to this interpretation, the concept of 'political justice' is distinct from the concept of 'psychological justice': the first determines how a city organizes its citizens, the latter how a soul organizes its parts.

The influence of the top-down holistic concept of justice is pervasive. In one of its cases, it plays the role of an implicit premise held among those who read the *Republic* as a pamphlet of political propaganda (an attempt to persuade people to obey a general and distinctly rigid normative system). According to this interpretation, the *Republic* posits a project of domination. Here, the political proposal offered by the text constitutes the generation of a closed society, a totalitarian system *avant la lettre* characterized by an absolutist dynasty of philosophers with strong social control to guarantee the proper obedience of the citizens.[14] As a consequence, the *Republic* does not provide a theory of justice as we understand it, that is, one that involves equity, exercise of citizenship, fair laws and impartiality in courts. In fact, in this reading, the text would appear to defend a concept of justice in which 'harmony' stands for 'oppression', given that most of its citizens are deprived of rights and are, technically, not fully human.

One strong objection to this reading is that, according to the priority established in T1, justice cannot be a duty that the city imposes upon its citizens. If justice is a character trait of a city, this must be derived from the presence of just citizens who themselves possess the principle of acting justly: duties must be grounded in the principle of action in persons, and not vice versa. It should come as no surprise that those who defend the holistic interpretation conclude that there exists a central inconsistency in the theses defended by Socrates in the *Republic*; those who attempt to avoid these inconsistencies in order to save his proposals subsequently end up generating increasingly strange theories about what a person, a city and justice are. Their basic problem is this: if psychological justice is the internal harmony of the parts of the soul, but a person who is psychologically just is not, in fact, a just citizen – as political justice is a duty imposed by the city to its citizens – a just city would not, therefore, be grounded in the principle of action of the people who live in it. T1 is therefore incompatible with the top-down holistic reading, which, if pursued, leads to the conclusion that the *Republic* is inconsistent. The principle of charity thus leads us to conclude that the top-down holistic reading should be dropped.

On the other side of the coin, there is what I call the holistic psychological interpretation. This reading, at its core, supposes that only philosophers are just, for only they are capable of refraining from committing injustice on account of their own peculiar personality. This approach has different versions. The first of them assumes that a just city in the *Republic* is the one in which all other human beings live under close inspection of these few intrinsically just individuals, their 'big brothers'[15] who surveil and brainwash them from committing unjust acts – as if this kind of despotic vision would not itself be an injustice. So while the philosophers may live in a just

---

[13] There is an academic consensus in committing the Socrates of the *Republic* to a top-down-holistic conception of justice: see, for instance, Demos 1957: 170 ff.; Cross and Woozley 1964: 132; Aronson 1972: 384; Williams 1973: 196; Irwin 2011: 92. For the implication of duties, see Robinson 1951: 493; Cross and Woozley 1964: 78; Vlastos 1969a: 513; Benardete 1989: 84.

[14] For the connection between the *Republic* to totalitarianism, see Hoernlé 1938: 168–70, 181–2; Popper [1945] 1966: 4, 74, 77, 80, 89, 127 ff.; Russell 1947: 7–8; Ryle 1947: 168; Robinson 1951: 492; Bambrough 1962: 111; Brown 1998: 24; Taylor 1997: 32.

[15] For the 'big-brother' readings, see Bobonich 2002: 62–8; Sauvé-Meyer 2005: 229–30.

community among themselves, a different code of behaviour towards other human beings, on whom they obviously depend for their basic needs, is expected. According to this interpretation, the *Republic* would conclude that political justice is impossible. An alternative version of this approach asserts that the whole point of the dialogue is to convey the message to the 'chosen ones' – the philosophers who master the relevant codes – that it is better for philosophy not to meddle with politics, as if justice is necessarily evil.[16]

A second subgroup of interpreters argue that philosophers are not selfish but are, by definition, moral human beings who act for the benefit of others: rather than 'big brothers', they are the *salvatore mundi*.[17] All other human beings, however, are regarded as completely incapable of learning, of benefitting themselves, and of knowing what is good for them – they are simply good sheep that will follow their leader in the belief that providing their champions with food and shelter is a benefit to themselves. This interpretation is unable to explain several puzzling aspects: the grounds on which the people are persuaded to become 'good sheep' remains obscure, and, even more pressingly, it is unclear how these non-philosophers, who by definition cannot be just, will do the right thing among themselves. If citizens are simply producers, they might exploit their fellow citizens, overcharge for services, be cruel to family members or even steal. How could these *salvatore* actually save them?

A third strand of the holistic psychological interpretation claims that justice in the soul is the only philosophically relevant point made in the *Republic*, which therefore becomes a work of moral psychology – or, better put, a work in which moral psychology stands independent of its political counterpart.[18] Though philosophically relevant, this point nevertheless turns out to be irrelevant to the problem that Socrates is addressing. If the challenge is to demonstrate that it is in our best interest to perform just actions, and Socrates' answer is that justice is a form of psychological well-being, he thus fails to prove both that this well-being is sufficient to cause my just actions, and that my just actions have this psychological state as their end.[19] Indeed, Socrates does not even state that psychological well-being is sufficient for flourishing; instead, the text makes it clear that he understands that there are external goods, such as free time and inalienable material items, that are necessary factors to our flourishing.

A further variety, the 'both wholes at once' thesis – that is, the 'analogical interpretation' – claims that, since the soul and the city are two individuals with similar structures and components, the dialogue employs an analogical method which attempts to determine both what they are and what justice is in each of them.[20] Although it is acknowledged that the text explicitly talks about how these 'wholes' relate to each other (as in T1), this interpretation asserts that the analogical method, being inherently comparative, precludes the dialogue from addressing this interrelation. The analogical method is, quite simply, not heuristic and does not aim at demonstration – its goal is simply to persuade. Interpreters who assume this perspective acknowledge the critiques

---

[16] Readings divorcing philosophy from politics are found in Strauss 1964: 103, 109–18, 123–8; Bloom [1968] 1991: 408–15, 426; Benardete 1989: 87–91 149; Rosen 2005: 85, 111, 133, 142, 277, 355.

[17] Readings of the holistic psychological approach in which philosophers are the *salvatore mundi* are found in Cooper 1977: 155; Irwin 1977: 202; Penner 2005: 11.

[18] Among those who see that justice in the *Republic* is nothing but a discussion of morality, and that the idea is for the proposal simply to be 'psychologically possible' are Nettleship 1906: 4; Prichard [1928] 2002: 23; Guthrie 1975: 470; Cooper 1977: 151; Waterfield 1998: xvi; Menn 2006: 34; Penner 2007: 23; Brown 2007: 46; Hitz 2010: 126; Woodruff 2012: 90–1. Narcy 1997: 238 characterizes it as a post-Kantian interpretation; for defences that the term *dikaiosunē* should be translated and understood as justice; see Vlastos 1968; Annas 1981: 12–13.

[19] See Foster 1937: 386; Sachs 1963: 153; Aronson 1972: 393–86.

[20] Supporters of the analogical reading of justice in the *Republic* are Demos 1957: 174; Neu 1971: 249; Irwin 1995: 230; Ferrari 2005: 61; Keyt 2006: 349; Blössner 2007: 349. A more moderate position is taken by Anderson 1971: 23 ff..

which are traditionally made of the method as a result of these limitations, and, in response, assert that the *Republic* should be classified as a protreptic dialogue, that is, a rhetoric pamphlet aiming at converting the reader to philosophy; after all, there is no other way to be just and to flourish. Questions of how citizens interact with each other, and what kind of political action is expected from philosophers, are simply irrelevant to this purpose.

As this discussion demonstrates, all variants of the holistic readings deny that the *Republic* is about the *politeia*, the shared life of human beings. Instead, each supposes that it is either about individuals being internally happy or about governmental institutions imposing norms. In the latter case, based on the assumption that the states act like individuals, they read into the text the idea that political power is always exerted by individuals who usurp and use it as they see fit. Given these premises, a general disappointment with the dialogue is not surprising.

If holistic top-down approaches result in such awkward interpretations, why do interpreters insist on proposing them? One obvious reason is textual evidence, as some passages do seem to support this view. One such passage is the following:

[T2] What we are going to investigate is not trivial, and, it seems to me, requires precise observation. Since we are not that smart, I said, I believe it is necessary to carry out the enquiry on it as if we did not have sharp sight and were asked to read small letters from a distance, and then realized that the same letters were elsewhere in a larger size and on a larger support. It would seem a godsend, I believe, to be able to read those first and then to examine whether the smaller ones were in fact the same.

It would indeed, said Adeimantus, but how is this similar, Socrates, to the enquiry on justice?

I'll tell you, I said. We say justice belongs to a single man, and presumably also to an entire city?

Certainly, he said.

And isn't the city larger than the single man?

It is larger, he said.

So perhaps justice is larger when it exists in what is larger and easier to understand. If you will, we shall first examine what it is in cities. Then, we will also investigate it in one person, examining the similarity to the form of the larger in the smaller. (368c8-369a4)

According to the holistic interpretation, this passage states the following: (i) there is justice in the city and in the soul; (ii) justice in the city is more easily identifiable; (iii) Socrates first intends to investigate justice in the city and then compare it with justice in the soul, determining their similarity. My primary objection is to how the holistic interpretation understands (i). From the assertion that justice is predicated both of an individual and of a whole city, it does not follow that (a) they are discrete objects of the same ontological kind, as two different substances for instance; (b) the kind of predication is the same in both cases. Before I address these points, however, I will discuss (ii) and (iii).

Thesis (ii), which states that justice in the city is more easily identifiable, does indeed describe the claims levied in books II and III but does not adequately capture the whole account. Education through gymnastics and *mousikē* is not, as we shall see, simply about how a city becomes just: it is an equally important component of the education of a just individual (see 441d7-442a2). The method that defines political justice is the same that defines justice in the soul – it consists in investigating how human beings interact. Regarding (iii), it is true that comparison between city and soul adequately describes a methodological procedure that occurs in book IV, as, following the description of the just city, Socrates then proceeds to investigate the soul. This procedure begins, however, with T1. As indicated earlier, this passage offers an argument for grounding and not for comparison, because the action principles in each of us generate different kinds of city. This, in my understanding, explains why political justice is more visible: the principles of action being internal to the agents, it is the state of affairs in the world that results from human interactions. In other words, political justice is the verifiable product of the citizens' psychological states.

When the holistic interpretation subsequently interprets T2 as postulating two definitions of justice in order to preserve the analogical method – *first* we see what justice means for a city, *then* we see what it means for a human being – it makes Socrates' project nonsensical. If we are searching for a single concept with a single definition, identifying it in the city alone should be sufficient to pinpoint what it is.[21] A subsequent investigation to ascertain what constitutes justice in the individual is therefore superfluous, unless there are significant differences between the two concepts. And indeed, if there are significant differences, then it is not the same concept and the enquiry has been in vain. In order to understand the relationship between these supposed two concepts, a proper understanding of the metaphor of the letters is required. Some clarification about this issue is found in the following passage:

> [T3] But then it is, I said, like learning the letters: we are competent when we understand that they are few and recurrent in all texts, and we do not neglect any of them as unworthy of attention, whether written small or large. Quite the opposite, we are motivated to identify them everywhere, because we will not be literate before we have this ability.
>
> It is true.
>
> And what about the images of the letters, if by chance they appear on water surfaces or in mirrors? Will we identify them before we have known the letters themselves, or [don't they belong to] the same expertise and exercise?
>
> Sure, they do.
>
> But by the gods!, I said, then we will not be cultured (*mousikoi*) – neither ourselves nor those who we said we must educate, the guardians – before we know the forms of temperance, courage, freedom, magnanimity and all their sisters, as well as their opposites wherever they occur; we can notice both them and their images, and we do not neglect them neither in the small nor in the large things, for we understand that they belong to the same expertise and exercise. (402a7-c8)

T3 re-employs the metaphor of letters to reinforce the notion that reading is the ability to identify the same elements, that is, the same forms of virtues, across different media. The purpose of testing small print against large print is in identifying the same thing *despite* differences in size, surface and reflection: the metaphor depicts the process of defining the same individual seen in different instances. As the object of this enquiry, justice must therefore be expected to be the same across instances *despite their being different*. The central premise of the method is that there cannot be two different concepts of justice. The conclusion confirms this premise: 'justice is such a power that yields such men and cities' (443b4-5). The 'letters' we learn are those which explain our interactions and thus account for what both a just person, and, as a result, a just city are.

---

[21] For previous versions of this objection regarding two definitions of justice, see Benardete 1989: 45; Rosen 2005: 124.

If I am correct, neither T2 nor T3 entails two analogous concepts of justice. One can see, for instance, how this notion of two concepts emerges from Williams's awkward 'analogy of meaning': 'the explanation of a city's being F is the same as that of a man's being F (the same *eidos* of F-ness applies to both)' (Williams 1973: 255-6). If Williams intends to imply here that justice, being the same, has the same meaning in both the city and the soul, he mistakes predication for analogy, and, worse, reference for meaning.[22] T2 and T3 posit a single concept, regardless of its instances, as the object of enquiry, and nothing suggests that the two individuals are *analogous* simply because they are instances of the same concept (if we concede, for the sake of the argument, that a city is a substance independent of the people in it).

I shall now return to point (i) and the claim that justice is the same in the city and in the soul. My argument goes thus: T1, T2 and T3 are in fact compatible if we assume that cities arise from the interaction of human beings. T1 clearly states that there is no other place from which types arise in the city than from the soul[23]: as Socrates puts it, the city is the cohabitation of human beings (369c1-4) and the soul the principle of human life (353d9). A certain region up north, or even the Athenian territory, would not have a certain character were it not for the presence and interaction of people there. Territory alone does not constitute a city for two reasons. First, territory is established by borders that are outcomes of human interaction. Second, when human beings interact while living together in the same place, they involve their environment in their actions. A city is therefore neither an aggregate of people in a territory, nor a substance on its own: its existence is grounded in the nature of human beings as political living beings. What follows in this book is predicated on this understanding: a city is the state of affairs produced by the power of each human being to accomplish the ends of their action.

Cities arise from human nature, and human beings always live in cities. This is not a logical necessity but a natural one, grounded in the intrinsic teleology of human actions. A city does not have the same unity as a soul, for instance. It does not pre-exist the people that form it, and the people that form it can cease to be in it by, for example, founding another city. A city is therefore generated and perishable.[24] It is, by its very nature, a divisible unity. The components of cities, souls, cannot, on the other hand, be decomposed: the parts of the soul neither pre-exist it, nor can they be disaggregated (611a10-b8). For this reason, the kinds of truthmakers involved in statements such as 'Athens is just' and 'Socrates is just' are distinctly different. As I go on to show, while the truthmaker of 'Socrates is just' is the state of affairs produced by the interaction of the parts of his soul, the truthmaker of 'Athens is just' is, by contrast, the state of affairs produced by the interaction of the Athenian citizens *according to the power of each of them*.

Human beings are political living beings. So when an individual acts according to the interaction of the parts of their soul, they are interacting with others. As others, in their turn, are also doing the same, the state of affairs caused by the interaction of the parts of one agent's soul is obtained according to their interaction with others, and may or may not correspond to the end

---

[22] That justice is one is an established interpretation since Proclus (*Commentary to Plato's Republic*, I, 12.16–19). I think Williams's analogy of meaning is a case in which the assumption that 'meaning determines reference' is catastrophic to the interpretation of Plato (see cogent arguments in Penner 2005: 62–4 and in Barnes 2012: 43). For Platonic forms as meanings, see Kahn 1972: 568–70. Others who defend the analogical reading have a more refined concept of analogy. Ferrari, for instance, works with the stricter concept of proportional analogy, such as A:B::C:D. (see Ferrari 2005: 40).

[23] For some more textual evidence, see the argument at 500a5-501c3, where the philosopher, as a producer of virtue (500d7-9), transfers the virtuous character to people both in an individual and in a public way (500d6). This makes him a designer of *politeiai* (501c6-7).

[24] For the difference of souls and cities, see Barker 1919: 187; Joseph 1935, p. 41 ff., 81 ff. For the remark that there is no form of the city in Plato, see Strauss 1964, 92–3; Burnyeat 1992: 177.

of the agent. This explanation goes as follows: in pursuing their own ends, human beings may compete or cooperate. In both cases, the interaction may make them moderate their ends in order that they be accomplished or it may simply result in an outcome that does not correspond to the end originally intended. Thus, once it is established that human action constitutes interaction, it becomes evident that human ends are obtained according to human power.

A city is the state of affairs which results from this power across all its citizens. Emerging *with a certain form* from the interaction of its citizens, a city is thus neither an object distinct from interaction nor pre-existent to it in any form. Because individuals pursue different ends and also have different powers to obtain these distinct ends, there exists a multiplicity of ends and powers which cause there to be uncountable forms of *politeiai* (445c4-7). This, in my view, is the explanation of how the different *politeiai* emerge from the principles of action, as enumerated in T1. For instance, it may be true that Socrates is just due to the end he pursues and the mode in which he pursues it, but a lack of power caused by interacting with unjust Athenians may preclude him from obtaining a just outcome of his actions, making Athens an unjust *politeia*.

My interpretation does not precisely align with Williams's 'predominant character rule', that is, 'a city is F if, and only if, the leading, most influential or predominant citizens are F' (Williams 1973: 259).[25] Power is not, I suggest, the end pursued by predominant citizens, but is what each citizen (including the predominant ones) has according to the state of affairs obtained by their interaction. While predominant citizens may be F, they may also make concessions to achieve power; in this case neither the citizen has full power, nor is the city F. Where Williams sees serious obstacles for the predominant character rule and for the so-called analogy of the city and the soul as a whole, I see an oversimplification of a much more refined conception of politics which is expressed in the *Republic*, and therefore a compelling reason to abandon the supposition that is based on a comparison between 'wholes'.

I intend to show that predominance is a relation between ends, and that power is a relation between an end and the state of affairs obtained by an action, as a form of interaction. The character of a person is primarily rooted in its predominant end but can also be described by the mode of its prevailing, as well as the power the individual has to obtain the end. A city, on the other hand, is described by the state of affairs which results from the power of its citizens to obtain their end. This power may require the employment of devices dedicated towards conflict control in the form of 'institutions' which stabilize the city, for instance a code of laws. Institutions are therefore grounded in the power of citizens, and not vice versa.

It is something similar towards which Payne (2017: 7, 10) gestures when he distinguishes between the end that motivates the action (an intentional teleology) and the natural end of the action (a functional teleology). According to his interpretation, actions have an intentional end but, when they take place, they obtain unintended ends which result from the action's function. On this understanding, a just city is therefore the unintended end obtained by agents whose intentional end was psychological justice (Payne 2017: 141). While I agree with Payne's assertion that the just city is the result of actions which aim at flourishing, I dispute that the just city is an unintended end which is distinct from the original intention, at least in relation to Plato's *Republic*. Rather, I argue that there are three important features in describing an action: an end, the mode of predominance of this end and the power to obtain it. In my view, the Socrates of the *Republic* is committed to the claim that we have different modes of pursuing an end, and that there may be compromises in our ends depending on the power we possess.

---

[25] The predominant character rule is tacitly accepted by Lear 1992: 190; Cooper 1977: 153; Ferrari [2003] 2005: 79; Barnes 2012: 47 (the latter also see problems similar to the ones pointed out by Williams).

If the relations of power between citizens describe the city, the city is something constantly in flux. It may find stability when institutions created by this interaction are established, though these are stable only for as long as the resulting power allows. The most stable institution is, as Socrates argues, that which stabilizes the powers of all the citizens: justice. Political justice is a stable state of affairs because there is no quest for more power than what is obtained by each citizen. As each citizen consented to moderate their ends to correspond to their power, the state of affairs is satisfactory to all. As a result, they flourish cooperatively. If political justice thus promotes the flourishing of all individuals through their own action, it immediately follows that this is the answer to why we should always want to be just. This is why justice is a good.

It is striking that countless interpreters of a work entitled *Politeia* do not bother to ask who the *politai* (the citizens) are.[26] A brief overview of the occurrence of this term throughout the dialogue indicates that the most basic form of Plato's city contains four citizens, all of them producers (370c8-9), and all of them, as we shall see, responsible for shaping the *politeia* (see also 375b11, 389b9, 416b2, d1, 417b1, 423d3, 466c7). No one would challenge the fact that the dialogue's guiding line unfolds along the education of the guardians: the best among the citizens (456e1-2). But its argument collapses if the rest of the population is deprived of the education by *mousikē*, gymnastics and dialectical training. The aim of citizens is to found a community in which the pleasure of some does not entail the pain of some others (462b4-464a7), therefore they must develop empathy and reach some agreements. If every citizen must agree on who should rule, they must control their love for money through the exercise of temperance (compare 431e4-5 and 555c8, and also 501e6-502a2). This basic civic agreement thus requires justice, the practice of having a certain relation to other people in which their ends matter for our own ends: a *politeia* is just only when its citizens cooperate in friendship and concord (351d4-5), for which they must all be educated.

My aim in the first part of this book is to explain Socrates' interactive theory of action. Chapters 1 and 2 argue for what I would call an interactionist concept of the soul. According to this interpretation, our actions are explained both by the activities that desire, reasoning and *thumos* have by themselves, *and* their activity relative to others. This relation is described in terms of predominance and its modes, which can be either cooperative or conflictive: there is always a prevailing element which determines the end of our action, as well as a non-prevailing part which determines the mode of our action. *Thumos*, in particular, causes an emotional assessment of ourselves as agents or patients of actions according to our notions of flourishing; as such, *thumos* adds pleasure or pain to actions and is highly influential in the process of establishing a character and, therefore, a personal identity.

The subsequent two chapters address the role of cognitive powers in determining our actions. The function of our reasoning is, above all, to learn, which entails the constant scrutinizing of our beliefs in order to ensure that we possess only those which are true based on everything that we have learnt – that is to say, beliefs we can trust. However, desire may prevail over reasoning due to the presence of an unreasonable belief, a controversial concept explained in Chapter 3. Chapter 4 then explains the regular function of our cognition, from perception, apprehension of appearances, and belief up to knowledge. In order to avoid unreasonable beliefs, I shall argue that one should have a specific trait of character: endurance in learning. I point out that the difference between knowledge and belief lies in two factors: the first is that belief is the judgement

---

[26] A praiseworthy exception is Prauscello 2014: 21-4, although her assumption that the *Republic* is a work of political propaganda transforms the whole matter of citizenship into an attempt to deceive people.

of appearances of forms, while knowledge is only about forms; the second is that belief is an intermediary power, since it does not obtain its end.

Powers are the theme of Chapter 5, which analyses how knowledge and belief differ and offers a general account of the uses of the vocabulary of *dunamis* throughout the dialogue. I assert that a power is always ascribed to an agent due to a state of affairs obtained, which, as it admits degrees, is particularly relevant for assessing success in pursuing a particular end. Our personal powers are restricted by the powers of others which determine what is and what is not feasible. The first part of the book then ends with the concept of personality: pleasure and pain obtained in our actions, including the possible restriction of the power to obtain our ends, may lead us to repeat them (or not), which creates habits that reduce internal conflict and stabilize our identity. Here, I analyse some personalities that are particularly relevant to the arguments in the *Republic*, and show that both the end and the manner in which they pursue it matter to their description. Lovers, for instance, are obsessed with their beloved. But love is not the only means of pursuing the good; decent people do so as well. Some personalities establish a rule of living for themselves, like the democrats, while others fail to establish their own identities, as the tyrannical individual.

The second part of the book takes the analysis of interaction to the next level by investigating how action always constitutes interaction with others, and thus explains how a *politeia* comes to be. Chapters 7 and 8 pertain to Thrasymachus' speech, which posits the following thesis: *politeiai* are the outcome of the motivation of those who prevail in cities. There are some inconsistencies in Thrasymachus' speech, which I ascribe to his conception of power. He mistakenly assumes that prevailing in a city implies power. The inconsistencies derived from this mistake become clearer in Chapter 8 with Socrates' counterarguments. These are based on the notions of the good of others, cooperation and obtaining equitable states of affairs.

From this debate, we gain the conceptual tools to understand Socrates' account of evil. Chapter 9 begins by explaining the concepts of connatural good and evil and demonstrates that, for Socrates, every good and evil is peculiar to something. Evil is a power of dissolution and destruction of natural beings. While souls are singular in not being destroyed by their connatural evil, in cities, sedition causes its degeneration by gradually annihilating its peculiar good, which is the community of pains and pleasures. This chapter ends by locating the kinds of evil enumerated in books VIII and IX as centred in different figures of the privatizer, the person that considers their flourishing unconnected to the flourishing of others.

Chapter 10 then gives us the reasons to live in cities, which I previously described as the first stage in the persuasion strategy of the reader. It begins with Glaucon's version of social contract: on this account, fear is the reason why human beings live in cities. For the sake of safety, individuals give up their expectation to flourish and obey the law, unless, of course, they are powerful enough to avoid punishment. Socrates then offers a counter version of the social contract, in which citizens subscribe to it so as to flourish. In this form, the constitutional principle states that each citizen must do one activity by means of which they both commit themselves to doing the good of others with fairness, and find a fulfilling life. As Glaucon is unimpressed, for he does not see how this political way of living would lead to flourishing, Socrates is prompted to open a new argument to demonstrate that a city has to commit itself to the constitutional principle to become good. This is the second stage in the reader's persuasion strategy.

Chapter 11 finally brings us to justice. It argues that, according to Socrates, justice is not the constitutional principle, but is in fact the excellence of the citizens. Here, I claim that the three political virtues are actually institutional principles of government, and that the so-called political justice and psychological justice consist of the same: to have cooperative parts of the soul. This, I argue, is sufficient cause for being a cooperative person. As cooperation is the excellence of every person *qua* citizen, personal flourishing depends on the flourishing of the city.

The third part of this book explores the consequences of this definition of justice, that is, what it means to be a citizen. Chapter 12 details the concept of popular virtue in order to counter the dominant interpretation according to which an individual cannot be just without knowledge of the form of the good. It also introduces the distinction between popular virtue and other kinds of virtue, in particular, the philosophical. Chapter 13 then explains Socrates' communitarian proposals which form the third stage of the persuasion of the reader. It demonstrates that the political participation of women is deduced from the definition of justice, and that this commits every citizen to reject the *oikos* as the structural unity of the *polis*. I argue that, while all citizens take part in the community of women and children, the community of material goods is restricted to rulers in order to ensure popular legitimation of the government.

Chapter 14 confronts the problem of knowledge of the form of the good. It opens with a precise interpretation of Adeimantus' challenge, which voices the objection that people may cooperate to do evil. Socrates' response is the need of laws deduced from the knowledge of the form of the good. On the basis of this, I argue that the form of the good is an object of knowledge that unifies the peculiar good of everything: because good is a relative concept, the form of the good thus encompasses everything in the world according to the formula 'being good for'. Moreover, because the world is stable, something is only good for something else if this is according to the stability of the world. I conclude with a defence of a concept of good that is all-encompassing and sustainable.

The subsequent two chapters deal with the problem of feasibility: how might justice and flourishing be achieved? Here, we arrive at the fourth stage of the reader's persuasion. Socrates' preferred course of action is the Philosopher-King proposal: a king to whom the citizens listen might become a philosopher and persuade them to begin a new educational project with the children. Equally, there is the reverse scenario in which the people call for a philosopher to become king. The first difficulty of the proposal is that it is based on the chance of such a king or philosopher existing. But the devastating argument against it, pointed out by Socrates himself, is that education is a communitarian action. A non-philosophical *politeia* hinders the education of philosophers, eliminating the chances of their casual existence. Chapter 16 addresses the alternative that rests between the lines of Socrates' argument. The name *Kallipolis* refers to a city that would supplement the cooperation of its citizens with a second citizenry, namely, the philosophical *politeia*. Given that the *politeia* is the way of life of the citizen, I shall defend that *Kallipolis* is a two-citizenry model under which one part of the citizenry cooperates, promoting their own good and the good of others, while its counterpart seeks knowledge and is thus in charge of scrutinizing the principles of public education, as well as giving justification to all the citizens for why this is the best political life. In comparison to the Philosopher-King proposal, *Kallipolis* is a long-term alternative for generating a just city. As opposed to the chance involved in the former model, it is an institutional project which promotes justice through an education in dialectic, a curriculum that begins in childhood and ends with the formation of rulers who know the form of the good.

The last chapter pertains to flourishing and opens with Glaucon's challenge to Socrates: how can real justice make us flourish? The first point is to clarify the terms of the challenge, in particular the difference between accomplishments and rewards of justice. Following this, I analyse Socrates' final response, which, in book IX, comes in the form of three arguments: each,

I claim, discusses one level of accomplishment of justice, and together – and only together – they explain what flourishing means. The first of these arguments demonstrates that flourishing depends on political life; the second, that it depends on good judgement; and the third on serenity. Socrates' response thus concludes that we may only flourish cooperatively. To do so, we must be just.

Please follow me as I connect these dots.

Part One

Interaction

1

Desire and reasoning

Politeia is the civic organization that emerges from the interaction of citizens, whose characters are each explained by principles of action. Principles of action are the theme of this chapter.

[T4a] The difficulty is this: [a] is it by that very same [type] that we perform each action or [b] with the three [types] that are distinct from each other? [Is it the case that] [c] we learn by one, are impetuous by another of our [types], and desire by a third one of them, which is related to the pleasures of nutrition and generation, as well as their kindred? Or [is it the case that] [d] it is by the whole soul that we act according to each of them, when we move? These are the difficulties that a worthy argument shall distinguish.
I think so too.
Let us then try to determine if these are the same or if they differ from each other.
How?
It is clear that the same thing will not accept to do or bear opposites simultaneously according to the same thing and in relation to the same thing, so that, if we discover that this occurs in any of the cases, we will know that they are not the same, but more than one. (436a8-c2, my brackets)
[T4b] Therefore, no statement of this sort shall disturb us, nor any more persuade us that the same thing can, simultaneously, according to the same thing and in relation to the same thing, bear, be or produce opposites. (436e8-437a1)

T4b simply rephrases the conclusion of T4a, with the important addition of the verb 'to be' that justifies its quotation. T4a is the sequence of T1, which identified different political types as a brute fact about human mores, for instance, the Egyptian love of riches in contrast to Phoenician impetuosity, through which their differences in character may be identified. In T4a the difficulty is how to account for this diversity of personalities. This is introduced in the form of a dilemma regarding how these different types explain our actions.
This dilemma has been interpreted in different ways.[1] On one reading, it is set in the distinction between 'acting with the soul' or 'acting with a part of the soul', a reading which supposes that [d] 'the soul as a whole' is the explanation of [a] 'the same'. In doing so, however, it ignores the demonstrative pronoun ('*that* very same') in the first line of T4, which must refer to the concept of 'type' introduced in T1 (hence my addition in brackets). This demonstrative makes it clear

---

[1] Interpreters who understood the text according to the first version are, for instance, Robinson 1971: 45-6; Woods 1987: 30; Bobonich 2002: 225; Brown 2012: 57. This reading supposes the alteration of *touto* for *toutōn* proposed by Adam 1902: I, 246. The second version is found, for instance, in Allen 2006: 133 and Price 2009: 1. The third version was adopted by Lorenz 2004: 85 and Kamtekar 2017: 130. In this case, *ousin allo allō* is a predicate of *trisin*; both *allo* and *allō* refer to types, and the dilemma is not established between *hekasta* and *allo* (with each type *versus* with other type), but between *tō autō touto* and *trisin*.

that [d] must explain [b] instead of [a], because [a] explains how the type is different, not the same. An alternative reading suggests that we either perform every action with [a] the same [type]; or [b] another [type]. The dilemma cannot, however, be between [a] 'it is by desire that we desire' and [b] 'sometimes we desire by another type', for the alternative (b) contradicts the definition of type as the principle that explains our desire. The best available translation for [b] is 'do them with three different parts', wherein 'doing something with the whole soul' means to do it with all the three parts, rather than merely one. The difficulty is therefore whether or not the non-relevant types are involved in the explanation of actions. Is learning simply the action of the rational part of the soul, or does it also involve certain actions by desire and *thumos*? Naturally, in order to answer it, one needs to determine the identity and the difference between parts. Nonetheless, as I shall defend, the argument does not aim primarily at a division of the soul, but rather at an explanation of the soul as an interactional entity.

One must begin by noting that the difficulty is set in an already complex conceptual framework. First, the assumption made from the brute fact stated in T1 is that there are at least three principles of action in our souls. The difficulty is therefore not about determining whether principles of action exist, but about explaining how they account for our actions.[2] Second, we are given the definitions of two of these principles of action which must be taken into account throughout the whole argument: T4a states that the rational type of the soul is the one by which we learn, and that desire is the correlative of nutritive, reproductive and further related pleasures. Third, it is assumed that, as agents, we are a soul that moves. The problem is thus located in explaining *how* types in us act when we move – that is, whether our action happens through the action of a single type or through the interaction of types.

To negotiate this difficulty, Socrates introduces a famous principle that holds that the simultaneous presence (compresence) of opposites entails unacceptable contrariety. It has been argued that there is an inconsistency between the principle and what it is supposed to explain:[3] the principle seems to support the inference that, if the soul desires and does not desire according to the same, in relation to the same, and at the same time, it would not be one soul but two other things. If it is not a soul, then it is true neither that the soul desires nor that it does not desire. This inconsistency can be avoided, for it is possible to read the principle as an analytical rule for individuation.[4] According to McCabe, an individual is a basic, unified, countable item, self-identical and different from others, from which we organize the world of our experience.[5]

---

[2] Interpreters who have assumed that the argument aims to prove the existence of the types are Bobonich 2002: 224; Price 2009: 2; Kamtekar 2017: 131. Lorenz 2004: 85 suggests that the types are presupposed.

[3] See Crombie 1962: 345; Robinson 1971: 48. I take the inconsistency to be as follows: If p is the case for X, X is not X, but Y and Z. If the apodosis, 'X is not X' is true, the protasis 'X does (bears or is) contrary...' can only be false. If there is no X about which p is the case, then p will never be the case for X.

[4] It cannot be a principle of non-contradiction (as argued by Adam 1902: I, 246; Nettleship 1922: 155; Rosen 2005: 152), because 'the same thing' is not a proposition but an agent, a patient or a subject of properties. Although it is stated as a principle to distinguish opposites (as it is called by Woods 1987: 30; Bobonich 1994: 5; Lorenz: 2004 88), its application, as I shall show, entails the principle of the excluded middle (see Robinson 1971: 39; Irwin 1977: 327; Stalley 1975: 125; Vallejo Campos 2013: 192–3), therefore something as principle of non-contrariety (Price 1995: 39) or principle of contraries (Bobonich 2002: 223) would be more appropriate. Nonetheless, I think Socrates aims to establish a more general principle for positing individuals whenever there is inconsistency between two propositions about the same individual, so the argument is valid to posit *eidē* in general, which function as explanatory principles (*aitia*, see T1).

[5] See McCabe 1994: 3. Individuals are the ultimate agents of their activity; their activities are not something the soul does, they simply happen in the soul. On the other hand, it is not the case that that they are subjects of intentional actions, as if they could do something different from the activity that individuates them. My use of 'individuals' may correspond to what Price (2009: 7) called 'agencies' or what Shields (2001: 146–7) understands as 'conceptual parts', on the condition one should not transfer the parts' activities to the soul. In

In my understanding, the principle establishes criteria to disqualify (or qualify) something as an individual in the following terms:

1) For all X, if X, non-p is the case for X.
2) If p, then p is not the case for X, but for Y and Z.
3) For all Y and all Z, if Y, non-p is the case for Y; and, if Z, non-p is the case for Z.

In this formula, p is to do (or to bear, or to be) contraries [Φ and non-Φ] simultaneously, according to the same and in relation to the same. For it to be valid, however, non-p must have a restricted description that specifies that 'Z non-Φ' is an action Z does (or either a property Z bears, or what Z is) that is incompatible with ZΦ. In other words, the principle entails the principle of the excluded middle. What is interesting about this proposal is that, following the basic statement that 'the same thing will not accept to do or bear opposites simultaneously', p is never the case of X, Y and Z. As such, a particular advantage of this reading is that it avoids the regress that would threaten the explanation should parts Y and Z have internal conflicts (in which case they would have subparts, which could again have further subparts).[6] The reading I suggest avoids this regress by defining X, Y and Z as individuals, and non-p as sufficient for being an individual. This therefore produces the following scenario:

1. For all X at moment *t*, according to the same and in relation to the same, either 'XΦ' is true or 'X non-Φ' is true.
2. If it is the case that Φ and non-Φ at moment *t*, according to the same and in relation to the same, then 'Y Φ' and 'Z non-Φ'.
3. For all Y at moment *t*, according to the same and in relation to the same, either 'YΦ' is true or 'Y non-Φ' is true; for all Z at moment *t*, either 'ZΦ' is true or 'Z non-Φ' is true.

What connects premises 1 and 2 is the principle of individuation. For each action at each moment of time, there is an agent (or bearer, or being, that is, an individual). Whenever incompatible actions occur at the same time, there are necessarily two agents (individuals). For every action, property or essence, there must always be an individual that accounts for it – that is, its *aitia*. On this interpretation, X, Y and Z are acting simultaneously: though Y and Z are each performing an action opposite to the other, this is compatible both with X performing another action and with both Y and Z not performing, each of them, simultaneously opposite actions.[7] The soul, as

---

translation I follow certain vagueness in the use of term 'part' (*meros*) which is freely replaced by type (*eidos*, 435c1, c5, e1, 437b8) and by kind (*genos*, 435b7, 441c6, 441d8, 443d3).

[6] Some interpreters have thought that the principle is liable to regress (for instance Williams 1973: 256; Annas 1981: 142; Irwin 1995: 218; Bobonich 1994: 14, 2002: 248–54); some others also find in it some further evidence that the parts of the soul behave as homunculi (Annas 1981: 142–5; Price 1995: 54; Bobonich 1994: 4; 2002: 219; Kamtekar 2017: 144, 152). There are three main justifications for this hypothesis: some passages suggest that parts of the soul have beliefs (see 442c9-d2, 602e4-603a8); some that non-rational parts are capable of means-end reasoning, arguing with each other, and being persuaded (553b7-c7, 554c11-d3); some that there is a kind of pleasure connected to each part (580d6-581a1). I shall address the two first points in Chapter 4, and the latter in the Chapter 6. For now, I would say that my answer lies in this interactive approach of the soul, in which reasoning is the source of information for non-rational parts, and desire may be channelled out of its proper end. For interpreters that do not posit the homunculi thesis but find Plato faulty for blurring the distinction between desire and reasoning, see Joseph 1935: 52; Moline 1978: 15; Cooper 1984: 5; Woods 1987: 37; Burnyeat 2006: 13.

[7] I would take one step further Macé's thesis (2006: 14) that 'every action involves an agent and a patient' as *the most basic* principle in the Platonic analysis. I understand that the most basic principles are 'action implies agent', 'effect implies bearer' and 'essence implies individuals'.

an example of X, acts (or bears, or is) something – say Δ – simultaneously with the contradiction between YΦ (reasoning commanding 'no') and Z non-Φ (desire commanding 'yes') because this contradiction does not preclude the soul from performing an activity that individuates it.[8]

Moving forward in our analysis, it is worth noticing that this principle is only valid given two restrictions on relations – internal and external – and a restriction on time. The restriction about external relations is expressed more generally as 'in relation to the same thing' (*pros tauton*, 436b10), which includes all the external relations of X. It is posited so as to ensure that analysis of X's action (or bearing or being) does not include different circumstantial variables. This restriction is in place to avoid objections along the lines that X is not an individual because, for instance, X is larger (XΦ) than A and smaller (X non-Φ) than B. Relation to two different external relata is not a case of non-p. The restriction concerning time states that Y and Z are inferred only when Φ and non-Φ occur *at the same time*: this aims to ensure that 'XΦ' and 'X non-Φ' may only both be true if they happen at different moments of time.

The final restriction pertains to internal relations, denoted by the expression 'according to the same thing' (*kata tauton*, 436b9), which functions as the key determinant of individuals in the argument that follows. This restriction states that, if 'XΦ' according to something in X, and 'X non-Φ' according to something else in X, it is not the case that both 'X Φ' and 'X non-Φ' *simpliciter* are true. This avoids an objection posed by an anonymous interlocutor imagined by Socrates, who offers two counterexamples to the principle:

In the first example (436c9-d2), the objector argues that a man who is standing while moving his head and hands is an example of an individual both at rest and in motion *according to the same thing* (436c6). This, the objector claims, demonstrates that p is true about him. But Socrates responds that p is not true because he is not simultaneously at rest and moving *according to the same thing*:[9] the man rests *according to* his legs and moves *according to* his hands and head, which is equivalent to stating that his legs stand, and his hands and head move.[10] The first example thus concludes that whenever Φ and non-Φ are simultaneously the case, Φ is *kata* Y (and YΦ), and non-Φ is *kata* Z (and Z non-Φ). In the second example (436d4-e5), the objector claims that a spinning top is both in movement and at rest. Once again, Socrates responds that p is not the case for the spinning top because it does not rest and move *according to the same thing*: it rests according to its axis, and it moves according to its circumference.[11] Given this analysis, we should

---

[8] In my reading, the alternatives 'act', 'bear' or 'be', must be applied simultaneously to X, Y and Z. Some interpreters claim that while Y and Z *do* opposites, X is the *bearer* of these actions (Lorenz 2004: 86–7, 94; Renaut 2014: 158). This seems to me to result in a fallacy by equivocating p, because, when applied to Y and Z, Φ means to do something and, when applied to X, it means to bear something.

[9] It is true that *kata* is not mentioned at 436c9-d2, but this does not mean that restrictions are irrelevant to the example (see Lorenz 2006: 23). There is a clear parallel between *estanai* [. . .] *kai kineisthai* [. . .] *kata to auto* (436c6) and *to men ti autou estēke, to de kineitai* (436d1) (see Delcomminette 2008: 9).

[10] The text says that something of the man rests (which I assume is his legs), and something else (hands and head implied) moves; so, the application of the principle suspends the judgement about the truth of the previous statement that man is at rest (Price 2009: 3; against Bobonich 2002: 228, who claims that the conclusion is that it is false that the man is at rest).

[11] Some interpreters insist on the difference between the two examples, mostly arguing that one should not infer parts from the example of the spinning top, but simply some aspect of the movement. The reason is that the whole top is in movement and there is no part of it that is still (Cross and Woozley 1964: 116; Stalley 1975: 112–13; Woods 1987: 34; Price 1995: 39–40, 53; Bobonich 2002: 229; Lorenz 2004: 89). I would minimize the difference, not because I disagree with their observations, but in order to stress the continuity in the argument so that throughout it 'parts' are posited for explanation, not for composition. I offer three arguments for it. First, to hold that the two examples differ, interpreters must either deny that *kata* X was the determinant key in the case of the man, or suppose that *kata* changes its meaning from one paragraph to the other (compare 436b9, c6, d8). Second, the objector cannot argue that the top as a whole rests without resorting to *kata* clauses, which makes this a weaker objection than the first. Third, the conclusion is that 'the axis' is what rests and the

expect that whenever we find opposite actions (sufferings or properties), these are not *according to the same individual*.

From these basic premises, we may infer two conclusions about Y and Z as both individuals and parts. The first is that being an individual does not entail existential independence of others. They are individuals, but not necessarily, if I may use an anachronism, distinct substances. The second conclusion is that, as individuals, their action is determined not by X, but by their own action: Y and Z are individuals whose action occurs in X, which, in its turn, is an individual whose action is distinct from those performed by both Y and Z. Y and Z are parts of X only because they result from the analysis of X when opposite actions, which are not X's actions, occur in it. If this is the case, then doing (or bearing or being) Φ or non-Φ in those circumstances is what defines Y and Z as individuals respectively. It is their activity or property or essence that marks them out. I therefore submit that the results from the application of the principle are such as stated in Table 1.

Table 1 The Principle in *Republic* IV

(a) every action entails an individual agent;	(b) every property entails an individual bearer;	(c) every essence entails an individual entity;
(a') there is no individual agent of opposite actions;	(b') there is no individual bearer of opposite properties;	(c') there is no individual entity that has opposite essences.

This is a general principle applicable to not only Socrates' account of action but equally to his metaphysics. I shall return to it in what follows,[12] for now, I restrict myself to an analysis merely of how this result may clarify the difficulty of how the parts of the soul work. It does so as long as what is termed 'internal conflict' is a case of *p*. The example of internal conflict which Socrates offers is of an agent who is thirsty and does not drink (439b3-7): he associates this situation with the principle of individuation through a specific example of *p*, where someone who resists drinking when thirsty is like an archer whose hands pull the bow in opposite directions. Thus, although his individual parts perform Φ and non-Φ, in this case, pushing forward and pushing backward, the action that must be attributed to the archer is Δ, because the archer is at rest (439b8-c1). Notice that the principle does not explicitly state anything about how the action of X relates to the activity proper to Y or Z. Even so, we know that, if Y and Z occur in X, there is an X in which 'YΦ' and 'Z non-Φ'. If there is such X, which is an individual, thence there is Δ, such that it must be true that 'XΔ'. On the other hand, if Y and Z are the *aitia* of our actions, Δ is explained by 'YΦ', 'Z non-Φ' and the interaction of Y and Z. This is our next topic.

'circumference' is what moves, and that they are both in the top: *auta . . . en autois*, 436d9-e1 (see Price 2009: 2–3). I also note that in the *Parmenides* (137e3-138a1) Parmenides explicitly states that axis and circumference are two different parts of a shape: as such, nothing precludes that, as with the head and the hands of the man, the objector would suppose parts of the top at the outset. A supplementary argument would be that to distinguish aspects rather than individuals would leave Plato with a bad argument for claiming that there are parts in the soul (see Shields 2001: 148). What is remarkable about the spinning top is that it introduces an important feature of Socrates' argument: that the motion of the top is nothing but the interaction of its parts.

[12] It is worth noticing the consequences of the principle for the case of bearing properties or having an essence (cases in which the verb 'to be' replaces the general action of X, Y and Z). It commits Socrates to a strong metaphysical thesis: whatever has opposite properties/essences, according to the same and in relation to the same, is not in itself an individual. In 479b8-9 it is said of things that are and are not at the same time, that they are not individuals; as we shall see in Chapter 4, they are instead the appearances of opposite forms (476a1-9). The principle applies in this case as follows: (1) For all X at moment *t*, according to the same and in relation to the same, either 'X is Φ' is true or 'X is not-Φ' is true. (2) If it is the case that Φ and non-Φ at moment *t*, according to the same and in relation to the same, then 'Y is Φ' and 'Z is not-Φ'. (3) If, we claim Φ is what Y is, and not-Φ is what Z is, so that it is never true that 'Y is not-Φ' and 'Z is Φ', then Y is the form Φ and Z is the form not-Φ.

Further detail is required to explain the internal conflict in the example of thirst: first, that thirst is a desire linked to nutrition (436a10-b2, see T4a), and therefore to pleasures connected to the survival and preservation of our organic functions. As mentioned, desire is not the correlative of pleasure *tout court*, but merely a certain kind of pleasure which Socrates later terms 'bodily' (485d11-12), a pleasure which has its origin in our personal survival needs, even if it evolves into luxurious demands. The second note is that desire is always both object-driven and affirmative in its response to its object (437c3-4, 437d7-e6); on the other hand, it neither assesses nor evaluates it (see 474c8-10). Thirst, for instance, is neither specifically for a cold nor hot drink, nor for too much nor too little. Desire is simply guided by the basic information that an object will fulfil its end. This information comes from our cognitive apparatus and beliefs. Third, being thirsty implies internal movement – a motivation (ΥΦ) – to an 'external' action (ΧΔ) to either move towards the object that quenches thirst, or to bring the object to oneself (see 437b8-c2). Desire is the principle of motion, but it does not move the soul by itself: it moves it in interaction with other parts.[13]

A fourth note is that, because desire is defined by its natural objects (nutrition, reproduction, etc.), it cannot be defined by a good specimen of these objects (437e7-8). As a result and in the case of thirst, one simply desires a drink rather than a *good* drink. The reason for this is that desire and its objects are correlatives (438a7-b2).[14] Socrates proceeds to detail the logical rules of this category: a correlative is an object implicated in the definition of another, as, for instance, knowledge is knowledge of an object (438b4-d8). Specimens subordinated to a correlative correspond to subordinated specimens of their counterpart. Medicine is knowledge of health (438d9-e1), for example. But a correlative is part of the definition of its counterpart and not one of its properties. Medicine is not healthy; rather, it is the science of health (438e1-10). Given the definition of desire, its object cannot be further restricted to good specimens of its nutritive and reproductive objects.

As a consequence, though it is true that the activity of desire is intentional and, as such, may be expressed propositionally as an assent in the form 'X is a good for desire', this does not entail that desire has a faculty of judgement of its own, capable of judging that X is a good. The reason is that a capacity of judgement requires the ability to believe the opposite, so that the beliefs that result from it can be either true or false. This is not a capacity of desire, which is merely a one-track agent. In order to distinguish between a good and a bad drink or to conclude whether 'this drink is a good for me' is true or false, it is necessary to have learned from prior experience. By definition, desire does not learn. Learning is a capacity of reasoning alone. If, therefore, internal conflict is incompatible with the premise that all the desires are for good objects on the one hand,

---

[13] Some interpreters suppose that each part of the soul is a different principle of motion, each a desire towards a different object aiming at a different pleasure (see Cross and Woozley 1964: 118; Woods 1987: 37; Price 1995: 40, 86; Bobonich 2002: 239; Lorenz 2004: 99; Burnyeat 2006: 15; Ferrari 2007: 165; Delcomminette 2008: 6; Kamtekar 2017: 134). One of their reasons is that they see Socrates as attempting to establish the principles by which we move (*hormēsōmen*, 436b3 in T1). In my view, however, by nature, only desire moves us (see *horma* at 439a9-b1). Another reason is that the opposition between desire and reason is described as 'pulling' and 'pushing' (see 437b1-4). As I see it, this does not entail that reasoning move us, but only that it brakes desire when it tries to determine an unreasonable end for the motion of the soul. A last and more substantive reason is a passage in book IX in which Socrates states: 'It seems to me that, there being three (kinds in the soul), the pleasures will also be three, one peculiar to each part. The desires and the principles of action are also in the same number' (580d6-7). To this I would say that the context matters. On some occasions, I shall argue, desire can be channelled and diverted from its correlative objects. In these instances, the internal conflict ceases, giving rise to different kinds of desire (see Chapter 6).

[14] For this passage as the first definition of the category of the relatives in the History of Philosophy, see Santa-Cruz 2013: 74.

it is, on the other, compatible with the premise that all desires are based on a (true or false) belief about something being good; a belief, however, that is not produced by desire as such.[15] We shall now proceed to the explanation of the activity of desire within the internal conflict.

> [T5] So we say that there are thirsty people who are not willing to drink?
> Certainly, he said, there are many, and this often happens.
> What, I said, would anyone say about them? Is it not that there is an urge in their soul but, on the other hand, there is a brake to drinking, which is distinct from the urge and *prevails* over it?
> It seems to me so, he said.
> Well, doesn't the brake in such cases, when it does arise, do so from reasoning? And are the stimuli and impulses that thereafter occur caused by passions and pathologies?
> It looks like it.
> It would not be unjustified, I said, to consider them as two, and distinct from one another – calling the one by which one reasons the rational element of the soul; and the one by which one loves, is hungry, thirsty, and excited by all other desires the unreasonable part, i.e., the appetite, a companion to certain satisfactions and pleasures.
> No; it would indeed be plausible, he said, to consider the issue in this way. (439c3-d9, my emphasis)

The man who does not drink while thirsty does so due to the activity of reasoning. The cause of this restraint is, according to T4a (436a9), something he has learned. If, for instance, the liquid available to drink is sea water, he possesses two conflicting pieces of information once he identifies it. The first is that, because it is water, it is an object towards which he should move on account of his thirst. The second is the information that there is salt in it. From all he has learned about this object, he thus believes that this is not an object that will fulfil his end.[16] In this situation, *he does not drink while thirsty*. But if the water available had been drinkable, reasoning would have identified it as something beneficial and therefore assented to his movement towards it. This suggests that reasoning and desire may cooperate in the sense that both may perform their own activity simultaneously without conflict. In the latter case, reasoning identifies the end of the action based on its learnings while desire moves the agent towards the object. Nonetheless, in this scenario it is not possible to identify the distinctive features of each part. This is only possible when conflict occurs.[17]

Desire is a principle of motion (see *horma* at 439a9-b1) naturally disposed to obtain the objects necessary for our survival. It commands the whole soul to move towards X – 'X is good for desire' – however, sometimes the correlative object of desire is not compatible with our

---

[15] For belief-based desires, see Gill 1996: 57; Carone 2001: 120; Moss 2008: 39–40; Singpurwalla 2011: 286; Kamtekar 2017: 134. For the incompatibility between the internal conflict and a desire capable of judging something as good, see Irwin 1977: 192; Price 1995: 48. We shall come back to this topic in Chapter 3.
[16] In my interpretation, desire does not learn from experience that a certain object may fulfil its proper end (like for instance in Cooper 1984: 12); it depends on reasoning and our cognitive apparatus to do so. Because it does not have a cognitive faculty, it is not capable of making distinctions about the object available.
[17] In contradistinction to the analytic validity of the principle of individuation, internal conflicts are episodic. We can only identify parts of the soul if and when they are in conflict (see Shields 2010: 159). Conflict emerges when the correlative of desire is taken as an intentional end and not due to any analytical point. Duncombe's (2015: 46) attempt to explain the conflict in terms of correlative opposites cannot prove more than a conflict between two unreasonable desires, in terms of drinking or not drinking when reason says no – which does not correspond to the description of the internal conflict – and yet it does so by confusing correlatives with intentional ends.

good. Because desire is by definition a one-track agent, it may insist, and this is how the internal conflict occurs. Internal conflict is therefore caused by a single object and two different ends of action:[18] 'X is good for desire' does not entail that 'X is good for the soul', and if desire were not a one-track agent and was instead capable of judging whether an object is in fact good *all things considered*, there would not be such a conflict. It is for this reason that every internal conflict arises from desire and never from reasoning: reasoning does not move us; it simply shows us the end of our action.[19] Conflict only occurs when desire causes us to move towards something that shifts it out of a state of cooperation with reasoning.[20]

T5 implies that neither the activity of desire nor the activity of reasoning is by itself sufficient for action, that is, $Y\Phi$ does not entail that $X\Delta$, nor does Z non-Φ entail that $X\Delta$.[21] As the aim of this enquiry is to establish whether action is motivated by either a single type, or by the interaction of types, T5 is an integral passage in indicating that it is the interaction of Y and Z that determines the action of X. 'Predominance' (*kratos*) and 'to prevail' (*krattein*) are two crucial terms to explain how reasoning and desire determine what the soul is doing – in this case, that the man does not drink while thirsty. '*Kratos*', as Émile Benveniste reminds us, 'means neither "physical strength" (*iskhus*, *sthenos*) nor "strength of the soul" (*alkē*), but "superiority, prevailing" whether in combat or in assembly.'[22] The significance of this claim is to stress that predominance is a comparative concept, which therefore denotes a relation and lies in contradistinction to the concepts of force or strength, which are mere attributes of a substance. This point establishes that the predominance of reasoning is not due to some property of reasoning itself, for instance, that it is *strong*,[23] but instead describes how reasoning and desire stand in relation to each other: predominance is the mode (or the outcome) of their interaction.

This understanding of predominance gives us an interactive interpretation of the soul that avoids an important objection raised by the alternative interpretation that is based on the attributes of the parts. As the objection goes there is something missing in Socrates' explanation,

---

[18] Since Proclus (*Commentary on Plato's Republic*, I, 225.3–227.27), it has been often objected that there may be a conflict between appetites, for example, spending money on treats versus accumulating it. As we will see, these are very common events in vicious personalities, and the reason why appetites are both various and multiple. They do not, however, fit the form of the most basic internal conflict because they describe conflict about two different objects, and not about the same object being either a good or not a good (see Lorenz 2004, 113). This means that a conflict must be put into forms such as 'is this treat good for me?'; 'is accumulating money good for me?'. Basic internal conflict is the one that gives rise to appetite, that is, when desires, opposing reasoning, become unreasonable. Internal conflict, therefore, happens before the agent yields to the end of appetites, in the person's hesitation to do so. See 554d9-e2 and 559e9-560a2 for Socrates' description of an hesitation between desires, which is the fundamental reason why, a little later, he will distinguish between necessary and unnecessary desires.

[19] Notice that it is the end, not the action, that matters in the account (see Renaut 2014: 160): reasoning leads someone to undertake a variety of actions by directing desire to move towards a certain end, and it does so because it learns.

[20] Some interpreters think because the conflict begins with desire, reasoning is a second-order principle (see Irwin 1977: 327; Cooper 1984: 13; Price 1995: 45; Lorenz 2004: 16). Although this is correct about the conflict itself, I would rather say that the cooperation between desire and reasoning is prior to the conflict; otherwise, desire would not be informed about the presence of its correlative object (more on this point in Chapter 3).

[21] Price agrees with the interactive thesis but supposes that it means that the parts must have consciousness of each other (Price 2009: 7–8). My argument is that parts are agents only of their proper activities, but, being so, they also interact with others, since they 'co-habit'. One part suffering the effects of the action of the other does not require co-consciousness, simply an interdependent existence.

[22] Benveniste 1969: II, 71. The comparative meaning can denote both momentary superiority and lasting prevailing (Lefebvre 2000: 47), the latter, as demonstrated in Chapter 6, is denoted also by the metaphor of 'ruling'.

[23] The force model is read into this passage by, for instance, Cooper 1984: 7; Bobonich 1994: 7, who regrets that Plato does not give any content to the concept of strength; Blössner 2007: 360; Price 2009: 5–6; Kamtekar 2017: 147 ff..

namely, the factor that gives strength to reasoning: what later philosophers term 'will'.[24] Accounts based on will generate an entirely different explanation of internal conflict, according to which X acts either on the basis of the 'strength of the will' and thus follows the end indicated by reasoning, or on the basis of the 'weakness of the will', wherein the end followed is that motivated by desire. This account posits the resulting Δ action as based purely on the character of the will, and thus makes the distinction between reasoning and desire useless. Introducing the concept of will in Plato's model therefore reduces it to nonsense.[25]

There is a further reason why it is important to emphasize predominance as an interactive concept. Predominance is one of the central psychological concepts which Plato applies metaphorically in the *Republic*, that is, by transposing the exact same meaning from one situation to another. In its basic use, the term refers to the interaction of people in a city, to mean, as introduced by Thrasymachus, not force (see 338c7-d1), but an individual's being superior or excelling over others. When reasoning is said to prevail in an individual, what is meant is that their reasoning is superior to desire, which thus causes them to act according to the former. The similarity ends here, however. Because both reasoning and desire are explanatory concepts – and their being is determined by their activity – they cannot, as an individual in a city may, do another activity or do it otherwise. As such, 'prevailing' is not an additional activity of these parts; it is, by definition, what they do as they perform their characteristic activities, that is to say, it is their characteristic activity *in relation to other* parts.

In explaining how Plato understands the concept of predication, Meinwald draws the following conclusion: 'Predications of a subject *pros heauto* hold in virtue of a relation internal to the subject's own nature. Predications *pros ta alla* on the other hand concern individuals' displays of features, which Plato takes to involve a relation to natures – that is, to other things' (1991: 70).[26] I would like to suggest that the activity proper to each part of the soul, such as 'reasoning learns', is said of it *pros heauto*. This is important because a part is defined by this activity and not by any other. On the other hand, there is an activity that it performs in relation to others *in performing its proper activity*, for instance, 'reasoning prevails'. This is not an extra activity the part performs, but the activity it performs *pros ta alla*.[27]

The prevailing of reason may occur in different ways according to the action of the non-prevailing part. As a result, there are different modes of actions in which reason prevails. If we take the simple case of not drinking while thirsty, we can see that it has different modes. In one scenario, understanding that the available water is salty is sufficient for the agent not to consider drinking the seawater anymore. While they may still experience the internal movement caused by thirst, the agent remains resolute in not drinking. They do not go back and forth about

---

[24] Cross and Wozzley (1964: 129–30) claim that in the absence of an 'I' that makes the choice in the moral conflict, Plato has to abandon the notion of personal responsibility. Since he does not abandon it, they conclude that his analysis must be mistaken. In response, I would say that the action of the soul is sufficient for self-identity and responsibility, no will is required; for different arguments in this direction, see Gill 1996: 11–12; Penner 2007: 5; Brown 2012: 54–5, 70, see also Adkins 1975: 116–18.

[25] In contradistinction to what Hume claims (1888: 415), here reason is not a slave of desire because it can determine the end of the action, whose movement desire will accomplish. Desire can also establish the end of the action, in which case it makes reasoning instrumental.

[26] I notice that these are two categories of predication and neither entails relative predicates. They consist of two ways of saying what something is, or, in the present case, what something does. On accounting for things based on their interrelation, see Proclus (*Commentary to Plato's Republic*, I, 207.14–211.3), where he explicitly mentions that ruling is the activity required of reasoning in interaction with others.

[27] Prevailing is how a part of the soul interacts with another because of its own activity. Were it a different activity, then there would be problems about the individuation of reasoning, for it depends on reasoning not being liable to internal conflict itself. For a different approach to this problem, see Cooper 1984: 6.

the action, although there remains a motivation to move towards some drink to quench their thirst. An alternative scenario is an agent that hesitates: in this case, when desire still insists even after reasoning has manifested itself against it, desire has become passionate, pathological (*dia pathēmatōn te kai nosēmatōn*, 439d1-2, T6), and thus fully unreasonable (*alogiston*, 439d7).

These are two modes of the predominance of reasoning. In the first instance, a device is found to re-establish the cooperation of reasoning and desire. In the latter, one is found to hold a non-cooperative situation that involves either an increase of pain or a decrease of pleasure. Both of these scenarios stand in contrast to the best-case alternative, which would be to simply drink water when thirsty, that is, a situation in which reasoning and desire had never been in conflict. In my view, the cooperation of reason and desire occurs by the activity of reasoning itself when it situates bodily pleasures within a wider notion of benefit that includes the individual as a whole, social mores and consideration of the good of others.[28] When desire prevails over reasoning, reason follows the end of desire in spite of itself; in this case its role is to calculate the means to decrease the pain – even if, given the circumstance, a certain amount of pain is inevitable.

Such unreasonable desire is desire for that which is opposed to what has been learned through reason to be the good for us – as such, it is the cause of internal conflict.[29] It is because of the existence of unreasonable desires that Socrates cannot accept that all desires are for what is good for us: some desires are merely for what is good only for the desire itself, that is, things that the desire sees as fulfilling its proper end which do not fulfil the end of the person themself. This division of desire is coherent with the distinction he introduces in book VIII between desires directed to objects that grant our survival by means of the fulfilment of our needs, and desires that are not grounded in need (558d8-559c2). The so-called inevitable desires are those (i) that are unavoidable due to our own nature and (ii) produce something beneficial to us when fulfilled (558d11-e3). One such example is healthy nourishment, which keeps us alive but also promotes the benefit of a well-being that goes beyond mere survival (559a11-b6). This passage complements the definition of desire given in T4a by showing that, when they cooperate with reasoning, nutritional and reproductive desires may constitute sources of good. On the other hand, book VIII also defines a form of desire that (i) is avoidable, and (ii) even if linked to nutritive and reproductive objects, remains harmful. Here, the example given is excessive food in both quantity and quality, which harms the body with disease and the soul with lack of moderation (559b8-c2). To avoid such desires, a good education from early childhood is required.

In conclusion, it is evident that human actions are always explained by the interaction of distinct parts of the soul. An action is always caused by the predominance of one of these parts which determines the agent's end, in conjunction with the non-predominance of a different

---

[28] When Socrates speaks of reasoning 'persuading' desire, and desire 'agreeing' with reason, this happens only when desire develops under reason's influence and is guided by it (431a5-7) such that unreasonable desires simply do not happen. For this view, see Price 1995: 63. For cooperative accounts of the soul, see Shorey 1895: 194; Joseph 1935: 49.

[29] Even if the term is the same throughout (*epithumia*), desire is 'divided' in two kinds by the internal conflict (see Carone 2001: 122; Lorenz 2004: 108). Unreasonable desires should properly be called appetites. In book IX Socrates explains how appetites develop from nourishment and reproductive desires: 'We called it "the appetitive part" because of the intensity of its desires for food, drink, sex and all the other things that follow from them, and also "the money-loving part", because it is by means of money that most of these desires are accomplished' (580e2-581a1). By childhood habit, desire identifies money as a 'good for desire' because it is a means. In Chapter 9, where it is established what a city is, it will become clear that every citizen knows that money is a means for exchange of goods; this is something they learn from living in a city. We do not have to conclude therefore that desire has a capacity for means-end reasoning (as defended for instance, by Annas 1981: 129–30; Price 1995: 62; Bobonich 2002: 244; Erginel 2013: 206), for it was simply shown to it that money is one of its proper objects, just as with all its others. On the other hand, it is clear that going through means-end conditioned paths is typical of desire: it identifies water as the 'means' to quench thirst.

part, which thus explains its mode. Understanding the effect of their interaction in terms of predominance, cooperation and the devices found in the absence of cooperation is just as important as identifying the activities that individuate each of them. In doing so, Socrates' argument avoids a top-down explanation of agency (e.g. it is not the spinning top that explains the difference between the axis and the circumference). Instead, we have an explanation of action as an outcome of the interaction of the parts of the soul. In the spinning top case, its axis rests and its circumference displaces itself. Because the circumference displaces itself around the resting axis, the top does something that is neither displacement nor resting: it spins. An action is nothing but the emergent outcome of the interaction of parts of the soul. Only on this basis does it become evident that we do things with the whole soul – that is, we act through the interaction of all its parts.

2

Thumos

The previous chapter concluded that the principle of individuation establishes that, if something acts, bears a property or is something, it is an individual. On these grounds, the soul as well as desire and reasoning constitute individuals. Desire, the principle of motion towards nutritive and reproductive objects (as well as others akin to them), may be reasonable when its object coincides with the end presented by reasoning. Reasoning is the learning principle that allows us to make distinctions about the objects in the world and guides our desires by presenting these objects as ends of actions. Equally, desire may be unreasonable when insistent on moving towards objects that reasoning shows not to promote our survival or well-being. As such, reasoning and desire can conflict. In the case of conflict, one part of the soul always prevails and, in doing so, determines the action of the whole soul in moment t. But because both desire and reasoning are involved in everything we do, our actions must not merely be described in terms of their end (determined by the predominant part). They must also be described by their mode, which is determined by the non-predominant part.

This chapter argues that an agent's good is diminished when there is internal conflict – even when they retain the power to obtain their end. It begins by making the point that the end of an action is not merely obtaining an external object (thus generating an external state of affairs) but also the well-being of the agent the object is able to generate. The latter, however, cannot be achieved in the presence of appetite or unreasonable desire. Under normal circumstances, appetite activates *thumos* causing a reduction of the agent's good. This is not the only situation in which *thumos* is triggered; it also causes anger when the agents find themselves in circumstances in which their well-being does not obtain. *Thumos*, I shall therefore argue, is an emotional self-judgement according to beliefs about our own flourishing. It is not an ill-designed part of the soul; rather, it is crucial to the formation of personality.

In Greek usage prior to Plato, the word *thumos* is associated with different types of emotion, such as anger, self-assertion and indignation. It is also associated with moods or modes of action, such as impetus, ardour and vehemence. Connected with the notion of 'hot' and abrupt action, it is further associated to motivations that stretch over time and thus with the notions of perseverance and determination, for instance, in cases of revenge.[1] From this point on, I no longer translate the term *thumos*. This is not due to the wide semantic variation (which is true of many terms), but because I hold that the *Republic* redefines the term by formulating a new concept.

The conception of *thumos* in the *Republic* still accounts for the emotions of anger (*orgē*, 440a6, c1) and indignation (*khalepainein*, 440c7); the mood of persistence (*hupomenein*, 440d1); and the motivation for victory (*nikē*, 440d1, 545a2) and honour (*timē*, 545a3, b6-7, 549a4). After

---

[1] For analyses of non-Platonic uses of *thumos* and their meanings see Jaeger 1945: 313–14; Hobbs 2000: 7–8; Frère 2004: 14–15; Renaut 2014: 11–12; Cairns 2014: 10–11.

mentioning it as the characteristic type of Thracians and Scythians in T1 (where I simply translated it as 'impetus'), Socrates begins his redefinition of *thumos*. This opens with an anecdote about a certain Leontius, son of Aglaeon,[2] a man who, upon his return from Piraeus to Athens, passed by an executioner depositing the corpses of criminals destined for exposure to putrefaction in the outskirts of the city.[3] The procedure was aimed at preventing crime by exemplary punishment. When faced with this scene, Leontius experiences internal conflict: while his unreasonable desire wants to look upon the corpses, his reasoning holds it back. I disagree with interpreters who assume that Leontius' conflict is between desire and *thumos*.[4] This is because it follows precisely the description of the standard internal conflict, in which unreasonable desire persists after the intervention of reasoning (see *para ton logismon epithumia*, 440b1). In the case of Leontius, desire prevails (*kratoumenos d'oun hupo epithumias*, 440a2), and he looks at the corpses. The outcome of the conflict is that the pleasure he experiences when he looks at the corpses *after the internal conflict* is mixed with anger against himself (440a6). In other words, the full pleasure that was the end of his desire is frustrated.

The stronger this activity of the *thumos*, the less pure the pleasure of fulfilling desire; that is, less free from the simultaneous feeling of displeasure or pain. By acting in face of the predominance of appetite in the soul, *thumos* causes the pleasure obtained to be mixed, a hybrid of joy and anguish. In Leontius' case this comes as self-censorship. The displeasure that accompanies experiences such as these can generate practical inferences and learning that will guide other choices in future actions. For instance, the anger Leontius feels may prompt him to avoid looking at the corpses the next time. This sort of mixed feeling seems to have been the precise aim of such Athenian exemplary punishments: the corpses are exposed to give visibility to the abject consequence of crime and thus cause the onlooker to feel exactly as Leontius. Though this experience of simultaneous pleasure and displeasure may not necessarily guarantee any moral improvement among the spectators, it may help.

In Leontius' case, *thumos* is activated as a protest against the predominance of unreasonable desire when the course of action has been taken and desire is no longer present: *thumos* does not participate in the internal conflict between reasoning and desire but merely reacts to its outcome.[5] As an emotion activated by circumstance, it is a second, or even third-order of internal activity, in case one would like to ascribe a second-order activity to reasoning when it reacts to desire. The *thumos* emotion depends on the agent's placement in their particular circumstances, in comparison to how they would prefer to be placed. If, in the case of Leontius, *thumos* manifests itself as anger, self-censorship and repulsion at the act itself, this is not, however, the only kind of manifestation of *thumos*.

In living beings where reasoning is absent, such as in animals and children, *thumos* manifests as aggressiveness against others for the purpose of self-preservation (441a5-b3), as attested elsewhere across the text. There, the central idea is that *thumos* makes animals fight well by

---

[2] A fragment of Theopompus (fr. 25), the comediographer, mentions someone called Leontius and suggests he had a physical attraction to cadaverous youngsters (see Aristophanes, *Birds*, 1406; Adam 1902: I, 255; Nails 2002: 186). I think it is irrelevant to the argument whether Leontius' desire was sexual, for the text leaves it clear that it is an appetite. Unreasonable pleasures connected to the abject do not need to be sexual, they can be related to death, as in the case of the tyrannical personality (see 571d3).
[3] See Liebert 2013: 180 for punishment by lack of burial and Allen 2000: 136 for the suggestion that the display of the corpses pleased the Athenians and would be demanded as a completion to the punishment.
[4] Among the interpreters that argue that Leontius suffers a conflict between desire and *thumos* are Bloom [1968] 1991: 375; Carone 2001: 137–8; Kamtekar 2017: 140. For views similar to my own, see Singpurwalla 2013: 44; Renaut 2014: 172.
[5] For *thumos*' activity as a reaction, see Delcomminette 2008: 15; Renaut 2014: 180.

removing fear and thus keeps them from being defeated or conquered (375a9-b3). *Thumos* is thus a factor of survival as well as desire. Yet it differs from desire in that it is not a movement towards objects for the fulfilment of a lack, but a movement against those that would attack the agent. This is the same principle that drives children's reactions to others. Naturally, this reaction can be educated, especially by *mousikē* – storytelling associated with music – and gymnastics (411c4-8). Children can, for instance, cease reacting to prohibitions with anger and physical reactions should their resilience and perseverance be improved by means of listening to stories of agents who successfully controlled their reactions (390d1-6) alongside music designed to invoke emotions of persistence (399b1-3). Endurance can also be developed through gymnastics (411a5-c3). Notice, however, that this education of the *thumos* advances in parallel with the development of reasoning, for benefitting from such role models entails learning. In cases when there is no set of beliefs against which to judge one's actions, for instance in animals, *thumos* simply reacts to external stimuli. It is only with the acquisition of a set of beliefs that children begin to educate their *thumos*, and so to gradually learn to judge their actions until such a time as they reach the 'age of reason' (402a3).

When reason is present, the agent's notion of her own self-preservation becomes more complex, as reason offers a greater end than self-preservation: flourishing.[6] In rational beings, the activity proper to *thumos* is the manifestation of an emotion when our present situation is held in comparison with a notion of ourselves that we aim to achieve. In this comparison, our present situation may be considered (a) from the point of view of our actions (when we are the cause by which *thumos* is triggered) or (b) from the point of view of our sufferings (when *thumos* is triggered by an external cause). Furthermore, because the activity of *thumos* is an emotional self-judgement of the agent, it may manifest in various different ways: when (a.i) an agent's action puts them in a situation that does not correspond to the model personally aspired to, the reaction is painful; (a.ii) when in a situation which does correspond to this model, the emotion of *thumos* is pleasant. When (b.i) the action of others contributes to obtaining the agent's notion of personal flourishing, the emotion is pleasant; conversely, when (b.ii) others hinder personal flourishing, *thumos*'s reaction is painful. In all these instances, time is an important factor. As already pointed out, *thumos* may be a momentary or long-term emotion, in which case it is more like a mood. Evidence for this classification may be found in Socrates' additional examples following Leontius':

> [T6] Furthermore, in several other cases, I asked, don't we perceive that, when the desires use violence for someone [to act] in opposition to reasoning, he reproves himself – his *thumos* acts for the sake of that in himself which suffered the violence and, just as when the two factions clash, *thumos* arises as an ally of reason? On the other hand, I think you would not assert to have perceived it cooperating with the desires to counter-act what reason has chosen must not [be done], either in yourself or in someone else.
>
> No, by Zeus, he said.
>
> What happens, I asked, when someone thinks they've done an injustice? Is it not true that the more noble he is, the less he is capable of becoming angry when enduring hunger, cold

---

[6] I understand that the proper end of *thumos* is personal flourishing according to a belief we acquire by education. This differs from interpretations that understand that its end is self-esteem or self-assertion (Cornford 1912: 264; Cooper 1984: 14–15; Kahn 1987: 83; Kamtekar 1998: 331–4; Hobbs 2000: 30) or fairness (*to kalon*, see Moss 2005; Burnyeat 2006: 11; see convincing arguments against this latter proposal in Singpurwalla 2013: 49–51). For a position similar to my own, see Gill 1996: 251.

and the like, imposed on him by someone he himself recognizes to act justly, with his *thumos* unwilling, as I say, to be roused in relation to this?

It is true.

But what happens when someone considers himself to have suffered an injustice? Doesn't the *thumos* in him boil, outrage and fight for what he believes to be just? Won't he endure hunger, thirst and all the rest until he wins, without giving up the noble actions until they are completed or he himself dies or yet until he calms down by a call of the reason in himself, like a dog under the call of the shepherd?

Indeed, he said, it seems to be as you say. (440a9-d4, my brackets)

The passage presents the different ways in which the activity of the *thumos* may be identified. The first describes general cases similar to Leontius' which fit standard (a.i). Here, the passage reinforces that these are cases of internal conflict between appetite and reason. The predominance of desire is explained by an internal act of violence, which is a device for non-cooperative predominance against which *thumos* reacts. Does it react because it is an ally of reasoning? In the present example, yes: Leontius feels remorse because he does not aspire to be someone with violent appetites. Here, the crucial factor is what is aspired. *Thumos* is an ally of reasoning only insofar as it is educated by rational role models. If, for instance, these agents regarded flourishing as the experience of violent appetites, the emotion of *thumos* would be pleasure added to their pleasure.

Being *by nature* (see *phusei*, 441a3) an ally of reasoning means that the acquisition of reason itself is the starting point for the education of *thumos*. The acquisition of reason is undertaken through learning from others, not only in relation to how to speak and think but also regarding what it means to be a good person and what it means to flourish. As such, the beliefs with which our *thumos* is educated and against which we then judge ourselves have their origin in others, in our community. The fact that *thumos* cannot cooperate with desire against an end determined by reason does not entail that *thumos* cannot be associated with the predominance of desire to reinforce the stabilization of such a personality (see 553d1-7). Rather, it means that this cannot be a *cooperation* – that is, there is no common action (*koinōnēsanta*, 440b4) between desire and *thumos*. As cooperation entails that every individual operates simultaneously, there is no common action when one part is not able to do its proper activity. This is most evident in the case of the oligarchic personality, in which the association between *thumos* and appetites is described as a kind of slavery (553d1-2).

The second case described in T6, a person who has committed an injustice punished by someone else (perhaps the city) who proceeds justly, exemplifies (b). In this instance, the nobler the agent is, the more their notion of flourishing entails virtue, the less *thumos* will provoke emotions of anger and self-censorship while enduring punishment. In those who are able to see suffering as a means to flourishing, *thumos* manifests itself as endurance and resilience, a mood that attaches mixed pleasure to the effort being expended (b.i). *Thumos* thus aids the achievement of rational ends. In this case, the end is perfecting one's character. But it does so only when the motivation for this improvement is pre-existent. *Thumos* helps to obtain flourishing but as an emotion and not a capacity for analysing and judging *otherwise*. It cannot decide what flourishing is.

This becomes clear in the counterpart example of the second case. Here, the less noble someone is, the less the agent conforms with the punishment for their injustice and, as a result, the more *thumos* reacts to add pain to the circumstance by stimulating anger and inspiring actions of revenge towards those who punish. With its counterpart, this constitutes two different manifestations of *thumos* that both depend on different personal notions of flourishing. Both are grounds to explain how *thumos*'s proper activity is self-assessment. The verbs which denote this activity are 'to have an opinion' (*oiētai*, 440b9); 'to consider' (*hēgētai*, 440c6); and 'to believe' (*dokounti*, 440c7). But as in the case of desire, this does not entail a faculty of judgement as *thumos* is not capable of judging otherwise, that is, against one's notion of flourishing. In the case of just punishment, the *thumos* will only react according to the 'nobility' of the person, that is, to their beliefs about flourishing.

These cases of just punishment also show the centrality of time as a factor in the manifestation of *thumos*.[7] The noble person who committed an injustice is likely to feel immediate remorse in the same way as Leontius, since, after all, committing an injustice is incompatible with their (noble) notion of personal flourishing. However, the momentaneous painful manifestation of *thumos* is subsequently replaced, in the endurance of punishment, by a manifestation that adds pleasure to the effort due to the presence of rational beliefs about flourishing. This is the explanation behind cases (a.i) and (b.i) that depict the manifestation of *thumos* as a momentaneous painful emotion and a long-term pleasant one. The shift between pain and pleasure occurs because the perspective of the agent shifts from having failed in their flourishing standard to being on their way to achieving it. In the inverse scenario, one of the change from (a.ii) to (b.ii) in the unjust agent, it is likely that the presence of appetites may account for the shift from pleasure to pain. The *thumos* of this agent may engender pleasure in obtaining goods through injustice, which, after all, corresponds to their notion of flourishing as obtaining appetitive ends. In being punished, however, *thumos* becomes an unpleasant anger against others, the agent having shifted their position from being on the way to flourishing, to having failed it.

The third case in T6 reinforces the relevance of temporality in the manifestation of *thumos*. In this example, an agent who considers themselves a victim of injustice appeals for justice and persists on the demand until reparation obtains. Here, the temporal shift from (b.ii) – the painful emotion of indignation for not being allowed to flourish – to (a.ii) – the added pleasure in enduring the quest for one's flourishing – is clearly evident. The most interesting feature of this case is that it does not matter for the manifestation of *thumos* whether what happened was really an injustice, nor if the subsequent appeal is just – all that matters is whether the agents themselves believe this to be the case. They could, for instance, believe their punishment to be unfair: in this case, their *thumos* would undergo a further change, adding pleasure to their efforts of revenge.

Another example of the shift from (b.ii) to (a.i) is the case of Odysseus (441b3-c2). Returning to Ithaca and witnessing the degenerate situation in his palace, Odysseus is angry and feels the impulse to immediately react to the injustice committed against him by attacking the suitors and his own female servants (Homer, *Odyssey*, XX, 17). This is an instance of (b.ii). But the presence within him of a notion of flourishing that entails excellence turns the activity of his *thumos* from anger into endurance (*karteria*, see 390d1-5), a case of (a.i). This shift corresponds to a change of the perspective in self-assessment: from suffering the action of others (b) to one's own action (a). Odysseus' change is therefore a sign of an antinomy of *thumos* (*heteron heterō epiplētton*, 441b6). Having been triggered by external hindrance to flourishing (b.ii), *thumos* causes a pain which motivates the actions that lead to an (a.i) situation. On the other hand, the actions so motivated do not correspond to those of the model of himself he aspires to. When an excellent agent is in this deadlock, his reasoning intervenes calculating which option is better or worse (441c1-2). The solution thus found brings the agent back to (a.ii) in spite of (b.ii), with the underlying premise that committing injustice is worse than suffering it. This is an action in which the best

---

[7] For time as a factor in the manifestation of *thumos*, see Ferrari [2003] 2005: 112; Singpurwalla 2013: 63.

option is not available, and the agent notwithstanding follows the end of reasoning. We shall come back to this topic of rational actions in the context of absence of the good in the next chapter. For now, I would like to conclude that the antinomy of *thumos* proves that it is distinct from reasoning, it does not have the capacity of judging otherwise and it can, like desire (439d7), be unreasonable (*alogistōs*, 441c2).[8]

Thumos thus has its own activity, reduceable neither to desire (most evident in the case of children and animals) nor to reason (as in the case of Odysseus). Some interpreters have suspected this not to be the case, as *thumos* is not argued for on the basis of the internal conflict.[9] Indeed, *thumos* does not take part in internal conflict, which occurs when desire aims to move us towards some unreasonable end. This is because *thumos* does not pose ends to us. It merely follows those that are already given to us. Neither is the role of *thumos* to control the desires,[10] because, as I have attempted to demonstrate, *force* is not an adequate metaphor to explain the interaction of parts of the soul. *Thumos* engenders emotions of pleasure or pain in addition to action; it does not act on desires. As such, it is neither a guiding nor a motion principle; it is an emotive principle which, by its self-assessment, reinforces the predominance of either reasoning or desire.

It is nonetheless a well-defined part of the soul, for what identifies a part of the soul is not internal conflict but the principle of individuation. This principle may be applied to the act of emotional self-assessment because it is a conflict between a situated self and an aspired self. If the same thing will not accept to do, to bear or to be opposites simultaneously – according to the same thing and in relation to the same thing – it cannot be the same thing both performing the action and rejecting it (see 437b1-4). *Thumos* is identified by identity conflicts that arise, not before someone engages in an action, but either during the action or after it. They are conflicts between *thumos* and the self as an agent, wherein the agent is not the one assessing the action. As Leontius' case demonstrates, this happens in (a.ii) cases where emotion leads to the identification not of himself, but of his eyes as the agent of the repulsive action (440a2-4). This also happens in (b.ii) cases, when, in failing to obtain what one supposes to be one's flourishing, *thumos* rejects oneself as the agent of the failed action.

If I am right, Leontius' case should be addressed as an identity conflict rather than a case of weakness of will; though it is clear that Leontius regrets his looking at the corpses, there are elements that distinguish this account from that of a standard account of weakness of will. Let us take, for instance, Davidson's (1969: 93) definition of weakness of the will: '(a) the agent does x intentionally; (b) the agent believes there is an alternative action open to him; (c) the agent judges that, all things considered, it would be better to do y than to do x.' In contrast to this definition, it is remarkable that Socrates does not claim that Leontius' action was intentional – in fact, there is a suggestion of compulsion to look at corpses. If the action is described as guided by desire and subsequently resulting in an identity conflict, it is controversial to affirm that the soul is the intentional agent of this action. It is at least necessary to describe the soul's intention as pursuing such an end *in a certain way*, that is, conflictedly.

---

[8] I see no evidence that the manifestation of *thumos* in Odysseus is a sign of his bad upbringing (see Cooper 1984: 15). On the contrary, the interference of his reasoning in the situation of antinomy is sign of virtue, which supports the mention of this passage in the *Odyssey* as one with positive influence in the education of youths (390d1-5).
[9] Interpreters who hold that *thumos* is posited with the extrinsic purpose of mirroring the tripartition of the city are Cornford 1912: 262–5; Penner 1971: 111–13.
[10] Interpreters who have reduced the activity of *thumos* to the mere control of desires are Penner 2007: 38; Brennan 2012: 106; Rothschild 2017: 122.

Moreover, if the explanation of the Leontius' case is established as an identity conflict, it is not clear that the agent judges that it would be better to do y than to do x, for two reasons: the first is that it is the *thumos*, rather than the agent who does x intentionally, which judges that y would be better (which is a premise *sine qua non* for the individuation of *thumos*). The second is that, rigorously speaking, what the *thumos* judges is actually that 'it would be better *to be the agent* of y than of x': *thumos*'s judgement is a self-assessment, rather than an action appraisal. Finally, as we shall see in the next chapter, the *Republic* is committed to the thesis that any action x can be described in terms of a belief that x is good. If this is true, then it cannot accept, based on the principle of individuation, that the agent that does x intentionally is the same that believes that y is better than x. The principle of charity, therefore, commands us to avoid reading the weakness of the will into the text, which, interestingly, reflects my previous point that the will is not an element compatible with the psychology of the *Republic*.[11]

I therefore conclude that identity conflict is proof of a third part in the soul. On the other hand, it would not be appropriate to regard such conflicts as the only function of *thumos*. Manifestations of the (b) type are important to show that our beliefs of personal flourishing are regulated by our interaction with others, which, as I shall argue, is involved in the manifestation of *thumos* in two ways. The first is in education, as mentioned earlier: personal notions of flourishing are primarily constructed by shared beliefs, on which basis the end of our action is accountable. The second form of involvement is in power: others may offer resistance to our obtaining our ends in various ways. This is why, in situations in which agents fail to obtain what they consider to be their personal flourishing, their anger is directed at others. Identity conflicts which are based on a lack of power may lead to a change either in the personal notions of flourishing (by moderating one's end such that it may be obtained) or in the means to obtain these ends (by resorting to alternative devices, such as violence, concealment, false appearance or lies).

The previous chapter began by pointing out that the difficulty to be addressed in an attempt to understand justice was whether the action is performed by only one part of the soul, or by all of them interconnected. The answer is clearly that they are all implicated in our actions, even while being distinguished among themselves. As this chapter has demonstrated, *thumos* is implicated in our action as an emotion that explains how there are such things as mixtures of pain and pleasure, both in the effort of pursuing some good, and in obtaining one's end – which is important in further actions, in long-term engagements, and in stabilizing character. Again, actions are not explained only by their end, but by their mode and their power to obtain a good, and, as such, require three explanatory principles. On the other hand, nowhere can we find the claim that there must be only three parts of the soul[12] – in fact, Socrates explicitly mentions the possibility of inferring other parts should this prove necessary (443d7-e1, see also 603d5-6). Desire, reason and *thumos* are, however, the most basic explanatory parts necessary to give a simple account of action.

---

[11] For the critique that the argument aims at explaining conflicts instead of weakness of the will, see also Ferrari 2007: 169.

[12] Interpreters who think that Socrates must commit himself to only three parts of the soul are, for instance, Bobonich 2002: 49; Lorenz 2004: 100. For a critique of this position, see Shields 2010: 159–60.

3

Unreasonable belief

The two previous chapters identified three principles of action. Two of these (desire and reasoning) were shown to be active in internal conflicts and the third (the *thumos*) in the formation of personality. Chapter 1 indicated that desire may cooperate with reasoning. But equally, its activity may also lead to internal conflict in attempting to make its correlative object the end of our action. Becoming unreasonable in conflicts does not preclude it from being described propositionally – that is, it 'assents' to some object (437b1, c3). This framework formulates the internal conflict towards X as appetite manifesting itself under the assumption that 'X is a good for desire' in contrast to reasoning's assertion that 'X is not a good'. I stressed that this should not be mistaken for the notion that desire possesses its own faculty of judgement. The power of judging belongs to the soul's cognitive apparatus. This apparatus, which will be the theme of the next chapter, informs all parts of the soul about exterior objects by learning – that is, through the powers of perception (with the different senses), apprehension of appearances, judgement, thinking and knowing. It is due to these powers that reasoning can do what desire and *thumos* cannot: it may believe otherwise. In other words, it may acknowledge some previous beliefs as false.

This chapter focuses on how false beliefs about something being a good may persist in spite of reasoning's better judgement, becoming therefore what I call an unreasonable belief. Here I shall argue that an unreasonable belief (one in which X is mistakenly believed to be good) is not to be conflated with the propositional description of the activity of desire ('X is a good for desire'). Rather, it should be described as 'X is a good for the person', since it results from the predominance of desire over reasoning. An explanation of this phenomenon is offered in book X of the *Republic*, where, in the greatest accusation against simulative *mousikē* (poetry and music), a second formulation of internal conflict is given:

[T7] So, in relation to which of the parts of a human being does [simulation] have the power it has?
What part are you talking about?
This: through vision, the same thing does not appear to us to be of the same size from close and from far away.
Of course not.
And the same thing [appears] crooked and straight when observed in and out of the water; the same thing [appears] concave and convex through optical illusions concerning the colours; and all this sort of disturbance is manifested inside us, in our soul. Because it takes advantage of this liability of our nature, chiaroscuro painting does not fall short of bewitchment, and the same applies to the special effects of spectacles and other devices of this kind.

It is true.

But do not measuring, counting and weighing provide us some rescue regarding these appearances, so that the apparent larger or smaller or more numerous or heavier does not rule us, but what has been calculated, measured and weighed?

Absolutely.

But this would be precisely the activity of the reasoning in the soul.

Yes it is.

Frequently, however, when it has measured and indicated that these things are either larger or smaller or equal to some other things, the opposites simultaneously appear[1] about the same[2] things.

Yes.

And did we not say that it is impossible to have opposite judgments simultaneously about the same thing?

And we were right in saying it.

Therefore, the part in the soul that has beliefs that oppose the measurements would not be the same as that which has them according to the measurements.

Of course not.

But what relies on measurement and reasoning is the best part of the soul.

Absolutely.

So, the part that opposes it is one of the inferiors in us.

Necessarily. (602c4-603a8, my brackets)

In discussing the effects of simulation (*mimēsis*), the argument begins with cases of optical illusion. These illusions are first described as the diachronical appearance of opposites. It is possible, for instance, for us to view the same object as small at distance at t1, but large when closer at t2 (602c7-8). X thus appears Φ in t1 and non-Φ in t2. Such cases of diachronic contradiction, even when clearly apparent, disturb the soul. In them, the disturbance is located at t2; in t1, when X and Φ first appear and thus when they are primarily learnt, it is simply believed that X is Φ. It is only at t2, when X appears to be non-Φ that, given the previous belief that X is Φ, doubt emerges regarding whether X is Φ (602d1-2).

A solution to this disturbance may only occur in t3, when we resort to mechanisms of comparison (measuring, counting, weighing, etc.; see 602d6-9). Here, the soul posits a standard unit for what it is to be Φ and subsequently compares it to both X's Φ and X's non-Φ, a process which, for reasons I will undertake to explain later, I regard as an act of *dianoia* – our thought, or discursive reasoning capacity. Positing what it is to be Φ does not change how X appears (which persists in appearing Φ at t4 and non-Φ at t5). However, positing units is a resource that pacifies

---

[1] I reject that the appearance to the reasoning part entails a belief that this appearance is true and consequently a division of this part of the soul (see Nehamas 1982: 64; Storey 2014: 83; Kamtekar 2017: 141). Some alternatives were suggested by Barney 1992: 286, Lorenz 2006: 66 and Moss 2008: 45–6. I would like to claim that appearance of opposites is not a reason for partition as long as it does not entail belief. The argument is that the opposite appearance may be present to our cognitive apparatus, which is usually guided by the reasoning part, and that this does not necessarily entail conflict of beliefs. The presence of the opposite appearance, however, may give occasion to the activation of desire or *thumos*, here described as a believing the opposite, and this may lead to the person's unreasonable beliefs.

[2] I think we could go without Lorenz's (2006: 66–8) suggestion of *peri taûta* and maintain Slings's reading *peri tautá*, as it is the contrast between *tanantia* and *tautá* that connects this passage to the principle of individuation in the next line. Based on my argument in the previous note, I think this can be done with no harm to Lorenz's thesis (ibid., 68) that the opposites do not appear to the reasoning part.

the soul[3] by establishing what it is to be Φ. It thus furnishes conclusions about whether X is Φ or not – in particular, *qualifications* such as 'X is Φ *in relation to* Y'. Once what it is to be Φ is ascertained, it is possible to judge that X appears to be both Φ and non-Φ, that is, under certain qualifications it is Φ, and under certain other qualifications it is non-Φ. For instance, once it is determined what it is to be straight, it is possible to judge that the stick appears both crooked (when in water) and straight (when not). At this point, the soul has learnt that both Φ and non-Φ are included in the appearance of X; it has not, however, reached the further stage of knowing whether 'X is Φ' is true. Nevertheless, opposite appearances are the first stage in the learning process, as they force us to posit what it is to be Φ; we build our beliefs about the world starting from appearances.

Opposites do not appear to us only diachronically. T7 gives the example of chiaroscuro painting, which uses synchronic opposite appearances (light and darkness) to depict objects in special visual effects for aesthetic purposes. Known in specialized literature as the compresence of opposites, this phenomenon is what grounds the fact that opposites may become diachronically evident to us. The reason for this is given in book VII, where Socrates introduces what I take to be his explanation of our power of appearance – our capacity to apprehend what appears to us. An appearance is the product of our perception (*tēs aisthēseōs ... poiusēs*, 523b3-4), the unity of sense data (*ta en tais aisthēsesin*, 523a10) that are distinguished by each sense (*hupo tēs aisthēseōs krinomena*, 523b1-2).[4] Socrates subsequently differentiates between two kinds of appearance. In the first, the unity of the data coming from our different senses is sufficient for a judgement on what the perceived object is: when we see three of our fingers, we are not at loss to say that they appear as something, that is, as fingers (523c4-d6). We do not have to posit some individual unit to explain why they also appear as non-fingers, for the appearance of fingers is not one which includes both Φ and non-Φ. Once we have learnt what a finger is, we do not need to establish any qualification in order to determine the truth-value of 'this is a finger'. The fact that we need to learn what a finger is so that our perception would suffice to our judgement may suppose a previous intervention of our thought or discursive reasoning (*dianoia*) in identifying the sense data, but this is a topic that does not concern us right now.[5]

The second kind of appearances is that of opposites. Opposites are the extremes of a scale that admits degrees, for instance, soft and hard (see 523e3-524a3), and appear to us because our senses are organized in such a way that each sense is set over both opposites; that is, it is the same sense, in this case touch, that perceives both hard and soft (524a1-3). This allows for comparison through which we come to understand different perceived objects according to their consistency; every time I touch an object, I situate it within a scale that goes from absolute hardness to absolute softness. On this scale, every object of touch is, at the same time, hard to a certain degree and soft to a certain degree. In other words, its degree of hardness determines its degree of softness. As in a chiaroscuro painting, contrast allows for identification. Unless I use my thought to posit units of measurement about the absolute degree of hardness and the absolute degree of softness, I cannot establish *the degree* of hardness and softness in an object

---

[3] It is not so clear, however, what kind of explanation Socrates would suggest in cases of the refraction of light in water, or of chiaroscuro in painting: neither seems to allow for measurement.
[4] I disagree with the thesis that perception itself judges; that is, it judges something either to be Φ or to be both Φ and non-Φ (see Barney 1992: 287, Storey 2014: 109). I claim that it offers the appearances that will be judged by our power of belief to be either Φ or non-Φ.
[5] See Turnbull (1988: 12) for the qualification of appearances by resorting to forms. For the risk of misjudging something as a finger, see Smith 2019: 161.

of touch, which remains something in between these extremes as simultaneously both hard and soft. Indeed, the structure of our senses is such that opposites are always grasped simultaneously in this way, hence why the compresence of opposites explains their diachronical appearance (the reverse order would be senseless). Although a good example to explain the compresence of opposites in appearances, optical illusions are just one instance of this frequent phenomenon (523b5-7).

The argument of book VII further substantiates this interpretation of the process of learning from opposites detailed in T7. After learning that X appears both soft and hard, for instance when X is placed in comparison with something harder and something softer, we are puzzled. Puzzlement (*aporia*) results from questions we put to ourselves, such as 'what does perception indicate, when it tells us "X is Φ and non-Φ"?'; 'What is it "to be Φ"?'; 'What is it "to be non-Φ"?' (compare to 524a5-9). Appearances of opposites, states Socrates, summon our intelligence (523a10-524d5) – in particular, our discursive reasoning (*dianoia*, 524d2). *Dianoia* is activated to posit individuals by which we may calculate and reason (see *logismos* at 524b4) about what appears to us, so as to explain the degrees of mixture in appearances. In this process, the task of our thought is to determine whether a particular appearance is of a single thing (as of the finger) or of two things (as of the hard and the soft) that are both present in it (524b3-5). As demonstrated in Chapter 1, the principle of individuation asserts that something cannot *be* opposites simultaneously (see T4b). Still, no restrictions apply to objects *appearing* as opposites. Following this principle, our intelligence thus posits two individuals (Φ and non-Φ) to explain the appearance of opposites in X, and to determine what X is. Φ and non-Φ are conceived as self-identical items after which we organize appearances and ascribe being; these individuals posited by our intelligence are not the same in kind as those which appear to us, as, unlike the latter, they do not admit opposites. This is the basic distinction between what is visible (or perceived by our senses), and what is properly an object of intelligence (524c10-14).

T7 takes the conclusions of this argument a step further, to point out that, after puzzlement and the subsequent positing of individuals that allows for the activity of reasoning and the attainment of a true belief, opposites still appear to us. Crucially, this appearance activates our non-rational part, which, on its turn, may engender what T7 describes as an unreasonable belief.[6] This is not to be taken as a capacity of judgement desire has, but simply as the activity of desire, which is equivalent to the statement 'X is good for desire', and after which conflict takes place. In the case of the prevailing of desire, this may be described as the person adopting the belief that 'X, that is good for desire and not good according to reasoning, is good for me'.[7] Take, for instance, the case of chiaroscuro painting. Even after the realization that it is an optical illusion, we may continue to desire to illude ourselves in order to enjoy the work – in doing so, we surrender to our desire

---

[6] I do not see that the text supposes that appearing entails believing (as Storey 2014: 98 puts it). As Storey (idem, 85) himself points out, there is a gap between the conflict of a belief and an appearance, and the conflict of two beliefs. As I understand it, the latter happens when desire is activated by the appearance. Storey suggests that this reading would invalidate the argument because it aims to prove the partition (idem, 100), but this does not seem the purpose of the argument: it both states that the aim is to show what is the power of simulation and does that by resorting to what has been previously said about simultaneous opposite beliefs. The argument assumes that internal conflicts can be described as belief conflicts. On the other hand, in insisting that appearing entails believing, Storey commits himself to the thesis that there is internal conflict in every perception (ibid., 114). Were this the case, the non-rational part of the soul would not be a principle of action, but just a capacity for judgement, and the whole division of the soul would be jeopardized.

[7] I follow Gill (1996: 59) in the understanding that these do not have to be a conscious self-address. Conflicts may be expressed in propositional formula, but they do not need to be.

of simulation⁸ and are led to believe something we know is not true. This highlights something important about internal conflicts: the dispute between desire and reasoning is not only about the end of the action but is also about our beliefs about the good.⁹ If desire prevails, it obtains not only an action but also the belief that 'X, which is good for desire and not good according to reasoning, is good for the soul'. The agent then adopts an unreasonable belief, that is, a false belief that is not grounded in ignorance, but rather in the prevailing of the appetite. A belief that is held *despite* the conclusions of our reasoning is, says Socrates, a kind of bewitchment.

The regular activity of our cognitive apparatus does not allow us to have an unreasonable belief (602e8-9 in T7). It dictates that we either believe that it is true that 'X is Φ'[10] or we are at loss when X appears unqualifiedly both Φ and non-Φ. There is no such thing as the belief that our present belief is false, which would constitute a misdescription of our present belief. This is because our cognitive apparatus is truth-directed:[11] beliefs realized to be false are always relinquished and, whenever we are perplexed, we posit some standard that allows us some true belief to soothe our souls. In the latter case, the true belief may simply be the qualification for X appearing either Φ or non-Φ.

Socrates is committed to the thesis that beliefs produced by reasoning in our cognitive apparatus are either true or false, a third option being excluded. If false, our reasoning discards them. Unreasonable beliefs, however, are engendered by the interaction between reasoning and the non-rational parts of the soul (603a1-7, T8), and thus constitute false beliefs about the good and the end of our actions. Socrates explains how true beliefs are replaced for false beliefs in book III:

[T8] It seems to me that a belief is expelled from our thought (*dianoia*) either with or without consent (*ē hekousiōs ē akousiōs*). The false belief is expelled with consent when we learn better; all the true beliefs are expelled without consent.

I understand the case of consent, he said, but I have yet to learn about the case without consent.

What it is then? Don't you too consider, I said, that it is without consent that human beings turn away from good things, and it is with consent that they turn away from bad things? And isn't being deceived about the truth a bad thing, and possessing the truth a good thing? Or don't you believe that to possess the truth is to judge that things are what they are (*ta onta doxazein*)?

---

⁸ Annas (1981: 339–4) and Nehamas (1982: 64–5) criticize the connection between desire and optical illusions, but this is precisely the point about simulative art: even after realizing how the illusion of the chiaroscuro painting was achieved, we come back to illude ourselves (to believe that X is Φ, even after learning that it is not), in order to enjoy the work.

⁹ T7 supports the thesis that all our actions are based on beliefs about the good. Interpreters who have taken it otherwise (Kamtekar 2017: 141) have assumed that it states that we do not always follow the beliefs of the proper activity of reasoning. If my interactive approach to the soul is correct, we still follow beliefs produced by our cognition (for we cannot do otherwise), but of a reasoning misdirected by the predominance of desire. My position follows Reeve's (2013: 85–6) cooperative account of believing: belief's content is made available by our cognitive apparatus to which reasoning naturally assents, but the prevailing of desire may lead to the assent to an unreasonable belief based on opposite judgement of appearances, which are also provided to us by our cognitive apparatus.

¹⁰ See Silverman (1991: 134, 137) for belief in the *Republic* as a top-down imposition of concepts on appearances.

¹¹ See Price (1995: 43, 49): all beliefs aim at truth as correspondence with reality. However, because beliefs are subjected to the principle of the excluded middle, one should not accept Price's concept of half-belief (see Price 1995: 43). For this same reason, the division of beliefs in two kinds is a not division of the rational part of the soul (for interpreters who have considered it as such, see Murphy 1951: 39; Nehamas 1982: 65; Singpurwalla 2011: 285).

> You are right, he said, I do consider that it is without consent that one is deprived of a true belief.
>
> Isn't it so that those to whom it happens were either robbed, or bewitched or victims of violence?
>
> Now, this I don't understand.
>
> I am probably speaking in too tragic a way. I mean that those who were stolen are those who either changed their convictions or forgot about them; the latter forget because of time, the former because of an argument that removed them. Do you understand it now?
>
> Yes.
>
> By victims of violence, I mean those in whom great pain and affliction forced their changing beliefs.
>
> This I also understand now, he said, and you are right.
>
> The bewitched, I suppose you would say, are those who change their beliefs because they were seduced by some pleasure or terrified by some fear.
>
> It seems to me, he said, that all bewitchment is an illusion. (412e9-413c4)

First, it must be noted that the replacement of our beliefs is undertaken in two different modes, conveyed by the terms *hekousiōs* and *akousiōs* which express commitment of the self to action.[12] When the agent consents to such change, they act *hekousiōs*. The agent is committed to the move, for it is seen as a pursuit of a good – even if effort is required in the task. In the *Republic*, examples of consented actions are peaceful actions (399b3-4) and contracts (556b1). By contrast, actions without consent are those in which the agent performs an action *despite* themselves and thereby deprives themselves of a good (see 381c2-5). These actions are still performed by the agent but, since they do not obtain a good, are those from which the agent would prefer to be divorced. Examples of such actions include moral faults, such as manslaughter (451a5-6). Although this was not the vocabulary in which the case of Leontius was described, it is clear that his was a case of an action despite himself (what I called identity conflicts occur in actions done despite the agent). As such, we should expect *thumos* to be triggered in these modes of action.[13]

In book IV, Socrates explains how the general notions of self-commitment to actions fit his strict psychology. By all general accounts, temperance occurs when a person prevails over pleasures and desires. Accordingly, the majority of Socrates' contemporaries (*hoi polloi*), who suppose that we are all motivated only by our desires, define temperance as 'prevailing over oneself' (430e5-6). Socrates, however, argues that this definition does not make sense (430e6) (it is ridiculous, 430e9). His argument goes thus: if our prevailing end determines our personality, our self cannot be that over which we prevail. This is because it is simply not possible for something to prevail over itself. Dissatisfied with the account of the majority, he therefore refines the expression to offer a stricter definition of temperance: 'But, I said, it seems to me that the

---

[12] See Adkins 1960: 12–13; Vernant and Vidal-Naquet: 1972 [2005]: 56–7; Rickert 1989: 5, 127–8. The terms *hekousiōs* and *akousiōs* are usually translated by 'willingly' and 'unwillingly', or 'voluntarily' and 'involuntarily'. In the previous chapters I made a point about the inaccuracy of ascribing a concept of 'will' or *voluntas* to the moral psychology of the *Republic*: my argument was that there is no third element which gives strength or weakness to reasoning. A translation for 'voluntarily' thus suggests an interference of the will in our reasoning and cognitive functions. Moreover, if 'willingly' implies intention, it is hard to understand how we could 'unwillingly' be persuaded by an argument. My proposal of translating the terms as 'with' and 'without consent' (or in spite of oneself) will allow us to make better sense of the passage, and to better explain the identity conflict. For alternative arguments which support my choice, see Vernant and Vidal-Naquet: 1972 [2005]: 46.

[13] For unconsented actions as the explanation for unreasonable beliefs, see Carone 2001: 131–2; for an alternative way to see the activity of *thumos* in them, see Wilburn 2015: 8–9.

expression means that in the same person there is regarding her soul one individual that is better and another that is worse, and when, by nature, the better prevails over the worse, this is termed "prevailing over oneself"' (431a3-7). This is Socrates' definition of the temperate person: one in whom reasoning prevails over desire. This person is someone who engages with the actions they perform, who pursues their intended ends and does not act *despite* themself, that is, led by unreasonable desire. This means that, even if the intended good is unavailable, their reasoning engages in what is less bad. In Leontius, on the other hand, desire prevailed over reasoning and his *thumos* judged him according to the belief that he should be temperate. So, he was not able to engage himself in his action and he blamed his eyes.

The unconsented action of replacing a true belief with a false one may happen in a variety of ways. The first is by a defect of our own reasoning. We may, for instance, have deficient memory – in that we do not have present the information we already learnt to be true – or accept the conclusions of a flawed argument without noticing its flaws. It seems clear that replacement of this form is deeply connected with the most basic way in which to possess false beliefs (as opposed to replacing true for false ones): ignorance (see 382a7-b4; 535e3-4). On the one hand, forgetfulness is a process of reacquiring the state of ignorance; on the other hand, accepting a fallacy comes from ignoring the methods of inference. In this sense, both ignorance and misfunctions of the cognitive apparatus may give us false beliefs. However, these are not unreasonable for they are not beliefs that persist against those gained by reasoning. Instead, they are merely beliefs gained by our own (faulty) reasoning.

The second way in which a true belief is replaced for a false one is through suffering violence. Here it must be assumed that only extreme experiences of pain and affliction cause the genuine expulsion of a belief learnt to be true. This could not even be compared to, for example, a simple false public statement to avoid suffering such as the one made by Galileo. It would be comparable only to a situation in which Galileo would actually have changed his mind about heliocentrism. As such, it is a very rare phenomenon. In this more strict case, changing one's belief is imposed from the outside on someone, who then acts against themself without any alternative. The agent thus becomes a victim who loses their own agency, the basic feature of their being.

The most usual category of unreasonable beliefs is that which is due to pleasure or fear, the case of bewitchment or illusion as stated in T7. In T8, the discussion of these forms of expulsion of true belief is presented in the context of the enquiry on the character of a good guardian, one who must care the most for the city. A person only cares for what they love; and to love entails believing that one cannot flourish without the flourishing of the beloved (412c10-d8). Though we shall return to these themes of love and cooperative flourishing later, for now, the most important claim is that guardians should be tested for their personal commitment to this specific belief that their flourishing is bound to the city's flourishing (412e4-7). These tests are conducted by exposing the candidates to circumstances of effort, pain, fear and pleasure (413d3-4, 9-e1, later on simplified to pleasure and pain, 503a1-2) to see whether they relinquish this true belief in favour of some other, unreasonable belief about their personal good to the detriment of the city. Becoming bewitched by such factors proves that a particular candidate is not a good guardian of themself, and thus that they are not ready to care for others (413e1-5): bewitchment by pleasure and pain is an occasion in which one does not guard oneself. Instead, one gives in or lets oneself go – an action despite (and without the consent of) the self.

In the selection of guardians, these circumstances for proving one's character are artificially created in the same way as the abject spectacle of Leontius' corpses was intended as a moralizing spectacle for Athenian citizens. This is also the case, as I now proceed to argue, of the employment of appearances in simulative *mousikē* in T7. In all these cases, the production of appearances that may lead to unreasonable beliefs is used as an educational tool. Let us then return to T7. I think we are now in a better position to assume that this passage redescribes the internal conflict between reasoning and the non-rational parts of the soul as a circumstance similar to the tests for guardians. We know that, based on the compresence of opposites in appearances, the spell of pleasure and pain may cause us to judge something as good even after having learnt that it is not. In the T7 case, however, the appearances of opposites do not summon our intellect. Instead, they provide occasion for adopting unreasonable beliefs.

In order to understand the adoption of unreasonable beliefs, says Socrates shortly after T7, we shall leave the case of painting (introduced merely as an image designed to make the case; 603b10-c1) aside and focus on how thought interacts with simulative poetry. By definition, this poetry simulates one object exclusively: an agent in either consented or non-consented actions (603c5-8).[14] However, the audience of this poetry feels the same pain and pleasure as its characters (its agents); that is, they experience compassion (*sumpaschontes*, 605d3-4). To be a spectator of poetry is an activity performed, not in view of some end, but for its own sake; to be a spectator requires neither commitment to truth nor prudence (603a9-b3); it is something we do simply for pleasure (see 605b7, 606a7, 606b4). This pleasure requires that some beliefs be temporarily assumed to be true in order to fully experience the world created by the artist. Though these are technically not false beliefs, they are simulated – beliefs that are considered true *during* our simulation and for the sake of the simulation. This is precisely the reason for Socrates' concern: that the reception of poetry may inadvertently generate unreasonable beliefs after the simulated ones.

He explains how this happens through the example of the spectator feeling grief for the loss of someone dear, such as a son (603e4-6).[15] Grief is a psychological pain that motivates us towards our own self-destruction. The case analysed by Socrates, the one of a decent man, is one who despite such pain remains serene and does not change his behaviour (603e8-604a2). This attitude, says Socrates, is stable when supported by the regard of others. But when alone and unobserved, retaining serenity is more challenging. Alone, the decent man may let himself go by saying and doing the opposite of what both his reasoning and others urge him to do – things he would be ashamed to do in public. Here, he may experience the conflict (604a9-10) in which desire leads him to give in to the 'hunger for tears' (606a4), while his reason and his mores (*nomos*) attempt to hold on to serenity. In Chapter 1, I sought to emphasize that the soul is always in activity, for it is an individual as well as its parts. Based on it we can understand that, in this conflict, the individual in action may be either crying or not crying. In both cases, the *thumos* interacts with the course of action taken by assessing the agent and adding either pleasure to the act of not crying (thus prompting endurance) or pain to the action of crying (causing remorse and self-criticism). In the decent man, *thumos* supports the shared mores because he holds that his flourishing lies in acting in accordance with them. Because others agree that flourishing lies in not crying, the presence of others supports the activity of his *thumos* and the decent man endures. As such, the activity of *thumos* is enhanced by the presence of others because (and only when) there is a shared notion of flourishing involved.

In the decent man, his reasoning provides the end of his action through having learnt what is good for him on the basis of the mores (see *logos kai nomos*, 604a9) of the shared political life that

---

[14] For poetry as simulation, see Else 1958: 78, 81; Nehamas 1982: 56–8; Palumbo 2009: 239. For the importance of agents as poetry's object of simulation, see Moss 2007: 430.
[15] There is no need to determine what the non-rational part of the soul is. The argument aims at both (see Lorenz 2006: 70; Moss 2008: 42–4), one in short-term acquisition of unreasonable beliefs, the other in acquisition of beliefs about flourishing which are held in the long term.

educated him. This is how he learnt that it is good to avoid disturbance (604b7-8) and to remain as serene as possible in adversities. Here, the end of reasoning and the mores match. Following the mores is justified based on the following reasons (604b7-c3): (i) it is not clear whether the situation is good or bad, for we cannot know if death is something bad; (ii) intensifying the suffering will not engender less pain in future situations; (iii) the human condition is not worthy of being considered with such austerity (a point which will be discussed later); (iv) the pain prevents the fast recovery of our sound deliberation. There is nothing we can do about adversities themselves, but there is something we can do to preserve ourselves when facing them. In doing so, we may resume our flourishing as fast as possible by turning our efforts towards what is good for us. There are thus true and justified reasons to moderate grief. Having learnt from mores that this is good, the decent man justifiably believes minimal grieving is good for him (604c5-d1) and so follows his rational ends. This supports his resilience, which is assessed positively by his *thumos*,[16] and thus he should be expected to overcome his conflict.

The case of the decent man was introduced in book III (387d4-6) (along with that of the decent woman; see 387e11-388a1) within the discussion of lamentation. There, they are described as self-sufficient for the most part.[17] Not in *need* of others, they are therefore more capable of facing adversity. However, it is also stated that the formation of such a personality would be compromised if poetry were to present divine or heroic role models in lamentation (387e10-388a3). The effect of such poetic role models would be that, with time, these decent people would not rebuke or feel shame at feeling these destructive emotions and would be less disposed to control themselves (388d2-8). The reason is that simulative poetry causes decent people to experience unreasonable beliefs, even if 'merely' by simulation.

This experience happens because simulative poetry does not necessarily depict the most admirable characters – agents who, in either consented or unconsented actions, do the best thing. Indeed, virtuous characters, due to their serenity and imperturbability, make a hard object for a poet to simulate and for a diverse audience to understand and to empathize with (604e1-6). Although simulative poetry could technically do otherwise (a topic Socrates discusses at length in books II and III) its popularity and success (605a4) stems from its depicting those who experience internal conflict in their actions, on account of simultaneous opposite beliefs (603c11-d6). By depicting heroes who in distress cry, lament, beat their breasts and suffer vividly, poets like Homer and the tragediographers attempt to inspire compassion for these heroes (605c9-d5). In doing so, they associate such actions with the pleasure the audience feels in simulation. Though the decent man believes that it is, in fact, good for people in adversities to remain serene and to endure (605d7-9) (as his mores have rightfully taught him), in his simulative reception, he also believes that the hero is an honourable person (605d4). Therefore he is led to understand such actions as not only understandable and not shameful but also typical of a good man (606b2).

The simulation of heroes in suffering is a test to the decent man, one he may not be ready to pass. This is because the pity felt for the characters (*eleos*, 606b3, 606b8, 606c5) – a pity purposely provoked by the poet – is transferred to himself (606b5-8), who then exerts self-pity (606b7-8). Under the effects of the simulation, the decent man believes that it is good and honourable for him to grieve intensively. The decent man whose virtue depended on the shared mores and the presence of others now begins to adopt a new system of belief regarding his personal flourishing

---

[16] For different accounts on the role of *thumos* in the resistance of the decent man to simulative poetry, see Naddaf 2002: 118; Destreé 2011: 277 ff.; Liebert 2013: 197–8. Ferrari (2007: 181) associates the spectacle with the case of Leontius, but also considers that the decent man keeps his appetite controlled by force (2007: 180).

[17] See note 6 in Chapter 12.

(605c5-6).[18] This is how compassion for the heroes fosters unreasonable beliefs about what human beings are; what is noble about them; what it means to flourish; and what is the good or wrong course of action (see 603c5-9).

Let us recapitulate for a moment. We saw that non-rational parts do not have the capacity for judgement. Their activity may nonetheless be described in propositional form, for instance, as 'X is good for desire', which allows us to understand how desire may cause us to adopt unreasonable beliefs through the association of pleasure or fear with one of the opposites which appear to us. This association of emotions with appearances may lead desire to prevail over reasoning. When this happens we act under a bewitchment, a self-deception, that amounts to trust in an unreasonable belief and perform actions from whose agency we would like to divorce ourselves. When desire thus prevails over reasoning, it does not only lead us to its end but submits reasoning to a false belief about our good. Unreasonable beliefs are beliefs of a *misdirected* reasoning caused by the predominance of the appetite.

Now I would like to add that there is a difference between sporadic non-consented actions, such as Leontius', and the effect of simulative poetry on the decent man. In scattered occasions, agents act in spite of themselves through actions that do not identify with their notion of flourishing and trigger their *thumos*. However, if the pain added by *thumos* is not superior to the pleasure felt in the action, the agent may be willing to repeat such kind of actions. Repetition may engender habituation, which, on its turn, may lead to decrease the emotion caused by *thumos*, and, most dangerously, may lead to a ceasing of conflicts altogether. In this case, a vicious personality is generated, which stabilizes itself after the adoption of a new notion of personal flourishing with which the *thumos* judges the agent. Adopting a belief about personal flourishing distinct from the one with which one was educated, as may happen to the decent man during the performance of simulative poetry, is a significantly larger step than momentarily adopting an unreasonable belief. It is not simply about the conflict regarding the end of some occasional action. This is a second-order conflict of beliefs, which resets the parameters according to which our *thumos* judges ourselves. This is singular life-changing experience. When a true belief is adopted and a false one abandoned, we engage in a virtuous life (the topic of Chapter 15). Conversely, by adopting an unreasonable belief about flourishing we engage in vice (the topic of Chapter 9).

The insidiousness of the simulative poetry, however, does not limit itself to exposing the decent man to vice. Evidently, it is not simply about an emotion that surfaces when the decent man is alone without the support from others for endurance. It is about an experience of collectively challenging the shared mores. When a large group of citizens adopt unreasonable beliefs about what is good for them, this ultimately entails that a different notion of flourishing may begin to guide their collective conduct. Rather than motivating each other to recover from grief, the group now shares the belief that excessive grief is not shameful and pities collectively, praising and reinforcing the pain (606b1-3). When many share this pleasure of simulation and begin to demand more of such experiences, thus begins the vicious circle of poetry encouraging unreasonable beliefs.

As indicated, the depiction of conflicted protagonists is not intrinsic to simulative poetry, but a contingent choice made for the purposes of popularity stemming from the pleasure of the simulation it offers (see 605a7-c3). It is in the attempt of this kind of art to sell itself to the pleasure of the majority, Socrates claims, that its proper activity is distorted (605a9-b5). When simulative poetry makes concessions to the desires of the majority by depicting agents guided

---

[18] Ferrari (2012: 107) is certain that the decent man will fail the test, assuming that his education is precarious. I do not believe that Socrates would call him 'decent' and 'the best of us' (605c9), if that were taken for granted.

by unreasonable beliefs as role models, it nurtures the non-rational parts and misdirects the reasoning (606d4-7) of the whole community at once. Socrates mentions a possible antidote (see 595b6-7) to this phenomenon. He indicates that knowledge of what simulative poetry is enables us to resist compassion, that is, the transference of the sufferings of the character to ourselves (606b5-7).[19] However, this is something few can do (606a7-8). In this sense, the audience of simulative poetry has an educational experience that is the reverse of the test for the guardians. Instead of being tested in their resistance, the audience has an experience of bewitchment that leads to the collective adoption of unreasonable beliefs about flourishing, harming the thought of the spectators (595b5-6). This is the 'greatest accusation' Socrates levies against simulative poetry (605c5-606d7): it is a form of miseducation.[20]

---

[19] The antidote is said to consist of knowing of what poetry is (595b6-7), which some consider to be philosophy (see Belfiore 1983: 62; Ferrari 2012: 112). Halliwell (2011: 246), however, claims it to be some non-epistemic agency. I agree with Halliwell because it seems to me that the text leaves open the possibility of an education of character that could resist unreasonable belief: were the decent man really abiding by the justified mores he may do it. More on this point in Chapter 13.

[20] I follow Janaway (1995: 133 ff.) in understanding that the four arguments against simulative poetry in book X should be considered as two pairs: two about the lack of knowledge of poets (598b8-601b8 and 601b9-602b11); two about the parts of the soul (602c1-605c4 and 605c5-606d7). I consider the latter two as forming the greatest accusation. For a different perspective, see Halliwell 1998b: 9.

4

Cognition

Chapter 1 introduced the concept of internal conflict between reasoning and appetite, that is, unreasonable desire. Chapter 2 subsequently discussed *thumos* as the third part of the soul which furnishes emotional reactions as judgements of ourselves in relation to our own notion of flourishing. Finally, the immediately preceeding chapter presented the process of how unreasonable beliefs (false beliefs about the good) cause desire to posit ends contrary to those that are rational. This potentially leads *thumos* to possess mistaken conceptions of flourishing. Its emotional response in such cases is to stop favouring our own good, resulting in the agent performing consent actions that should be considered unconsented. Unreasonable beliefs are not produced by any standard functioning of our cognitive apparatus, but rather by miseducation that associates our ends with non-genuine goods. In standard functioning, the compresence of opposite appearances in perceived objects would generate puzzlement and summon the intellect. Because the agency of the intellect entails effort in dealing with puzzlement, endurance is required for enquiry and learning. In the absence of endurance, however, we simply give in to the easiest way to overcome puzzlement: to assume an unreasonable belief that identifies pleasure with minimal effort and risk, therefore dropping intellectual enquiry.

This description shows that the acquisition of an unreasonable belief is preceded by internal conflict, as stated in T7. Our cognition does not decide the part of our soul that prevails in such conflict. This is not only because reasoning is only one of the contenders but also because desire is based on appearances provided by our cognitive apparatus. The conflict is about the real good, and it happens at the start of our intellectual enquiry: Are we going to endure the effort to understand reality, or simply follow the easier path of taking some beliefs for granted? In circumstances of puzzlement, to determine that further enquiry on the matter is a good necessarily supposes the prevailing of reasoning – that is, the judgement on what is good for us precedes our acquisition of a knowledge that begins with opposite appearances. One only pursues knowledge due to a belief that knowledge is a good; that is, that truth is something we aim at.[1] This is the topic of Chapter 13. The present chapter addresses the standard functioning of our cognition and how Socrates understands our learning process. This begins with T9:

> [T9] Does someone who has cognition (*gignōskei*) have it of something or of nothing? Answer me just like he would answer.
> I would answer, he said, that he has cognition of something.
> Of something that is [something] or that is not [something]?

---

[1] Delcomminette (2008: 39) understands that it is knowledge that allows reasoning to prevail over other parts. I regard the process as the opposite: the prevailing of reasoning results in someone trusting that enquiry is a good, and by enquiring, the agent obtains knowledge.

Something that is [something]. For how would someone have cognition of something that is not [something]?

Let us thence hold this as granted. If we now investigate further, then what perfectly is [something] allows perfect cognition, what is not [something] at all prevents cognition in every way, right?

Granted.

Let it be then. So, if something is such that it is and is not [something], wouldn't it lie in-between what purely is [something] and what in no way is [something]?

In-between, of course.

Since cognition is set over what is [something] and the lack of cognition (*agnōsia*) is necessarily set over what is not [something], then one must search for something in between ignorance (*agnoia*) and knowledge (*epistēmē*) that is about what is in-between [what is and what is not something], if there is something like that?

Absolutely. (476e7-477b3, my brackets)

The first step stipulated in T9 is that cognition[2] (*gnōmē*, 476d4, *gignōskei*, 476e7) is always about an object; it has a correlative. Its second step is to grant that this correlative is not the end of cognition – in contrast, perfect cognition requires us to know perfectly what this correlative is. At the other extreme, lack of cognition (*agnōsia*) or ignorance (*agnoia*) of an object entails that nothing *appears* to our cognitive function (478b11, c3). T9 then posits the existence of something in between these two, where Socrates expects to place the appearances of simultaneous opposites (see 479a5-6): what appears to us is not what this thing fully is, but is something about which we possess beliefs.

My translation and subsequent reading of T9 is far from orthodox (hence additions in brackets). The justification for my alternative approach lies in some important studies on the Greek verb 'to be'. As Brown (1986) demonstrated, there is no difference in its meaning in monadic (i.e. without a predicate) or dyadic (i.e. with a predicate) forms of the verb 'to be'; in fact, she makes it very clear that the monadic form may also be expanded with the addition of a name and without changing the meaning of the verb. The result is that for the Greek verb 'to be', there is no semantic distinction between what was once considered its existential and predicative meanings. In other words, 'X is' necessarily implies 'X is something'; 'X is Φ' therefore necessarily implies 'X is' (Brown 1986: 69). This understanding of existence differs from our post-Aristotelian sense, which entails that some individuals (like substances) exist, while others (like mythological entities) do not. The Greek language can also express this strong sense of existence, such as when Adeimantus challenges the existence of the gods (365d8). However, this meaning requires an indication in its context (see Kahn [1973] 2003: 300 ff.) and, in my view, this contextual indicator is absent in T9.

When Socrates asks (476e10) whether the thing we cognize either is or is not, he does not use any special sense of the verb 'to be';[3] instead, he simply asks for agreement about a point for clarification. The point is that when we cognize something, we do it *qua* being something. Cognition begins with this association between something that appears to us and our

---

[2] Cognition is taken here in a broader notion than merely knowledge (see Schwab 2016: 80; Moss 2021: 51). Cognition includes all the aforementioned powers: perception, apprehension of appearances, belief, thought, enquiry, knowledge.

[3] See Kahn [1973] 2003: 101–2. This is not to claim that the verb 'to be' has an overdetermined meaning. It has the specific meaning of 'being something' which is predicative in form, imports some existential meaning, and also entails that the identity statement 'X is X' is true about its subject. I claim that it is more charitable to the text to assume this sense of the verb 'to be' for it provides Socrates with a better argument.

identification of it as being something. This is an interpretation of 'being' as 'being something' (*ti*), which is compatible with the elliptical predicative form of the verb 'to be' of T9. For this reason, I have inserted 'something' in brackets throughout the text.

An alternative approach holds that the monadic use of the verb 'to be' conveys existence in the post-Aristotelian sense I mentioned. In this case, knowledge is about what fully exists. Were this the case, Socrates would be committed to the partial existence of the relata of belief as well as to the conclusion that for them 'to be' and 'not to be' should be understood as 'exist' and 'do not exist'. This has been termed the 'two-world theory', a complex theory in which sensible things have their own partial mode of existence.[4] The problem with this strong distinction of worlds in the context of T9 is that Socrates aims to show how beliefs alone do not qualify an individual to rule; this power requires knowledge (473c11-e3, 476a10-d3). As such, the purpose of the argument implies that knowledge be applicable to particular actions, people and circumstances, whilst the two-world theory would confine the existence of such items to a realm of reality unapproachable by knowledge. If knowledge is useless for ruling, Socrates' argument collapses. It is only by avoiding this stronger concept of 'existence' that the argument remains plausible.[5]

Another further reading of the monadic syntactical construction employs the veridical sense of the verb, that is, 'to be' meaning 'to be the case that p'. This reading associates cognition with propositions and claims that knowledge is about propositions that are true, while belief is about propositions that are either true or false. That is, knowledge picks up a set of only true propositions; belief, which corresponds to the 'in-between' category mentioned in T9, picks up a set of both true and false propositions. Under this description, the two sets overlap and the distinction collapses. Some interpreters have attempted to avoid this consequence by committing to the claim that knowledge is the set of necessarily true propositions and belief is the set of circumstantially true or false propositions. But this stronger distinction still falls prey to the same objection about ruling: politics does not provide occasion for necessarily true propositions. Similarly, the overlapping version of the veridical reading must suppose belief picks up a group of propositions that obviously cannot be simultaneously false and true. Yet the text explicitly states that belief is set over what simultaneously is and is not (478d5-6). Propositions are regulated by the principles of non-contradiction and the excluded middle and, as we saw in the last chapter, appearances (the objects of belief) are not.

I therefore suggest the predicative syntax reading as a means to understand the argument as distinguishing appearance from the being of what appears (what perfectly is). On this understanding, our cognition has a correlative object (without which it cannot occur) and an intended object (the one it aims to reach). This means we are not dealing with propositions, but

---

[4] Interpreters who claim that the *Republic* is committed to an unacceptable notion of partial existence are Cross and Woozley 1964: 162, 164; Stokes 1992: 125. For the difficulties involved in the notion, see Vlastos 1965: 8; Smith 2012: 62. Interpreters who claim that there is a way in which partial existence makes sense are Allen 1960: 158; Gonzalez 1996: 258–62.

[5] Although we see some references to a so-called predicative meaning of the verb 'to be' in this passage, I find the formulation misleading. There are two syntactical constructions and two different meanings of the verb, leading to four lines of argument: (a) monadic syntax with existential meaning, which entails existence in the strong sense (see Cross and Woozley 1964: 172; Stokes 1992: 125; Fronterotta 2014: 54); (b) monadic syntax with veridical meaning, which entails that cognitive states relate to propositions (Gosling 1960: 122; Fine 1978: 124; Baltzly 1997: 267); (c) dyadic syntax with existential meaning, which entails that the predicate is a form understood as a specific ontological object (Allen 1960: 158; Cooper 1986: 240–1; Gonzalez 1996: 258–62; Vogt 2009: 14) (d) dyadic syntax with veridical meaning, which entails that the predicate is a form understood as a cognitive reliable object (Vlastos 1965: 7; Annas 1981: 198, 199; Smith 2000: 159–60; Ferrari 2000: 403). I shall argue for the latter line.

with objects: the appearance and the being. Strictly speaking, these are not distinct substances in the sense of each of them existing separately. Rather, appearance is a mode of being: the real being of things appears, so that the appearance is the appearance *of being*. As became evident in the previous chapter, appearances allow for the compresence of opposites and can only be understood by positing individuals (the forms) as the being of these appearances, after which one begins to investigate what this is. Appearances are forms in connection with bodies, actions and other forms. Forms thus do not appear as what they are; the appearance combines what they are with something that they are not:

> [T10] Since fairness and unfairness are opposites, they are two.
> Indeed.
> And since they are two, is it also the case that each of them is one?
> This also.
> The same account holds also in the case of the just and unjust, the good and bad and all the forms: each of them is one, but because they *appear* everywhere in connection to actions, bodies and with each other, each of them appears as multiple. (476a1-8, my emphasis)

T10 introduces the ontology entailed in the description of learning through puzzlement in book VII and in the distinction between kinds of cognition in T9. In this ontology, forms are individuals that answer to the true being *of what appears*. Here appearances, in their turn, are described as the compresence of opposite forms, suggesting that the compresence of opposites is a case of connection of forms with each other. Also introduced are variants on the appearances of forms, for instance, the connection of forms and bodies (a finger is a form that appears to us in connection with a body that is perishable) and the connection of forms and actions (just actions are an appearance of justice). What this implies is that appearances are not ontologically independent of forms and, as such, that this is not an ontology of two worlds: there is no such thing as a world of appearance, because what appears is certain forms in certain connections.[6]

If the ontology in T10 is compatible with the description of the summoning of the intellect in book VII, we may suppose that the distinction between fairness and unfairness mentioned here may well result from the intellectual discrimination acting over the compresence of these opposites: a fair action or a fair body also appears unfair, hence why we can judge them otherwise. In this sense, the central principle of T10 is also the principle of individuation. This is why the inclusion of the verb 'to be' in T4b is relevant. According to the principle, whatever has opposite properties/essences, according to the same and in relation to the same, is not in itself an individual. Although appearances may have a unity as the correlative of a kind of cognition (just as the soul has a unity given by its action), they lack the unity specified in the principle for

---

[6] It is puzzling why Fine, arguing against the 'two world theory', avoids explaining what is the ontology involved in this passage by putting it into cognitive terms: 'one can have knowledge, but not beliefs, about forms; and beliefs, but not knowledge, about sensibles' (Fine 1978: 121). I endorse the view that cognitive distinction of objects does not entail two independent sets of existent things. For appearances depending on forms, see Allen 1960: 150; Gonzalez 1996: 254, Smith1996: 34. Interpreters who refuse this ontological dependence, read this passage as suggesting that particulars *actually have* – as opposed to appear to have – these appearances of forms (White 1978: 145; Smith 2000: 151–2). As for me, I do not see (i) how the text allows for any inferences about particulars and their reality and (ii) how this could lead to the conclusion of the argument about the objects of belief.

they exhibit a contradiction in terms of parts, relations or time.[7] This lack of unity is precisely the reason they summon our intellect. But T10 gives another reason for forms: they allow us to understand multiplicity, that is, multiple instances of the same form. Socrates addresses this mode of appearance later in the *Republic*:

> [T11] We shall come to an agreement, I said, and remind ourselves of what was said before as well as on many other occasions.
> What is that? he said.
> We say, I claimed, that multiple things are fair and multiple things are good, and so on with each of them, and that we mark them off by means of reason (*tō logō*).
> We say it.
> Then also fairness itself and good itself, and thus with everything that we then posited as multiple, we now conversely [mark them off] according to one single form of each, positing it as one single essence, and referring to it as that which each of them is.
> This is so.
> And we say that the things that are seen are not intellectually apprehended, and the form that is intellectually apprehended is not seen.
> Entirely in agreement. (507a7-b10, my brackets)

Socrates seems to suggest that this is a thesis he has often repeated and one familiar to his circle (507a7-9): we shall postulate individuals to account for multiplicity. The concept of multiplicity, as the recurrence of a unit, entails the concept of unit. If we are to acknowledge multiple cases of a thing, we must determine what repeats itself. The so-called 'one over many' argument[8] (as in T11) is different from T10's argument 'from opposites' for appealing to the first type of appearance mentioned in the previous chapter. There, the appearance could have a unity sufficient for judging what the perceived object is (as in the case of the finger). But now, we are in position to see how such a judgement is made: we 'perceive' a finger because we recognize in it a form with which we are already acquainted. Let us consider the case of the form of fairness. In T10, the compresence of fairness and unfairness caused puzzlement leading to their being posited as individuals; with the 'one over many' argument in T11, however, it becomes evident how this individual may be employed to collect a multiplicity of items (see also 479a3).[9]

T11 also shows how collection is done by means of reason. Items may be marked off under a certain form with a certain name in order to be distinguished from those collected under a different form. In positing forms, we stipulate the individuals through which we explain the world.[10] By identifying the recurrence of the form in different particulars, we are able to collect

---

[7] Robinson (1971: 39) is right in understanding that the principle of individuation entails the denial of the compresence of opposites. But, in my view, he mistakenly claims that the principle is not applicable here. His inference is that, because at 479b8-9 Socrates says that opposites are acceptable in appearances, the principle is not valid for them, rendering the passage in book IV incompatible with the one in book V. They are not. The unity ascribed to appearances is the unity of their apprehension (see 478b9), not of their being. It is for this reason that they summon the intellect (see White 1978: 146; Cooper 1986: 230).

[8] For the one over many argument see Fine 1980; Dixsaut 2005: 235.

[9] The neutral plural *polla* may have the sense of a collective of items of the same type (see Gosling 1960: 116), but this does not exclude the possibility that they may refer simply to tokens (see White 1978: 128).

[10] 'Positing is only that kind of believing in which we deliberately and consciously adopt a proposition with the knowledge that after all it may be false' (Robinson 1971: 98). While I agree with Robinson on the methodical purpose of positing (*etithemen*, 507b5; *tithentes*, b6) I disagree that this is restricted to propositions. Positing a form is supposing that there is something that is the essence of multiple items. In a certain way this has a propositional form – I posit that X is φ – but this entails positing the existence of φ.

items under it to both learn more about what it is, and to verify the truth of our beliefs about it. True propositions refer to what forms are, even when they are about a specific item that falls under them.[11] Whatever we learn, this is a form. We learn that forms appear, how they appear, what they are, and how they relate to other forms. Although T10 and T11 specify different items as forms and introduce two different arguments for their function, it is possible to employ an inclusive approach that brings both of them together within the third argument for forms introduced in T9 – the 'object of knowledge' argument.

According to my understanding of T9, identifying appearances as *something* is ground zero for our cognition. This identification is not a given. It occurs with our own act of judgement, by means of which the appearance falls under a specific form, such as when we judge someone to be a friend (334c1-2), or a particular object to be beneficial (340c3-4). It is for this reason that it is so hard, under this account of cognition, to precisely distinguish beliefs from the apprehension of appearances. Sheer appearance would not present us *something*. As such, the power of apprehending appearances connects us to *no-thing* (not a unity, 477a10-11). In this case, we can say either that we have no cognition (*agnōsia*, 477a10) or that we have ignorance (*agnoia*, 478c3) of what the appearance is.[12] This is a cognitive process that only begins when we believe it to be something (Φ or non-Φ or both), that is, when we posit that this is an appearance of something that is, a form.

A belief is not the apprehension of an appearance but the assertion that an appearance is an instance of Φ.[13] As demonstrated in the previous chapter, the beliefs in our cognitive apparatus operate according to the principle of the excluded middle. So, we do not believe simultaneously that an appearance is both Φ and non-Φ. While appearances are therefore never 'mistaken', beliefs often are. The interesting element of beliefs is that they employ forms to judge that an appearance is Φ; therefore, they can always be scrutinized by our knowledge of forms. When knowledge of forms is lacking, on the other hand, we trust an appearance to be something by 'guessing' which form it is (the concept of 'guessing' will be explained later, see *manteuomai*, 506a6).[14]

The context of T9 in book V is such that Socrates' purpose is to show an enthusiast of simulative poetry,[15] the spectacle-lover, that he does not truly know what fairness is (*auto kalon*, 476c7) as he merely possesses beliefs about it, having failed to use his thought to identify its nature (476b4-7). Glaucon, who is made to answer on behalf of this character, accepts that a perfect cognition of something entails the perfect identification of what it is (477a2-4). Socrates then associates knowledge with perfect cognition: given that this something is Φ, knowledge, by its nature, is set over Φ (*epi tō onti*), and identifies what it is to be Φ (*hōs esti to on*, compare 477b11-12 with

---

[11] For forms as reference of names and truthmaker of propositions, see Wieland [1982]1999: 95–105; Graeser 1975: 231; Penner 2005: 20–8; Franklin 2012: 497; Rowett 2018: 11. This claim entails that, in Plato, meaning does not determine reference of terms; forms are always the reference of propositions.

[12] Annas (1981: 201) and Smith (2012: 64–5) emphasize this predicative syntax in understanding ignorance. I disagree that ignorance is a false *judgement*, for I understand that this is the definition of false belief. Instead, I insist that ignorance is a state in which something appear to us, which we are, however, not able to identify because we have never learned it before.

[13] For the difference between belief and apprehension of appearance, see Delcomminette 2008: 29–30.

[14] For beliefs being set over appearances but judging having forms as standards without acknowledging them as forms, see Gonzalez 1996: 272; Smith 2000: 155. Guessing should be understood in contrast with positing, previously described as consciously adopting some assumption on the essence of Φ as the basis of one's judgement that X is Φ.

[15] There seems to be here a dialectical requirement that the interlocutor must find the argument acceptable (see Gosling 1960: 121; Fine 1978: 125; 1990: 87). For the critique of the terms of the requirement, see Benitez 1996: 532; Baltzly 1997: 243; Vogt 2012: 58–62.

477a10). Here Socrates' argument contains the important twist. Whatever appearance I judge to be Φ, I can only perfectly cognize it if I know not that it is Φ, but what Φ is (in other words, the essence or *ousia* of Φ; see 479c7).

There is, of course, a difference between cognizing this as a finger and being able to identify what is Φ for fingers in the sense of their essence or nature. If I am to classify animals according to dactyly, for instance, I am expected to respond whether horses are monodactyl or not, that is, if their hoof actually exhibits a 'finger'. This is precisely the problem towards which Socrates' examples of the use of ambiguities in enigmas point (479b10-c5): is a pumice stone a stone? As it appears to be both a stone and not a stone, what is it? This example is not categorically different from that of the horse hoof, as both refer to a further stage in the process of learning: knowledge as perfect cognition because it is cognition of essences.[16] Socrates' interlocutor agrees. On his behalf, Glaucon declares that knowledge is infallible (477e7). For infallibility we are to understand that knowledge necessarily obtains cognition of essence, which is its correlative object. There are no degrees of knowledge, since knowledge is an activity whose end is obtaining its correlative. We shall come back to this point.

By now it is important to stress that, on the other hand, there are degrees of cognition furnished by the different powers. Glaucon accepts that beliefs are fallible (477e7) and may even be false. The correlative of a belief is not, therefore, the being of things; rather, it must be something else (see 478b1-2). The lover of spectacles may not have known previously what this relative is, but Socrates offers a suggestion: appearances *qua* opposites *appear* fair as well as unfair, just as well as unjust, and pious as well as impious (479a5-7). As such they are like optical illusions, in which we judge something that appears both double and half the size it is (479b2-3). Beliefs judge what appears both Φ and non-Φ as being either Φ *or* non- Φ. Therefore, what explains that beliefs are fallible is that they are set over appearances while 'guessing' their form. They are neither ignorance nor knowledge.

I previously used 'set over' to express how our senses are organized in such a way as to simultaneously apprehend opposites (see 524a1-3 in Chapter 3). It is also used to express the way knowledge has 'what things are' as its correlative (477b8-13). The fact that knowledge, belief and ignorance are each 'set over' different objects is what marks them off as different cognitive powers[17]: While they hold a parallelism for having a correlative, I argue that they differ regarding their accomplishments in relation to these correlatives. My reason for doing so is that the 'objects' of our perception and the objects of our belief seem to coincide. Both are appearances. But while the first simply provides us an appearance that is *no-thing*, the latter engages with it in order to judge it (see *doxazein*, 477e3) by guessing its form. I shall detail how this proposal fits the argument against the spectacle-lover in the next chapter. But first, it is necessary to discuss how this distinction between two different accomplishments related to the same object becomes clear in the contrast Socrates draws between knowledge and belief in the image of the divided line (509d6-511e5).

At the end of book VI, Socrates uses the image of a vertical line, proportionally divided into four segments, to explain the distinction between objects of belief and objects of cognition

---

[16] Knowledge is the grasping of what something is (Rowett 2018: 7) – that is, its 'nature' (see 490b1-3, Schwab 2016: 42), its 'being' (Moss 2021: 93).

[17] The argument aims simply at explaining the difference between these three cognitive states. One might want to add explanations, for instance, of the use of knowledge to judge appearances in a kind of knowledgeable judgement – that is, the kind of knowledge required for ruling – or yet about how forms are posited along enquiry. These are, however, speculations on topics that are not addressed here.

(510a9). Though this may sound awkward since beliefs are part of our cognitive apparatus, one must not forget that beliefs may be formed by misdirection of our learning processes. Thence the divided line supposes that beliefs may or may not lead to the end of cognition. Divided unequally into two and then divided again by the same proportion of inequality, the line is composed of four segments.

The lower segment is described in visual terms relating to images (*eikonas*, 509d10) or appearances (*phantasmata*, 510a1) in the technical sense I have been using throughout. Socrates' examples here include optical phenomena concerning light (in the same sense in which he refers to the optical illusions in T7, although these phenomena are not necessarily deceptive in the same way), such as shadows and reflections. As such optical phenomena are simply a case of the appearance of opposites occurring due to the functioning of our senses, I understand that Socrates resorts to such examples in the divided line to explain appearance *qua* a component of our cognition. This reading is supported by Socrates' own conclusion that the diagram of the line represents different cognitive states obtained in the soul (*pathēmata tēs psuchēs*, 511d7) rather than different kinds of being. For this reason I would like to submit that what I have been referring to as the power of apprehension of appearances is, in the divided line, termed *eikasia* (511e2).[18]

Proceeding to the next segment, Socrates resorts to items around us (animated and inanimate) to explain belief. The contrast between this and the lowest segment is compared to the distinction between things and the shadows or reflections of them. This illustrates the claim that, in our beliefs, we identify appearances *as something* – just as we can identify something as a shadow when we know what it is the shadow of. We do not identify anything in appearances before judging them to be Φ or not Φ. The second segment also stresses that, since we cannot believe simultaneously that something is both Φ and non-Φ, in judging we must take a stand. Entailed in any judgement about appearances is the trust that some proposition is true about them: this is why the cognitive state involved in this second segment of belief is trust (*pistis*, 511e1).[19]

The trust we have in our beliefs may be called into question when we are faced with other occurrences of Φ that show our assumptions to be false: moments of puzzlement. Puzzlement

---

[18] Because the text points out very clearly that the line aims to posit four different cognitive states of the soul, I do not see good reasons for insisting that the two inferior segments are simply explanatory for the two upper ones, and that *eikasia* is nothing but a place holder, as classically defended by Sidgwick 1869: 102; Jackson 1882: 150; Shorey 1895: 229; Ferguson 1921: 136. I understand that *eikasia* is a different stage from trust (*pistis*, 511e1) because we are able to distinguish our perceptual apprehension from what we trust – as in the case of puzzlement due to optical illusions. On the other hand, I do not see it possible for us to have beliefs that would correspond to *eikasia* – such as a conjecture– in contradistinction to other beliefs that would correspond to the other section of the divided line (for this reading see Nettleship 1922: 241; Cross and Woozley 1964: 218–20; Irwin 1977: 221; Lafrance [1981] 2015: 195; Smith 1997: 188; Gutierrez 2017: 35–47, Storey 2020: 21). To have beliefs we must trust something to be true, for which *eikasia* is insufficient. Any attempt to classify *eikasia* as a kind of belief leads to the thesis that it would be contrasted to *pistis* as false belief is to true belief, which leads to the false assumption that one can only trust true beliefs. I also reject the thesis that *eikasia* is a form of failure in distinguishing between appearances and objects (see Cross and Woozley 1964; Lafrance [1981] 2015; Fine 1990: 102; Wilberding 2004: 129), for such a failure would not result in a state of the soul. In sum, the position I assume is that the two lower segments have as objects the appearances of forms, and they distinguish themselves by two different affections of the soul: it is affected by exterior objects, and it affects itself by judging and obtaining a belief in which it trusts. For similar positions, see Stocks 1911: 77–8; Paton 1921-22: 76; Hamlyn 1958: 17; Hall 1980: 75–6, Moss 2014: 221–2.

[19] I do not see textual evidence for either describing *eikasia* as a mode of *learning* (Dominick 2010: 1), or for distinguishing apprehension of images and trust in terms of direct and indirect grasp of sensible objects, as, for instance, in Ferguson 1921: 144–5; Cooper 1966; Storey 2020: 19. My position is that direct apprehension of sensory data is a component of belief, for this is what we judge as being something: there is no grasp of what something *is* without a judgement (see Wieland [1982]1999: 203–5).

summons our intellect, which thus puts an enquiry in motion about what follows from positing Φ (510b4-5). Positing Φ means supposing, as opposed to unknowingly guessing, that appearances are the appearance of what Φ is. This assumption allows us to make inferences, for instance, the conception of a measuring system with which to explain phenomena such as something appearing as being large under certain qualifications while small under others (see T7). Socrates describes this activity as overcoming puzzlement (*poreuomenē*) based not on the principle but on the end (510b5-6). I understand that this obscure formulation means that such perplexity was caused by a problem that is solved simply by positing forms, not requiring their grounding. The end is to solve the specific problem (see 510d1-3).

This kind of solution has two sorts. One entails using the forms for practical trouble-shooting. This is how, for instance, a carpenter uses the form of the couch (596b4-8). The second is a properly theoretical enquiry about the properties of specific forms (510d7-e1) that establishes the field of theoretical deductive sciences, such as mathematics. Its value lies in making clear what these specific forms are (511a8-9). In both procedures, the same cognitive state is present: knowledge obtained by enquiry, that Socrates terms 'thought' or 'discursive reasoning' (*dianoia*, 511d8). Just as appearances and trust were both involved in the power of belief, thought and intelligence are both involved in the power of knowledge:

> [T12] Due to habit we have often referred to the cases of expertise (*technai*) as knowledge, but another name is required. They are clearer than belief and more obscure than knowledge. In a previous argument we defined it as thought (*dianoia*): as such, let it be so. It seems to me that we are not to dispute about a name when there is so much more lying before us in this investigation. (533d4-9)

In this passage, Socrates refers to a habit of supposing that expertise is knowledge. This is not technically wrong but remains imprecise. Strictly speaking, expertise proceeds from positing forms in order to infer consequences either about the appearances or by means of appearances (not to enquire what forms themselves are) and should therefore be termed thought. Such a distinction of kinds of knowledge corresponds to the division between the third and the uppermost segment in the line. The latter approaches forms by aiming to ground them in a principle that is not posited (510b6-7). This is what Socrates calls dialectical knowledge, the mere contemplation of intellectual objects, or simply intellect itself (511b3, d8). Such an approach takes forms not as something posited to explain appearances – deducing more information from them – but as something that requires an explanation of their own. In other words, an account is required (*logon didonai*, see 510c6-7) about what these posited standards are. The relation of forms among themselves is precisely what this kind of investigation addresses (see 510b8 and *allēlōn koinonia*, 476a7 [T10]). The cognitive state that results is, according to T12, rigorously, not merely loosely, termed knowledge (*epistēmē*).

The divided line distinguishes discursive thought and knowledge by the following criteria: (i) the former take an hypothesis (the positing of a form) as the principle of its investigation (510b5) and proceeds making inferences about the rest of things (510d1), while the latter departs from its hypothesis, that is seen as provisional, and enquires after a non-hypothetical principle of each thing (510b6-7, 511b3-5); (ii) the former includes images (of forms) in its procedures,[20] while

---

[20] I understand that the images are included in the inferences made after the positing of forms (they are not the principle from which they are deduced); therefore, I reject that a different kind of object is introduced in the third segment, be it mathematical objects, as claimed by Proclus, *Commentary to Plato's Republic*, I, 291.21-25, and Adam 1902: II, 159, or some other image of forms, such as in Boyle 1973: 6 or Smith 1996:

the latter deals only with forms (510b7-8) with no use of perception (511c1, 7-8); (iii) the former does not give an account of what the posited form is (510c6-8), while the latter does it by means of the power of dialectic (511b3); (iv) the former aims at agreement (510d2), while the latter aims at forms (511c2); (v) the former is typical of a series of practical procedures (*pragmateuomenoi*, 510c3) involving reasoning (*logismos*, 510c3), including expertise (511b1, c6) and geometry (510c2).[21]

Book V has shown us that belief and knowledge are set over different objects. But the illustration of the divided line specifies that, on the one hand, belief is set over the same objects as appearance (i.e. what appears) and, on the other, that there are two ways of conceiving of knowledge, both related to the same objects (i.e. forms).[22] For this reason, appearances and beliefs can be grouped under the term 'belief', and knowledge and thought under the terms 'knowledge' and 'intelligence' (see 534a1-2),[23] as general conceptions formulated according to what the soul does in respect to their particular objects. Appearances may be apprehended or judged; forms may be posited or defined. Indeed, Socrates sees a certain correspondence between these attitudes. Apprehension is akin to positing because neither entails further individuation of their objects. In contrast, judgement and intelligence both involve processes of individuation in the form of either guessing or defining their objects. Furthermore, apprehension is necessary for judging and positing for defining.[24] It is for this reason that he concludes that 'as intelligence is to belief [referring to the two concepts in general], knowledge relates to trust as thought relates to appearance' (534a4-5, my brackets).

The image of the divided line helps us to understand why every cognition is, in a sense, cognition of forms. Beliefs judge by guessing some form. Thought acknowledges that forms are being posited. Intellectual contemplation aims at explaining forms based on their relation to each other. On the other hand, the argument in book V stresses the different stages of cognition as different powers. Obtaining an undifferentiated appearance is the power of ignorance. Judging it to be *something* is the power of belief, while the power of knowledge is knowing what this something perfectly is. Power is a central concept in the explanation of interaction in the *Republic* and the theme of the next chapter.

---

28. For interpretations similar to mine, see Stocks 1911: 85; Cross and Woozley 1964: 230, Robinson 1971: 195. Images, in my view, are appearances of forms, so that the inferences drawn from the positing of forms are about perceptible objects in general.
[21] I emphasize the connection between discursive thought and practical knowledge. The introduction of the example of geometry has in view the inferences that it allows about shapes in general, which are basic objects of sight (see 477c7). For the practical use of geometry and mathematics in general in Socrates's time, see 522c6-8, 522e1-523a3, 525b1-c6, 526c11-d5, 527a1-4. For views that insist that expertise and practical knowledge in general are simply belief, while discursive thought is proper of theoretical investigation see Murphy 1951: 186–7; Lafrance [1981] 2015: 192–3. For views closer to mine, see Nettleship 1935: 252–3; Wieland [1982]1999: 211–12. More on this topic in Chapter 12.
[22] I hold that the line supports the thesis that there are two different accomplishments for the same kind of objects. While the two lower segments of the line describe two components in belief (the accomplishment of apprehending appearances and the accomplishment of judging them), the two upper segments of the line describe two modes of knowledge: grounded knowledge in a strict sense, and knowledge based on assumptions. An important tradition among interpreters reads the divided line as displaying correspondence between different existent objects and different cognitive states (see Adam 1902: II, 64; Wedberg 19551955: 99–103; Lafrance [1981] 2015: 185; Smith 1996: 28) Another important tradition has shown, however, that the argument of the divided line emphasizes differences of approach to the objects of belief and cognition, and does not entail ontological differences (see Bosanquet 1895: 251; Nettleship 1935: 239; Hackforth 1942: 1–2; Crombrie 1962: v.1, 126).
[23] In another synecdoche, Socrates gives the name *noēsis* (511d8) to one kind of the intellectual realm (*noēton*, 509d4, 510b2). At the recapitulation of the conclusion at 533d4-534a1, he uses the word *epistēmē*.
[24] This does not mean that the knowledge resulting from inferences from forms in the third segment is a requirement for the enquiry that gives justification about them. Although one of course needs to posit forms in order to investigate what they are, one does not need to investigate the inferences that may be drawn from them regarding perceptibles. More on this topic in Chapter 16.

5

Power

The previous chapter offered an overview of our cognitive apparatus to explain how we learn. Cognition begins with judging appearances to be something, a judgement that commits us to some state of affairs we believe to be true. A further judgement on these appearances may, however, suggest that this first is wrong. This generates puzzlement. The path out of puzzlement begins with positing forms as the being of what appears to us, by means of which we obtain standards for identification, counting of multiplicities, measuring opposites, etc. Even unknowingly, we use forms to cognize appearances and as the truthmakers for our beliefs. However, we can acknowledge that this is what we are doing and thence investigate both the kind of inferences we can make from forms and what forms are. In the latter case, we seek definitions and explanations by determining the connections among forms themselves.

This theory of cognition is introduced in the argument at the end of book V that aims to prove to the lover of spectacles that he does not possess the cognitive position of knowledge, and that therefore he is not a good candidate for ruling a just city. Built on the difference between knowledge and belief as powers as a means for showing the interlocutor that his cognition is set over appearances as opposed to forms, this argument concludes that the lover of spectacles is liable to false judgement and therefore does not possess a cognitive position sufficient to qualify as 'knowledge'. The lover of spectacles already agrees with Socrates that knowledge is different from belief (477b6-7), that it is set over the being of things (477b11) and that it is infallible (while beliefs are fallible (477e7-8)). What remains to be shown to him is that *his* cognition is fallible because it is not set over the being of things. Only in acknowledging this will he be able to accept that he is not in a condition to undertake certain accomplishments, that his power is limited. It is for this reason that powers are central to the argument.

This chapter explains the role of powers within this argument as well as more broadly along the *Republic* as a whole. Though the cognitive powers involved in the argument at the end of book V form one specific kind of power, I argue that 'power' generally denotes the accomplishment of an agent, and particularly denotes the contrast between this accomplishment and the end pursued in action. In this comparison we may individuate the relation between the state of affairs obtained in an action and the end that the agent aimed at, measuring their success or failure. Within this broader sense of power, the argument directed at the spectacle-lover consists of establishing that his cognitive state falls short of the end he aimed at because it is not set over forms. Let us begin with this argument about what cognitive powers are:

> [T13] We claim powers to be a certain kind of beings, indeed those because of which we can do whatever we can do, as well as everything else that could do something. For example, I say that vision and hearing are powers, if you understand what I mean by that kind.
>
> I understand, he said.

So, listen to what I think about them: of powers I see neither a certain colour, nor a shape, nor any any of those features found in many other beings, [features] which, when observed, allow me to distinguish outside myself that some are such and some are different. Of powers I rely on one single feature: what they are set over and their accomplishment, thence I call each of them a power: the one that is set over the same object and accomplishes the same, I call the same [power], the one set over a different object and accomplishing something different, I call a different [power]. (477c1-d5, my brackets)

Power is what allows us to do something (477c1-2); it is the attribute that qualifies beings as agents. Because this is a real attribute, with causational explanatory features, powers are real beings, whose presence and absence alter phenomena. The pronoun *hais* (translated as 'because of which') in the second line of the quote was read as an instrumental dative, entailing that powers are a means by which we may do things.[1] My objection to this reading is that it gives us a circular description of powers: power is that by means of which we have power. I shall argue that powers are grounding explanatory principles, and not independent beings that are instrumental to events. For instance, when Socrates asks, 'does the musician have the power of making someone averse to music *because of music*?' (335c9), he is not referring to a means, but to the attribute whose presence explains something the agent does or, for that matter, does not do.[2]

The argument begins by introducing four cognitive powers.[3] These are vision, hearing (477c3), knowledge and belief (477b6-9). Unlike other powers, cognitive powers are not verifiable by a state of affairs in the world; they are inferred from some accomplishment regarding an object[4], thence being a more problematic case. How is it possible to verify that someone other than us (see 'outside myself') has the power to see? Powers such as vision do not obtain a state of affairs in the world, but rather an internal state of affairs. This is a cognitive (or psychological) state (see *pathēmata tēs psuchēs*, 511d7) that cannot be individuated by some direct verification, though it may be inferred. I cannot, for instance, observe that someone is blind. But I may infer this based on how this person performs certain actions, for sight is a power that allows, for instance, displacement. Cross-examination, in its turn, is one way of inferring what the beliefs and knowledge of others are. To distinguish between cognitive powers themselves, one must compare the cognitive states obtained.

There is only one (*monon*, 477d2) criterion for individuating powers in general: the relation between the objects they are set over, and their accomplishment, that is, the state of affairs obtained. Socrates is not claiming that there cannot be two powers set over the same objects with different accomplishments;[5] he is also not saying that objects alone answer for the

---

[1] For the interpretation of powers restricted to means, see Lefebvre 2018: 236.
[2] For other uses of the dative to designate powers, see 341a9-b2; 345a5-6; 348a4. For the causal function of powers, see Bury 1894: 298.
[3] Although cognitive powers are those envisaged by the argument (this is why Bury 1894: 298 and Gosling, 1968: 122 insist on not translating it for faculties or soul's capacities), the definition is valid for powers in general.
[4] The prefix *ap-* in the verb *apergazesthai*, translated as 'accomplishment' at T13, indicates complete achievement by reference to the end that describes the action. See 374c3; 381e6, 420d7, 433c5, 457a1, 464c6 and Harte 2018: 149–50.
[5] Some interpreters (Gosling 1968: 129; Fine 1978: 128; Crombie 1962: 57; Stokes 1992: 119–32; Szaif 2007: 263–4), who have supposed that the text argues for two criteria for the individuation of a power – object and accomplishment – criticized this claim on the basis that the same object could allow for different ends. But this is not what accomplishment means, for it entails the achievement of an action over certain objects. Identifying powers by the state of affairs allows us to find new powers in other accomplishments over the same objects. As

difference between powers.[6] Instead, he asserts that accomplishment and object together are what identify a power.[7] While some interpreters have regarded this premise as insufficient to provide a reasonable argument to the spectacle-lover, I would like to point out that, before this point about powers was introduced, the spectacle-lover had already agreed with the following: (i) knowledge is perfect cognition (477a3, b1); (ii) it is of what perfectly is [something] (477a3); (iii) it is a different power from belief (477b6-10); (iv) it is the accomplishment of cognizing what perfectly is (477b11-12). All that this argument must explain is why belief is a different power (by identifying *both* its accomplishment and object), more specifically, that it is an intermediary cognitive power (*tē metaxu dunamei*, 479d7) rather than a power the spectacle-lover himself describes as the most robust of all (*errōmenestatēn*, 477e1), and then situate the spectacle-lover within the realm of belief-lover. He is not a wisdom-lover.

As previously mentioned, what is peculiar about knowledge is that its end coincides with its correlative, that is, the being of things.[8] Because being is intrinsic to the definition of knowledge (see *pephuken*, 478a14), the action of knowing what being is either obtains or does not obtain, a third option being excluded. There is no such thing as partial knowing or knowing a not-being. As such, there is no such thing as mistaken knowledge, knowing otherwise or obtaining knowledge to a certain degree. The power to know reaches its end only when it obtains its correlative object.[9] Whenever we know what it is for something to be (478a7), this psychological state obtains and, thus, we have the power to know.[10]

The action involved in accomplishing beliefs is judging (477e3, 478a9). It is this, rather than the exclusivity of objects to powers, that is the central point of the argument in my view. Belief and knowledge are distinct powers because judging must allow for mistakes (477e7-8) and therefore its correlative must allow for opposites. One must be able to judge X to be Φ or X to be non-Φ (as in T9, see Chapter 3). That is to say, a belief is something about which the opposite may be true and therefore may be abandoned once such an opposite is found to be the case. This

---

argued in the previous chapter, the subdivision of the divided line indicates different accomplishment over the same objects.

[6] Some interpreters reduce the difference of power to difference of objects: Moss (2021: 50) inverts the text by claiming that 'powers and their accomplishments are individuated by their objects'; Crombie (1962: 57) and Szaif (2007: 263) do the same through the opposite path: by claiming that the objects are intrinsic to the accomplishments, they conclude that objects determine power.

[7] For insistence on taking the accomplishment together with the object, see Santas 1973: 39; Prince 2014: 101 ff.; Payne 2017: 40; Harte 2018: 142; Delcomminette 2008: 32.

[8] Smith (2000: 148) explains what I see as the difference between the end and the correlative, as a difference between the content of a cognitive state that results from simple contact and the object that it is of/about. He, however, does not reach the same conclusion as I because his interpretation understands that the distinction entails exclusion – being is the content, but not the object of knowledge, which in this case can be particular items. What I propose is that end and correlative coincide in the case of knowledge.

[9] Hintikka (1973: 10, 13) points out that the confusion of relatives and ends is the cause of the fallacy in the argument, which concludes that the objects of knowledge are the products of the faculty of knowledge. As I see it, the states of affairs accomplished by cognitive powers are *states of the soul* which obtain from their being set over some objects. In the case of knowledge, the end is the same as the correlative (so it either obtains or not), but this is not valid for belief. The correlative of cognition is not the same as its end (see note 17 in Chapter 1), as a relative entails its correlative by definition and not the end: a relative may fail to obtain an end, but it cannot happen without its correlative. What I am arguing is that, as it is clear in book IV, knowledge has forms as its correlative, but cognition in general has forms as its end.

[10] For positions that restrict knowledge to forms for reasons different from mine, see Schwab 2016: 79; Moss 2021: 111. Other interpreters present arguments to claim that knowledge is not exclusively of forms (see Vogt 2012: 64; Harte 2018: 142). I think they are correct in assuming that nothing precludes different powers from having accomplishments over the same object, but the argument on the exclusivity of forms to knowledge does not depend on it. Though I agree one can have beliefs about forms and appearances, I understand that connecting both in a statement is the basic form of judgement.

means that belief may still occur while failing to obtain its end. The end of belief is truth since when we judge, we trust (we have *pistis*) its content to be true even if we cannot know for certain. But this end is not its correlative, as in the case of knowledge. Its end is truth about whether 'X is (non-)Φ'. If belief and knowledge share the same end, the correlative of belief is different from the correlative of knowledge, for X admits opposites while Φ does not (478b1-2, d5-6, e1-2). As their 'accomplishments cum objects' differ, they are different powers. The spectacle-lover is therefore able to be persuaded by this difference as it rests on a distinction he already supposed. His consent about some clause for exclusivity of objects is not required as the difference in powers is sufficiently persuasive.

The next goal is to make the spectacle-lover see himself as differing from those who pursue wisdom. He acknowledges that to possess a belief is to judge that something is one (*hen ge ti doksazei*, 478b9), and that it is correlative to what it judges. Socrates then proposes to him this correlative to be the appearances (*phaneiē*, 478d5) which partake simultaneously of opposite forms (478e1-2). Because all spectacles are judged to be either fair or unfair (479a5-6), he is led to conclude, by the 'argument from opposites' (T10), that they are judged based on forms. As he acknowledges that this judgement allows for opposites and mistakes, he must accept that he is not devoted to the knowledge of these forms, but only to judging the spectacles (see 477e7-8). The spectacle-lover is on the wrong path for learning. He loves to judge spectacles rather than enquiring about the truth of fairness. He would not, for instance, engage in a conversation such as the one that takes place in Cephalus' house (475d4-6). The spectacle-lover thus cannot avoid false beliefs because he is not concerned with how to obtain truth (479a9-b1). It is safe to assume that Socrates does indeed succeed in showing him that he is not concerned with this matter, and that therefore he falls short of the power of knowledge, as well as of other powers for which knowledge is instrumental, such as ruling.

It is now pertinent to broaden our perspective on the concept of power, which is central to the *Republic*'s account of action as interaction. Here, I shall argue that Socrates supposes an agent's power refers to the state of affairs obtained in an action. This can be compared to the end of the action, a comparison that allows us to assess how much power the agent has to obtain their end. The end of an action is always the state of affairs in which the agent acquires a good. But the state of affairs actually obtained may, nevertheless, fall short of this. How it falls short is that power admits degrees. The agent may either not obtain their end at all or obtain it partially, obtain it by a certain device, or obtain it fully. Because the agent is the cause of a certain state of affairs when pursuing an end, the power to obtain it is ascribed to the agent as a dispositional attribute they have. Whenever the circumstances are similar, the state of affairs will obtain. This conclusion is engendered by analysis of a range of phrasal variations that address the concept of power (as a verb, adjective or noun) in the *Republic*, to which I shall now proceed.

The simplest verbal structure denoting power is the use of the verb *dunasthai* in conjunction with another verb.[11] This is the most elementary phrase because powers are defined by accomplishments. As for the evidence that the state of affairs obtained is the central feature in individuating a power, it comes from the absolute use of the verb where Socrates refers, for instance, to 'some other rich men considered to have great power (*mega dunasthai*)' (336a6-7).

---

[11] For this simplest structure, see also 327c12; 336e9-337a1; 338b7; 349b10; 361d7; 440c2 (with adverb indicating degree), 517c5 (with an expression indicating conditions); 522e2, 565b2-3, 574b4, 590c3-5, 620b7. It is worth noticing that there is no restriction to the kind of action – the same verb *dunasthai* is employed with active and passive verbs, as well as verbs denoting state.

Here, 'having power' simply means that they obtained their end, whatever this may be.[12] That powers are individuated according to the state of affairs obtained may be explained as follows. Given the principle of individuation, a soul is an individual because it is always doing something (either Δ or non-Δ). If so, its actions may be undetermined if not circumscribed between a beginning and an end. In the case of human beings, the beginning is the agent. Action begins with the prevailing end in the agent's soul, which then moves towards obtaining this end that is always described as the state of affairs in which they acquire some good. The action ends only when some state of affairs comparable to the end of the action obtains. As a measure of success or failure, powers are defined by this state of affairs and in contrast to the original end of the agent. It is fair to say that actions begin with an end, and end with a state of affairs where the agent is acknowledged as having the power that corresponds to this state of affairs (as opposed to the end).

As expressed in T13, both accomplishments and objects matter to powers. It must be noted, however, that there is no term in Greek for 'object' and that the concept is introduced to designate a variety of roles played by items in an action.[13] What determines how an object relates to the accomplishment is the action itself. One kind of object is that on which the action causes change (the 'patient' of an action). For instance, Polemarchus challenges Socrates by saying, 'Do you have power to persuade us?' (327c12). Here, the 'us' is the object on which the 'you' will act in an attempt to obtain an end. But it would be false to suppose that 'persuasion' in expressions such as this would not also be an object, because it was something obtained by the action. In the argument on the powers of knowledge and belief, it became clear that correlatives had different roles in each kind of power. Now, it is possible to build a wider view based on the textual evidence that the objects of powers are determined – both in number and in kind – by the state of affairs obtained by the power itself.

To make a simpler example, when Socrates states that 'the washing ... has the power to remove the purple from it [the wool]' (429e2-3, my brackets), both the purple and the wool are objects in this state of affairs. Objects are as many as those included in the state of affairs thus obtained. Further evidence for this global understanding of the object as the set of items included in the state of affairs comes from a very particular use of the pronoun 'something' (*ti*) to describe the object of a power as the whole action: when Thrasymachus challenges Socrates by saying 'trick this argument and accuse falsely, if you have power to do something' (341b8-9, see also 351c8-9), 'something' is not one single particular item. Rather, it is a set of items previously mentioned.

Distinct from objects are the means employed in obtaining the end of the action, precisely because they are not part of the state of affairs obtained. Sometimes, however, mentioning the means matters in the explanation, particularly in those instances where absence of the relevant means was the reason why the end was not obtained. This is clear in Glaucon's statement that 'I shall defend you by means of the power I have' (*amuno hois dunamai*. 474a6-7). The instrumental use of powers is not to be mistaken with the causal explanation powers provide. The latter accounts for something being the agent of a certain outcome and therefore explains why it may be used as a means to another end. The power of means is not the power of the agent; the former is a necessary condition for the latter, but it is not included in its definition. This explains a general use of the term *dunamis* as a resource to be used in actions, such as in

---

[12] For other absolute uses, see 366a8, 474a7-8.
[13] For different kinds of objects, see also 395a3-6, 400c8-10, 429e2-3, 486c7; 507a1; 516a2-3; 516b5-6; 517a5-6, 528a3, 529b3-4, 577a2; 599a7-8. For the difficulties of assigning specific kinds of objects to powers, see Benson 1997: 88–9.

the expression 'vicious people who have wealth and other powers' (364a6).[14] An individual may acquire, have or lose these resources. In the latter case, the absence of power in the means causes the failure of obtaining whichever end one pursues.

By far the most common way of expressing power in the *Republic* is by qualifying the agent with the adjective 'powerful' (*dunamenon* or *dunaton*), which is also frequently used as a noun. In these cases, we should understand that the other elements relevant to the action, if not mentioned, are implicit. Extreme cases of implicit content are those that do not even mention action, such as 'mustn't they be prudent and powerful?' (412c13, see also 451d7). Alternatively, there exist cases in which only the action is mentioned, such as 'those who are greatly powerful to accumulate' (344a1-2).[15] At the other extreme, some statements express the whole state of affairs obtained, such as 'those who are completely unjust are powerful to oppress cities and groups of human beings' (348d5-6).[16]

As previously mentioned, 'power' may express the *décalage* between the intended end and the state of affairs obtained. As such, being powerful admits degrees. One individual has more or less power than another, meaning that one agent may obtain the end of the action more completely than the other. The most extreme degree on this scale is, of course, being entirely powerless. This is expressed in statements such as 'they are powerless to act in common with themselves' (351e1-2).[17] Comparative instances are expressed by either the adverb 'more' (as in 'you are more powerful than they are to take part in both'; see 520b8-c1) or the comparative (*dunatoteros*, 351a2-3, 352b7-9) and superlative forms (*dunatotatos*, 332d10-11, e3-4, 472e7-8, 516d1-2).

Degrees of power explain why the term is often used in 'restrictive' expressions.[18] These formulae entail that the power of an agent determines the limits of what they may achieve, such as in 'I will pay as much as I have the power to' (338b7). Very common to the Greek language, these expressions suggest that any positive statement about power (e.g. 'X has the power to Φ') is also a restrictive statement in the sense that 'X has the power *only* to Φ'. This is why expressions that designate power also denote allotment. These expressions establish limits or boundaries for their bearers according to the state of affairs these agents obtain. Powers denote some mapping of reality according to who was the cause for what in the whole state of affairs.

This leads us to the more basic use of the noun *dunamis*. As said, power is the mark of the agent; the attribute agents have for having obtained a certain state of affairs.[19] As an abstract noun, power becomes primarily an explanatory principle that grounds the qualification of the

---

[14] See also 423a3-4, 591a7-8.
[15] For the description of being powerful for a certain action, see also 359b2-3; 361b2, 368a6-7, 368c2-3, 402d4, 432c4, 476c2-3, 489c1-2, 493c6, 519d9 (with the verb 'to be'), 536d1, 573c4-5, 575b9, 577a6, 577b6-7.
[16] For the description which includes the whole state of affairs obtained, see also 394e8-9, 398a1-2, 401c3-5, 402a2-3, 407e1-2, 476b9-10, 476c7-8, 479c3-5, 479d10-e4, 484b4-5, 484b9-10, 484c6-d2, 503a1-4, 511a5-7, 519e4-520a2, 531e3-4, 533c3, 559b3-4, 9-10, 559d7-8, 573e8-574a1.
[17] For the use of powerless, see also: 352a7-8, 352d1, 358e7-359a1, 359a7, 359b8 (which refers to *adunamia*) 362d8-9, 366d2-3, 368b4-5, 392e1, 395b5-6, 476b6-7, 514b2-3, 515c8-d1, 518a5, 533c2, 537b3, 551d9-10, 568d1. For degrees of power see Macé 2006: 58–60.
[18] For the restrictive use, see Lefebvre 2018: 161–2. There are different restrictive expressions, using power terms with 'as' (*hōs*): 367b2-3, 434e1-2, 450c8, 504b1; 'in such a manner as' (*hopōs*): 368c3-4, 466d7; 'as much as' (*hosos*): 338b7, 374e12, 509c9-10; 'according to' (*kata*): 429e7, 460a5, 466c9, 469b10, 507a6, 535a11-b1, 619a7; 'as far as' (*kath'hoson*): 534b1, 565a6-7; 'to the extent of' (*eis*): 366d3-4, 381c7, 427e1-2, 458e3-4, 464d3-4, 500d2, 587a1-2, 590d5-6; 'to the point that' (*eis hoson*): 607a1-2, 613b1.
[19] Bury (1894: 298, 300) insists that *dunamis* is a necessary quality of every member of a correlated pair, and a self-externalizing explanation. Souilhé (1919: 149) describes this as the designation of a peculiar constitution that locates the beings in different groups, therefore being a principle of diversity.

agent as powerful.[20] For instance, the shepherd 'tried the ring to see if it had that power' (360a5-6), that is, to make its user invisible. Another less common way of expressing the presence of a power in an agent is to use the dative, as in Cephalus' statement, 'If at least I was empowered (*en dunamei*) to easily make my way to the city' (328c7; see also 567b1-2). This approach to powers as abstract individuals matters for a variety of accounts, among them to explain the transference of power between agents. Returning to the example of the ring, for instance, it is important to establish that it has a power in order to, subsequently, be able to refer to it as 'the power they said was given to the ancestor of Gyges of Lydia' (359d1-2). Powers are properties that agents may have, acquire and lose.[21]

Up until this point, powers have been addressed as concepts that explain action. One important reason for singling out powers as individuals, however, is to turn them into an object of enquiry in order that they might be properly defined. For instance, we first learn that the city 'has the power to preserve in all circumstance the belief about what is dreadful' (429b8-9), that is, we learn about how this power obtains a certain state of affairs. We may then isolate this power the city has in order to prompt an enquiry on what it is: 'Such a power of preservation in all circumstance of the right and lawful belief about what is and is not dreadful I call courage, and posit it to be such, unless you don't have something else to say' (430b3-5).[22] By positing powers as objects of enquiry, we may avoid conceptual mistakes regarding which power accounts for which state. It prevents, for instance, the attitude of Thrasymachus who, as Adeimantus puts it, 'ludicrously inverts the powers of [justice and injustice]' (367a8-9). The argument addressing the distinction of knowledge and belief aims precisely at this kind of enquiry (see 477b6), as well as the comparison between the power of vision and the power of intellect (see 507c6-8, 532a2-3).

The enquiry into powers leads to an enquiry into the relations they hold between themselves, despite being different from each other. Powers may be connected by their end, as in the case of knowledge and belief; they may have similar features, as in vision and intellect; they may also be instrumental, as are the cognitive powers. The *Republic* presents a very interesting way of approaching this relation of powers as the means for other powers. First, it introduces a power for action with mention of the means required for it to obtain its end: 'Does the city that prevails over others have such a power without justice?' (351b7-8). This is followed by an account of this kind of means as being a power itself: 'if (. . .) injustice arises in one individual, will its power be destroyed?' (351e7-8), a notion of instrumental power already discussed. Finally, it introduces information about the power this power has, such as 'doesn't it seem that injustice has the power [. . .] to make one powerless to act with oneself' (351e10-352a2). Justice and injustice are alternatively addressed as being powers (433d7-8) and as having powers (358b4-6, 588b6-8).

This idea of powers of powers is highly reminiscent of what has become known as Molière's regress.[23] This is the power to have the power to have the power to have the power and so on. Yet there is a simple way to avoid this conundrum when we are reminded that powers are defined by the state of affairs they obtain. The power that justice and injustice have is to obtain a certain state of affairs. If they are the powers that accomplish it, they are the powers that they have. At least

---

[20] For the philosophical coinage of abstract nouns, see Havelock 1978: 312–14. For power as the attribute of agents, see Souilhé 1919: 91, 149.

[21] For acquisition of power, see 366c1-2, 494c2, 546d4-5, 591a7-8; for transference of power, see 364b6-c5, 391a7-8, 433b8-9, 443b4-5, 618c2-3. Of particular interest is the transference of power of the sun and the form of the good, see 508b6-7, 508d10-e2, 509b1-3. For losing the power (*a contrario sensu*), see 351e7-8, 518e2.

[22] The same kind of shift happens about the learning subjects: they are powers for certain states of affairs (see 522e1-2), and they have the power for certain states of affairs (see 521d1-2). Payne (2017: 40) calls these 'self-transmitting powers'.

[23] See Molière, *Le malade imaginaire*, troisième intermède.

two instances of textual evidence substantiate this notion that the power a power has is the power it is. The first is Adeimantus' statement on the power of justice and injustice, which is 'what each of them does by their proper power in the soul of the person who has it' (366e5-6). This implies that the power justice and injustice have is whatever power the person who has them possesses. The second piece of evidence is in the first line of T7: 'So, in relation to which of the parts of a human being does [simulation] have the power it has?' (602c4-5, my brackets). In other words, the power simulation has is the attribute a part of the soul possesses due to simulation (and not a different one). This is sufficient evidence to avoid any regress and thus return to the question of different relations powers hold among themselves.

As previously stated, the restrictive expressions of power inspire a notion of allotment within which each agent obtains some part of a whole state of affairs. The idea of mapping different roles applies to powers themselves, in describing what powers there are and how they relate to each other. This approach is evident in the following passage:

> [T14] Don't we say that each expertise differs from others for having a different power? And, my dear sir, do not answer against your belief, so that we may conclude something.
> They indeed differ in this, he said.
> Isn't it also the case that each of them provides us a benefit that is peculiar to it, and not common, for instance, medicine [provides] health, navigation safety in sailing, and so on with the others?
> Absolutely.
> Doesn't the reward expertise provide rewards, for this is its power? Or do you call it medicine or navigation? And if you want to make rigorous distinctions, as you propose, if a captain recovers his health because sailing in the sea is beneficial to him, would you for this reason call this power medicine?
> Not at all, he said. (346a1-b6, my brackets)

The previous chapter evidenced how expertise (*technē*) is a form of knowledge that allows for inferences; in particular, it is the form that makes practical inferences: it leads us to accomplishments that are good for us. For this reason, every expertise entails a power.[24] Notice that T14 emphasizes how powers are not individuated by whichever state of affairs is the case – only by those obtained in actions with a certain end. The captain does not become a doctor when he recovers his health by sailing, because health was not the end of his action. As human agency entails purposiveness in action, so do human powers.[25] Although some powers are not determined by an end, such as that of the ring of invisibility, human power is always determined according to the end of the agent and what they obtain.

It is precisely because the end of the action is part of the definition of a power that an expertise may be knowledge as well as power – that is, knowledge of the state of affairs to be pursued in order for the agent to succeed and be powerful. This association of knowledge and power is welcome within the theory of action as interaction in the *Republic* – not because an agent will learn how to accomplish whichever end they set themself, but rather because they will learn how to restrict their ends. It is typical of unproductive individuals to set ends without considering their power to obtain them (458a1-b1). In contrast, experts are those who learn what they do and

---

[24] For expertise defined by power, see 454a1-2, 532c4-d1 and Payne (2017: 39).
[25] For human action explained by purpose, see Cross and Wozzley 1964: 89. I disagree with Harte (2018: 153–4) about a power having atypical results because in my view powers explain agency. Atypical results should be explained by different concurrent powers obtaining a certain state of affairs.

do not have the power to accomplish. As Glaucon puts it, 'the smart expert discriminates what in his expertise he has power to achieve and what he doesn't' (360e5-361a1).

When determining our ends, our reasoning takes our power into account. As mentioned in Chapters 2 and 3, we may have consented actions even when our good is not available. In these cases, our reasoning scrutinizes the circumstances to verify what kind of end they allow us to obtain, and thus to point out a *pis aller*, which is nonetheless the end to which the agent commits themself. This is what I term a power device. Our reasoning is capable of compromising our ends according to the power we possess: rational ends are determined after considering their feasibility. By the end of the *Republic*, Socrates insists that we must engage in learning about what gives us power to 'always choose in every circumstance the best within the feasible' (618c4-5). This means that, for agents in whom reasoning prevails, ends are set according to power such that they are powerful and satisfied with their accomplishments. Because desire does not have the capacity of assessing the ends it pursues, in actions in which desire prevails, rather than moderating their ends, the agent engages in enhancing their power. Therefore, power is in itself a good for desire. For this same reason, as Socrates will argue, for agents guided by appetitive ends, power devices result in failures and dissatisfaction, because, after obtaining a state of affairs, these people continue to aim for more.

Given the general picture of the uses of power expressions in the *Republic*, it is reasonable to conclude that the translation of expressions, such as *dunaton/dunata* and *adunaton/adunata* as 'what is possible' and 'what is impossible' when referring to states of affairs is too vague in comparison to their meaning. When used in action explanation, these expressions entail that certain states of affairs are (or are not) to be achieved by some agent under certain circumstances. They imply a notion of causation that should not be mistaken for the concept of modal possibility.[26] For instance, when Thrasymachus answers '*adunaton*' at 335c10, he refers to the power a musician lacks rather than to the impossibility of some event.[27] Of course, this does not preclude us from saying that something is impossible *because* there is no power available to cause it. But a much more accurate translation would be 'unfeasible' or 'not accomplishable'.

As a matter of fact, it is structural to the argument of the *Republic* that showing a state of affairs to be feasible (*dunaton*) is to show that it is not against nature (*ou para phusin* – 375e5).[28] In other words, what is not accomplishable (*adunaton*) is against nature. Nature, the proper movement of natural beings, has laws that describe phenomena that are neither necessary nor inevitable. However, these laws determine that some events are against nature, in which case they are not accomplishable and impossible.[29] If the nature of an agent does not preclude them from obtaining a certain state of affairs, the state of affairs is feasible and the agent in question may have or acquire the power to accomplish it. Again, the power of the agent is still what grounds the fact that the state of affairs is feasible. The only difference with the previous account of powers is that, by referring to the nature of the agent, we may determine what is not feasible for them. In this case, we also determine a law of nature. It is for this reason that investigating whether the community of women and children is a feasible concept (450c7-8) coincides with determining whether the nature of women is such that it precludes them from obtaining a certain state of affairs (452e3-453a5). This argument will be covered in more detail in Chapter 10.

---

[26] For possibility as what can be accomplished by action of an agent that causes it, see Faust 1931: 46–8; Menn 1994: 98.
[27] For an outcome being 'impossible', see 335d2, 353e1-3, 370e5-8, 374a6, 375c10-d1, 381c2-8, 391e1-2, 392a10, 436c6-7, 467b5-6, 555c7-d1, 566a12-b2, 582c7-9.
[28] For the connection of power and nature see 395b4-7, 621c3-4 and Souilhé 1919: 158–9.
[29] For what is unfeasible, see for instance 424e6-425a1, 456c1, 583e7.

Finding the causes of (un)feasible states of affairs for agents has interesting consequences for the way we account for the interaction of powers. For instance, when Adeimantus states that 'relative to the gods nothing has the power of being either unnoticed or violent' (365d7), it becomes evident that agents who may attempt to accomplish these feats will certainly fail due to the power of the gods (see also 612c8-9). The gods' powers are greater than ours such that their accomplishments cause us to lack power in our own. The restriction the power of others imposes on one's power is what we should understand as political power at 473d3. One has political power (*dunamis*) when one is able to obtain one's end without restriction caused by the power of others in the city, though this should not be mistaken for political prevailing or predominance (*kratos*).

Chapter 1 demonstrated that predominance is a superiority in conflicts or competitions. In internal conflict, predominance is ascribed to whichever part of the soul determines the end of an action, though the mode of this action is determined by the part that does not prevail. The power each part has, however, does not depend on prevailing; it depends on obtaining a good state of affairs. Desire may obtain its end under the prevailing of reasoning if they cooperate. On the other hand, in general it does not obtain its end when it prevails, because an agent guided by appetite tends not to be satisfied with the state of affairs obtained. One may predominate without being powerful enough to obtain its end. Predominance is determining the end of others, while power is obtaining the state of affairs described in this end. Power admits degrees and may be intermediate, restricted, or partial; predominance, however, does not admit degrees, it is always either true or false; one either is superior, or is not. Prevailing results from a competition to gain the single winning position; power, on the other hand, is not established like this: different powerful agents may obtain the same state of affairs simultaneously. If they have the same end, agents may be compared among themselves as more or less powerful, but this is not a competition for one single position relative to others; it is only to measure their success in obtaining their end.

This chapter has put forward a significant amount of evidence of the uses of the concept of power in the *Republic*. While I do not claim that all these are philosophically relevant uses, they lay down the premises for a theory of action, interaction and justice. Above all, it is relevant for understanding the *Republic* that power in it is not a modal notion, but objective and determined by the state of affairs obtained in the world. Because it gives relevant information about the agent's particular success in obtaining their ends, power is what provides us with information about their action and interaction. Its relevant role is to point out the results obtained, the objects and agents involved, and how the agent qualifies as a cause of something. Power matters for flourishing. Yet before I demonstrate how, it is first necessary to understand how an individual's personality is built on these concepts. This is the topic of the next chapter.

6

Personality

Thus far, the following has been established: within us exist reasoning and desire which may either cooperate or conflict with each other; in addition to *thumos* that may approve or disapprove of our actions according to our beliefs about our own flourishing. Each of them is informed by our cognitive apparatus, which may go astray should desire prevail in us. While these are the explanations of singular actions, *thumos* also has a role in determining our tendencies in future actions for it adds pain or pleasure to our present actions. Habit formation is the recurrence of actions, with their ends and modes. We form habits because conflicts add pain to our experience; we then hesitate when appetites arise and do not fully engage in the action when *thumos* manifests itself. Acquiring a stable personality is therefore a device for suffering less. On the other hand, personality is also a very powerful explanatory concept in building a theory of action and interaction, as it gives standards of different outcomes of interaction. This is the approach that is favoured in the *Republic*.

The personality approach responds to a deadlock in the dialogue between Socrates and Cephalus at the opening of the *Republic*. Socrates infers from Cephalus' testimony about his own life that he thinks justice is an attribute of certain actions, such as speaking the truth and giving back what was once taken from someone (331c2-3). However, these same actions may be both just and unjust (331c4-5): if a friend, in rage, wants returned the gun that he left with us in order to kill someone, the just thing to do may, in fact, be to lie to him and not return the gun (331c5-8). Actions are appearances of forms (see T10 in Chapter 4). As such, they admit opposite qualifiers and are therefore not a good place to look if trying to make a point about justice and flourishing. A schematic personality that, by definition, will take the course of action considered to be just (or unjust) in every circumstance provides a much better explanation than singular actions. Because it follows what is *considered* to be justice (or injustice), it will highlight our basic assumptions about this kind of behaviour. Such personalities are therefore very useful to test our beliefs about flourishing.[1]

A good example of how this works is furnished by the case of the decent man in Chapter 3. This man is someone in whom reasoning and desire cooperate: he has a tendency to maintain serenity, which is beneficial in facing adversity, such as the loss of a beloved one. For him, *thumos* is very important in his endurance because, as it is based on a belief about flourishing in accordance with the mores, he finds support to overcome his pain in the presence of others. What a man of this personality does when he is alone, however, is an open question. How dependent is he on the presence of others? Does he really trust that his flourishing lies in refusing self-pity? And is this trust strong enough for him to be a spectator of tragedy without letting the principle of serenity go? Let us suppose that this is the peculiarity of this personality: no one can be sure

---

[1] On the personality approach – as opposed to the action approach – of the enquiry on justice, see Keyt 2006: 352.

about the extent to which he is virtuous apart from his community, whose customs are beneficial to him. This uncertainty suffices for Socrates to argue that he should not be exposed to poetry that simulates base characters. On the other hand, however, no one can say that, together with others in his *politeia*, he is not virtuous.

The decent man is therefore one of the explanatory personalities in the *Republic*. The central focus of the dialogue, however, lies in a group of different personalities, the lovers:

> [T15] We called it 'the appetitive part' because of the intensity of its desires for food, drink, sex and all the other things that follow from them, and also 'the money-loving part,' because it is by means of money that most of these desires are accomplished.
> Rightly so.
> But then if we said that its pleasure and love (*philia*) are for profit, it was mostly because we could thence ground our argument in one main point that would make clear to us what we refer to when talking about this part of the soul, and also because it would be correct to call it money-lover or profit-lover, wouldn't it?
> This is how it seems to me, he said.
> And so, what? Didn't we say that *thumos* is related to prevailing and always moves as a whole towards victory and reputation?
> Absolutely.
> And if we refer to it as a victory-lover and an honour-lover, would this be appropriate?
> Most appropriate.
> Then it is clear to all that the part by which we learn is always disposed towards knowing where the truth lies, and cares the least for money and reputation.
> The least.
> On this account would we call it learning-lover and philosopher [wisdom-lover]?
> Of course.
> Isn't it so, I said, that it also rules in the souls of some, while the others [rule] in the souls of others, whichever happens to be the case?
> This is so, he said.
> For this reason, the three prime kinds of human beings are the philosopher, the victory-lover and the profit-lover?
> Absolutely. (580e2-581c6, my brackets)

T15 introduces us to a specific process of personality formation, one that results in the 'three prime kinds of human beings'. Socrates' purpose in describing these personalities is to map their 'locations' relative both to each other, as well as to justice and flourishing (548c8-d4, 587d12-e4). There is something schematic about their description, clear in the way they are simply depicted as 'part-like' people. For these people, their good is that this one part obtains its end and they experience no kind of conflict, hesitation or remorse. The activity of a part of the soul was previously described in a specific technical sense: an object is taken as the end of its activity, and the part expects to obtain pleasure when the whole soul obtains this end. Because parts of the soul cannot have faculties or internal conflicts in themselves, they cannot opt to cease to move towards their objects, or to move towards different kinds of objects. This is not the case with people in general, who can have different ends. What makes the personalities described in T5 so exceptional is that they have one single motivation; they emerge by a specific process in which one part of their souls does not simply prevail but rules (581c1-2).

Prevailing and ruling are two intrinsically connected concepts, though they differ in duration and in regard to the activity of *thumos*.[2] When Socrates talks about ruling, he refers to a long-lasting predominance in which the end of the prevailing part is set as a default for our actions. The ruling of a part entails that our beliefs about our flourishing, according to which our *thumos* judges our actions, follow the end of the prevailing part, whichever it is. Thus when desire prevails in an action and *thumos* reacts against it, for instance, this is a sign that this agent believes their flourishing lies in pursuing rational ends. In this person, desire may occasionally prevail – but reasoning still rules in the long run. On the other hand, in personalities in which desire rules, *thumos* judges by adding pleasure to actions guided by desire. This person believes that her flourishing lies in the quest for unreasonable ends.

Although T15 does not make it explicit, Socrates needs a notion stronger than ruling to account for the personalities he is interested in there: as he puts it elsewhere, a 'part-like' person is not simply someone with a ruling part in their soul, but with a part that occupies the throne of the soul (553b7-c1), that is, that rules hegemonically. These are one-dimensional people: obsessed, predictable and able to do whatever it takes to obtain their end. These are the lovers.

Lovers are a prime kind of personality precisely because they emerge from the simplest process for personality building: one single object over and above everything else. In Chapter 1, we saw that prevailing ends were not enough to explain an action alone; that the mode of the action was also significant, and that it was determined by the non-prevailing parts. As such, it is the soul as a whole (not simply one of its parts) that acts. If modes matter in prevailing, they therefore also matter in ruling, that is, in accounting for personalities; a good example of this is the decent man, who is virtuous *in a certain mode*. However, the inclusion of mode generates a multiplicity of personalities that does not favour Socrates' schematic approach to the matter in T15. A whole encyclopaedia would be required to describe them all. Lovers therefore make excellent explanatory devices for this kind of general argument precisely because of their simplicity and predictability.

The concept of desire can explain a variety of lovers since, although the object of desire was earlier identified as nutritive and reproductive, it also included other objects akin to these. This factor makes the unity of the object pursued by people ruled by desire problematic. As a matter of fact, a multiplicity of lovers may be conceptualized as such. This is precisely the case in the *Republic*: we learn of the lover of youths (474d3), of wine (475a5) and of food (475c4) – not to mention the spectacle-lover (475d2) with whom we have already been acquainted. Socrates' schematic approach in T15 replaces them all for the 'the money-lover', a kind under which other lovers do not fall, but which offers a good median within a distribution chart of desire-like people, where money is the means for many of them to obtain their goals. The money-lover rigorously speaking is also termed the oligarch (548a6). He is not someone who seeks money for other ends, such as food, drink and sex. Rather, he is motivated by an appetitive desire of a certain kind: he is obsessed with money. The money-lovers turn their reasoning into an instrument to obtain this end only; their *thumos* judges accordingly (553d1-7), and therefore they do not have any internal conflict. Their reasoning is simply present to calculate what kind of appetitive pleasures to have because they fear spending too much on them.[3] They dismiss honour

---

[2] In explaining ruling as a metaphor for long-term ends and personality, some interpreters include the idea of a personal *choice* of life and values that, to my view, is not compatible with the kind of psychology we find in the *Republic* see Kraut 1973: 221; Klosko 1988: 344; Blössner 2007: 363. For a critique of this position, see Johnstone 2011: 152–3.

[3] Because money-lovers love money as an end in itself, they constitute evidence that desire is not capable of means-ends reasoning, as some interpreters have thought (see note 29 in Chapter 1). Were desire capable

and victory if these entail spending money, in which case they prefer to be a loser (555a1-6). This is the avaricious personality (554a5-8, c11-d3, see 558d4-5), one not disposed to splurge their goods on other pleasures.

Neither is the object of a *thumos*-like person easy to unify. T15 states clearly that *thumos* is related to prevailing and associates it with winning and reputation. In Chapter 2, we saw that *thumos* reacts positively when either our action or our situation corresponds to our beliefs about our flourishing. As such, it seems a *thumos*-like person would find pleasure only in obtaining what they believe to be their flourishing. However, we also saw that in cases of the antinomy of *thumos*, in order to have this pleasure, one must both act according to their belief of flourishing *and* avoid situations in which this flourishing is obstructed by others. Flourishing in a way that others would accept, that is, a shared concept of flourishing, is therefore a decisive factor for a *thumos*-like person to obtain a kind of win-win outcome: they do not simply wish to win, but to win in such a way that others acknowledge as fair. Victory and reputation may be conflicting ends, but, since a lover does not have conflicts, a *thumos*-like person must aim at their intersection by following the shared belief about flourishing: they are, therefore, victory *and* reputation lovers. I take this to be the meaning of the claim that *thumos* moves towards victory and reputation *as a whole* (581b1).

In Greek, all these lovers are designated by names beginning with the prefix *phil*-, which we still similarly associate with obsessions in words such as 'philatelist' or 'bibliophile'. Among the lovers mentioned in T15 is the wisdom-lover, the *philo-sopher*, on which the *Republic* primarily focuses.[4] This is how this personality is introduced in book V:

> [T16a] Do you remember, I asked, or do you need to be reminded that, if we say that someone loves something and if it is rightly stated, he must not appear to love part of it, and not another part; but instead he must adore everything?
>
> It seems that you will have to remind me, for I do not have it very clear in mind. (474c8-11)
>
> [T16b] Didn't we say that the philosopher is the one who desires wisdom – not only this one and not that other one, but all of it?
>
> It is true.
>
> Then someone who has restrictions about learning some topics, especially if he is young and has no justification about whether they are useful or not, we shall say that he is neither a lover of learning, nor a philosopher; just as we shall say of someone who rejects food neither that he is hungry, nor that he desires to eat, nor that he is a glutton, but rather that he is actually a bad eater.
>
> This is right. (475b8-c5)

I begin by mentioning that, in the interval between the two cited passages, Socrates gives a list of various examples of lovers that includes the ones already mentioned. T16 identifies these lovers by three features: (i) unrelenting desire; (ii) one-dimensional character and (iii) love for a kind. First, they have a constant desire for X: such people never reject X and, above all, never have

---

of means-end reasoning, money-lovers would not aim at accumulation of money, but at its use as a means. Therefore, instead of allowing for inferences about different capacities desire has, T15 simply states that, because it aims at objects connected to our nutritive and reproductive activities and it cannot learn which of them are good for us, desire is activated towards a multiplicity of objects. For other arguments against the desire means-end reasoning, see Lorenz 2006: 158–15; Parry 2007: 406.

[4] For the description of characters designated by *phil*-, see Burkert 1960: 172–5 and Moore 2020: 250–6. For the object-directed *eros*, see Halperin 1985: 164–5.

enough of X. They continue to desire it. In this sense, being a lover is opposed to being a hater of X, just as the philosopher is opposed to the wisdom-hater (456a4). It is also opposed to being indifferent to X, just as the glutton is opposed to the bad eater (475c2-4).[5] Second, this is not an occasional desire. It is reiterated to the point of constituting a personality. The youth-lover's obsession, for instance, is not described in terms of episodes of passion, but rather in terms of what kind of person he is (*aner erōtikōs*, 474d1-2).[6] Third, the object of desire is the kind rather than particular instances: haecceity does not matter. Particulars are as replaceable[7] as a glass of wine easily exchanged for another. The same goes in the case of philosophers: they do not aim at one single learning, but at all of them (475c6-8). A lover desires all the items that fall under the kind of object they love (475b5).

It is remarkable that a psychology based on different principles of action can accept that there are such one-dimensional people, but there is an explanation for how lovers come to be. It focuses on the case of the philosopher:

[T17] It is completely inevitable that someone who is a lover (*erōtikōs*) by nature delights in everything that is congenial and akin to his beloved.
This is correct, he said.
Would you find something more akin to wisdom than truth?
No, he said.
And is it possible for the same nature to be a lover of wisdom and a lover of falsehood?
Absolutely not.
Therefore, the true lover of learning must straightforwardly pursue the whole truth to the fullest from a young age.
Absolutely.
But when in someone desires flow strongly in one direction, we know that they will be somehow weakened in the other directions, like a flow of water that is channelled.
And so what?
So, when in this person [the desires] flow towards learning and everything related to it, they are [directed] to the pleasure of the soul itself and according to itself, abandoning the bodily pleasures, if he is not a fake but true philosopher. (485c6-e1, my brackets)

According to Kahn (1987: 97-9), this passage claims that *eros* is an undifferentiated psychic energy that may be channelled. That is to say, it may change its objects. In his view, this contradicts the theory of desire presented in book IV of the *Republic*, in which each part of the soul has a desire for a peculiar object. Kahn entertains that the thesis on the channelling of *eros* should not be attributed to Plato, despite its mention in such a crucial argument as the deduction of the philosopher's nature from the definition of philosophy. But, as Scott (2007: 13) points out,

---

[5] A lover has a variety of opposites: the philosopher is opposed to the wisdom-hater (456a4) based on the contrariety of desire and aversion. They are the opposite of the falsehood-lover (485c12-d1) because of the contrariety of its peculiar object. They are also contrasted with honour-lovers and money-lovers (581a2-581b11) because it is impossible to channel desire to different ends. Finally, they differ from the belief-lovers for being truth-lovers (475e4, 501d2). Truth, as we know, is secured by knowledge only.

[6] According to Halperin (1985: 170), Plato is the first philosopher to distinguish between appetite – which is gratified by the possession of the object – and desire, which cannot be satisfied in acquiring the object. On obsession, see Scott 2007: 136 and Parry 2007: 397. On *eros* as dangerous and difficult, see Halperin 1989: 38.

[7] For denial of haecceity see Vlastos 1981: 31; Nussbaum 1986: 181; Araújo 2017: 232-3. For the opposite claim, according to which *eros* has a tendency to possessiveness, see Ludwig 2007: 209.

eros is the channelling of desire (*epithumia*) and it is not *eros* itself that is channelled. A further argument against Kahn's reading is that the channelling metaphor does not require some 'basic matter' or 'psychic energy'. It is perfectly intelligible as a theory that allows for different types of motivation that may eventually conflict with each other, but which also considers ways to solve these conflicts. There is no need to postulate a concept of psychic matter or energy that is displaced from one activity to the other; we may simply suppose that the flow of desires happens when other ends lose their importance. Because philosophers organize their life and time such that they can learn more, their interest in other types of objects diminishes.

What is the channelling of desire? First and foremost, it is an account of habit formation and the decrease of internal conflict. While it associates pleasure with some actions, it also disassociates it from other ends, reducing the frequency of internal conflict and determining habit with increased pleasure of a certain kind. This is desirable because internal conflict diminishes our pleasure. Although the philosopher in particular is described as someone who diverts their desire towards learning in general,[8] we are to expect the channelling of desire in every lover to include the pleasure of learning more about their specific objects. In describing what it is to be both a philosopher or a gymnastic-lover (456a1-5), for instance, Socrates refers to the way both sets of people easily learn about their object of desire – they memorize it, are capable of making inferences and of discovering more about it (455b5-8). Moreover, they care about their bodies in order that they be fit for their purpose (455b8-c1): the philosopher in T17 may neglect their body in their love of knowledge, but the gymnastic-lover will take special care of it in order to obtain their ends. In book III, Socrates describes loving as caring for a particular object (412d2), and so 'to consider that the same things suit himself and the beloved and that if the beloved fares well, he will also fare well, and if not, he will not' (412d4-7).

We are now in a better position to see what the hegemonical ruling of a part of the soul means. The channelling of desire allows lovers the unification of the parts of the soul, not by a cooperation in which each of them would obtain its end, but in the elimination of the differences between parts: there is only one end, which corresponds to the belief about flourishing that they pursue at every occasion. Lovers have no internal conflicts because for them reasoning and desire never disagree, whichever their end is. As such, a lover cannot differentiate their desire from their reasoning as they are merged together. Once again, this demonstrates that parts of the soul are explanatory principles of the soul's movements, as opposed to substances or components. They allow us to explain, for instance, the difference between a lover and conflict.

The channelling of desire allows for pleasures of anticipation, that is, the pain of the lack of the object is diminished by some pleasant feeling of being on the move towards obtaining it (see 584c7-9). This kind of mixed pleasure of anticipation is crucial for explaining the habit formation of lovers: their desire being unrelenting means obtaining their end will not cause the desire to cease. They thus constantly repeat the pursuit because it is accompanied by the pleasure of expectation. This pleasure concomitant to the effort in the pursuit of its object is characterized as *philoponia* (the love of the effort, 535d1-7) and can be explained as the endurance that comes from the positive support of *thumos*. A gymnastic-lover or lover of hunting, for instance, would gladly submit themself to physically strenuous activities (535d3-4), while lovers of enquiry love mentally exhaustive investigations: were they to hate the effort, they would not be true lovers (535d4-6). Therefore, their flourishing lies in the pursuit itself, rather than in obtaining these objects. On the other hand, it is unlikely that the beliefs about flourishing held by a lover may be shared with

---

[8] For the specific description of reasoning in the circumstance of channelled desire of the philosopher, see Lane 2007: 50–1; Ferrari 2007: 191; Obdrzalek 2013: 219.

non-lovers. This feature of their personality can put them in delicate situations while interacting with others; situations in which they can perceive others as hindering their flourishing. I conclude that the channelling of desire is a specific process of habit formation resulting in *eros*.

There is more to personality than simply being a lover, however. A democratic personality, for instance, is not a lover. It is born from the opposite experience; rather than being a desire channeller, it is a desire disperser (see the emphasis on *pollai* at 560b1 and 560d7). Here we have a complex and long-lasting process of habit formation that involves a significant amount of suffering. A democratic person's early age is marked by a tumultuous experience of a myriad of different motivations for different kinds of pleasure (561a6-7). Their problem is how to pursue multiple ends, or as many as they can. These individuals are not hesitant, as this is not a case of internal conflict (see note 18 in Chapter 1), but simply of having many desires at the same time (see 561b1-2), causing what Socrates describes as a frenzy, an internal turmoil (561b1-2). Concurrence of ends seems to bring anxiety, and adds the pain of missing some pleasures to the pleasures actually experienced. Socrates suggests that the chaotic fight among pleasures (see 561b1-2) leads to an escalation of licentiousness (see 560d9-561a4), and hence why he regards as good fortune should age furnish them with a certain device to deal with the situation (561b1).[9]

The democrat's personality arises when they discover the device of treating all pleasures as equal (561b3-4). The ruling principle in them is the constant alternation of the ruling principle (561b4-5); that is, there is no structuring of action according to means and ends, as in avoiding a present pleasure for the sake of a future pleasure. Rather, it is about avoiding the prevailing of one particular end and the formation of a habit; a purposeful obstruction to channelling. To avoid becoming lovers, democrats must distance themselves from the prevailing end of their actions. Ends must be pursued, not because they are good or bad (561b8-c4), but simply because a particular course of action is the occasional end – an end ascribed not by the agent themselves, but by luck of a draw (561b4-6).[10] Each day brings a different end. There are days when such a person is interested in drinking, others not; there are times when they practice physical exercise and when they are lazy; sometimes they do philosophy and sometimes they exercise civic duties (561c6-e2). A democrat is a presentist (561c6),[11] one who seizes the moment for experiencing a different pleasure. It is likely, therefore, that *philoponia* is incompatible with this personality as such an individual is not someone willing to endure. Moreover, their default attitude is to not have anticipatory pleasures. They fight against *eros* because they fight against an end-directed habit formation, both of which are regarded as causes of pain because they restrict the amount of ends pursued.

A third kind of personality results from failure both in the channelling of desire and in finding a device to unify a personality: the tyrannical personality. While *eros* is the channelling of desire towards specific objects, tyrannical *eros* is a strong motivational flux towards a multiplicity of appetitive ends (573b6-7). It is a personality which experiences the kind of frenzy and turmoil that the democrat lives with at an early age but is not lucky enough to discover a device to deal with it. For the tyrannical personality, the solution is simply to resist any solution (573a8-b4) and to place the whole soul in this erratic state of flux (573d4-5). Socrates characterizes the tyrannical

---

[9] It is not simply that democracy is the prevailing of appetites; it is also the resistance of the prevailing of a single appetite; see Scott 2000a: 23–6; Santas 2010: 62.
[10] There is a tendency in the literature to describe the democrat as a lover, in particular a 'desire-part' lover; see Scott 2000: 23–6 and Burnyeat 2006: 16–17. I also disagree with Johnstone's (2013: 147–8) theory that this is an anarchic character (see later about tyrannical personality) because a democrat follows a regulatory maxim.
[11] A defence for this kind of presentism was found in Aristippus; see Irwin 1991: 57 and Lampe 2015: 64–73.

character as mad (573a8), frenzied (573b1, 577e1), drunk (573b9, c9), atrabilious (573c9), disturbed (577d13-e2), insatiable (579e2-4) and as one whose life has no ruling principle or law (575a1-2). Rather than structuring its choices according to the object of its obsessions, such a personality lives for its obsession: it is a motion without an end – an anarchy (575a1).[12] This person is not a lover, for a lover moves towards its object; the lack of an end, however, moves the tyrant by sheer force, where what they desire is the intensity of motion – perhaps in the form of a strong sensation resulting from the mixture of pain and pleasures – rather than obtaining something good.

These differences show that the channelling of desire occurs in the case of the formation of a lover, but not in other kinds of personalities. The democrat shows that adopting a certain single maxim of conduct, taken as a device to minimize pain, is also sufficient for structuring a personality, while the tyrannical person demonstrates that personalities may lack unity, and may be diffused, complex and contradictory. The clearer and more unified the ruling end of a person is and the more hegemonically it rules, the more consistent they are, the more we may know and anticipate about them, and the more they may know and anticipate about themselves. The less unified and more in flux a prevailing end is for an individual, the less consistent the personality is, hesitating to repeat previous experiences that mixed pain and pleasure. If this may still constitute a personality, we are not to expect its flourishing – a movement towards some self-fulfilment.

There are different ways in which a personality may grow, but all of them are based on experiences of pleasure and pain and the inclination to repeat them, and all emerge from the interaction of the parts of the soul. The inclination to repeat pleasant actions is stronger when desire is channelled, forming solid but one-dimensional personalities, but personalities may also be built out of the mores shared by the community, the adoption of a certain maxim of conduct and even the simple use of force in the place of prevailing ends. Not every personality flourishes. The tyrannical suffers; the democratic rejects a single belief about flourishing; lovers may find resistance from others in their interaction and the decent man may fail himself when alone. Personality is not the attribute of an enclosed whole; rather, it is an outcome of the interaction with others. Others influence our experience of pleasure; they can, for instance, limit our power to obtain our ends. Yet having a personality grounds the expectation others have of our actions; it is the way they can 'know' us. Part Two is devoted to explaining this interaction and how we move from agents to cities, from personalities to *politeiai*.

---

[12] *Anarchia* is a term used specifically to the tyrannical personality, meaning lack of a predominant end; see Hitz 2010: 112; Obdrzalek 2013: 217–18. Alternative accounts are the tyrant is a lover of: (i) appetites in general: Larivée 20052005: 181; Johnstone 2015: 428; Arruzza 2019: 179–80; (ii) lawless appetites: Reeve 1998: 47; Scott 2007: 140–1; (iii) sex: Barney 2008: 369; Parry 2007: 395–6; (iv) power: Blössner 2007: 361.

Part Two

Politeia

7

Thrasymachus

The first part of this book was devoted to presenting the key concepts used to explain action in the *Republic* in an attempt to demonstrate that action is explained by the interaction of individuals. The first chapter introduced desire and reasoning as two different parts of the soul which may conflict in regard to the end of an action; whichever prevails determines the end taken by the soul, while the non-prevailing part determines the mode of the action. *Thumos* is an emotion that reacts to a state of affairs regarding either an action performed by the agent or a situation in which they are in, based on self-assessment according to individual beliefs about flourishing. The two alternatives of *thumos* activity – action and situation – may lead to an antinomy while reasoning presents ends for our action according to what we learn about what is good for us.

Our learning begins with the appearances that come to us through perception. Due to the structure of our perception, these appearances allow for the compresence of opposites which we judge to be either Φ or non-Φ. Opposite beliefs about X being Φ generate puzzlement, which subsequently summons the intellect for an enquiry about what Φ is. Because beliefs aim at truth, we cannot believe in opposites about Φ. Our beliefs about the good, however, are more complex, because in this case true beliefs can be expelled from thought by pleasure and pain without rational consent. In these cases, we possess unreasonable beliefs, which mistake more pleasure or less fear for the good. Initially they occur out of desire, but, since the tendency to repeat certain experiences may change our beliefs about flourishing, *thumos* may subsequently adopt them. Another key concept in action is power, an attribute acquired due to agents obtaining a certain state of affairs as a result of their actions, which may be expressed according to degrees when the accomplishment of an action is compared with its prevailing end.

Cognition, predominance and power explain our actions by the interaction both between the parts of the soul, and between the agent and others; they are also basic blocks in building our personality. The simplest kind of personality is the lover, who is characterized by unrelenting desire for a specific kind of object and described as hegemonically ruled by one part of the soul. Ruling has, however, different modes. It may, for instance, occur based on habit sustained by the mores of the community, as well as based on practical maxims or merely based on force.

Having addressed the explanatory concepts of action one by one may have led to the impression that they are isolated pieces of an isolated agent; they are not. Reason and desire always interact with each other and with the agent's environment; *thumos* always interacts with states of affairs caused by actions; we are always dealing with the lack of power to obtain certain ends and constantly learning about the world. Every action is an interaction, and the purpose of this Part Two is to enlarge the scope of the previous enquiry to show precisely how these concepts explain interaction between the agent and others – in particular, with other agents. The significance of this enquiry is that justice is an interactive concept and cannot be understood otherwise.

* * *

The best point of entry to the question of justice is Thrasymachus' speech. It introduces some of the basic concepts of interaction in a theory encompassing human motivation and *politeia*. He expresses some key assumptions about how we obtain our ends and how this brings out a state of affairs that involves other agents also pursuing their ends. Thrasymachus opens his speech by declaring that 'justice is what suits who prevails' (*kreittōn*, 338c2-3). As has already been pointed out, Socrates explains the action of a person who suffers the internal conflict as the prevailing of a part that determines the end of the action, and the activity of the remaining parts that determines the mode of the action. Chapter 1 mentioned that this idea was taken from Thrasymachus, as the following text demonstrates:

> [T18] Isn't to prevail in each city this: ruling?
> Definitely.
> Each government establishes the laws aiming at what suits it: democracy establishes democratic laws, tyrannies tyrannical and so with the others. Once established, [laws] display to the ruled what is to be just, i.e., what suits the rulers, and they punish anyone who goes against it as unlawful and unjust. This is, my dear friend, what I say is the same in every city: just is what suits the established government. Once it has somehow prevailed, it follows from a correct reasoning that everywhere the just is the same, what suits who prevails. (338d9-339a4, my brackets)

T18 explains the statement 'justice is what suits who prevails' as the principle that in every city, to prevail is to rule (338d9). A democracy is a *politeia* in which the *dēmos* prevails; in aristocracies the 'better' establish their end to be obtained at the detriment of the ends of others, while tyrannies are the prevailing of a single individual (338d6-7).[1] All *politeiai* emerge from predominance, that is, the prevailing of a party who thence determines the end of others. The difference among them is simply 'who'. Like Socrates, Thrasymachus does not feel the need to explain what it takes for one party to prevail over the other; it is simply a brute fact that one of them will be superior. However, this account should not be mistaken for a simple report on facts of reality, it is rather a theoretical explanation of what a *politeia* is. Since Thrasymachus accepts that different parties may prevail in a city, he also seems to accept that the prevailing party may change in the same city – thence 'to prevail' would mean 'to seize a certain winning position'. In every city some party is superior, and justice is that other citizens acknowledge this fact by rewarding it with government.[2] Thrasymachus' first definition of justice is therefore foundational: justice is accepting the political organization based on the institution of ruling, and distinguishing the ruler and the ruled according to the principle that the ruler should be the superior. This definition establishes justice as the principle of sovereignty.[3]

---

[1] In using aristocracy instead of oligarchy, Thrasymachus seems to superpose the two traditional ways of classifying the *politeiai* in six species according to the number (one, few, many) and the quality (good or bad) (see Romilly 1959: 82). In doing so he avoids the issue of whether a tyranny is a good form of government.

[2] Interpreters who see Thrasymachus as simply reporting brute sociological facts at this point are Hourani 1962: 112; Harrison 1967: 30; Harlap 1979: 354; White 1995: 322; Everson 1998: 122; Chappell 2000: 105–7; Santas 2006: 126; Wedgwood 2017: 47. Another line of reading, engaged in preserving Thrasymachus' coherence, dismisses this first definition as rhetorical (Kerferd [1947]1976: 560; Nicholson 1974: 219; Anderson 2016: 15). In my view, both these perspectives miss the important construction that Thrasymachus makes about 'being superior', in whichever context of mores, and the 'natural' right of operating the governmental system. For more attentive views, see Henderson 1970: 221; Maguire 1976: 146.

[3] Describing the principle of sovereignty as 'Might makes right' (Cross and Woozley 1964: 29; Rosen 2005: 39–41; Penner 2009: 201) is at once too vague, in the sense that it does not specify the distinction between

This principle asserts that government is a certain institution that exists in every *politeia* (338d9, 338e6-339a3). It consists of legislating or establishing a system of laws, through which the ruler presents his own ends as commands that the others must obey (338e1-4),[4] and punishing or eliminating the power of action of those who do not pursue the ruler's end (338e4-6). Laws determine that everyone must pursue the end of the predominant party (338e2-5) by making clear what this end is, while punishment enforces the law (338e4-6). The universal presence of punishment institutions in cities indicates that the use of coercion is always necessary, as law alone is not sufficient to guarantee justice. Indeed, I shall argue that such institutions are needed to assure the power of the rulers, for, as we already know and Thrasymachus does not, predominance does not entail power.

By introducing the institution of government, Thrasymachus restricts the otherwise more general notion of the *politeia*: it is now a collective of people organized according to government, and divided between the ruled and the rulers. Moreover, if 'what suits who prevails' is a statement about the way in which all human beings live in every city (338e6-339a3), and if this is what justice is, everyone lives under the sovereign principle and therefore in just *politeiai*. Justice constitutes the difference between ruled and ruler, the latter determining the end of the action of the former by institutional means which give him power: predominance gives government; government gives power; power shapes a *politeia* in which the ruled pursue the end of the ruler.

There is an ongoing debate regarding whether the principle of 'what suits who prevails' is proposed as a definition of justice, and whether it is a good one.[5] Indeed, the text makes it explicitly clear that this is Thrasymachus' answer to the question 'what is justice?' (336c3-6), and that he considers it universally valid. On this basis, it seems that there is no room to assume that Thrasymachus is not committed to it as a definition. However, there are reasons to suppose that it is not a good definition. According to Thrasymachus, his *definiendum*, justice, is the universal form of the *politeia*. It is common to all peoples inasmuch as people co-habit a territory. But his *definiens* mentions only part of the citizens, only those 'who prevail'. Socrates' first objection stresses this limitation: isn't the obedience of the ruled justice too (339b9-10)? Thrasymachus agrees and subsequently introduces a second clause in the definition: 'justice is also the ruled obeying (*peithestai*) [the rulers]' (339b9-10). *Peithestai* is an ambiguous verb meaning 'to be persuaded', 'to be won over' or 'to obey'. Whichever Thrasymachus' intended meaning, this is what rulers must obtain: the ruled must act according to the end of the ruler. As Socrates puts it, Thrasymachus' definition is in fact 'what suits who prevails [which] will be accomplished by those who are prevailed upon' (341b6-7).

---

predominance and power, and too restrictive, for in contradistinction to the principle of sovereignty, as we shall see, it does not allow for a form of government that promotes the shared good.

[4] Despite my note 4 in the Introduction, I see that the context of the argument, with a system of governmental law-enactment and punishment, does not allow for a translation of *nomos* in a less institutional way. For a different view, see Sparshott 1966: 426.

[5] There is a great deal of debate on Thrasymachus' definition of justice in two ways. In the first one, the question is what is the definition? (a) 'what suits who prevails'; see Sparshott 1966: 430; (b) 'obedience to the law'; see Hourani 1962: 112; or (c) 'the good of others'; see Kerferd [1947]1976: 560; Nicholson 1974: 22; Annas 1981: 46. In the second, the question is what counts properly as a definition in the Platonic context: whether it should be analytical (Hourani 1962: 112; Everson 1998: 107) or synthetic (Kerferd 1964: 13; Shellens 1953: 486; Boter 1986: 264; Chappell 2000: 107). What I intend to show on the second topic is that there are no empirical premises in Thrasymachus' discourse because he starts from the concept of political system as a universal principle (338d9, 338e6-339a3). As for the first, I see that Thrasymachus considers both (a) and (c) as definitions, and his word should be our standard. I believe that Thrasymachus gives reasons for (b) to be a mistake regarding his thesis.

Socrates' second objection stresses the end of rulers: Can they be wrong about the end they pursue (and yet enforce others to promote it) (339c1-2)? Thrasymachus has no problem in admitting this much (339c3): what justice grants to those who prevail is the power to obtain their end, not that these ends are good – indeed, they will obtain the end they establish, whether it is good or not (339d1-3, compare with *beltistou* at 339d7 and *kaka* at 339e3). Socrates' suggestion is thus that justice should be redefined as the power to obtain what is genuinely good to whoever prevails.

Cleitophon intervenes in the discussion by attempting to grant Thrasymachus the opposite thesis: it does not matter if the state of affairs obtained by ruling (and by the obedience of the ruled) is good for the ruler; all that matters for something to be just is that it is what the rulers considered to suit them, being proclaimed by law and obtained by the obedience of the ruled (340b6-8). Laws express what is just, no matter the outcome of the ruled actions (340b7-8, see also c4-5). In Cleitophon's eyes, Thrasymachus' justice is simply the *politeia* (340b6-8), the state of affairs generated by the rulers, the ruled and the legislative and punishment system. It is not necessarily good for the rulers, even if this is their end when legislating and punishing.[6]

Some interpreters have ascribed Cleitophon's position to Thrasymachus,[7] but this is an approach he clearly rejects when retracting his first statement about rulers (339c3) and instead introducing another interesting claim: one cannot be said to prevail if one is wrong about one's end (340c6-7). What does Thrasymachus mean by this?[8] His inductive explanation is as follows: someone who makes mistakes about sick people is not called a doctor; someone who makes mistakes in calculating is not called a mathematician (340d2-6). The inference is that professional agents are, in general, identified by their power and, as such, it is the state of affairs obtained that makes them what they are. Mistakes would result in a different state of affairs and therefore disqualify them as those who prevail (340d6-e3). In retracting his first response about mistakes, opposing Cleitophon's position, Thrasymachus assumes that the state of affairs obtained is sufficient to show others that such an agent acted according to such an end, and thus has the power to obtain such a state of affairs. The outcome grants the reputation given by others and justifies the agent 'being referred to' (340e1), or 'being called' (340d3) (i.e. identified) as such and such.

We do not know what Thrasymachus thinks knowledge (*epistēmēs*, 340e3) is, but he clearly makes the claim that those who are *said* to have it – that is, professionals in general, wise men, rulers – genuinely possess it (340e2-7). If those people are reputed to have knowledge because of some results obtained in their action, Thrasymachus clearly infers the presence of knowledge from the presence of a certain power. He seems to suppose that knowledge is an unmistakable understanding both of an agent's end as being good for them, and of the way to obtain it. Whoever has power cannot be mistaken about their end being good. I shall call this kind of clear-cut good, one that does not even allow for internal conflicts, a Thrasymachean good. If agents do not err about what is good for them, pursuing a Thrasymachean good, all there is to an agent's action

---

[6] Cleitophon's position has been considered a defence of positive law or legalism (Kerferd [1947]1976: 549; Hourani 1962: 115). This is not incorrect, but it seems too reductive. His claim is that the just is what is obtained by the actions of the citizens following the laws proclaimed by the ruler.

[7] For readings that ascribe Cleitophon's position to Thrasymachus, see Hourani 1962: 114; Strauss 1964: 75; Hadgopoulos 1973: 208; Maguire 1976: 155; Everson 1998: 113. Critiques of this attribution, for different reasons, are found in Kerferd [1947]1976: 549; Nicholson 1974: 226; Bloom 1991: 327, 329.

[8] Penner (2009: 205) suggests that this is a science of good and bad. Henderson (1970: 224) sees a distinction here between people and functions. This is correct: rulers and ruled are functions and not the people who occupy these positions, but Thrasymachus' thesis includes a justification for why such people occupy such functions. My position is closer to that of Nawar (2018: 365-6), who argues that the expertise abandons the agent when they err, so that no error is committed with technical ability. However, I go further in attributing to Thrasymachus the premise that power entails accomplishment and recognition by others.

is the different degrees of success they have in obtaining it. On these grounds, I argue that the thesis that a ruler does not commit mistakes about his end (340d2-341a4) is not an ideal, utopian and unreal position of Thrasymachus:[9] it simply follows from an implicit premise that we are all pursuing Thrasymachean goods.

Socrates reacts to Thrasymachus' explanation with an argument on the relation between predominance, knowledge and power to conclude that experts prevail because they have the power to obtain the good of others (341c5-342e6). I shall address this argument within the bulk of Socrates' arguments against Thrasymachus in the next chapter. For now, I shall focus purely on Thrasymachus' response in which he introduces what seems to be a different definition of justice: the good of others (343c3-4). From one perspective, this is an 'expanded' version of the definition of justice as 'what suits who prevails'. As we saw, Thrasymachus includes reference to all the citizens in his expanded definition – 'what suits who prevails [which] will be accomplished by those who are prevailed upon' (341b6-7) – thus 'the good of others' may be read as a paraphrase of what is accomplished by the ruled. However, 'the good of others' also introduces a new consideration. As Thrasymachus clarifies, justice is the good of others (what suits who prevails and rules) *and self-harm*, because it is accomplished by means of one's obedience and servitude (343c1-d1). I shall argue that this addition of self-harm makes Thrasymachus' two definitions inconsistent with each other.

The conjunction of good of others *and* self-harm matters for Thrasymachus' inference that no agent obtains a good in a just action. Indeed, Thrasymachus clearly advises against this kind of altruism; it is an act of obedience and servitude, a nonsensical naiveté (339b9-10, 343c5).[10] Justice thus does not promote our flourishing; it promotes the flourishing of others (343c7-d1). Those who flourish are therefore unjust, because injustice is the appropriation of the good of others (344a7-8). When we try to accommodate this new information with the previous concept of justice as the principle of sovereignty, it becomes evident that this distinction establishes different roles for different citizens: the ruled give the good to others (the rulers) and are just; the rulers get the good of others (the ruled) and are unjust.

Phrased in this way, this formula differs from the principle of sovereignty. The new definition states that the end of the rulers must be such that it precludes the ruled from obtaining their end, for they must give their good to others. The principle of sovereignty, in its turn, allows for the ruled to be persuaded that acting according to the laws will let them obtain their own good while still obtaining the good of the ruler; that is, it allows for a kind of cooperation based on a shared or common good. The introduction of the second definition, however, eliminates this possibility by claiming that the ruled are slaves of the ruled (*andrapodisamenos doulōsētai*, 344b6-7). As a result of this addition, every *politeia*, the universal form in which human beings live together, is a form of oppression of the ruled and against their best interest.

A very important feature of the second definition is that it clearly supposes a zero-sum game scenario in which justice is the transference of the good of the ruled to the ruler. It therefore supposes that goods are owned and transferable. Thrasymachus refers to these goods as 'what others own' (*tallotria*, 344a7) and gives the treasury of temples, private property and public funds (344a8-b1) as examples, summarizing them as 'the riches of the citizens' (344b6). This is

---

[9] Readings of an idealist Thrasymachus are Adam 1902: I, 33; Harrison 1967: 31; Maguire 1976: 145–6; Klosko 1984: 15; Nicholson 1974: 224; Barney 2006: 48.
[10] There is a line of interpreters that sees in the thesis of the good of others a convincing theory of justice as natural justice (Kerferd [1947]1976: 558) or equality (Boter 1986: 265). Thrasymachus, however, never associates justice with either motivation or the common good. For positions that emphasize the harm caused by justice, see Chappell 1993: 11; Harlap 1979: 350; Boter 1986: 265; Everson 1998: 114.

good evidence for what a Thrasymachean good consists of: material items owned by someone in a determined quantity, whose ownership and accumulation is the good of the agent, whilst their lack is to their detriment. As previously mentioned, Thrasymachus supposes that having a Thrasymachean good is an unmistakably good end for the agent, and there is no internal conflict that may raise the question about its being worthy. What this means is that we all pursue Thrasymachean goods, we all want the same thing, and this is clear to all of us. Because its quantity is limited and we desire to accumulate it in large quantities, rather than internal conflict, external conflict results: every human being is in conflict with every other to obtain more Thrasymachean goods. So, every acquisition of a good must be made against the owner by means of stealth or violence. In this dispute for the same good things, we differ among ourselves: those of us with the power to obtain them will flourish, while those of us who are powerless are condemned to deprivation.[11]

We are now in a better position to see the difference between Thrasymachus' first and second definitions of justice. The second reduces all conflict about prevailing ends, either internal or external, to the conflict to obtain Thrasymachean goods: rather than being in conflict in regard to what is good, we are all fighting for the power to obtain something that is an objective and unquestionable measure of our flourishing. Every Thrasymachean good is commensurable with every other; we may count the goods within one single scale, marking off the agents who obtained more of them from those who obtained less. The Thrasymachean good allows for a purely mathematical basis to account for power, justice and injustice, and their unequal distribution is easily verified, whilst the dissatisfaction of those deprived of them can be solved simply by redistribution (which will, of course, cause the dissatisfaction of those whose goods will be taken). Thrasymachean good is at the basis of Thrasymachus' implicit definition of injustice as *pleonexia*:[12] to have the good of others, to take the good of others and to have more goods than others.

Translations of *pleonexia* are precarious. The term denotes one specific kind of motivation, such as 'greed' or 'ambition', but does so by denoting the state of affairs that results from actions accomplished under such a motivation, that is, the situation of inequality in which one of the parts has more (*pleon echein*) than the other, which has less (*elatton echein*, compare 343d3 and d6). This shall not be considered an ambiguity of the term; rather, it is a key feature for understanding how Plato in particular, as well as the Greek language in general, explains human motivations by the end of the action. The motivations of others are not simple to identify – in general, they are determined by some justification, that is, some account of a fact which traces the outcome of an action back to the agent responsible for it. For Thrasymachus, this explanation is done straightforwardly in terms of power: the end is the outcome; that is, reputedly wise men are wise because of the state of affairs they obtained; someone is said to have *pleonexia* not because of some intention, but because their actions resulted in the unequal distribution of goods. *Pleonexia* is both a motivation and the state of affairs obtained in interaction, precisely because it is a power. As we have seen, powers are the attributes of the agents *because* they achieve a certain state of affairs. Since powers admit degrees, we may say that this particular *pleonectic* person aimed at a state of affairs but failed to obtain it to a certain degree. Now, we may see how

---

[11] For Thrasymachus' commitment to reality reduced to a power struggle in a zero-sum game see Anderson 2016: 20; Wedgewood 2017: 40.

[12] There is a tendency to emphasize the psychological character of *pleonexia*, see Boter 1986: 265; Burnyeat 2006: 21; Fissell 2009: 35. Psychological descriptions run the risk of attributing to Thrasymachus a dispositional theory (see Henderson 1970: 220). The problem I see in it is that Thrasymachus never argues modally: it is not that a certain agent may cause the exploitation of others under the right conditions; his thesis is that the unjust agent never fails. Even Boter (1986: 266, 269) recognizes that there is an objective state of affairs of inequality designated by *pleonexia*; see also Joseph 1935: 32.

powers explain the relation between the city and the soul and, in particular, how the principles of action in the soul cause the city to be a certain *politeia*. When citizens obtain their prevailing end in their interaction, the *politeia* is reorganized according to it: others suffer the impact, the goods are differently distributed and conflict is established. A *politeia* is the outcome of the citizens' powers in their interaction.

Evidence for this assumption is found in Thrasymachus' explanation for how to find (see *heurois* at 343d5) a just and an unjust agent. His claim is that 'the just man everywhere has less than the unjust' (343d3), and he provides three different contexts in which this can be verified. The first is the interaction between a just and an unjust man in the peculiar case of contracts (*sumbolaiois*, 343d4) established on common purposes (*koinōnēsē*, 343d5). These are contracts assumed on a win-win basis: both parties engage in them with the end of obtaining a good that belongs to the state of affairs aimed at by the contract, which Thrasymachus simply calls a 'community' (*koinonia*, 343d6). When this community ends, he claims, we find a state of affairs where there exists the unequal distribution of goods, from which we infer that one is the just agent because he has less and the other is the unjust because he has more (343d6).

The second context in which one may find a just and an unjust agent is in the practice of citizenship, that is, when individuals act towards the city. While citizens were expected to equally (*apo tōn isōn*, 343d8) give the good to the city in the form of paying taxes, this is not the state of affairs obtained. Instead, the just citizen pays more taxes and therefore ends up having less Thrasymachean goods. The unjust citizen, having paid less, has more; he acts based on *pleonexia* (343d7-e1).

The third and final context is in ruling, where Thrasymachus supposes that there are just rulers who, when ruling, neglect their own affairs (343e3-4), do not benefit from public funds (343e4), are hated by friends for not unjustly benefitting them (343e5-6) and sometimes are punished for being just (343e1-7). The just ruler, he concludes, is the one who ends up having less Thrasymachean goods. In contrast, the unjust ruler is described as having the greatest power to have more (*ton megala dunamenon pleonektein*, 344a1-2), having used ruling to accumulate goods.

In all the three levels, we find a state of inequality – the unjust has more goods and the just has fewer goods – obtained by a powerful agent (the unjust) motivated by *pleonexia*, *despite* his partner's purpose to obtain a different state of affairs, and *because* this partner is powerless to make it happen. Injustice is *pleonexia*, both in the sense of the motivation of an agent (greed) and in the sense of a certain state of affairs obtained – unequal distribution of Thrasymachean goods.

Another important feature of Thrasymachus' account of injustice is that he addresses the power struggle on two different levels. According to his argument, a partially (*merei*, 344b1) unjust agent obtains only some of the Thrasymachean goods. It is safe to assume that, in Thrasymachus' first example of a contract between a just and an unjust agent, the latter who simply obtains the good of the just partner is partially unjust. The same applies to the unjust citizen who pays fewer taxes than the just: they obtain some of the public Thrasymachean goods. Partial success in injustice occurs also in the case of crimes (344b5), which consist of an unlawful or violent appropriation by an individual of the property of another individual, a group or the city itself. They include assault of the temples (which kept the public treasury), kidnapping, home invasion, stealing and theft (344b3-4).

The interesting point about this is that crime is a form of injustice if, and only if, it is practised with sufficient competence so as not to be punished: it must employ what I called a 'power device', that is, an artifice to obtain one's end in circumstances in which others are harmed. Thrasymachus states that a partially unjust agent must use the devices of violence and stealth

(344a7-8) because, if caught, the crime is subject to public punishment and reproach (344b2), and thus the agent fails. Because the bonus of the Thrasymachean good obtained does not exceed the burden of punishment, in these cases, the agent has less and, having less, is therefore not unjust. Every action aiming at an inequitable state of affairs must employ some power device.

The second level of power struggle, according to Thrasymachus, is the one involving government. An agent is completely (*teleōtatē*, 344a4) unjust if he obtains all the Thrasymachean goods, including the citizens, who become his slaves (344b6-7), something only accomplishable if power devices are added to the power of political institutions. Perfect injustice is therefore the ruler's accomplishment of inequality. With all citizens under control, the perfect form of injustice is autocracy, the rule of all by an individual who can thus obtain all the goods of others. Thrasymachus calls this tyranny. Everyone, he claims, verifies the state of affairs obtained by the action of the tyrant – the *politeia* that emerges from his ruling – and considers the tyrant blessed (344b7-c1). Of course, there is a problematic assumption here. Thrasymachus supposes that government allows for the employment of power devices because it controls the system of punishment and, by laws, the reactions of other citizens. He assumes that political power can be completely taken from other citizens to the point that they will admire the tyrant rather than reacting against him. Socrates will pick up on this point: the fact that a tyrant prevails in a city does not lead us to infer that he has power to obtain his ends. This reflects the difference between predominance and power. It is one thing to assume that there are predominant individuals and that it is just that they should operate the government. But it is something very different to assume that they will have political power; that is, that their end will obtain. The power device is employed precisely because there is resistance. Thrasymachus commits himself to this confusion when he takes the ruler to be an expert and assumes the tyrant to have complete power.

The agents of both complete injustice and partial injustice have the same end and the same personal motivation, *pleonexia* – only complete injustice, however, leads to what Thrasymachus understands as flourishing (see *eudaimones*, 344b7), that is, the possession of all Thrasymachean goods. He takes a prescriptive position on complete injustice:[13] it is necessary for human beings both to aim at *pleonexia* and to have power to obtain it in order to flourish. Some interpreters see here a wake-up call for individual enlightenment about the rules of political life.[14] I disagree. Thrasymachus' concept of flourishing supposes the control of political institutions that guarantee the submission of others (343c5-d1). So, no one can flourish without the *politeia* just as no one may flourish without having others engaged in obtaining his own end to the detriment of their own.[15] Two important points follow. The first is that Thrasymachus must concede that personal flourishing depends on others for it depends on the others' servitude. The second is that if one must occupy a political position that fits only one individual in order to flourish, this enlightenment comes hand in hand with a great amount of pessimism: all but one of us will fail.

---

[13] For the prescriptive attitude of injustice, see Cross and Woozley 1964: 32; Chappell 1993: 7–10. Surprisingly, this interpretation is not unanimous; see White 1995: 322. *A contrario sensu* his thesis on justice is descriptive, see Sparshott 1966: 423; Chappell 1993: 3–4; Flew 1995: 438.

[14] For 'Enlightenment' versions of Thrasymachus, see Barker 1918: 181; Shellens 1953: 485, 491–2; Reeve 1985: 259; Sparshott 1966: 438; White 1995: 322; Anderson 2016: 2.

[15] Because Thrasymachus' concept of flourishing depends on government, his thesis cannot be sustained at all without the principle of sovereignty. His notion of justice cannot be the simple defence of selfishness, egoism, immoralism without political power (as defended for instance by Sparshott 1966: 436; 2017: 42). Neither can his thesis allow for a gap between morality and politics (Maguire 1976: 163; Harlap 1979: 364). If Thrasymachus' conclusion depends on his two definitions, we must assume that he is committed to both and to their inconsistencies.

This conclusion demonstrates that Thrasymachus' concept of flourishing commits him to the two definitions of justice he proposed: in order to flourish, one needs the good of others *and* sovereignty. I shall now argue that, if he is genuinely committed to both, some inconsistencies follow.

The first is the argument of the just ruler. According to this argument, (i) from 'justice is what suits who prevails' follows that the just ruler obtains what suits him/her. But (ii) from 'justice is the good of others and self-harm' follows that the just ruler obtains their self-harm.[16] Following from (i), justice is that the ruler always practices injustice and, from (ii), justice is that the one who prevails obtains self-harm. Thrasymachus could try to avoid this inconsistency by dropping 'what suits who prevails' as a definition of justice, assuming that there is no such thing as justice as a sovereignty principle, and simply sticking to justice as the good of others and self-harm. But, in doing so, he would also have to drop his concept of flourishing which depends on this principle.

Thrasymachus' strategy to distinguish crime and tyranny in terms of degrees of power may also lead him to inconsistency. The criminal who has power to conceal his actions takes the good of others and avoids punishment, while the ruler aims to take this same good by operating the system of punishment against the criminal. Criminals and rulers dispute the same Thrasymachean goods, and the state of affairs obtained depends on the power of each of them. Thrasymachus therefore has a dilemma: he must either agree that there are no criminals in tyrannies, or that there is some loophole in tyranny's institutions that allows for criminals to remain unpunished. There is no sign he takes either alternative. Nonetheless, the point remains that, if every conflict is a power struggle for Thrasymachean goods and the success of some entails the failure of others, either there is a complete unjust agent or there are partial unjust agents, a third option being excluded.

Thrasymachus' account is also inconsistent in regard to justice. Justice, the opposite of injustice, must be the opposite of *pleonexia*. However, Thrasymachus never states that justice is – with the excuse of the neologism – *elattonexia* or the motivation to have less. Instead, he says that having less is the outcome of the interaction between a just and an unjust agent, or a comparison between how they deal with the city and others in general. On the other hand, he says that the just agent establishes contracts expecting both parties to obtain a good; that is, their end is not to have less, but to have a common (or shared) good. The just agent who pays taxes to the city, for example, expects taxation to be based on some equality of all the citizens; they are not simply motivated to have less. The just ruler aims neither at being deprived of goods nor at being punished. In all these cases we see that the just agent's end, which is the opposite of *pleonexia*, is something like a common/shared good or an equal distribution of goods. Yet the just agent fails to obtain this end; they lack power and obtain a state of affairs that is less good than the end aimed at. So, the agent has less.

Thrasymachus supposes that every just agent lacks power as they are never to obtain their end. For this reason, justice is self-harm and a naiveté (343c4-6), an assumption grounded on the concept of Thrasymachean goods. If whoever obtains a good is taking it from others, there is no such thing as a common or shared good. Every acquisition of a good happens by means of power devices, such as stealth or violence, and there is no such thing as cooperation and win-win contracts. Thrasymachean goods reduce the end of all human actions to *pleonexia* and grant

---

[16] For different versions of the objection of the just ruler, see Cross and Woozley 1964, 39: 41; Henderson 1970: 218; Nicholson 1974: 213; Annas 1981: 46; Chappell 1993: 6; Everson 1998: 116; Barney 2006: 45. The only way out of the objection of the just ruler is to claim that Thrasymachus is not committed to one of his definitions – in general, interpreters who have taken this position have dropped the principle of sovereignty as a definition of justice (see Sparshott 1966: 451; Jang 1997: 192; Maguire 1976: 146; 2017: 50).

Thrasymachus poor explanations for facts he assumes to exist, such as communities, just citizens and just rulers. But why should we suppose that all that is desired are Thrasymachean goods? In fact, Socrates' account of internal conflict shows us that we do not have to suppose this, and, indeed, that there are more goods available to us than Thrasymachus assumes. It is therefore time to see what Socrates has to say in response to Thrasymachus' arguments.

8

Socrates against Thrasymachus

The previous chapter discussed Thrasymachus' argument that 'what suits those who prevail' is a universal definition of justice as the principle of sovereignty, as well as his addition of a second definition, according to which justice is the good of others and self-harm, and injustice is inequality (*pleonexia*). He also argued that injustice can be obtained partially or completely: only a tyrant achieves complete injustice by controlling the ruling system to take possession not only of the goods of others but of the citizens themselves, thus avoiding punishment. This account of justice and injustice presupposes a specific concept of good (a Thrasymachean good), which is the sum of transferable material items owned by an individual, the possession and accumulation of which allow them to flourish. The introduction of the second definition, alongside the pressuposition that every good is a Thrasymachean good, generates a series of inconsistencies in Thrasymachus' speech.

Socrates presents five arguments of different importance against Thrasymachus' position. The first, the care argument, takes place between Thrasymachus' two definitions (341c5-342e6). The following four are delivered after his conclusion. The first of these, the argument on rewards (345b8-347e6), is a follow-up to the care argument, therefore, I shall analyse both as a single argument on expertise and the good of others. The remaining three pertain to the concept of virtue or excellence (*aretē*):[1] the knowledge argument (348c1-350c11), the argument on common action (350d5-352b5) and the argument of the peculiar virtue (352d2-354a11). I shall address these in this order, indicating how Socrates builds them on Thrasymachus' concepts of *politeia*, prevailing and power. My understanding of Socrates' response is that he is particularly interested in refining Thrasymachus' expanded first definition of justice in terms of the power given to rulers to always obtain their end.

(a) Expertise and the good of others: the care argument (341c5-342e6) and the reward argument (347b8-347e6)

Thrasymachus retracts his first statement that rulers may fail (339c3) by claiming that they obtain unmistakably good ends (340d2-341a4). His argument for this latter claim is that professionals in general, wise men and particularly rulers are acknowledged as such because they obtain a certain

---

[1] I alternately use the terms 'virtue' or 'excellence' to translate the term *aretē* because neither has the same extension of meaning of the Greek term: *aretē* is the noun formed from the superlative *aristos*, the best, from the adjective *agathos*, good, always indicating the characteristic of the one who is better than the others, therefore the excellence of the one who stands out among others (see Adkins 1960: 31). The *Republic*'s great task, however, is to show that justice is an *aretē*, and that it is by being just that we flourish, that is, we become *eudaimōn*. As the concept of justice is incompatible with the notion of inequality associated with excellence, in his response to Thrasymachus Socrates fits into a lineage of Greek thinkers who endeavoured to show that virtues are not only competitive but are also cooperative. (See Adkins 1960: 37-8, 70-9.)

state of affairs – a fact he assumes sufficient to infer not only that they have power to obtain this outcome, but also that they unmistakably know this end to be good. Earlier, I emphasized that this argument is based on the social recognition of their accomplishment rather than on what it takes to know something: Socrates' first argument aims at clarifying this latter point.

Such social recognition, claims Socrates, lies not in the fact that these professionals are wage earners. It lies in that they care for others (341c6-8; see *therapeutēs* at 341c7). They are experts in promoting something good for other people. The expertise of a captain, for instance, lies in ruling the sailors by pursuing and providing what suits them (341c10-d10). This expertise, which I call care expertise, achieves its end and is complete (*telean*, 341d12) in providing others with what suits them (341d11-12): the doctor who cares for the sick, the captain who cares for the sailors and the ruler who cares for the ruled. Care expertise was discovered (*hēurēmenē* – 341e5) because human beings are not self-sufficient (see *exarkei* at 341e2, 5) and so not able to provide themselves with everything they need. These experts thus developed ways to provide something others lack (*prosdeitai*, 341e3, 342a3). Medicine, for instance, is a care expertise discovered to provide our bodies with what they are not able to provide for themselves when it comes to health (341e4-7).

If care expertise was discovered as a means to obtain a given end that was lacking, the expertise itself does not lack anything. After all, its *raison d'être* is to be powerful enough to obtain its end (342a4-5).[2] Thrasymachus is therefore right in qualifying experts as powerful (340d8-9; see Chapter 7). On the other hand, if an expertise does not require further expertise to provide it with an end (342a6-b2), there is no such thing as an architectonic expertise: the end of the captain is to provide the sailors with something they need, not to benefit their own expertise (compare to 342c1-6). The reason is that, since expertise is a power, the argument against the Molière regress holds for it: there is no such thing as a power of power or an expertise of expertise. Powers must be defined by the state of affairs obtained by the agent, and an expertise must be sufficient to obtain its proper end (342b2-6). This, of course, does not preclude there being instrumental powers which an expertise uses. But instrumental powers, as we saw, are part of the circumstance that allows a power to obtain its end or not. They explain conditions for not obtaining the end of a power and are not part of the definition of the expertise as such.

Socrates' point is that if experts are powerful, their end is not to supply themselves with something they need; it is to supply others with something good (342c1-6). Rulers came to be because there was a need for the ruled to be provided for – their end is to obtain the good of others. However, Socrates draws a stronger conclusion: they provide *only* what suits others *and not* what suits themselves (342c10-d2). He seems to infer that because an *expertise* does not lack anything, *experts* themselves do not lack anything and so the activity of an expert brings him no good. This is a faulty inference, and Thrasymachus is right to object (343a7-8).

Here, Thrasymachus offers the counterexample of shepherds and cowherds (343b1-c1), which picks up on Socrates' own example of the horse-breeder (342c4-5). The cowherds care for their cattle aiming *solely* at their own good (343b1-4) just as rulers in respect to the ruled (343b4-c1). Thrasymachus is right to claim that care expertise has only one end for, as we saw, this is a requirement of its definition as an expertise. He is also right about there being some motivation in the expert to engage in this activity. But pushing for the exclusion of the good of others leads him to the other extreme position, according to which the ruler takes it all and the ruled get nothing (343c4-6). He then proceeds to introduce the definition of justice as the good of others and self-harm (343c3-5) analysed in the previous chapter. When it comes to the question about

---

[2] In my view, Socrates' argument is not a faulty induction, as seen by Cross and Woozley 1964: 48; Barney 2006: 49–50. It is rather a justification for the discovery of such practices.

why experts engage in their expertise, the dialogue leaves us with two extreme positions that do not help our understanding of justice.

After Thrasymachus' conclusion on injustice as *pleonexia* and tyranny as complete injustice, Socrates picks up where he left off: the 'shepherd' objection and identification of the motivation for caring for others. In this argument, he distinguishes the care expertise from the wages that the expert receives, which are produced by what he calls reward expertise (*misthōtikē*, 346b1).[3] This concept has been regarded with suspicion[4] for the reason that it seems to deny the general principle proposed by Socrates, according to which an expertise does not need another expertise to provide it with an end (342a6-b2); that is, there is no architectonic expertise. However, such suspicion is unfounded. The expert of such activity is the one who rewards, and the end of such an expertise is what suits the other expert, the good of others.[5] Reward expertise is knowledge of the good to be given in return for goods received, where one expert provides the good for others who themselves provide the expert with rewards. Rewards matter because – and on this point Socrates and Thrasymachus seem to agree – no one would rationally consent to care for others on a purely altruistic basis (345e5-6).[6] Care expertise is exercised within a common purpose contract with a win-win basis, according to which, for every good an expert provides, the beneficiary gives him a fair reward. The contract is extrinsic to the activity of expertise, whose end is not to benefit the expert.

The theme of contracts was introduced in an argument Socrates made to Polemarchus before Thrasymachus' interruption (332d7-333d2). At that point Socrates was examining Polemarchus' proposal that justice is promoting the good of friends and the harm of enemies (332d7-8), and, in an attempt to explain how justice may secure the good of others, they explored cases of care expertise – the doctor and the captain (332d10-e10) – to infer that they produce the good of others. However, they conclude that the good they produce is not justice: being a doctor or a captain is not the same as being just. The quest for justice leads Polemarchus to suggest that the good obtained by justice lies in contracts with common purpose (*sumbolaia koinōnēmata*, 333a14), for example, the hiring of a builder to make a house (333b4-5). While Thrasymachus saw these situations as a typical occasion in which the just person has less and the unjust has more (343d3-6), Polemarchus identifies them as the ones in which we should look for a just agent.

But in the discussion with Polemarchus, Socrates does not mention reward expertise. Rather, he takes a one-sided view of the matter to claim that we establish contracts when we hire an expert (333b1-6) – not necessarily a just agent. Even where this contract gives money to an expert, in this case the horse-breeder that would give us a horse, Socrates avoids the subject of

---

[3] Notice the contrast between the reward expertise and the money-making expertise (*chrēmatistikē*, 341c6, 345d11). These are not to be mistaken for each other, because the latter is the 'expertise' required to obtain profit, which, as it does not promote the good of others, will not be accepted in contexts of justice (see Campese 1998: 257–9).

[4] I reject the thesis that the expertise of reward is a type of ubiquitous architectonic expertise (see Bloom 1991: 322, 333; Benardete 1989: 24) because it is restricted to the contexts of rewarding the action of an expert. The agent of a reward expertise is the beneficiary of another expertise. A further reason is that Socrates explicitly denies the existence of an architectonic expertise (342a6-b2). For the claims that the reward expertise is inconsistent with Socrates' assumptions, see Dorter 1974: 33; Jang 1997: 194; Reeve 19851985: 260; Vegetti 1998: 248; Nawar 2018: 381–2.

[5] The verb *mistharneō* is best translated as 'to be paid', 'to be rewarded', so, although it has an active sense, it describes the action to receive, not to pay (see 346b8-12). The verb *proschraomai* at 346c5-7 shall be translated as 'to avail' the benefit of the reward expertise.

[6] This means that for Socrates justice is not pure altruism, as supposed by White 1979: 103; 1986: 46; Klosko 2006: 119; Weiss 2012: 183; Rowett 2018: 132. For a claim similar to mine, see Jang 1997: 196.

an expertise that would establish the value of the horse cared for (333a11-c3). Socrates' dialogue with Polemarchus may therefore be aporetic due to this partial approach to contracts, as the expertise of those who have contracts with experts is not acknowledged. This is not, however, the occasion to consider the aporetic route of the argument. I simply wish to point out that both Polemarchus and Thrasymachus, in their approach to justice, are attempting to place just actions within this kind of cooperation according to contracts.[7]

Returning to Socrates' argument against Thrasymachus, here he claims that all those professionals[8] who produce goods for others, care experts included, only benefit by means of the rewards expertise (346c9-11). With this argument, he agrees with Thrasymachus that there is no rational motivation for doing the good of others. This kind of expertise follows the general points introduced earlier. It is a form of knowledge, it has an end peculiar to itself (a specific good of others) and it is a power (346d5-6). On the other hand, if its expert obtains no benefit, no one would rationally consent to accomplish it (346e8). Rational motivation to produce the good of others occurs within common purpose contracts in which the agent expects their partner to employ reward expertise, valuing their work and rewarding them with money, honour or, should they refuse, punishment (347a3-5).

Socrates claims that the threat of punishment is the only way to motivate the best experts to care for others, especially in the case of ruling. The best experts in ruling are neither honour-lovers nor money-lovers (347b2-4) and do not wish to be recognized as one who rules *for the sake* of either money or honour, as this is how honour-lovers or money-lovers operate (347b7-10). The best agents do not engage in common purpose contracts because, being good, they have no interest and no need of the most common form of reward – money and praise – and so place themselves somewhat outside a community based on win-win contracts; they cannot be rewarded in the standard ways. The only way to have the best agent to produce the good of others is to threaten their own good.

> [T19] For them to be willing to rule, it is necessary that the inevitable befalls them, as well as a punishment. This is probably why it is considered shameful to engage in ruling with consent and not wait for it to be inevitable. The greatest punishment, if one is not willing to rule, is to be ruled by someone worse. It is with this fear, it seems to me, that decent people rule when they rule. They approach ruling not as if they were approaching something good or something that would do them some good, but as something inevitable, given that there is no one better or similar to them to whom to entrust it. If there should ever be a city of good men, there would be battles not to rule, just as there is now to rule, so it would be clear that the real and true ruler does not naturally aim at what suits him personally, but what suits the ruled. Therefore, everyone who knows this would rather be benefited by others than take trouble to benefit others. (347b10-d8)

Good agents rule despite themselves, in inevitable (*anankē*) circumstances. But the description of the situation shows that that ruling is not an evil. It is simply undertaking a lesser good to prevent an evil – that is, being ruled by someone worse than oneself. Inevitable circumstances do not entail that the course of action is determined. There are alternatives, but none of the alternatives is good.[9] In this case, an excellent agent would opt for the lesser good – and we

---

[7] For Socrates' assumption that just actions are cooperation, see Sparshott 1966: 438; Payne 2017: 37.
[8] I understand that *dēmiourgos* has the more general meaning of experts who produce the goods of others.
[9] We shall resume the topic of the relation of ruling and *anankē* in Chapter 15; for now, I would like to point out that the general meaning of *anankē* is the unavoidable, the inevitable, with a variety of subspecies (see Rickert

should pay attention to the kind of inference that happens here as there is an important difference between being virtuous while being ruled by someone worse, and being virtuous and ruling. Bad government can actually harm excellent agents. This suggests that even if their bad political environment may not compromise their excellence, it compromises their flourishing to the point of placing them in a situation of being urged to rule. When faced with such circumstances, ruling avoids the worst-case scenario for a good agent. Another feature of the argument is Socrates' assumption – in agreement with Thrasymachus – that ruling is inevitable in every city.[10] Even if all the citizens were excellent, they would still require someone to rule them, an assumption we shall consider in the third part of this book.

For now, we may conclude that this first pair of arguments claims that at least some kind of expertise was discovered because it promotes the good of others. It does not benefit the agent, so there is no rational motivation intrinsic to it. Rather, experts are motivated to promote the good of others within common purpose contracts that generally reward experts with either money or honour. But excellent agents who are not motivated by money or honour would only engage in such contracts in circumstances of inevitability as a way of securing a lesser good. It is worth noticing that, at the end of this argument, Socrates, despite not agreeing with Thrasymachus that justice is whatever suits who prevails, states that he will leave this enquiry on what justice is for another occasion, on the grounds that it is more pressing to know whether we should live the unjust life or the just life (347d8-e4). He will come to regret this move at the end of book I (354b1-9).

(b) The argument on knowledge (349b2-350c11)

Socrates' next three arguments deal with Thrasymachus' prescription of injustice, which entails that injustice is excellence (*aretē*) and our best option for flourishing (348b8-349a4).[11] Thrasymachus claims that the perfectly unjust agent, the one with political power, makes good choices and is prudent (*phronimos*) and good (348d2-6). In his attempts to refute this thesis, Socrates mobilizes basic assumptions on mediocrity and excellence to point out certain absurdities that Thrasymachus has committed himself to. In order to do so, he applies a method introduced by Thrasymachus (compare 344a4-c9 to 348d3-350c11) which consists of describing just and unjust agents as personalities (see Chapter 6). Both Thrasymachus and Socrates understand that they can find what complete justice and injustice are by following what is supposed to be the default actions of these characters (see 348b9-10).

In the first argument of this series, Socrates claims that knowledge is incompatible with *pleonexia*. His starting point is that while the unjust personality aims at having more than anyone in any action (349c7-9), the just personality does not aim at having more than another just

---

1989: 15–34, 60): (i) it can indicate both a circumstance in which there is no alternative and one in which the alternatives are not good; (ii) its cause can be violence or the threat of violence; compelling social practices or an actual absence of alternative; (iii) in these circumstances the agent can both engage themselves in the action (act *hekōn*) or act despite themselves (act *akōn*). To this list, Shields (2007: 27–32) adds that compulsion can be internal or external, proper or improper; a variety of cases is also present in Barney (2008: 10–11). Weiss (2012: 107–12) mentions the diversity but supposes a fixed meaning.

[10] Objections about the need for a government are raised by Penner (2009: 202). Socrates' answer is far from clear: if the need for the ruling expertise comes from the deficiency of the ruled, one would expect that in the city of excellent citizens that he imagines in 347d2-6, government would no longer be necessary; however, this does not happen, and the reward system is still maintained, although it has been converted into a punishment system (347b10-c2). I would like to leave this question open for now, as it will be answered in Part Three.

[11] This is not an actual inversion of values because Thrasymachus never states that justice is vice, simply that it is a non-sensical naiveté (see Chappell 1993: 11). However, he does claim that justice does not promote our flourishing, while injustice does; this is sufficient for the opposition (see 348e1-3).

agent (349b2-3). As the previous chapter indicated, this was one of the faults in Thrasymachus' account of justice – his neglect of the hypothesis that the just agent is motivated by shared or common goods. On the other hand, a just agent, claims Socrates, considers themself worthy of having more than an unjust agent (349b8-9). As I understand this statement, it refers to a situation in which, having acknowledged an unequal state of affairs obtained by the unjust agent, just agents demand redistribution. Why this appears to be the best reading is that, according to Thrasymachus, no one would be an unjust agent without having obtained an unequal state of affairs. Socrates' inference would therefore appear to be that, while the unjust always aim at having more than anyone else (a point on which he agrees with Thrasymachus), the just agent aims at having equal distribution among equals. This includes redistributing whatever unequal distribution an unjust agent might have obtained (349c11-d1).

Against Thrasymachus' claims (348d2-9; 349d4-5), Socrates aims to show that someone who is prudent and good pursues an equal state of affairs. His argument is controversial. From Thrasymachus' thesis that it is the state of affairs obtained that allows us to acknowledge someone as an expert (340d2-6), Socrates infers that every expert must aim at the same state of affairs (350a6-9, compare with 340e2-7). The premise seems to be that such an end is intrinsic to their expertise (see 350a8-9).[12] This, of course, depends on Thrasymachus accepting Socrates's argument on expertise and the good of others, which he seems reluctant to do.

Yet that is not the only problem with the argument. It is reasonable to suppose that experts are identified as such because they all obtain the same state of affairs, that is, the state of affairs for whose accomplishment the expertise was discovered. But this does not grant Socrates' inference at 350b7-c5, that they all obtain an *equal* state of affairs. Socrates himself opposes this kind of conclusion in his argument to Polemarchus where he claims that, when we hire an expert, we expect to obtain the good they can produce and not necessarily the state of affairs a just agent can produce, that is, a win-win outcome, the equal distribution of goods (333b1-6). But now, he seems to suppose that our expectation in contracts is to obtain not only something we lack but also a win-win state of affairs. In other words, we do not look for an expert *simpliciter*; we look for a just expert. Is there a hidden premise in this argument? I think there is.

I have already mentioned that the claim that all experts aim at the same end holds or falls depending on the acceptance of the previous argument on expertise and the good of others. In this argument, expertise is the power to obtain the good of others and the expert is motivated to exert their expertise due to common purpose contracts. In a common purpose contract, the role of the expert is to provide their partner with a good. It is by providing the good of others that experts are just; it is by rewarding them as expected that their partners are just. It is by this co-operation, that is, in each of them simultaneously performing the action expected in their contract, that both obtain a just state of affairs. Socrates' hidden premise is therefore that experts who do the good of others do their part to obtain an equal state of affairs in common purpose contracts. In claiming that they all have the same end, Socrates may be suggesting that all experts aim at win-win state of affairs, because he supposes that they are invested in common purpose contracts.

It is remarkable that Plato purposely omits Thrasymachus' response to this point (350c12-d2). We also miss a second speech he would have given in response (350d9-10), which makes it evident that Thrasymachus is not satisfied with this argument (350c12-d2, d8-9) – most likely because he does not accept that expertise is committed to the good of others and that the expert's motivation lies in the reward given by the expertise of others. Thrasymachus insists that rulers obtain their own good by ruling, even if they still need the ruled to accomplish it for them.

---

[12] For this distinction between the end of the expertise and the desire of the expert, see Annas 1981: 51–2; Penner 2009: 210, Barney 2006: 53.

(c) The cooperation argument (350d5-352b5)

Socrates intends to refute Thrasymachus' claim that injustice is more powerful and stronger than justice (351a2-3). On Thrasymachus' assumption, a city is perfectly unjust for enslaving other cities (351b1-5), that is, for taking their goods and enslaving their citizens without being punished (see 344a7-c3), and so Socrates' question is whether this prevailing city has the power to do it with or without justice (351b7-9). This is his argument:

> [T20] Do you think that a city, an army, a militia, a gang or any other group that intends to do something unjust in common has power to accomplish it if its members are unjust to each other?
> No, not really, he said.
> What if they are not unjust? Would they better accomplish it?
> Certainly.
> For injustice, Thrasymachus, generates sedition, hatred and strife among the members, while justice generates harmony and friendship, or not?
> Whatever, he said. Lest I disagree with you.
> You do very well, my good man. So, tell me this: if the outcome of injustice is to generate hatred wherever it occurs, whether among free men or slaves, will it make them hate each other, engage in strife and be powerless to act in common with each other?
> Yes.
> And what happens if it arises between two people? Won't they diverge, hate each other and become enemies both to one another and to the just agents?
> They will, he said.
> If, my admirable man, injustice arises in one individual, will his power be destroyed, or will he lose nothing?
> He won't lose anything, he said.
> Well, but doesn't it seem that injustice has the power, wherever it arises, be it a city, a family, an army or whatever, first to make this agent powerless to act with himself due to strife and disagreement, and then to make it an enemy both of itself and of that which is in every way its opposite, the just agent?
> Indeed.
> And also in an individual, as it seems to me, its presence brings about its natural accomplishment: first it will make him powerless to act, because he is in strife and does not agree with himself, then he becomes an enemy of himself and of the just agents. Isn't it so?
> Yes. (351c7-352a10)

The basic premise of the argument is that the unjust agent needs power to obtain their end, a thesis to which Thrasymachus is committed. In the first step of his argument, Socrates spells out how power works in the case of ends that require the action of others to be obtained: a city's action towards the enslavement of other cities, for instance, is an action with common purpose, a cooperative action among its citizens (351c7-9). The citizens get involved because they expect that, once the end of the common action is obtained, each of them will obtain their own end (351c8-9). A city which rules over another probably achieved this position because of the engagement and the success of its army in war. Indeed, fighting a war is an action soldiers do in common, with the single end of defeating the enemy, an end which, once obtained, generates a state of affairs that benefits each of the soldiers. Actions in common or cooperative actions are those whose end is to obtain a state of affairs in which the end of every agent is also obtained: they aim at a win-win outcome. It is not necessary for a cooperative action that all the agents will obtain the same end. In the case of contracts, one partner obtains the good produced by an expertise; the other obtains the product of the reward expertise. Similarly, members of a gang may associate with different ends. Some may act for the sake of revenge, others for the sake of money. However, they see the state of affairs that would result from this action as obtaining each of their ends: the goods are different, but they are all the outcome of a common action that is more properly understood as a co-operation or the joint operation of different agents towards a state of affairs.

In the second step, Socrates claims and Thrasymachus agrees, that in obtaining inequality, injustice always generates hatred and strife. Inequality (*pleonexia*) is what injustice produces by its own Thrasymachean definition; hatred and strife are the individual reactions of the agents involved in this state of affairs obtained by injustice (351d3-4, 8). Strife is described as the situation in which the agents involved have opposite beliefs about the state of affairs obtained in an action. Some believe it is good; others that it is not (352a1-3). This disagreement leads the dissatisfied to hatred (352a2-3). It is most likely that Socrates would account for hatred as the activation of the *thumos* as anger about one's personal situation in the resultant state of affairs. The hatred one feels thus turns others into enemies, and so, as in Simonides's statement which is discussed by Socrates and Polemarchus, what we should do about our enemies is to hate and harm them (332a7-10 and *misein* at 334c5).

By causing inequality, strife and finally hatred, injustice accomplishes a state of affairs in which there is a strong rejection of the win-win end of cooperation (351e1-2, 352a1-2). It is for this reason that agents within these political and psychological circumstances consider any just agent as their enemy (351e5; 352a1-3, 9): anyone who does not comply with their own purpose is to be fought. The argument Socrates puts to Thrasymachus is that situations of inequality resulting from previous actions destroy the power for cooperative actions (351e7-8) because they generate hatred in the agents involved and thus the emotional rejection of any win-win end. Inequality does not merely generate disagreement; it generates a vicious cycle of revenge which tends to perpetuate itself. If so, and if, as Socrates claims, some cooperation is required for complete injustice (351c8-9), then complete injustice never obtains (352c7-d1).

In this argument Socrates concedes to Thrasymachus that justice has an instrumental role in the power of injustice.[13] However, they disagree about what sort of means justice provides: a cooperative or a subordinative one? Socrates claims that the power to obtain one's end lies in having an end that includes the end of others, while Thrasymachus claims that the power to obtain one's end lies in having means to make others obey. Socrates struggles to convince Thrasymachus that an unjust individual would have less power to act, but the latter simply responds that 'he won't lose anything' (351e9). Because he supposes interaction is a transference of Thrasymachean goods, he understands violence and stealth as the sole means to power. Cooperation is not in his vocabulary. If he ends up yielding to Socrates' insistence about injustice generating strife and hatred even in one person (351e10-352a10), it is probably because he does not see that hatred would preclude someone to serve the ruler. After all, we have no reason to suppose that Thrasymachus admits such a controversial thesis as a divided self.[14] In

---

[13] For the interpretation that cooperation is a means instead of a virtue, see Strauss 1964: 82. On this topic see Chapter 14.

[14] Interpreters who see the argument depending on the assumption that a human being is a component of parts are, for instance, Dorter 1974: 39, Barney 2006: 55 and Nawar 2018: 386.

my understanding of the argument, no matter how much hatred they possess, the ruled have no alternative because they are powerless. Tyrants win wars and dominate other cities with armies of slaves; the cooperation of the soldiers is not required.

Thrasymachus does not have to agree with Socrates that justice is necessary for a perfectly unjust action (352c4-d1). If Socrates can prove that political power depends on cooperative, instead of subordinative, actions, he may refute Thrasymachus' thesis that perfect injustice is attainable: the tyrant would have to share some of the goods in order to remain in power. Socrates could also propose some restrictions to Thrasymachus' first definition – justice is what suits who prevails. If the cooperation of others matters for the maintenance of power, it does make a difference (in spite of what Thrasymachus has suggested) to what kind of laws rulers enact, how they are enforced and the degree of support and social legitimation they find. Political systems are not universally just.[15]

(d) The argument on excellence (352d2-354a11)

Socrates opens his last argument to Thrasymachus with the premise that there are activities performed peculiarly well by certain agents, or that there are agents that are exclusively apt for certain actions (352e3-4). In these cases, these agents are primarily identified for their ability to carry out these actions (353a9-11) like eyes that see. I hold that this claim anticipates the stronger thesis of the individuation principle we saw in Chapter 1: some actions are sufficient for the identification of individuals as their agents. When an agent is associated with a peculiar activity and solely under this condition, his excellence is excellence in this activity and not another (353c5-7).

Socrates evidently believes that the soul is such an individual. We identify the soul by certain activities that cannot be attributed to any other individual, such as caring, ruling, deliberating (353d4-7) and also the activity of living (*zēn*), which is its most basic function (353d9-10, see *malista*). The excellence of the soul is what allows these activities to be done well (353e1-2).[16] But more fundamental to it is the notion that the excellence of the soul is to live well (*eu biōsetai / eu zōn*, 353e10, 354a1). Those who live well flourish (354a1-2).[17] Thrasymachus, of course, had objections to Socrates' argument on caring (343b1-d1). However, he pointed out, supporting Socrates' present claim, that deliberation and ruling were components of the human excellence

---

[15] See Sparshott 1966: 427–47.
[16] I disagree with Butler (2008: 234) that Socrates understands that excellence is profitable in the same terms that Thrasymachus supposes that injustice is excellence and profitable, for the simple reason that, in linking excellence to the excellence of what something is, Socrates aligns it with the nature and definition of something, and not with the acquisition of external goods. While according to Thrasymachus, excellence can be described as simply material success or prosperity, Socrates rejects this hypothesis in favour of the notion of flourishing.
[17] Cross and Woozley (1964: 68–9) assume that the soul may perform well the function of living, that is, remaining alive, without performing the function of living well, that is, caring, ruling and deliberating well. In doing so, they assume there is a difference between natural good and a moral good, which is the modern standard of dealing with the matter. They also suppose that all teleology entails that a function was assigned to something by something else, in the case of the soul, by God. Santas (1985: 227 ff.) also points out a possible inconsistency between what he calls a functional theory of the good, displayed here, and the Form of the Good, in particular because performing one's function well does not amount to 'being happy', or to being closer to the best individual of a kind, which is the theory of the good he sees in the form of the good (idem, 230, 241–2). I understand that such problems arise in insisting on there being some peculiar function something has, as opposed to what something is (see Singpurwalla 2006: 328). Life is not a function of the soul, but what it is, and its flourishing is the fulfilment of what it is. In the next chapter I shall argue that Socrates is committed to a notion of natural peculiar goodness.

that in turn leads to flourishing, that is, the best life (348b8-c4). Socrates' disputed premise is that justice is this human excellence (353e7-8). This point comes about in the conclusion of the argument on knowledge (350b7-c5), where Socrates infers from the fact that all experts have the same end, that they all aim at an equal state of affairs. I underlined that this inference depended on his previous argument that all expertise aimed at the good of others, and that the motivation of experts to practise their expertise came from the rewarding expertise of their partners in common purpose contracts. Thrasymachus had objections to all of these conclusions; as such, it is far from clear why he now states that he agrees that justice is human excellence (353e7-8).

Though we can see that Thrasymachus was not properly refuted, the argument on excellence still connects the dots between all the arguments Socrates made to Thrasymachus to give us a sense of how they would cohere, if they were to align. Socrates claims that caring, ruling and deliberating are activities peculiar to the soul and therefore only a soul may excel in them to become a care expert. Given that all of Socrates' arguments about caring expertise emphasize that it always aims for the benefit of others, we may hold that the benefit of others is involved in our flourishing. Equally, one may think that these soul activities are also directed to the soul itself: self-care, self-ruling, deliberation about what is best for oneself – especially because Socrates pointed out that ruling others is not a good for the agent. Are we entitled to assume that the benefit of others is excluded from these activities now? There are plenty of points requiring clarification. But if we are to assume this much, then the good of others, knowledge and cooperation are all involved in justice as human excellence. As Socrates puts it, Thrasymachus' aggressiveness made him react like a glutton failing to savour the banquet of arguments. But rushing through them does not mean Socrates himself is not committed to the main theses of these arguments. As we shall see in more detail, they introduce his central theme on which variations will follow.

9

Evil

In the previous chapter we saw that Socrates claims that the unjust ruler has no political power because it requires a cooperative action which someone motivated by *pleonexia* cannot undertake. There I offered a precise concept of cooperation: agents acting concurrently in pursuit of their ends without preventing each other from doing so. I claimed that cooperation does not entail a common end to all, but being committed to obtaining a state of affairs in which the end of all is obtained, which I termed a win-win state of affairs. On the other hand, T12 stated that injustice results in hatred and strife. I suggested this implies that wherever inequality is the state of affairs, there is evidence that powerful agents are motivated by *pleonexia*, which destroys the trust of others and any further possibility of cooperation (351d3-352a10). The presence of unjust agents generates the unjust *politeia* where hatred and strife are its characteristic symptoms: its citizens do not cooperate. But if political power comes from cooperation, completely unjust rulers do not have political power. I argued that Thrasymachus disagrees with this argument, claiming that political power does not depend on cooperative but rather on subordinative actions – actions in which the ruler uses power devices to force the ruled to obtain what they have prescribed.

This chapter aims to explain Socrates' account of evil in the *Republic* and show how his theses about *politeiai* and personalities are based on interactions between people. Such theses (i) employ the set of concepts we have been working with to argue that, in the case of evil, predominant ends are unreasonable; that is, they are related to unreasonable beliefs about flourishing and are obtained only through power devices; (ii) they take evil as a power and therefore an attribute of an agent for some state of affairs obtained; consequently (iii) they reaffirm the thesis in T1 that soul explains city; (iv) they follow Thrasymachus' explanatory standard, according to which there is a partial and a complete way of obtaining one's end, whose difference depends on the use of the institution of government; (v) they add to this difference between partial and complete modes of obtaining one's end, the partial and complete modes of evil in a certain state of affairs, forming degrees of degeneration. These analyses aim to show that unreasonable ends result in state of affairs that are harmful to all, including to the agents themselves. Before addressing them, however, I shall analyse two important passages on the good and the evil of a person and a city in order to argue that the *Republic* has a natural approach to good and evil: its central concepts are items like flourishing, excellence, life and human beings. The first of these passages occurs almost at the end of the dialogue:

> [T21] Do you call something a good and something an evil?
> I do.
> Do you think about them as I do?
> How?

> That evil is what destroys and corrupts, and good is what preserves and improves.[1]
>
> I think so, he said.
>
> And beyond that? Would you say that there is good and evil peculiar to each thing? Like ophthalmia in the eyes and disease in the whole body, blight in the grain, rot in wood, rust in bronze and iron. In sum, is there, as I say, for almost everything an evil, a disease, which is connatural to it?
>
> I think so.
>
> Isn't it then the case that, when one of these happens in something, it makes that in which it happens bad, and, if it achieves its end, it dissolves and destroys it as a whole?
>
> Absolutely.
>
> Then the connatural evil and the degeneration of each thing destroy it, and if they do not destroy it, there is nothing that would destroy it. For neither a good would ever destroy something, nor something that is neither evil nor good.
>
> How would it? (608d11-609b3)

This passage is the clearest statement of Socrates' assumptions about good and evil throughout the entirety of the *Republic*. It states the general thesis about what is good and evil for natural items, and proposes that all good and evil are peculiar to what each thing is, that is, their being. Natural beings have connatural evils that are an alteration *of what they are*; they generate an internal process of dissolution until the complete destruction of their counterpart results. We may now see how the difference in degrees of evil corresponds to degrees of the power of this evil over its bearer. This suggests that, when something is affected by its connatural evil, its existence depends on a power struggle. If evil has power to obtain its end, it destroys its bearer. If somehow the bearer has power to preserve itself, it remains in existence, even if in bad condition. The presence of a connatural evil is sufficient for bad conditions and necessary for its bearer to cease to exist;[2] every natural being is destroyed through this process of ongoing degradation until dissolution, when the power of the connatural evil reaches its complete accomplishment, obtaining a state of affairs in which its bearer is destroyed.

A connatural good, on the other hand, is also accounted for by degrees. In its zero stage, the connatural good of a being is simply what preserves it from destruction – a preservation that is not an alteration as the good lies in something remaining *as it is*, possibly by resisting change. Health would be a good example of this sort. But there is more to connatural goods than simply this. Some goods do more than preserve us: they contribute to self-development and make us flourish. This is not an alteration *of what something is* but is an enhancement of it. Flourishing is also explained in terms of power, in this case the power to obtain self-improvement. Whilst connatural evil is the power whose end is the whole destruction of its bearer, the end of a connatural good is to cause its flourishing. It is not hard to see that the end of the connatural good is the proper end of its bearer. Although there may be a variety of external factors accounting for their presence, the main factor, the explanatory principle of good and evil, is the bearer being

---

[1] An objection can be raised about my translation of *opheloun* for 'what improves', since it may mean any kind of benefit or convenience. I have two reasons for translating it thus. First, I believe that there is a parallelism between the effects of the good and the effects of the evil – in which *opheloun* is parallel to *diaphtheiron* –, which refers to a destructive effect in something. Second, it is clear by the examples that we are dealing with natural kinds, and that no notion of moral benefit would fit in the argument.

[2] My analysis is indebted to Brown 1997: 216–18.

what it is. Although good and evil are opposites based on these natural processes, they are both correlative to what something is – that is, to the being of their bearers.[3]

T21 opens the *Republic*'s argument on the immortality of the soul (608d2-612a7). The argument aims to conclude that the soul is immortal because the evil peculiar to it, vice, does not trigger a process of dissolution leading to its destruction (609b9-d3). Vice does not kill us (609d4-8) and not everyone who dies is vicious (610c5-d4). This conclusion amounts to the claim that the death of humans is not the death of the soul for while humans are natural beings, the soul is not. Indeed, the soul has a peculiar evil (I shall not call it connatural for we are to assume that the soul is not a natural being) that causes it to deteriorate but does not destroy it. However, the proof of this is problematic for many reasons. The primary reason is that its central premise – all destruction is caused by connatural evil – is controversial. If, for instance, something were to cease to exist due not to its connatural evil, but to the destruction of something else on whose existence it depends, then the soul may perish because the body perishes.[4] Nevertheless, Socrates remains committed to the truth of the controversial premise primarily because, for independent reasons, he is committed to the thesis that good and evil are relatives to the being of things. Chapter 16 will be devoted to analysing his arguments for this claim.

Socrates is also committed to another controversial thesis: our death is the separation of the soul from the body (609d6-7) where the body undergoes its own dissolution by disease (609e5-6). This entails that human beings are composites – a soul to which a body is attached (see 611d2-5). This may restrict the notion of a tripartite soul (analysed in Chapters 1 and 2) to living human beings and suggest that conflicts and parts are the case only for the incarnated soul.[5] Since it is beyond my present purposes to address the question of this bodyless soul, I shall simply assume that Socrates is committed to two theses: (i) we are natural beings and as such have internal conflicts and parts; (ii) our good is correlative to the kind of natural beings we are, that is, ensouled bodies.

The notion that a good is correlative to what something is indicates that, when Socrates referred to an activity being peculiar to something in his response to Thrasymachus (353c5-7), he was not referring to a function imposed on it by some external end. Rather, he was referring to an activity that individuates an agent – that is proper to what it is.[6] Regarding human beings, this activity is life and its peculiar good is what leads to our flourishing. Flourishing determines the goods we are to acquire, and not vice versa. Socrates' concept of connatural human good therefore diverges from the Thrasymachean good, which in contrast was the sufficient cause of our flourishing according to Thrasymachus. But there are some points of intersection between the goods of Socrates and Thrasymachus: food, for instance, is a material and transferable good that is connatural to all of us as it preserves our existence. While Thrasymachus supposes that the accumulation of this kind of good is our flourishing – that is, that our good is to stuff ourselves with as much food as we can get – Socrates defends the reverse explanatory order: he claims that it is our health that determines which foods, and in which quantities, are our good. That is to say that health, which is the connatural good of our species, determines the measure according to which food is a good.

---

[3] For opposite relatives, see Duncombe 2015: 53–4.
[4] For the objection, see Annas 1981: 345. At this point Brown (1997: 226) ascribes to Plato a more controversial claim: if the soul were to be destroyed, it could happen in the moment when it separates from the body. I find this claim harder to sustain.
[5] For claims that the tripartition is not intrinsic to the soul, see Shields 2001: 149–51; Fronterotta 2013: 176–7.
[6] For the intrinsic relation between good and what something is, see Santas 1985: 242 and Singpurwalla 2006a: 322.

If these are good indications about what good and evil are for a person, I shall now address a key passage about what they are in relation to a city:

> [T22] But then isn't it a start towards agreement to ask ourselves what we would say is the greatest good for the organization of the city, the one that the legislator must target when enacting the laws, and what is the greatest evil? And next, to examine whether that which we just described fits into these characteristics of the good and into those of the evil?
> Yes, this is prior to everything else, he said.
> Do we have a greater evil in the city to mention than that which fragments it and makes it multiple instead of one? And a greater good than that which ties it and makes it one?
> We have no other.
> And isn't the community of pleasures and pains that which binds it, when all citizens celebrate or mourn the same events and losses as homogeneously as possible?
> Exactly.
> And what dissolves it is the privatization of these [mournings and celebrations], when some [of the citizens] rejoice while others suffer regarding the same state of the city or of its inhabitants?
> Sure. (462a2-c1)

T22 describes the evil of a city as what dissolves it, as opposed to the good as what preserves its unity. This suggests that the flourishing of a city supposes its unity. The city is a collective of interacting human beings sharing the same living space (369c2-4; we shall come back to this point in the next chapter). In contrast to the deathless soul (610e10-611a2), a city may cease to exist through a process of fragmentation, that is, its connatural evil is more powerful the weaker is the bond between citizens. This bond is its connatural good, which Socrates calls the community of pleasures and pains.

The meaning of this expression has been highly misunderstood by interpreters who have taken T22 as evidence for Plato's commitment to an organic and holistic view of politics. This is justified by the comparison, introduced right after the passage, between the community of citizens and a person (462c9). Socrates says that an event in the city should be felt by the citizens in the same way we feel a cut in our finger (462c9-10). Since these interpreters suppose a person to be a unified organism, of which a finger is simply a part without independent existence, they thus conclude that we have here an organicist theory of the state.[7] But this is not exactly what is found in the text. Socrates begins by declaring that, rather than an organism, a person is a *community* that stretches itself from the body up to the soul (462c10-11) – a composite (*suntaxin* at 462c11) whose unity is only given by the component that rules in it (462c11-d1). This whole description of the human being appears in political terms: there is no unity to the whole except the arrangement determined by the ruling principle, its prevailing end.

All the 'community' perceives the cut of the finger, but does so in different ways: the finger is distressed (*ponēsantos*, 462d2), while the whole composite condoles with it (*sunēlgēsen,* 462d1-2). Socrates marks the difference between that which feels the pain and that which interacts with this fact. Holistic interpretations assume that Socrates' city is an organism because they read into the text a holistic account of a person. However, the unity of a person as well as that of a city is

---

[7] I note the bias in Grube/Reeve translation: 'the entire organism that binds body and soul together into a single system' (Grube/Reeve, 462c10-11). For the claim that it amounts to an organic theory of the state, see Popper [1945] 1966: 212. For a defence of the lack of personal unity in this argument, see Kamtekar 2001: 209.

given not by the whole, but by a ruling principle that establishes its movement and its character – a principle that, as we know, prevails among others. Personality and *politeia* are therefore unified by the state of affairs generated from the *interaction* of their components.

We are not, therefore, justified in reading T22 as claiming that all the citizens must have the same feelings and emotions at the same time as if the whole city were a single, sentient individual. Socrates' point is that, facing the same state of affairs resulting from the interaction of citizens, they ought not to have opposite emotional reactions. In other words, they should have the same beliefs about what is a good and a bad political state of affairs, being able to associate pain with the bad and pleasure with the good.[8] This results from some crucial assumptions: (i) all citizens should have the same beliefs about what constitutes a good and bad state of affairs; (ii) all citizens should see themselves as implicated in the state of affairs of the city; (iii) none of them should associate the wrong belief and feeling with the state of affairs obtained (recall the risk of compassion in the decent man's reception of a poetry that simulates the actions and reactions of base personalities).

Following the analogy with the person, the community of pleasures and pains among the citizens is not committed to the thesis that the city is a sentient individual. Rather, it refers to a compositional unity in which citizens empathize with the pain of others. Though we do not find a specific word for empathy in the *Republic*, I would like to suggest that this is what we should understand for the community of pleasures and pains.[9] It should be noted that empathy is to be distinguished from the compassion introduced in the case of the reception of simulative poetry. In compassion, a person lets themselves go, by associating belief and emotion in spite of themselves. When engaged in empathy, on the other hand, someone is involved in understanding this association of belief and emotion. Empathy allows us to understand the feelings of others *based on our true beliefs*, that is, beliefs about the good we learned through the regular functioning of our cognitive apparatus. When citizens empathize with others, they do not necessarily *feel the same* joy or sorrow (although this may be true), but they do not *feel the opposite*. What matters is not the spread of the same feeling, but the understanding that the situation justifies (or not) the emotions of those involved for the same belief about good and flourishing is shared.

T22 tells us that the community of pleasure and pain is the end of every legislator. Laws therefore should aim at preserving the city and making it flourish, rather than punishing individuals. This means that laws should aim at (i) actually being the expression of the mores, so as to ensure justice by preventing injustice; (ii) establishing shared beliefs about what is pleasant and painful and what are good and bad states of affairs; and (iii) educating individuals to see themselves as agents of the state of the city – the *politeia* – as well as agents implicated in it; (iv) obtaining empathy among citizens. If this is so, therefore, obeying the law is the same as acting as a citizen. We know that pleasures and pains are the basic factors for habit formation, and we also know that *thumos* contributes to it by adding pleasure and pain to our actions based on our beliefs about flourishing. We are therefore to expect that the lawgiver would like to guide the activity of our *thumos* with a specific notion of flourishing – an empathy-based notion of cooperative flourishing. In sum, a good city has citizens who have a shared belief about their

---

[8] I see no problem in some citizens being indifferent to the state of affairs obtained in interactions in which they are not implicated, but this does not preclude that, once informed about the state of affairs, they must follow the shared beliefs in assessing it. Arruzza (2011: 221–2) describes it as 'collectivist arrangements', with which one can identify private interests with common interests.

[9] Nussbaum (2013: 145) defines empathy as 'the ability to imagine the situation of other, taking other's perspective'. Bloom (2016: 27) first defines it as 'the act of coming to experience the world as you think someone else does', then makes the distinction between 'cognitive empathy' and 'emotional empathy' to go on to argue against the latter. For the community of pleasures and pains entailing empathy, see Singpurwalla 2006: 279.

flourishing, more fundamentally one that states that their flourishing involves the flourishing of others. When all the citizens see themselves as akin, the best *politeia* and the best kind of citizenship ensue (*hē aristā politeuomenē polis*, 462d7).[10]

The opposite of the community of pleasures and pains is their privatization (*idiōsis*, 462b8). Socrates explains this concept as citizens diverging in their assessment of a certain political state of affairs, in such a way that their difference in belief leads them to suppose that they are not concerned in how this situation reflects on the pains and pleasures of others (*to te emon kai to ouk emon*, 462c3-4). The privatizers see others as alien (*peri tou allotriou*, 462c4) and not as akin (*oikeia*), and so believe their flourishing is not connected to the flourishing of others. This is the origin of the fragmentation of a city. Some lines later, Socrates describes how conflicts based on non-shared beliefs about the good operate like a connatural evil, degenerating the city by strife (470d4-5) and causing the destruction of the whole territory (470d5-9). This seems to correspond to what the previous chapter described as the power of injustice: hateful citizens reject any kind of cooperation, generating more injustice and a cycle of hatred that tends to perpetuate itself (see 547a5-6).

My next goal is to argue that this injustice is described as the prime kind of evil in books VIII and IX. Before proceeding to it, and after understanding more about good and evil in a person and in a city, it is worth stressing that book VIII introduces its account of evil by reminding us that, as clearly stated in T1, the evil in the soul explains the evil in the city and not vice versa:

[T23] Do you understand, I said, that there are necessarily as many types of human way of life as there are *politeiai*? Or do you think that *politeiai* arise from oak and stone and not from the customs in the city which, inclining it in one way, drag the others with them. (544d5-e2)

There is no other way to account for kinds of *politeiai* except by explaining how the way of life of individuals set some customs which, in their turn, obtain a certain state of affairs that is of consequence to others. Though of course they resemble each other, personalities and *politeiai* are not simply analogous.[11] The *politeia* is the state of affairs obtained in the interaction of citizens with their peculiar personalities, and depends on the power each of them has.[12] Neither T1 nor T23 claims that, for an end to prevail in a *politeia*, all the citizens must have the same character; nor do they claim that the majority of the citizens must have the same way of life, although they do not deny these options. They also do not claim that a ruler with a specific character is sufficient for such an end to prevail in a *politeia*, or that a hegemonical ruling is required for this purpose (although, once again, they do not deny these alternatives). As mentioned before, a prevailing end allows for different modes of prevailing, and in a city these modes vary according to the power each citizen has. This is why evil kinds of personality and *politeia* are of unlimited number (445c6). As explaining each one of them would be an insurmountable task (548d3-4),[13]

---

[10] As the text points out, the community of pleasures and pains is the goodness of a city; see White 1979: 39, 114. There are interpreters who suppose other criteria for the goodness of a city, such as its organization (Annas 1981: 110), its good functioning (Santas 1985: 241–242; Keyt 2006: 345) and the maximal happiness of its citizens (Reeve 1988: 84).

[11] The merely analogical reading of books VIII and IX was defended, for instance, by Demos 1957: 172, 174; Ferrari 2005: 61. For an argument against this approach, see Blössner 1997: 153.

[12] My interactive proposal considers all citizens as the agents who produce a *politeia*. In this sense, it varies according to the power each one has. My proposal is therefore different from explanations such as 'externalization' (Lear 1992: 190) or 'projecting the soul onto the city' (Ferrari [2003], 2005: 79), which, lacking an account of the concept of power, end up committed to the model that it is the predominant citizen who shapes the city.

[13] See also the reference to other forms of *politeia*, such as dynasties and purchased monarchies, in 544d1-3.

Socrates takes the schematic approach mentioned in Chapter 6 (548c8-d4) and discusses only four prime kinds of evil personalities and *politeiai*.

The narratives on vicious personalities explain the origin of a privatizer after an emotional life-changing experience that leads to the adoption of unreasonable beliefs about personal flourishing. As pointed out in Chapter 3, such experiences mark a moment of a second-order conflict which determines the belief according to which our *thumos* judges us, stabilizing our personality even if vicious. This contrasts with the instability of the degenerated *politeiai*, indicating the difference between what is destructible, the city, and what is not, the soul. An unreasonable belief about flourishing minimizes internal conflicts in the presence of unreasonable desires, as well as identity conflicts in actions pursuing unreasonable ends.[14] On the other hand, because these life-changing experiences cause the adoption of unreasonable beliefs on flourishing, they result in the increase and the intensification of the conflict with others. Socrates' point is to narrate the effect of the lack of empathy – the problem that arises from having a belief about flourishing in which it is disconnected from the flourishing of others – in the personal life of the privatizer. The narratives on evil personalities are framed in the context of partial evil, that is, without the power of government. They aim to show that the unreasonable belief about flourishing a privatizer has leads to the opposite of personal flourishing: pain, failure and regret.[15]

The narratives on vicious *politeiai* approach evil from the position of power, that is, when privatizers use the government to obtain their ends. In this case, the outcome of the interaction is strife in the city (its connatural evil). Since a city is a dissolvable entity and strife is a power struggle, the preservation of the city depends on maintaining some of its connatural good, that is, some shared beliefs about flourishing that allow for empathy among the citizens. The narratives on the *politeiai* show that one of the rulers' power devices consists in propagating an unreasonable belief about flourishing to the citizens in general. The strategy is this: if citizens believe in it, they will make the *politeia* last, even if it is an evil. The personalities with the same name as these *politeiai* are those who adopt this belief of personal flourishing and start living their private lives accordingly. It is because these people buy into this belief that they support strife. They are the cause of evil not because they are the rulers, but because by adopting this unreasonable belief they contribute to the conservation of a *politeia* that lives on from the flourishing of the few. Even if they are not politically engaged to obtain a certain *politeia*, their action, as the action of every citizen, causes an evil *politeia*. Let me give an overview:

In timocracy, rulers aim at accumulating money (548a5-b2) by propagating the belief that honour and victory constitute flourishing (548c5-7). The timocrat is thus the one who buys into the belief that his personal flourishing lies in honour and victory (550b6-7) and organizes his private life accordingly. Oligarchy, on the other hand, preserves itself by making others believe that money-making is flourishing (550e1-6, 551a7-10), a belief adopted by the oligarchic personality in his private life (553b7-c8). Democracy lives out of making people believe that

---

[14] For the special character of these life-changing experiences, see Irwin 1995: 284–7; Gill 1996: 256–7; Parry 2007: 391. Irwin and Gill consider that the adoption of new beliefs is a second-order reasoning. I understand that they identify such acts of deliberation as proper to a certain rationality; however, as pointed out in Chapter 3, adoption of false beliefs is considered an interference of desire over reasoning, a bewitchment that misguides it from its proper functioning. It also seems to me that Socrates explains these life-changing experiences in highly emotional and appetitive terms; they are occasions of turmoil, not of reflective reasoning. I am highly sympathetic to Johnstone's interpretation of a power struggle (2011: 152), but I find that power (*dunamis*) is not the right word. Internal conflicts dispute predominance of an end, not a certain accomplishment. In particular these are conflicts that ground the identity conflicts in which *thumos* judges our actions and situations.

[15] The cause of failure is not the lack of power to obtain the end of the action; it is the end of the action itself (see Blössner 1997: 94). The failure of rulers is, on the other hand, owed to their lack of power, resulting in constant strife.

flourishing is a certain kind of freedom (557b4, see 562b7-c2) and, as such, the democratic personality lives without chaining himself to any motivation whatsoever (561b8-c4). For tyranny to remain, it must make people believe they do not have any end to obtain, which cannot be the content of any propagated belief. Only a mad person would accept this – a sociopath perhaps, or someone with no belief or hope about personal flourishing. Tyranny lives thence out of sheer violence: stealing, killing, lying, torturing, etc. (567a6-7, 567d5-7, 569b4-6).

Privatizers ruin their own lives, but they also hinder the flourishing of others by adopting unreasonable beliefs about flourishing themselves. Beliefs about personal flourishing disconnected from the flourishing of others contribute to the dissolution of the *politeia* and are thus harmful to others and the community of pleasures and pains, even if restricted to a private life. Their presence empowers the city's connatural evil: strife based on lack of empathy. Once again, the explanatory cause is not in the city, it is in each privatizer for adopting this belief, either with or without political power.

The account of political evil as an evolving disease has been interpreted as Plato's conception of a Law of History[16] in which each kind necessarily develops from the previous. This is a mistake. It is true that his exposition follows a sequence of escalating intensity, because it follows the idea that strife is the city's connatural evil with different stages of dissolution before destruction. But nothing in the account suggests a necessity, irreversibility or sufficient reason that would characterize a law which determines how cities evolve. Rather, the transitions among the kinds are described as power struggles whose outcome is contingent. This notion of different degrees of power struggle – following the different degrees of the disease – is a point that Thrasymachus missed. As he considered that every good is a Thrasymachean good, he could therefore only accept one kind of power struggle. But Socrates shows us there are many, owing to the different beliefs about flourishing and therefore there are different privatizers and different causes of strife. Different privatizers were already enumerated among the personalities of Chapter 6. Here, therefore, I restrict myself purely to a discussion of the evil *politeiai*, and to how each of them instantiates the opposite of the community of pleasures and pains.

Timocracy and oligarchy restrict flourishing to the rulers – in both cases, through obtaining money. Timocracy enslaves its citizens through the application of war techniques as a power device;[17] oligarchy excludes them through stratification.[18] In the first case, evil lies in dividing citizens between masters and slaves; in the second, in their division between poor and rich, but, above all, in the generation of extremely poor citizens (552b5-6).[19] By contrast, we see Socrates

---

[16] Historicist interpretations of books VIII and IX suppose that there was a just city in a distant past from which History develops as degeneration; see Taylor 1939: 31; Popper [1945] 1966: 38; Strauss 1964: 129; Bloom 1991: 416; Vegetti 2005: 137. I also disagree with non-historicist, yet causational, accounts of the passage, such as the one defended by Helmer (2005: 158 ff.), who suggests an 'eidetic causality' or a 'dynamic typology'. Frede (2011: 195-7) offers some good criticism to this approach, although in my view she ends up ascribing a bad argument to Plato. By insisting on the diversity of descriptions, I disagree with recent interpretations that suppose that one single power device maintains all the different kinds of evil. Gavreliedes (2010: 206), for instance, claims that all forms of evil are unified by force and I do not see democracy as primarily depending on political force. For the thesis that the succession is explained by the different stages of power of evil, see Hellwig 1980: 75.

[17] Socrates identifies Crete and Sparta as timocracies (544c2-3), and the description seems to be made to fit. T1 mentioned the Scythians and the Thracians as peoples in which the *thumos* prevailed – they were impetuous, but not enslaved by their rulers as the citizens in a timocracy. One reason for this difference is the fact that non-rational parts of the soul do not have unified objects (see the problem of the antinomy of *thumos*). Another reason is that the power device is different: while Scythians seemed all to be impetuous, a timocracy employs war valour against its citizens. Because of this last detail, I cannot agree that there is any kind of courage about timocracy, or any kind of shadow virtue in the evil *politeiai* (see Hitz 2010: 119, 123).

[18] For oligarchy as exclusion due to stratification, see Helmer 2010: 139; Schriefl 2013: 197.

[19] The citizen in extreme poverty is called a drone (552b5-6, c2-4). He occurs when oligarchic laws allow citizens to buy and sell all one's property (552a7-b2, 555c1-5). Without any resource to produce anything, the extremely poor become idle citizens, who occupy their time with begging, stealing or more serious crimes (552d4-7).

committing himself, against timocracy, to the idea that freedom – in the sense of being the opposite of slavery – is a good. In contrast to oligarchy, we see him committed to the thesis that some money is required for flourishing and that there are some 'Thrasymachean goods' that are, in fact, inalienable goods. Flourishing therefore lies in being neither master nor slave; neither too rich nor too poor.

Democracy constitutes the *politeia* of excessive freedom[20] where each citizen has his/her own concept of citizenship (*politeia*):

> [T24] Because, due to self-determination (*exousia*), it [democracy] has all kinds of political life (*politeiai*), and it seems that whoever wants to organize a city, as we now do, will be forced to go to a democratic city, to pick the way of life he pleases, as if arriving at a market for political lives (*politeiai*), and, having picked one of them, to found a colony accordingly. (557d2-7, my brackets)

I would like to call attention to the role of the term *politeia* in T24. The *politeia*, as we know, is the life of the citizen. In claiming that each citizen chooses her/his political life, Socrates asserts that democracy allows its citizens to choose the practice of citizenship they prefer. In democracy, citizens are extreme privatizers – hence why it is considered so serious an evil. Democracies resist empathy and any kind of shared beliefs, least of all about flourishing.[21] They are a much more extreme case than the mere presence of privatizers. It is not simply about having a belief in non-shared flourishing; it is about not having a shared belief about flourishing whatsoever. It is an anti-*politeia* because there is no possibility of shared mores or laws (563d6-7).[22] Instead, its power device is a kind of systematic tolerance or forgiveness (*sungnōmē*, 558a10), which simply makes the shared life more intolerable.[23]

Tyranny is an autocracy in which one rules for the love of ruling, and so the means become an end in itself. In contradistinction to Thrasymachus, Socrates does not suppose that a tyrant aims at the appropriation of material and transferable goods. Rather, he is depicted as indifferent to whether goods are accumulated or destroyed (568d6-e1). In doing so, Socrates avoids

---

For the traditional association of the drone to individuals who do not work (*aergoi*), see Hesiod, *Works and days*, 302–6.

[20] *Exousia* and *parrēsia* echo two clearly recognizable features of the Athenian democracy, *isonomia* and *isegoria*, under less favourable descriptions. By turning *isonomia*, equality before the law, into *exousia*, the freedom to self-determination, and *isegoria*, right to equal speech, into freedom of expression, Socrates approaches democracy not from the perspective of its constitutional law, but from the perspective of individual rights. His reason, it seems to me, is to emphasize the abuse of individual rights due to the absence of enforcement of a constitutional law. On *exousia* as freedom in its negative sense see Solomon 1967: 189; on the difference between *exousia* and power, see Lefebvre 2018: 205-7.

[21] For interpreters who criticize Plato because they suppose that the democratic person is the citizen of a democracy, see Williams 1973: 260; Annas 1981: 301; Bloom 1991: 419. Plato does not generate this confusion. He does state that a democratic personality is the character whose proper mark is 'shifting', and that a democracy is a city with different personalities, but never that a democratic personality is the one who predominates in a democracy. Therefore Ferrari (2003 [2005]: 45): 'analogy does not peer into the souls of the individuals who make up the just city, but only into the soul of the individual to whom the just city is analogous.' There are two different points involved here. The first regards how the *politeia* is similar to the person: to this point I would reply that the power device each politeia uses is the same end of the correspondent personality (see a similar approach in Johnstone 2013: 140). My reason is that one of the power devices is always to propagate a certain belief about flourishing so that the citizens may adopt it and live accordingly. The second point is how the prevailing end of a city is determined: about this topic we must acknowledge that there is no single rule and the Plato seems to preserve the contingent character of the political game.

[22] Some interpreters suppose that, in arguing against democracy, Socrates argues against the public sphere; see Arendt 1958: 220; Popper [1945] 1966: 42. For a more rigorous reading, see Schofield 2006: 113.

[23] For tolerance, see Adkins 1975: 203; Schofield 2006: 111, 118–19. For the paradox of tolerance, according to which to tolerate becomes intolerable, see Popper [1945] 1966: 581.

Thrasymachus' confusion between the desire for political power and the desire for material goods, as well as the confusion between the desire to rule and the desire for pleasure.[24] A tyranny is the slavery of all citizens with the exception of the tyrant. Its power device to maintain such a situation is complex, involving violence, exile, death and the prohibition of *parrēsia*, etc. It is not hard to see that these are the means with which the tyrant, while assuring the elimination of his opponents, also eliminates his own political support (567e7-568a2). Tyranny is sedition in its most extreme form.

The tyrannical personality does not necessarily coincide with the ruler of a tyranny (a tyrant); indeed, Socrates introduces the extraordinary case of a tyranny ruled by a tyrannical personality in order to make this distinction clear (578b11-c4; see also 575d2-e1 and 576b6-8). This unlikely and unfortunate case (578c2, 575d2) is one in which the ruled are not only victims of violence but must also subjugate themselves to fulfilling the unlawful desires of the ruler (575e4-576a3). As such, it is the worst and least stable form of *politeia*. In it, no pain or pleasure is shareable with others and life in common is eliminated. If the tyrannical personality cannot individuate an object of love, and a tyranny uses whichever it takes as a power device, the tyranny of a tyrannical personality becomes the antipode of empathy and cooperation: a *politeia* in which no end is to be obtained.

The analysis of these kinds of evil is crucial for understanding how Socrates sees the relation between city and soul. Initially, he follows Thrasymachus in supposing that a *politeia* is defined by its predominant end, but he adds to this argument the assertion that, if its end is unreasonable, a certain power device will be required to sustain the regime. In contradistinction to Thrasymachus, Socrates therefore does not think that predominance involved in ruling entails power: rulers have more or less power depending on how much strife they face. As the politeia is the state of affairs obtained by the interaction of every citizen according to their power, political power thus lies in the soul of the citizens, who themselves are the cause of the *politeiai*. City and soul are not simply analogous, as analogy is but a mode of argumentation; rather, soul causes city, and city is a determinant factor in turning personal excellence into flourishing. This is the theme of the next chapter.

---

[24] For a reading that merges the desire for ruling and *pleonexia*, see Arruzza 2019: 172. For the tyrant as the lover of ruling, see Larivée 2005: 184.

10

Reasons for a city

Socrates understands a *politeia* to be the state of affairs which results from the interaction of citizens according to the ends of their actions and their powers to obtain them. I have argued that this is a point upon which he follows Thrasymachus. Thrasymachus has also argued that *pleonexia* is the only end of human action, and that tyranny is the state of affairs obtained when there is a powerful and unjust agent able to completely obtain his ends in a city. According to this argument, a *politeia* is the evident outcome of a prevailing end when it is given power. As such, *politeiai* are neither: (i) simply analogous to personalities; nor (ii) a bundle of people of a certain personality; nor (iii) the outcome of the end of the ruler. *Politeiai* are obtained according to the power of interaction. It is thus the unreasonable ends of its citizens that generate the evil of the city, which was the phenomenon discussed in the last chapter. In what follows, we now address the opposite question: what it is for a *politeia* to be good.

In order to introduce this discussion, we must first understand what a city is, why it is good for people to live in cities and be citizens and, most of all, why living in a city is our rational end. For that, it is necessary to address the account previously given by Glaucon to which Socrates' argument on what the city is and why it is a good for us responds. Both Glaucon and Socrates agree that justice is a central factor in human interactions, primarily because it guarantees certain expectations of the agents involved. But they disagree about what kind of factor it is: Glaucon claims that it is inevitable, while Socrates claims it is a good.

Glaucon allegedly defends the view of the majority (*hoi polloi* see 358a4-6) that claims justice is nothing but a contract among powerless citizens (359a2-5).[1] The majority supposes that every unjust action is an interaction resulting in a state of affairs with consequences both for the powerful agent and for others, who, being powerless, cannot avoid this outcome. Having suffered injustice from powerful agents, and judging themselves to be harmed by the situation, the powerless react to this state of affairs by imposing restrictions on powerful unjust agents: they enter in a social contract, which consists of the enactment of laws in order to avoid the unequal distribution of goods (358e6-359a2). This is the concept of justice according to the majority: just actions are those that preserve this contract (359a2-3). It is a compromise about the good (359a5-6, 359a7-b2) in which agents do not obtain their prevailing ends (the end of desire), but merely something intermediate (359a5-6). Justice is therefore a power device used by the powerless to prevent the unequal distribution of goods.

---

[1] For Glaucon's social contract see Cornford 1945: 40; Lee 1989: 90. I follow Kahn's view (1981: 93) that this can be taken as a theory of the social contract as far as it (i) assumes a 'state of nature' prior to political life; (ii) identifies an insecurity in this primitive state; (iii) traces the legitimacy of government and law to a contract between the parties. However, one may notice that there are a variety of contractualisms. Cross and Woozley (1964: 71-3), for instance, claim that Glaucon's version does not correspond to the social contract theory because the latter does not suppose a state of nature; instead, it is based on the premise that individual obligations are self-imposed because the agreement pays.

According to the majority, just actions are performed under *anankē* (358c3-4), that is, inevitable circumstances in which the good is not an available option. Only unjust actions obtain the good (358e4), but in suffering their effects lies a greater evil (358e4-6). The majority does not seem to accept Socrates' previous argument to Thrasymachus that there is a rational justification for committing oneself to the lesser good in inevitable circumstances (see Chapter 8). Instead, in their eyes, they join the contract in spite of themselves (359b7-9; 360c6-7), for, in their view, following the contract never leads to their flourishing (358c3).

Such an approach to justice has some specific premises. First, the majority shares Thrasymachus' assumption that we all have the same motivation, that is, that we are all disputing the same good, and that our flourishing depends on obtaining more of this good than others. They assume that human beings are driven by *pleonexia* (see 359c4) and aim at an unequal state of affairs; when some obtain it, others are dissatisfied. Second, because they suppose that we act by *pleonexia*, they assume that all good things are Thrasymachean goods (transferable items whose possession is good and whose lack is bad). Third, the majority also supposes that human beings have different degrees of power to obtain Thrasymachean goods (compare 359b2-3 with 7-8). As they dispute the same good things, the resulting state of affairs will always be unequal: good for the powerful and bad for the powerless. The contract therefore aims at preventing inequality by restricting the power of unjust agents to promote, the majority supposes, a more equitable distribution of goods.

The majority may have a good explanation for justice, but it is one that rejects the thesis that justice is an excellence or a good. It does so for two reasons. The first is that this concept of justice makes personal flourishing incompatible with being just: it assumes that only the powerful unjust agent flourishes, because he is the only one to obtain the goods (358c2-5). The second is that, as we shall see, laws are not powerful enough to obstruct the action of powerful unjust agents (359b2-5); the political organization provided by the social contract is introduced as an ineffective device. The powerless that create the contract are therefore doubly harmed by it as it hinders their flourishing, and does not promote a better distribution of goods. The majority must therefore assume, with Thrasymachus, that it is nonsensical for someone to be just unless justice may empower the agent to avoid political inequality or, better yet, to obtain some real good as opposed to mere compromise. It is for this reason that Glaucon wants to know from Socrates what power justice gives us when we are just (358b4-7).

With these claims, the majority must take upon themselves the onus of proving that our nature is such that we always desire to have more than others. On their behalf, Glaucon undertakes this task through the following 'thought experiment' (359b9-c1). Suppose that we had *exousia*, that is, freedom in the negative sense of being able to determine whichever end we pursue and power to accomplish it without any external restrictions (I recall that the previous chapter introduced *exousia*, 'self-determination', as a prime explanation for why democracy was regarded an evil). According to Glaucon, what we would all do in these circumstances would prove what human nature really is. This is a problematic assumption for supposing both that external restrictions are not part of our nature and that we would all have the same end in such conditions. The latter is the more serious, for it begs the question of what the argument was supposed to prove, as I proceed to argue.

The thought experiment proposed by the majority is as imaginative as a myth – whichever truth one may see in it comes simply from the fact that, the more it is repeated, the more people are persuaded by it without justification (see 415c7-d1 about myths). As the story goes, there was once a golden ring whose bezel, once turned towards the user, would make them invisible; once reversed, it would make them visible again (359e5-360a2). One of its owners was Gyges of Lydia, a shepherd who did not hesitate to use the device in order to seduce the queen, murder the king and take over the monarchy (360b4-c5). The moral of the story is that whoever had such a ring, whether a just or an unjust agent, would not refrain from taking the good of others and being unjust (360b4-c5). The majority assumes all human beings are equal regarding the end of their actions, and all are motivated by *pleonexia* (360c6-8). Glaucon uses the story's popularity to justify its plausibility without realizing that these two categories operate correspondingly without any relation to truth. He even appears to contradict himself in mentioning the exception of one who would still refuse to commit injustice even in the face of such an opportunity.[2] That person would be highly criticized by others for being the most wretched and senseless (360d4-7) and would be in the minority as the beliefs of the majority tend to be formed by popular narratives.

Glaucon's evidence about human nature is not improved when he abandons the magical condition of *exousia* and instead describes the actions of completely just and unjust agents (360d8-e5). Here he argues that, if one were to judge which life is better, the just or the unjust, all human beings would choose the latter. Here we find a much more reasonable account than the one offered by Thrasymachus, particularly because, in contrast to Thrasymachus' unerring expert (340e2-3), Glaucon's unjust man is capable of correcting himself when he misses his marks (361a1-2). The completely unjust agent is the one who is fully aware of his power – that is, what he can obtain or cannot obtain – because to proceed like an expert is to moderate one's ends according to one's power (360e5-361a1). Moreover, unlike Thrasymachus' perfect unjust man, Glaucon's version does not have the reputation of being unjust – rather, his success lies in concealing his identity as the agent of the unjust actions performed (361a2-5). Complete injustice therefore is not to obtain all the goods; it is an expertise to obtain the most goods without appearing to others as someone who violates the social contract. As justice does not lead to flourishing in their view, the majority strives to obtain the expertise of false reputation: being unjust while appearing to be just (361a6-b1). This involves developing some abilities of action, which include acute perception (361a1), the capacity to correct mistakes (361a2, b2), courage, strength (361b4) and a mastery of power devices such as persuasive speech and violence (361b3-4).

In order to make his point about reputation, Glaucon is forced to give an elusive description of what a perfectly just man is. So as to pair this with the artificial reputation of the unjust agent, the just receive the precise opposite reputation: of being unjust. It is for this purpose that he characterizes the perfect just agent in such an extreme manner. Once considered unjust, he will be whipped, stretched on a rack, chained, blinded and impaled (notice the degree of torture that the majority allows for punishing those who appear not to be committed to the contract). This seems incoherent because Glaucon is committed to power being ascribed to an agent according to the state of affairs obtained in action (see 359b2-4). Therefore, the just agent must at least have a partial accomplishment of justice in order to be just. On these terms, it is implausible that a just agent is not seen *by anyone else* as such. This will be taken into account when we address Socrates' final response to Glaucon in Chapter 17. For now, however, Glaucon merely wants to know from Socrates what power justice gives us when we are just (358b4-7), even if we do not have such a reputation.

The majority provides us with impressive images about the completely unjust agent, but not a consistent account of human nature and our need of protection and flourishing. I argue that Socrates therefore begins his response to Glaucon by establishing a different method to account

---

[2] Cooper (2000: 7–9) argues, based on 359c5-6, that Glaucon supposes that at least some people would honour justice and that this would be evidence enough for Glaucon to assume that justice is a psychological state. Although I agree that the psychological state is undeniable, I think it is clear that they do it *nomō de bia*, that is, out of compulsion, and eventually, under violence. If this is correct, this mention of a senseless just agent in 360d4-7 would be indeed a contradiction in the claims of the majority.

for our nature. This is not based on any assumption that we lack external restrictions (or use magical rings), which would lead us to wishful thinking in regard to our desire, and would beg the question about us being motivated by *pleonexia*. Addressing human nature must therefore begin with how humans live. Socrates agrees with Glaucon that we live in interaction with others, with power restrictions determined by the power of others, but this is not a reason for supposing that we do so in spite of ourselves. We are now in a position to understand the reasons Socrates gives for a city to exist. Rather than building his explanation on how we act under conditions of lack of restraint, he instead grounds it in our needs, in our differences and in fairness (*to kalon*). He accepts Glaucon's social contract theory but rejects that it is conventional. In fact, it is based on our nature, our life and our connatural good. We may therefore begin by analysing his basic principles:

[T25] Come on then, I said, and let's produce a city by means of reasons from the beginning. It seems that it is our need that will produce it.
Indeed.
But the first and greatest of needs is to provide nutrition in order to exist and live.
Perfectly.
The second is dwelling, the third is clothing and things of that sort.
This is true.
Come then, I said, how will the city be self-sufficient about these provisions? Is there another way than there being one farmer, one builder and someone else who is a weaver? Or shall we add there a shoemaker or someone else who provides care for the body?
Sure.
Would then the minimal city, that provides the indispensable things, emerge from four or five men?
So it seems.
And so what? Each one of them must put down the product of their work as something common to all? For instance, there being one farmer he will provide food for four, spending four times the time and the effort in producing food and then sharing it with the others? Or should he not care for them and only for himself, producing one fourth of the amount of the food in one fourth of the time; and spend the other three quarters of the time in producing a house, a cloak, shoes . . ., not having the things in common with others, but doing himself by himself his own things.
Then Adeimantus said: Perhaps, Socrates, the former option is easier than the latter.
This wouldn't, by the god, be absurd, I said. Indeed, now that you mentioned it, I realized that, first of all, each one of us is born not exactly the same as the others, but differing in nature, each one to carry out a different activity, don't you think so?
I do.
And then what? Would it be a fairer accomplishment if one person carries out multiple activities, or if each one carries out one?
If each one carries out one.
After all, I assume, it is clear that, if someone misses the right moment to carry out an activity, it is ruined.
That is clear.
For, it seems to me, what is to be done does not wait for free time of the agent; on the contrary, it is a necessity for the agent to attend to what is to be done and not take it as secondary.

It is a necessity indeed.

From this it follows that more things will be done, and fairer and more easily, if an agent does each activity according to nature and at the right time, having free time from having been released from other activities.

Perfectly. (369c9-370c7)

According to Socrates, there are two reasons for us to live together in a city. The first is that being alive imposes some basic needs on us. The second is that the city provides the fairest way to meet these needs. Basic human needs are identified as nutrition, shelter and healthcare (369d1-9). These are indispensable inalienable goods (369d11), goods that we must pursue and acquire due to our own human nature, and which establish four or five activities as basic for human species (369d11-e1). Having established what our nature as living beings demands from us, Socrates presents Adeimantus with two options. In the first of them, each of us would produce all these inalienable goods for oneself (369e6-370a4), living a kind of Robinson Crusoe's life. The second option, which Adeimantus understands as obviously easier, has each person engaged in one single activity and in sharing the products of this activity with the others (369e3-6). The minimal cell of a city is born.

Why is a city a better alternative? The first point of this answer comes in the assertion that we differ in our nature. Glaucon was the first to introduce the difference in nature by claiming that we have the power of injustice in different degrees. Socrates now rephrases it by claiming that we have different powers to accomplish different actions (370b1-3); a difference in quality. Widely considered the most anti-democratic and anti-modern principle of Plato's *Republic*, the notion that there is a fundamental difference in nature between human beings, and that an activity carried out according to the interests of the city must be attributed to each person, has caused many contemporary readers to criticize Plato.[3] I have two comments on this issue.

My first point is that the expression 'not exactly equal' (370b1-2) marks a restriction applied to a more general notion of equality (see Chapter 13). In building his city, Socrates did not forget his general claim on human nature, according to which we are beings naturally endowed with the activities of caring, ruling, deliberating and living (353d4-10). We are equal in species, but different as individuals (the differences in personalities do not deny our equality for a being person).[4] My second point is that there are ends that we all must, by nature, obtain (i.e. inalienable goods), although there are different ways we may pursue them. Socrates introduces one specific way in which we may do so: by living in a city in which the citizens share the goods they produce. A city is therefore an alternative – *one* of the ways we can pursue our inalienable goods – but not a compulsory way of life, as Glaucon has suggested. However, given our common nature as a species, and our different natures as individuals, it is our best alternative, because it allows for the

---

[3] Here is how Popper builds his argument: at first, he states that the principle of division of labour – the affinity between Plato and historical materialism – is grounded on an element of biological naturalism that defends inequality between human beings (Popper [1945] 1966: 70). Second, he claims that Plato identifies justice with the principles of class government and class privilege (idem, 90). Finally, he concludes that the argument, both in the *Republic* and in Plato's later work, is a claim against egalitarianism and humanism, principles that Plato hated (idem, 94). Against Popper's criticism, one may argue that individual difference does not deny anyone the right to inalienable goods and adds to them the benefit of fairness. Next, one may claim that Socrates does not argue in favour of social classes, but in discriminating professional activities, no specific privilege is attributed to any professional. Finally, by no reasonable method could one accept as valid an inference about Plato's emotive personal states from arguments in his dialogues.

[4] See Kosman 2005: 154 for justice as the principle of appropriate differentiation. For justice supposing relevant and irrelevant differences, see Santas 2010: 109.

performance of one single activity that befits our individual power. This not only makes survival easier but also results in a fairer way of life.

Various interpreters take this fairness that justifies the preference for the city as a principle of efficiency – something that resembles the principle of specialization in Adam Smith[5] – but these are not the terms in Socrates' argument. Instead, his emphasis is on how the agents use their time. The activity we do exclusively is better done because we may follow the rhythm of what needs to be done (370c1-2, see also 374e2); the right moment (*kairos*, 370b9) of each activity is a basic condition for it to be performed well. If we have to supply ourselves with all the other needs we have, our attention will be diffused. This will decrease the quality of our activity and, consequently, of the product we deliver to others. Someone providing healthcare, for instance, cannot stop a procedure because he needs to water the fields. But exclusivity is also a good alternative because it furnishes us with free time – leisure (*scholē*, 370c1 *a contrario sensu*) – without decreasing our attention on our central focus.[6] Exclusive activity structures our lives as a main axis without excluding leisure for secondary activities, so long as they do not compete with the rhythm required to produce a fair work. Associating free time with personal powers increases the quality of the products and services that supply our needs, as well as of the agent's use of time.

The Platonic argument for the division of activities is significantly different from Adam Smith's principle of efficiency on one crucial point: it is justified by the individual interest in exercising a certain activity – developing some of their powers – and organizing their time in relation to it. The activity that is proper to each person is determined by their own personality and the ease with which they accomplish some kind of actions. There is no reference to some end that the city itself would purport as an external agent, as in Smith's productivity thesis.[7] The individuals are the beneficiaries of the existence of a city, both by having their needs met by the exchange it allows, and by having only one activity. Socrates' argument for a city is therefore also different from Glaucon's contractualism. We do not live in the city just for safety, for fear of suffering injustice. This is not a circumstance of *anankē*. We live in the city as the natural outcome of the pursuit of our own flourishing, as the best development of our nature, the best option for our everyday life, which the Greeks called 'diet' (*diaitē*, 345a4-5). In other words, we have a natural and rational desire to be citizens.[8] It is in our interest to become a producer of goods for others, and inhabit a city, *because* we want the inalienable goods, the fairness and the

---

[5] See Smith [1776] 1977: 17–28. For this approximation, see Cross and Woozley 1964: 80 and Foley: 1974: 220–42. For some critique of the similarity between Plato and Adam Smith, for different reasons than those I offer here, see Helmer 2010: 43–4.

[6] To an objector who would hold that passage 370b11-c2 does not have the inversion I ascribe to it here, I would reply that nothing in the *Republic*'s argument would prevent us from inverting it. It does say that an activity cannot be confused with entertainment, but this does not deny some entertainment to citizens, nor a private life besides the public exercise of their activity. This is, unfortunately, not the occasion to deal with this theme, which finds an excellent formulation in Demos 1957: 164–74 (see also 374c1-3).

[7] Cooper (2000: 11) justifies specialization based on efficiency. For the claim that specialization distributes goods, see Vlastos 1977: 3. The latter is criticized by Kamtekar (2001: 194–200) on the basis that the principle refers to the self-fulfilment of citizens only regarding their work, which distributes only means and not goods. See also Woodruff (2012: 96–7) who claims that division of labour does not inevitably bring on fairness. For my part, I understand that a professional self-fulfilment, leisure and a fair environment (see next chapter) are goods, but I also think that this is not provided by the principle of specialization, and rather by justice.

[8] As Irwin (1977: 186) points out, the definition of justice offered by Glaucon already tells us that individuals have strong reasons for choosing a city as a common way of life (358e2-359a7), yet they do it *despite themselves* and do not engage in becoming excellent citizens. In my view, Socrates takes these reasons further in showing that cities promote our good by allowing us both to do what we are good at, and to have shared goods provided to us. Reeve (2013: 64) claims that grounding the city in natural differences of power makes it natural, as opposed to Glaucon's conventional approach.

free time it allows us. I shall call the sum of these three factors 'Socrates' constitutional principle' – the *raison d'être* of a city.

Before proceeding I would like to note that, in Socrates' account, the city is also organized by a monetary system that grants the correspondence in the value of goods produced – not just among those within the city, but also across different cities (370e5-371b11). Money was, as we have seen, one of the standard means (together with praise) of the reward expertise allowing the citizens to engage in common purpose contracts. Here money also appears as a means for exchanging and distributing common goods. It is not a good for accumulation, as any accumulation of production in a city should be used, according to Socrates, for importing goods that it cannot produce by itself (370e12-371a2). This is important to show that common purpose contracts are shared not only among the citizens but also among cities. They can be expanded to allow different people to take part.

It is under these guidelines that Socrates introduces his genuine city: the healthy city (see 372e6-7). It is a city that comes to be (see *hopōs gignetai*, 372e3) for the aforementioned reasons.[9] In their daily routines, its citizens are committed to fairly producing fair goods for sharing. There, even those individuals with disabilities in the intellectual activities required for expertise find a way of offering services to others (371d9-e4). When experts supply every inalienable good to all the citizens, the city reaches its end and is completed (371e8-9). Socrates describes how such a complete city fulfils the nutritive desire of its citizens with bread, wine and vegetables, and protects their lives with shoes, clothes and houses (372a5-b7). An important feature of this city is that its citizens find pleasure in sharing their life with each other (372b7-8). This is because their way of life is built on shared beliefs about pleasure and what state of affairs is good for all the citizens. A further relevant feature of the good of the city is that their reproduction must be controlled (372c1-2). Population overgrowth is a liability for any city as its ability to feed the population is limited. For this reason, population overgrowth traditionally leads to the demand for more territory, which leads to war (see 373d7-e4). As contraceptive methods were largely inefficient in antiquity,[10] one way to prevent undesirable reproduction was to control sex. While there is no intrinsic problem with sexual pleasure in Socrates' city, it is nonetheless governed by the imperative of not generating children that the city cannot nurture (372b7-c2).

This daily routine ('diet') just described is, according to Socrates, the place to look to find what justice and injustice are (371e11-12, 372a3-5).[11] This way of living shows, as Adeimantus puts it (372a1-2), how citizens interact by supplying goods to one another. It is their *politeia* itself. In a healthy city organized in such a way that all the citizens have their fair share of inalienable goods, fairly made, we find justice in the way these goods are distributed and in the pleasure these citizens have in living together. Strife, hatred and injustice are not found here. The city is unified.

---

[9] For the claim that this is Plato's true ideal city, see McKeen 2004; Morrison 2007: 251; Rowe 2017: 70.
[10] For contraception in antiquity, see McLaren 1992: 22–25; Jütte 2008: 12–13.
[11] Cross and Woozley (1964: 83–6) claim that Socrates drops the question of justice in the genuine city because there is no such thing as a practical agreement into which citizens have entered with each other in order that moral concepts may apply to the consequence of their actions. They suppose morality to entail a social contract. I see no reason why this would be a requirement. Ferrari (2003 [2005]: 40) suggests, on the other hand, that Socrates could go on to determine that justice is 'the efficiently cooperative manner in which each group provides for the needs of the collective', a view that I am ready to defend. But Ferrari thinks this is not what Socrates actually does, for, in his view, this route is left behind in order to introduce the comparative holistic analysis of city and soul.

Such a city is preserved because the citizen's desires are limited to those that are inevitable. But as Chapter 1 demonstrated, once our desire is engaged in its activity, it cannot draw a line between avoidable and inevitable pleasures (between objects that promote our flourishing and objects whose pursuit is unreasonable). Desire does not have cognitive capacities. Because Glaucon believes that every human being only pursues Thrasymachean goods, he supposes that we are all ruled by our desire; for this reason, he objects to Socrates' healthy city centred on inalienable goods (373a4-5). His objection is that human beings are not primarily rational. Rather, we are beings that primarily move towards objects of our desire for which reasoning is merely a means. We do not live with frugal meals and minimal shelter, claims Glaucon, nor do we restrict our sexual activity in order to control population growth so we might avoid war. On the contrary, we use our reasoning to create more objects of desire: couches, tables, desserts and so on (372d8-e1, 373a2-d3). Based on how the majority lives (and thus thinks a city is), Glaucon claims that human natural desires conflict with this constitutional principle. In failing to consider what our desire really is, Socrates would thus have gone astray from his primary purpose of arguing based on human nature. This is not an account of a city of human beings, but, complains Glaucon, of a city of domesticated animals: a city of pigs.

At Glaucon's request, Socrates now shifts his approach. In accepting Glaucon's objection about human nature, Socrates' new line of investigation aims, I submit, to show not why a city comes to be, but why a city is a good for us (see 427e7, 472d9-10). The purpose is to persuade Glaucon that a good city is not the way we live due *to our fear*, but the way we live as a means to our flourishing. If Socrates can show that we naturally desire a good city, then he may also demonstrate that there is a mistake in Glaucon's conception of human nature.

The city which arises from Glaucon's view of human nature is sick, fiery and swollen (372e8). The predominance of appetites leads to the demand for, and the production of, an enormous variety of things which requires an enormous variety of experts. However, because there is still demand for goods to be fairly produced, there remains the desire for them to be produced by experts. Desire requests fairness, but it rejects its restriction to inalienable goods. The variety of goods to be produced with expertise leads to a demand for population growth: various experts are required. This, in turn, causes the demand for territorial expansion and, finally, war (373d7-e4). The investigation into why a city is a good thus begins with a discussion of how to make war, a problem that picks up the argument on cooperative actions presented to Thrasymachus. How do individuals organize themselves towards a common end, which in this case is fighting a war enemy? It also picks up Socrates's constitutional principle – obtaining goods produced with fairness under common purpose contracts, and granting free time to all – in order to grant that warriors will do their job fairly.

The best way to fight in war, which will be a constant issue in a luxurious city, is to have experts in warfare to do so (374c8-d6). Even with his view of human nature, Glaucon is still led to recognize (374a7, e4) that warriors must be trained with free time; being released from other activities so they can work fairly against the enemies (374a5-6; b6-c3). As the very existence of the city depends on its success in war, if its guardians should fail, the whole city is destroyed. They are, in effect, the producers of the freedom (*eleutheria*) of the city (395c1).[12] They provide a more extreme case – a paradigm acceptable to the majority of the people – for why fair production matters to our desires. To put it more explicitly, it matters because fair goods are rational ends that also obtain the ends of our desire.

---

[12] In Chapter 16, I shall argue that this freedom does not refer only to preventing the city from being conquered by others but also to educating citizens that are themselves free.

Before concluding about the guardians, I would like to clarify why desire and fairness are not compatible as basic principles of the same *politeia*. According to the first, the citizens are motivated by *pleonexia* to obtain an infinite quantity and variety of acquisitive goods. According to the latter, each citizen is a producer of one of these goods. Each is involved in a network of product exchange in which the demand for fair products imposes on them a certain professional lifestyle, a routine 'diet' free from other worries and occupations. Later on in the dialogue, Socrates will give an example of this antinomy: a 'diet' of pleasure leads citizens to laziness and bad nutrition, a disease which the fair practice of medicine cannot heal (405c7-d5). The reason is that this constitutes a dysfunction of their souls, as opposed to their bodies, which does not fall under the purview of medicine (408e2-3). A life based on appetite is incompatible with the fair conduct of professional practice in such a way that these kinds of sick people, claims Socrates, should not be cared for (407d2-e3).

To a certain extent, this kind of incompatibility mirrors Glaucon's opposition of political law and human nature, but we must pay attention to the new phrasing. Once we compare the lifestyle of the producers of goods for others with the lifestyle of Glaucon's appetitive citizens, the opposition does not take the form of individual interest *versus* the city laws anymore, but rather the conflict of different interests of a single individual in their interaction with others. An individual may see other citizens as those who oppose their ends, or as co-operators in producing a pleasant, shared life. They may see the city as a means to protect them from the injustice of others; or they may see themselves as an agent that shapes the *politeia* by their own activity and the good of others they produce. It all depends on whether they see themselves as a cooperative producer of the good of others, or simply as someone who desires to obtain these goods for themselves – that is, on how they see themselves in interaction with others, and what kind of belief they have regarding their personal flourishing. This, I shall argue, depends on their education.

Examining the education of the guardians is not a digression from the topic of justice (376c8-d3) because it remains an investigation about the *politeia* and the 'diet' of the citizens: the fact that they are the prominent case in the argument does not imply that this education is not desirable for other citizens. Rather, guardians are the study case for all the other producers. Doctors and judges, for instance, will also be trained since childhood (408d8-9,409a1-2) and so, I argue, will all the citizens. Education purges the sickness in Glaucon's city both by enhancing the quality of exchanged goods and by causing people to be more satisfied with regarding themselves as cooperative citizens. Understanding that a city is a contract for the good, and therefore that it becomes a good for us when see ourselves flourishing as citizens, is a preliminary position for understanding what justice is.

11

Justice

In the previous chapter, we saw how Glaucon's account for the origin of the city is based on a problematic assumption that our nature is always motivated by *pleonexia*. Under this assumption, justice is a contract established by the powerless to forbid the action of the powerful. Only actions that prevent injustice and preserve the contract constitute just actions. The *politeia* that emerges from this contract bars all the citizens from obtaining their good: they are all citizens in spite of themselves. However, this is still an unjust *politeia*, for in it unjust agents still take the good of others, in particular by employing the expertise of false reputation. Socrates' response counteracts this account by arguing that a city comes to be after a different kind of contract – one in which all the parts obtain their good. His thesis is that, although we all have the same human nature, we differ in nature as individuals. We thus have different powers to accomplish different activities. The purpose of this chapter is to show how Socrates' concept of justice is directly inferred from his conceptions of human nature and city.

For this purpose, we shall temporarily pass over Socrates' account of the education of the citizens of Glaucon's fiery city (see the next chapter). Instead, we shall proceed straight to his conclusion: whenever we have educated citizens according to such constitutional principles, we have a city that is complete and good (427e6-10). This puts us in the same position we were in at 371e8-12 with regard to the healthy city. Indeed, the parallel between the two passages suggests that, having described how Glaucon's city educates its citizens to provide goods to each other, we may proceed in the quest to identify justice and injustice by looking for them in the 'diet' of the citizens (compare with 372a3-5). But before he proceeds in this direction, Socrates defines three further virtues that make the city good: wisdom, courage and temperance (427e9).

Wisdom is the knowledge (*epistēmē*) that allows for good decisions (*euboulia*, 428b7-8). The good city is full of a variety of knowledge types (428a10) for the simple reason that fairness in production is one key feature in the constitutional principle. Every citizen is an expert: the carpenter is the one who makes good decisions about wooden implements; the smith about bronze ones and the farmer about the generation of fruits from the soil (see 428b12-e10). A good city has knowledge as its predominant end: not only for ruling but also for citizenship. Knowledge of the city, in turn, concerns the best way for the whole city to interact (*homiloi*, 428d3) with itself and with other cities (428c11-d3),[1] and is peculiar to the ruling expertise. Strictly speaking 'the city has knowledge' equals, therefore, 'the ruler has ruler expertise' (428e7-429a3).[2] The reason

---

[1] The interaction of the city with itself makes sense only in a distributive meaning of city, that is, the way its citizens interact with each other. The interaction between cities includes war and the common purpose contracts mentioned in the previous chapter.

[2] I claim that the city is wise if all its citizens are wise in what they do, which includes the rulers being wise. This means that, for wisdom, Williams's rule of the predominant character (see Introduction) is an outcome of everyone in the city being wise (the whole-part rule). The same holds, I shall argue, for justice but not for courage. As a result, 'rules' for applying the same attribute to cities and individuals depend on the attribute.

why this is so, however, is that every professional position is ascribed to an expert, which is an inference from the constitutional principle of fairness in production.³

Courage of a city is the power to preserve the beliefs established by the lawgiver about what is fearful in all situations and, in trusting them, not to admit their opposite in circumstances of pain and pleasure, desire, or fear (429b8-d2). In Chapter 3, we saw that these are the circumstances in which an unreasonable belief replaces those that are reasonable in our souls. In Chapter 9, we saw that the lawgiver enacts laws aiming at the community of pleasures and pains. From this it follows that courage is simply self-commitment to the belief that personal flourishing is not apart from the flourishing of others (see 412d9-e2). However, rather than taking the general approach used in regard to the community of pleasures and pains, courage is considered here within a specialized scope (429b5-7): war (429b2-3). A city is courageous in virtue of having guardians who do not act in spite of themselves but maintain right beliefs through their actions, in particular in wartime, when the existence of the city is at stake. The city's courage results from ascribing a professional function, *not* according to expertise, but according to a character trait (as discussed in Chapter 3).⁴ It follows, then, from both the constitutional principle of fairness in production (since the warriors will have no other activity) and from the end of the legislator (since the preservation of shared beliefs about flourishing allows for the community of pleasures and pains).

Temperance is a form of attunement, harmony or good arrangement (430e1-3). It is based, as we saw in Chapter 3, on the prevailing of what is better. The temperance of a city is the ruling of the best (431b4-7) *in a certain mode*. This 'attunement' consists of both rulers and ruled sharing the same belief about who should rule (431d9-e2). This all-encompassing agreement (*homonoia*, 432a7) avoids conflicts in ruling; it is the opposite of sedition. Since this agreement concludes that the ruler must be someone with ruling expertise (431e4-5), and might also include the clause that guardians should be selected according to their personalities, one may infer that temperance is an outcome of the constitutional principle of fairness and possibly also of the end of the legislator, as pointed out in the case of courage.

Described as such, one sees that these virtues refer directly to the preservation of the basic institutions of the city: the offices of the rulers and the guardians. They determine the criteria to be met in order for people to occupy these offices, and for every citizen to agree with such an appointment so as to legitimatize such institutions.⁵ What is notable about this account of political institutions, in contrast to Thrasymachus' account, is both the absence of a system of punishment and the centrality of education or knowledge. This is because, for Socrates, institutional virtues are all grounded on the way of life of the citizens, that is, their justice:

---

³ It has been claimed that specialized knowledge of ruling is incompatible with political equality, because the latter suppose that citizens in general have sufficient intelligence to discuss public policy (see Keyt 2006: 346). I submit that the two proposals are not inconsistent once specialized knowledge of ruled entails dialogue with the citizens and a deliberation about what is better for all; see Chapters 12 and 16.

⁴ Sauvé-Meyer (2005: 24) supposes that only selected children would be submitted to this kind of test, but this would contradict the claim that the tests *are* the selective tools. For the tests being applied to youths, see Brennan 2005: 249; Rowett 2016: 70.

⁵ In claiming that political virtues sustain the institutions of ruling and warfare, I reject the assumption that they establish different social classes. The differences mentioned refer to individual abilities to perform some profession. See for instance Cross and Woozley, who see here a class-assignment system (1964: 111-16). On the one hand, they acknowledge that this is a cumulative pattern of personal virtue, in which all the citizens are temperate, warriors have the extra virtue of courage and rulers have two extra virtues, courage and wisdom (1964: 106). However, because they cannot include justice in this cumulative pattern, they conclude that it simply means to stay within one's class (1964: 125-6).

[T26] Then, I said, listen if there is something in what I say. Justice, or at least a certain form of it, is what we assumed from the beginning should be performed by all, when we founded the city. We have assumed, and in fact have repeated this several times, if you remember, that each one should have a certain activity related to the city for which their nature is most apt.

We actually repeated it.

And we also said that doing one's own and not interfering in others doing so (*polupragmonein*) is justice, and that we heard it from many other people as well as having said it ourselves many times.

We actually said that.

Therefore, I said, my friend, it may be the case that justice is a certain way in which doing one's own happens. Do you know what gives me evidence for it?

No, but say it!, he said.

It seems to me, I said, that what remains to be examined in the city – after temperance, courage and prudence – is what provides the power for all of them to happen, and which maintains their integrity, once they are obtained, for as long as it is there. Moreover, we said that justice would be what would remain after them, once we had found all three.

This is indeed necessary, he said.

But then, I said, if it were necessary to judge what would, once obtained, contribute the most to making our city good, that would be a difficult judgment: would it be the shared beliefs among rulers and ruled? Or warriors preserving the law-based belief about what is and is not to be feared? Or the prudence and guardianship of the rulers? Or would the greatest contribution to making the city good come from something existing *in* children, *in* women, slaves, free people, experts, rulers and ruled, namely that each one do its own and not interfere with others doing so.

How could it not be difficult to judge? he asked.

So, it seems, the power of doing one's own competes with wisdom, temperance and courage for being the excellence of a city.

Without a doubt, he said. (433a1-d9, my emphasis)

I would like to begin by stressing the contrast between justice and Socrates' constitutional principle, which is here described as each citizen being committed to performing the activity related to the city for which their nature is most apt. Various interpretations have characterized this idea as 'one man, one job', but I would like to claim that this is *not* what the *Republic* considers justice to be.[6] As T26 states, justice is 'at least a certain form of it' (433a3). On the other hand, Socrates claims that justice being 'doing one's own and not interfering with others doing so' (433a8-b1) has been repeatedly stated and heard from others. However, although related to justice, this thesis is also contrasted to it, when justice is said to be '*a certain way in which* doing one's own happens'.

This contrast is strengthened by the fact that the interlocutors in the *Republic* have, in fact, never claimed that justice was such a thing as 'doing one's own'. Indeed, there has only been one previous mention of 'doing one's own' in the text. It appears in the context of Socrates' reasons for a city at 370a4, in the formula used to express what I called the Robinson Crusoe alternative.

---

[6] For interpreters who have assumed justice to be 'one man, one job', see Kosman 2005: 156; Rowe 2017: 61. For arguments justifying the rejection of this expression as conveying Socrates's definition of justice, see Vlastos 1969: 509–10.

'Doing one's own' is, in this context, the opposite of the constitutional principle. If justice is a certain way of doing one's own in a city, this way must still be qualified. A good candidate for such qualification is Socrates' claim that every citizen in the city 'must occupy himself with only one activity that is his own' (423d3-4) because this is the activity for which they are naturally apt – in which case we could bring together the constitutional principle of the city with the formula 'doing one's own'. If this is so, one must suppose that 'doing one's own' is a way of 'doing the good of others', for this is the end of whichever activity each citizen should pursue in a city. I shall develop this point forthwith.

One new piece of information introduced by T26 is that justice is prior to other virtues: it provides the power for all three other virtues to occur. As previously evidenced, these three virtues relate to the preservation of the basic political institutions – the offices of the rulers and the guardians and the community of pleasures and pains – and justice is introduced as what gives these institutions the power to obtain their end. Political power, as we have seen from previous arguments, is diminished by the conflict and sedition promoted by injustice while enhanced by the cooperation promoted by justice. However, here Socrates extends this point by attributing to justice the role of *the* connatural good of the city. Justice preserves the city and, by providing power to its virtues, causes it to flourish. Cities may exist without the wisdom of the rulers, the courage of warriors, or shared belief about who will rule (the degenerated *politeiai* we saw in Chapter 9 lacked some of these qualifications). But if justice is the peculiar good of the city, it must be present in a certain degree in every city for as long as they exist. Thrasymachus was therefore right to claim that justice is intrinsic to *politeia*. His mistake was not to grant both that justice (being a power) allows degrees and may therefore be fully obtained in a good city. This shall suffice to conclude that justice is the constitutional principle *in a certain way*.

But a very important detail often missed in Socrates' account of the power of doing one's own in T26 is the preposition 'in' in italics, repeated twice and followed by datives: the greatest contribution to making the city good come from something existing *in* children, *in* women, slaves, free people, experts, rulers and ruled, namely that each one do its own and not interfere with others doing so' (433d1-4). Translators and interpreters who have assumed that the text says that justice amounts to enforcing children, women, slaves and so forth, to do a specific activity ascribed to them by the constitutional principle unfortunately miss the point. This is also the case for those who supposed that, according to Socrates here, slavery would be just and legal.[7] This is equally true of those who assume that Socrates presents two different definitions of justice – one for the city and one for the soul.[8]

Rather, Socrates' point is that all these people – that is, everyone in the city – should have the parts of their soul each doing their own and not interfering with the other parts also doing their own. Justice in a city is for all its citizens to have a certain character, regardless of their cognitive state, age, gender and the activity they perform. In all of them, reason, *thumos*, and desire should each be doing their own activity and not interfering with others also doing so. I shall argue that this is the connatural good of the city and the power that allows for the other three political virtues to develop, increasing thereby the good in the city. This conception entails that there is no difference between 'political justice' and 'psychological justice', and from it two conclusions

---

[7] For Plato on slavery, see Vlastos 1968: 294, and a critique in Calvert 1987: 371-2; both of them miss the reference to the parts of the souls here.
[8] For the problems of two definitions, see Vlastos 1968: 669-70, Barnes 2012: 44. For a different defence of a single definition, see Penner 2005: 11.

follow: (i) justice is not argued for after any kind of analogy with the city;[9] and (ii) justice is not a property of a whole regarding its parts, but of the interaction of individuals. A city is not just because it is structured in any particular way. It is just because all its citizens are just. As I shall subsequently argue, justice is a mode of interaction properly designated as a power because it accomplishes a certain state of affairs. In order to demonstrate this, I shall proceed to Socrates' account of justice in the soul:

> [T27] It is necessary, then, to remember that each one of us in whom each [part] does what is its own, will be just and will do what is his own.
> We really need to remember that, he said.
> Is it not appropriate for reasoning to rule, being wise and having a foresight over the whole soul, and for *thumos* to obey and fight at its side?
> Perfectly.
> But isn't it, as we said, the mixture of *mousikē* with gymnastics that makes them consonant, stimulating and nurturing the former through fair accounts and learnings, softening the latter through exhortations and making it gentler through musical modes and rhythms?
> That's right, he said.
> And these two, having been thus nurtured, having learned what is truly their own and been thus educated, will control the appetite, which in each person takes the largest part of the soul and is by nature the most insatiable for riches. They will watch over it so that it is not filled with so-called bodily pleasures, and thence become so multiple and strong that it does not do its own and instead tries to enslave and rule the others, not suiting it to do so, thus overturning the life of all of them.
> Perfectly, he said. (441d11-442b4, my brackets)

T27 opens with a reference to the 'in' introduced in T26: 'each one of us *in* whom each [part] does what is its own.' It subsequently connects the character of such citizens with the claim that they too will be just and will do their own. As such, T27 connects the dots that T26 left vague in regard to the manner in which justice is doing one's own. Still, the argument is hard to grasp, least of all to accept. As it stands, it seems to imply that if, in X, the parts do their own, then X is just and does its own. This thesis is awkward because it brings together three distinct levels: what the parts of X do, what X is and then what X does. We know that the disposition of X's parts, specifically the prevailing of an end and its mode, defines what X does and X's personality. But we have been told neither why an action in which all X's parts do their own is an action in which X does its own, nor why X is just in doing this. The first step to understanding this thesis is to clarify in which way 'doing one's own' is justice.

We know from T4a that the activity proper to reasoning is learning. T27 claims that, therefore, the end of its natural activity – its excellence – is to become wise. In particular, it is to know what is truly good for all the parts of the soul (441e3-4). Chapter 1 evidenced how: because reasoning learns what is good, it suits reasoning to give the ends that are truly good to all parts of the soul, that is, to rule (441e3). This leads to the more substantial conclusion that, for reasoning, doing

---

[9] Some interpreters hold that T26 establishes an analogy for a later inference about justice (see Vlastos 1968: 668–9). Others see that the definition of justice depend on the numerical correspondence of 'classes' in the city and parts of the soul (Blössner 2007: 348). Because these interpreters suppose that there is here a specific concept of political justice, they concluded that justice is an attribute of wholes regarding their parts (see Demos 1957: 170 ff.; Cross and Woozley 1964: 132; Vlastos 1968: 670; Kahn 1972: 571; Aronson 1972: 384; Williams 1973: 196; Irwin 2011: 92).

its own (441d11-12) has two sides: learning is 'doing its own' in relation to itself, while ruling is 'doing its own' in relation to others. A further conclusion supported by this claim is that the prevailing of reasoning is necessary and sufficient for X to do what is best for X (441e3-4), for it is the only way in which all the parts in X obtain real goods. As Socrates will state after T27, someone is 'wise, due to the small part that, in him, rules and gives such commands; which, moreover, bears in it the knowledge of what is convenient to each and all of its three parts in common' (442c4-7; see the next chapter).

Let us now analyse what happens to the other parts of the soul. For *thumos*, excellence is to associate emotions of self-assessment with the end indicated by reasoning. Indeed, it suits *thumos* to obey reasoning and fight on its side (441e4-5) because reasoning gives us true beliefs about flourishing with which *thumos* will judge us according to the best standards. On the other hand, as Socrates will soon explain, the excellence of *thumos* is courage or the preservation of the end of reason in circumstances of pleasure and pain (442b10–c2). In this sense, the excellence of *thumos* is adding pleasure instead of pain, to our actions. As its excellence depends on its interaction with desire, it therefore also suits *thumos* to command desire (442a5). *Thumos* does its own in relation to itself, it may be concluded, when it causes emotions according to the true belief about flourishing. In relation to others, it does its own when it causes emotions to obey reasoning and to command desire, that is, when it maintains this intermediary position between the two.

As for the part that moves us to nutritious, reproductive and related pleasures (436a10-b2), the excellence of desire is the preservation of the person and the species regarding the functions of the body (442a7-8). On the other hand, desire is insatiable (442a6-7). So for desire, excellence entails it not to be strenghtened, but commanded and ruled (442a4-b2). For desire, doing one's own in relation to itself is to move us to the objects of our inevitable pleasures and, in relation to others, to obey the end of reasoning and the emotion associated with it by *thumos*.

Because every action is an interaction, carrying out an activity implies interaction with the other parts of the soul. This means that 'doing one's own' is a formula for an excellence *that does not prevent others from being excellent*, which is introduced in T26 in the claim that justice is a way of doing one's own *and not interfering in others doing so (polupragmonein*, see 433a1-b1). The normative claim involved in the argument is therefore based both on the proper activity and on the interaction of individuals, so that the 'minorities' in the soul must also be excellent. I conclude that, in T27, 'doing one's own' entails doing so in relation to oneself and in relation to others.[10] This thus includes in the definition of justice the clause of non-interference in the excellence of others (see also 433d3-4, 434b6, 443d1-5, 444b2). Here, a note about non-interference is required. We have seen that the activity of each part of the soul is always an interaction with others; plus, in the first part of this book, I claimed that human action is always interaction with other humans and the world in general. If every action obtains a state of affairs that affects others, the claim on non-interference is qualified. It does not refer to refraining from interacting with others, but to refraining, while interacting, from hindering their excellence.

This is a detail that stands against the mainstream interpretation of the *Republic*, wherein 'doing one's own' is 'minding one's own business'.[11] The latter suggests that non-interference is simply restricting oneself to the activity one does *by oneself*. Pursuing one's own interests while leaving aside the care for others and the political life would, in standard Greek political

---

[10] We saw the same pattern of abbreviation in Thrasymachus' thesis on 'the good of others', which also entailed 'self-harm' (see 343c3-5).
[11] For justice as 'minding one's own business' see, for instance, Adam 1902: I, 237; Crombie 1962: I, 95; Dorter 2005: 344. For the critique of the expression, see Weiss 2012: 26.

vocabulary, be expressed by the term *apragmosunē*,[12] the kind of life that Odysseus was said to have chosen in the myth of Er at the end of the *Republic*. Recalling all the efforts of his life in his quest for honour, he subsequently chooses the life of an *idiotēs apragmōnos* or someone who would avoid visibility, reputation and political engagement (620c2-d2). Socrates also uses this term (*apragmōn*) to express the complaint of the *dēmos*, the working class. Their dissatisfaction comes from their lack of time due to the overload of work demanded by oligarchs in a lawless democracy; the situation thus turns them into *apragmōnes*, that is, having no part in political decisions (see 565a1-3). Understanding flourishing as 'minding one's own business' (i.e. carrying out actions without caring about the good of others) constitutes the practice of *apragmosunē*. This is *not*, according to Socrates, to be just.

While *apragmosunē* is one opposite of 'doing one's own', another opposite is found in the non-interference clause that accompanies it: *polupragmosunē* (433a8-9, d3-4, 443d1-5), which is also described as *allotriopragmosunē* (444b2) or 'doing what is alien'.[13] In Greek, *polupragmosunē* generally means to interfere in political life with consequences to the way others pursue their ends. As a proper mean between these two extremes, 'doing one's own' is a formula that says 'yes' to political activity as personal excellence and 'no' to interference in the excellence of others. To understand this point, we must advance in the definition of justice:

> [T28] But Glaucon, that it is right for someone who is naturally apt to make shoes to make them, and not to do something else, and for the carpenter to work on wood and so on in other cases was a certain appearance of justice – and this is why it was useful.
>
> It seems so.
>
> After all the truth, it seems, was that justice is something like that, however, it does not concern doing one's own externally, but internally, for this is what is truly about oneself and one's own, allowing neither each part in oneself to do what is alien (*t'allotria prattein*), nor to interfere (*polupragmonein*) in each other's activities. Instead, it is to establish well what is akin (*ta oikeia*) and ruling oneself, setting oneself in good order, becoming friend with oneself and harmonizing the three parts, as if, to put it roughly, they were the three points that determine a musical scale: the lower, the upper and the middle. And if by any chance there are other intermediate parts, all of them must be combined and become, in all senses, a unity from the multiple, temperate and harmonic. Thus, this person shall act – whether in obtaining wealth or caring for the body, whether engaging in politics or in private contracts – considering and calling just and fair the action that preserves this disposition and enhances it, wisdom being the knowledge that commands such an action. On the other hand, unjust is the action that always dissolves this disposition, and the belief that commands such action is based on the lack of learning. (443c4-444a2)

---

[12] *Apragmosunē* is one of the antipodes of justice. See Adkins 1976: 319, for the claim that *apragmōn* is someone who only votes in the assembly but does not take time in discussing policies and alternatives. Ferrari (2005 [2003]: 13) describes *apragmosunē* as the quietism that characterizes Glaucon, Adeimantus and a whole Athenian élite in their attempt to protect themselves against an intensely litigious politics, while also devoting themselves to a certain cultivation of their souls. For Pericles' reproach to quietism, see Thucydides, *History of the Peloponesian War*, II, 40, 2.

[13] The verb *polupragmonein* means to interfere in someone else's actions despite this person; it also means interfering too much in politics in order to obtain one's own interests (see 551e4). Ehrenberg (1947: 50) shows how, in Thucydides, this term always goes together with *pleonexia* without being confused with it. While *pleonexia* is greed for material goods, as we saw from Thrasymachus, *polupragmosunē* is the desire for domination of others. Ehrenberg (idem, 60) notes that Socrates, despite not interfering in political life, was *polupragmōn* in his own way, that is, by inciting people to virtue.

T28 opens by reaffirming a claim already made in T26: Socrates' constitutional principle (370b5-371e10, see also 397d9-e9) is an appearance of justice, not what it is.[14] As in T26, T28 claims that what justice really is is that each part in a particular individual does its own and not what is alien to them (*t'allotria prattein*) in relation to others: *thumos* will therefore neither leave desire unchecked nor judge it according to an unreasonable belief on flourishing. Equally, desire will not try to prevail,[15] thus allowing the others to flourish. This state of the soul is described in T28 as 'to well establish what is akin' (*ta oikeia*),[16] where 'being akin' is having something in common or being within the same kind (see 470b6-8, 470c1-3). To convey this idea of the opposite of interference (*polupragmonein*), Plato coins a very important neologism, *oikeiopragia*, the understanding of which requires us to return to the question of how justice happens in the city:

> [T29] Go ahead then, to see if you agree with me. If a carpenter tries to do the activity of a shoemaker, or a shoemaker that of a carpenter; or if they exchange their instruments and honours with each other, or one person tries to do both, or any change of this kind, do they seem to you to do a great harm to the city?
> Not at all, he said.
> But it seems to me that if an expert or someone who is a wage earner by nature, motivated either by money, by the support of the majority, by force or some other such factor, tries to enter the military sector; or if someone from the military sector tries to enter the deliberative and guardian sector without deserving it, or if these people exchange their instruments and honours with each other, or if one person tries to do all of these activities simultaneously, I think you may believe that such a change and interference (*polupragmosunē*) is destructive to the city.
> Absolutely.
> The interference among the three kinds, and the transformation of one into another, is the greatest harm to the city and most correctly referred to as the supreme evil.
> Indeed.
> Would you not say that the greatest evil to one's own city is injustice?
> Sure.
> So, this is injustice. Let us say it once again: the cooperation (*oikeiopragia*) of the wage-earner, the auxiliary and the guardian kinds, each of them doing their own in the city – this is justice, the opposite of injustice, and what makes the city just.
> It seems to me to be so, and nothing else, he said. (434a3-434c11)

T29 spells out the consequences of T26 on how justice in a city results from the citizens being truly just (having each part of their soul doing their own) and emphasizes that justice is not a principle of 'one man, one job'. It is irrelevant to the city if individuals change their activities so long as they still exert their efforts in an activity according to their nature, which aims at the good of others. Nature here refers not simply to personal abilities, but to the kind of motivation one

---

[14] Because I defend that there is only one definition of justice, I disagree with the interpretation that what is dismissed here is a previous definition of political justice as 'doing one's own social work' (see Cooper 1977: 153; Demos 1964: 398; Vlastos 1969: 515).

[15] By definition, parts of the soul cannot do an activity that is not the one they have by themselves. The only way they can do what is alien to them is not doing their own in relation to others.

[16] For *oikeiopragia* having two different routes – one's activity by itself and one's activity in relation to others – see Proclus (*Commentary to Plato's Republic*. I, 209.1-6). He also refers to the difference between *oikeiopragia* and *autopragia* (idem, I, 207.28-207.2).

has to do the good of others – one's second nature or personality. Some have a personality for which wages matter in their doing the good of others. Others, as we saw in Chapter 8, would not do the good of others *for the sake of wages*, but only because their good would decrease were they to do otherwise. These two constitute different personalities and, as we know, there are character restrictions that apply to those who will be professional guardians (429b5-7) and rulers (347b10-d8). So while having different activities does not hurt the constitutional principle, having non-qualified personalities in professions that require specific characters and expertise does. Though we are to expect different ways of doing the good of others, it is important to notice that exerting oneself in an activity for which one is not qualified is considered interference in the excellence of others for depriving them of the fair products obtained by the social contract. As Socrates puts it, 'justice is the possession of both what is akin and what is one's own, and the action [of both what is akin and what is one's own]' (433e10-434a1).

I thus infer that the attitude of being akin, *oikeiopragia*, has to do with one's own attitude relative to others. Further, I propose that the term should be translated as 'cooperation'. Cooperation is the concomitant operation of individuals pursuing their excellence without hindering each other's action. This does not suppose that all the agents involved aim at the same end, but it does entail that they aim at one single state of affairs that will provide the ends of all, as in win-win contracts. Cooperation may occur perfectly well with agents with different and independent ends, so long as they do not clash. It is therefore the opposite of the power struggle, which describes the action of connatural evil, being, in contrast, a power sharing. We saw in Chapter 5 how, in order to achieve a situation in which the end obtains, the agents avoid unfeasible ends. For cooperative citizens, flourishing is thus to obtain a feasible state of affairs that does not exclude the flourishing of others – therefore, their ends must exclude *pleonexia*. A character in particular, the one described as resulting from the cooperation of parts of the soul, is required in order for someone to be a cooperative citizen. Justice in a city is for every citizen to have this cooperative character, including women, children and slaves, etc., who therefore gain the status of being free and equal (see Chapter 16).

I suggest that an understanding of justice as cooperation would save Socrates from the classic accusation of fallacy made by Sachs. This accusation consists of two claims (Sachs 1963: 153). The first is that Socrates does not show that someone who has justice in the soul will necessarily perform what is vulgarly considered just acts. The second and stronger claim is that Socrates does not show whether those who perform vulgarly just actions have Platonically just souls. I begin by addressing Sachs's concept of vulgar justice: 'the vulgar criteria for justice consist in the non-performance of acts of certain kinds; and, of course, injustice, according to the vulgar conception, consists in performing such acts.'[17]

Socrates explicitly claims that being just is sufficient for agents not to commit vulgarly unjust acts (see *ta phortika*, 442e1), that is, committing crimes such as theft, rape, betrayal of friends, betrayal of the city, breaking of oath, adultery, neglect of the family, impiety, etc. (442e6-443a11). It is equally important, however, to characterize what Socrates' interlocutors in the *Republic*, without any Socratic assumptions, consider the just actions of a typically just person to be. First, Cephalus agrees that justice is cooperative in the form of giving back to someone what

---

[17] Sachs 1963: 143. Sachs's objection is considered valid by Kahn 1972: 574. Interpreters respond to it by either claiming that Platonically just people do not have the motivation to commit unjust actions (see White 1979: 398; Kraut 1992; Brown 2004: 290) or that Platonically just people only do what is objectively good (as opposed to what is good for all the parts of their soul, which they infer from knowledge of the form of the good) (see Annas 1981; Irwin 1995; Cooper 1977); or yet that the objection mistakes meaning for reference (Penner 2005: 3; Barnes 2012: 40). Singpurwalla' (2006: 271, 274) objects to the first approach by pointing out that omission is an unjust action; and to the second approach by stressing that it restricts justice to philosophers. I do not know of any response that challenges Sachs's conception of vulgar justice.

was previously received (332c1-3). Then, Polemarchus claims that justice is to benefit friends (332d4-6), specifically, as we have seen, through common purpose contracts (333a11-15). Thrasymachus also mentions common purpose contracts as something in which just agents would engage (343d2-6), while Glaucon defines justice as a kind of contract (359a2-5) more broadly. Adeimantus, on the other hand, believes the reputation of justice to be crucial to making associations and partnerships (362b2-5). Socrates' interlocutors thus appear to hold that just actions are not simply refraining from unjust actions, but that justice is a certain engagement in obtaining a state of affairs that is good for others as much as for oneself. This makes sense inasmuch as justice is a power, that is, an attribute of agents due to the state of affairs they obtain, rather than some 'non-performance' of certain actions. In his response to his interlocutors, Socrates is not expected to address whichever action an objector may consider just, but the actions that all his interlocutors consider typical of justice: cooperation.

A further methodological point may help. The first pages of the *Republic* have already dismissed the path of accounting for justice according to a classification of actions – such and such are just; such and such are unjust – in favour of a personality approach, as already discussed in Chapter 6. Sachs's objection, therefore, would be more properly formulated, if it would state that the just personality was not proved to be sufficient to prevent unjust actions and to guarantee the performance of just actions. I allow myself thence to have this formulation as the target of my response, which I shall do by rephrasing the claim of T26 in accordance with the conclusion that justice is cooperation: if the parts of X cooperate, X is just and X will cooperate with others. This is a more intuitive formula than the one to which we were first introduced, and renders the last inference of the claim (X is just; therefore X will cooperate with others) more acceptable according to the standards of Socrates' interlocutors: just people aim at a state of affairs in which others also obtain their end. If this is the case, a cooperative person cannot commit vulgarly unjust acts because they entail hindering others from their excellence. On the other hand, they remain individuals who will engage in vulgarly just actions – that is, cooperative contracts. A cooperative person is therefore what the majority considers a just person.

Nevertheless, it remains unclear as to how the parts of the soul are brought into the argument: why is a person with cooperative parts in their soul a cooperative person? This still appears to be a fallacy.[18] T26 makes precisely this claim: that people in whom each part does what is their own will be just and do what is their own. However, the apparent fallacy is read into the text under the assumption that, in order for someone to be cooperative with others, something other than the cooperation of parts is necessary. This assumption is not present in Plato's text; rather, T26 ratifies that the cooperation of parts of the soul is sufficient for a person to be cooperative: it is by having parts of their soul in cooperation that children, women, slaves, free people, experts, rulers and the ruled all cooperate and do not interfere in others pursuing their own excellence. A cooperative person is nothing other than someone who, ruled by reasoning, pursues what they have learned is good for themselves rather than any unreasonable desire: someone in whom *thumos* is an ally of the ruling of reasoning and has no unreasonable belief about their personal flourishing. In their belief that personal flourishing must not restrict the flourishing of others, this person aims at a win-win state of affairs. The alliance of reasoning and *thumos*, where desire is guided towards an end that is neither an unreasonable belief about the good, nor an unreasonable belief about flourishing, is sufficient for being a just person and, necessarily, cooperative. No one may cooperate with others while in possession of unreasonable desires about the good and personal

---

[18] See 'the soul is just$_1$, if it is just$_2$,' (Vlastos 1968: 670), where being just$_1$ is to be a just citizen, and just$_2$ is to be a complex of elements. See also Galis 1974: 291; Blössner 2007: 349.

flourishing. Rather, cooperation demands the rule of reason because it entails the moderation of ends according to power and to a win-win state of affairs. This happens, for instance, in their accepting the constitutional principle and so understanding that rulers must know what is best for the city; guardians, too, must have a particular commitment to the belief that their good is the good of the city. If this is true, there is therefore no fallacy about justice in Plato's *Republic*. Being a cooperative agent is nothing but having the kind of internal disposition that is metaphorically described as the 'cooperation' of the three parts, or yet as the 'ruling' of reason. Justice is not an attribute of wholes; it is a power of agents.

Being just is to have the power to obtain a state of affairs that contemplates the end of all the agents involved. Justice is the power that accomplishes a cooperative city by the agency of its citizens, who are thus cooperative people (443b4-5). Their just actions are not simply those that maintain the internal psychological order of the agent (see T27), but those which preserve the disposition of cooperation in the soul *because* they obtain a win-win state of affairs in the world (see also 433e10-434a1 quoted earlier), eliminating strife. A similar move was implied in Thrasymachus' concept of *pleonexia*, a character that obtains inequality in the city whenever given partial or complete power. Socrates thus concludes that it is best for anyone to live in a city in which they may do the good of others while still in pursuit of their own good: the best for everyone is to be a citizen and pursue a cooperative flourishing:

> [T30] However, and it is right to say now what I said before, if a guardian undertakes to flourish in such a way that he is not a guardian anymore, and that a moderate and safe life which we said to be the best, will no longer suffice him – or if an unreasonable and childish belief besets him, motivating him to take possession, through his power, of everything there is in the city, he shall know that Hesiod was really wise when he said that half is more than everything. (466b4-c2)

Cooperative flourishing is flourishing according to human power.[19] It is the best we may obtain without participating in the illusion of a happiness consisting of the acquisition of all the good of others and, as a result, a life isolated from others in the expectation that they may take revenge at any minute. The idea of being happier than others, or the happiest of all (see *eudaimonestatēn*, 466a5), is unreasonable. This is because our best rational option is to live in a city where we may share with others the outcome of our actions. Socrates' argument in the *Republic* is that justice is good because our best life is political and our flourishing is cooperative. The best for us, according to our powers, is to share everything in every way (466c9). Though there may be limits to this, as we shall see, flourishing *despite* others does not accord with our powers.

---

[19] Kamtekar (2001: 202–3) claims that it is the 'happiness principle' that distributes goods to the citizens, which she sees formulated at T30, but also at 420b4-8 and 519e1-520a4. By rejecting holistic conceptions of the city, she agrees that all citizens should be happy, but this is not grounded in what she considers justice to be, that is, what I call the constitutional principle. By claiming that justice is cooperation, I can propose a much wider notion of interaction than the citizen's 'duties' and activities, and I also do not need to concentrate it on a single agent who is the 'distributor'. Cooperative goods are produced and exchanged by citizens who are just and do not need someone else to enact justice in their place.

Part Three

Citizens

12

Popular virtue

This book has argued thus far that a *politeia* is the state of affairs obtained by the interaction of the citizens according to their power. According to Thrasymachus, it is identified both by the predominant end and by the government. His thesis opens with the claim that justice is what suits those who prevail. It thus implies that justice in every *politeia* consists of the principle of sovereignty, which Thrasymachus subsequently refines to include subordinative actions of the ruled and, later, to offer an altogether different definition. For him, justice is the good of others and self-harm. This breeds many inconsistencies in Thrasymachus's thesis, particularly due to his assumption that rulers have all the power to obtain the good of others.

Some of Thrasymachus' concepts are employed by Socrates in his account of evil personalities and *politeiai*. The first of these is the notion of evil as a power, which opposes the preservation and the flourishing of something. The second is that evil may have partial or complete power, depending on the use of the government institution. The contrast between Socrates' and Thrasymachus' theses lies in the variety of predominant ends, which cause different degrees of strife in the city and in the soul. There, I have argued that individuals are always the cause for evil by their adoption of unreasonable beliefs about flourishing, thus contributing to the maintenance of wretched *politeiai*.

Socrates presents five arguments against Thrasymachus. In the first two, he introduces the concept of care expertise, the aim of which is to provide the good of others. He also introduces the concept of reward expertise, which aims to reciprocate the good received with another good. That is the formula of the social contract that Socrates places at the origin of the city, as discussed in Chapter 10. On the other hand, Socrates responds to Thrasymachus with an important argument about cooperation designed to demonstrate that power depends on not finding resistance from others. Finally, Chapter 11 approached justice by evidencing how this is not to be mistaken for the constitutional principle employed by Socrates to explain the reason why cities come to be. Justice is not 'one man, one job', but cooperating with others, that is, pursuing excellence in one's activity without interfering with others doing the same. This theoretical framework entails that human flourishing must be cooperative so that we may both pursue our ends and avoid the reactions of others.

We saw that justice is the power of cooperation and the particular good of a city that, being present to a certain degree, grants its existence and, when fully present, allows for its flourishing. A good city is just insofar as its citizens are just, which allows for all of them to be able to achieve their ends cooperatively. This constitutes cooperative flourishing, the rational concept of flourishing that contrasts with the unreasonable belief that one should be happier than others (or even happy despite others, as Thrasymachus supposed a tyrant to be). Understanding that cooperative flourishing is the best for us – because it is the flourishing that lies within our power – requires an education. This education allows us to learn that life in the city is the best for us and that living in a good city is the best we can obtain. T27 indicates that just citizens, that is, those motivated by rational ends, are educated by *mousikē* and gymnastics. This must be added to the general thesis, already discussed, that, for a city to be just, it must educate *all* of its citizens. The third part of this book is thus devoted to analysing the political form of life that Socrates proposes in the *Republic* as a consequence of his concept of justice. We begin with popular virtue.

* * *

This chapter aims to argue that justice is popular virtue. I have already distinguished justice from the three political virtues that respond to the excellence of the ruling institution in the last chapter. Now, I would like to distinguish it from philosophical virtue and from the personal virtue of the guardians. My reason for doing so is to deny that philosophers and rulers are the only cases of justice. Instead, I wish to claim that the model of justice is the decent person. I shall do so by insisting on the just agent, who is also wise, courageous and temperate, as being the outcome of an education by *mousikē* and gymnastics. They are not people who know the form of the good, as some interpreters infer having in view of future passages in the *Republic*.[1] The important text is as follows:

> [T31] So we call this person courageous, it seems to me, due to one single part, when his *thumos* preserves through pains and pleasures the command given by reason about what is terrible or not.
> Correct, he said.
> He is wise due to that small part that rules in him and gives such commands; the one that, in addition, has in it the knowledge of what is convenient to each and all of the three parts in common.
> Perfectly.
> What about temperance? Is it not due to the friendship and attunement between them, when both the ruler and the two ruled share the belief that the rational element must rule and do not engage in strife against it?
> Temperance, therefore, he said, is not something different in the city and in the person.
> But then, the person is just due to what we have mentioned many times and in that way.
> It is very necessary. (442b10-d7)

T31 follows T27 to describe a specific virtuous personality in which the parts are friends of each other – a trait described in T28 as someone being a friend of himself (443d5). The just person, as we shall call them in abbreviation of the presence of the four virtues, is not a philosopher. This is because a lover, as we saw in Chapter 6, is a 'part-like' person, characterized by the channelling

---

[1] For the claim that justice requires knowledge of the form of the good, see Cooper 1977: 152–4; Irwin 1977: 202; Penner 2005: 11. See also its critique in Hall 1959: 149; Santas 2010: 143–53; Woodruff 2012: 91. In a later paper Cooper argues that philosophical reasoning is required because it is the only way to ensure that citizens in general possess 'ideas where their good does lie [...] that are true and correct' (Cooper 2000: 16) and that they have a firm grasp on those ideas. However, he then remarks: 'I don't suppose any of us could seriously think that justice demands that the contemporary philosophical profession be given any unique or even specially privileged place in investigating and directing social policy relating to this question' (idem, 17). See also Cross and Woozley 1964: 126–7; Lane 2007: 58.

of desire and the hegemonic ruling of a certain object.² The just person, in turn, is identified by the cooperation of the parts of his soul that is proper to justice, which, as we know, has friendship and agreement as an outcome (see 351d4-5). This indicates that, rather than being channelled, the desire of the just person is fulfilled in their actions. I recall how, in the previous chapter, T29 pointed out certain differences in the nature of citizens by suggesting that some would do the good of others in exchange for wages while others would not. Receiving a wage is just and proper to just agents engaged in common purpose contracts. It is likely that this is the kind of personality to which T31 refers when suggesting the friendship of reasoning and desire, and this is not a tendency found in philosophers. At the beginning of book VI when the philosopher is identified by the channelling of their desire, we find that this causes them to turn away from pleasures connected to the body and particularly those connected to money (485d10-e5). The philosopher is therefore not someone in whose soul desire and reasoning are friends. As we shall see in Chapter 16, a philosopher finds it shameful to receive money in return for the good they do.

The definitive point against the identification of philosophers and just agents is that the latter are a result of education through *mousikē* and gymnastics (441e7-8), while the end of the philosopher's education is learning the form of the good (505a2-b1). This brings us another problem. At first, this education was introduced as the best method to educate guardians (376c8-d3), whose fair job was of key importance for the flourishing of every citizen (374e1-3). In Chapter 10, I argued that examining the education of the guardians was not a digression from the topic of justice (376c8-d3) because it remained an investigation about the *politeia* and the theme of the citizens' 'diet'. The fact that they were the prominent case for the argument does not imply that this education is not desirable for other citizens. Now, I shall argue that the conclusion expressed in T31 commits us to a stronger position: that the educational project is for everyone.³ After all, there is a general argument offered by T26 in which Socrates states that everyone in the city – children, women, slaves, free people, experts, rulers and ruled – must have their parts of the soul in cooperation with each other. Moreover, T31 states that these same just agents are the outcome of an education in *mousikē* and gymnastic. This just person is therefore, by definition, not a philosopher (as a substantive portion of interpreters has taken them to be). The just person is simply the decent person whom we have followed since Chapter 3.

Before proceeding, I would like to briefly mention that *mousikē* is the standard education in oral cultures.⁴ It is an education that consists of telling and retelling stories about characters in action involving, in general but not necessarily (398c1-5), simulation (*mimēsis*, 393c5-6) of these characters. Stories are generally told in verse involving music and dance, melody and rhythm. The process begins in early childhood as an important feature of the interaction between

---

² See Singpurwalla 2006b: 280 for the difference between the philosopher and the just citizen as two ways of being ruled by reason. See Obdrzalek 2013: 219-20 for the claim that the philosopher's soul is not harmonious.
³ In claiming that all citizens in a just city are just, I oppose interpretations that hold that, in a just city, there are citizens who are either ruled by desire or by *thumos* (see Reeve 1988: 173; Bobonich 2002: 47-8; Rowe 2017: 65), as well as to interpretations that restrict *mousikē* and gymnastics solely to guardians (Cross and Woozley 1964: 78; Vegetti 1999: 51; Ferrari [2003] 2005: 46; Bobonich 2002: 47-8; Sauvé-Meyer 2005: 229-30; Brown 2004: 285; Rowe 2017: 60). For defences on how the universal education and the justice of all the citizens follows from the definition of justice, see Hourani 1949: 60; Vlastos 1968: 673; Brennan 2005: 247; Jeon 2014: 188-9; Rowett 2016: 93-4.
⁴ For *mousikē* as traditional education, see Brisson 1982: 114-38; Schofield 2010: 238.

children and caregivers (377c4-6). It continues to adulthood with youths retelling and restaging themselves these same stories.[5]

This involves compassion with the characters, as discussed in Chapter 3. *Mousikē* promotes a direct experience of ourselves as someone else. This explains the 'modelling' vocabulary used to describe it. It casts the soul of (very young) individuals after cultural moulds. Its efficiency in doing so is precisely the reason why it is so dangerous – we accept the experience regardless of whether it is good for us. In using *mousikē* in education, Socrates tries to use a powerful weapon towards a good end. He aims at redefining the poet's expertise with the commitment to use only characters that are good role models so that, in experiencing compassion, we can thus learn how to become better.

I now turn to examine the education for each of the virtues indicating how it targets citizens in general.

(a) Justice

If the audience of *mousikē* is to become good, the gods that are its characters must both be good and do the good (379b3, 379b11-16, 380b5-6). They must not commit injustice, and instead be just (378b2, 380b1). They must not harm others (379b5-10, 16), but be fair and virtuous (381c1, 6). As role models, gods can neither violate oaths (379e3) nor be contentious among each other (378b8-c6; d2-6; 380a1). They must punish only in order to benefit, rather than harm the punished (377e6-378a3, 380a9-b6). They are not to fight and plot against those who are akin (*oikeious*, 378c6). These are standards of behaviour expected from all citizens. As Socrates puts it, these are patterns necessary 'if they are to honour the gods and the ancestors and not to belittle the friendship among themselves' (386a2-4) and not to hate each other (378c4-8). One can see that this is part of Socrates' aim to establish friendship between the ruled and the rulers (547c1-2 referring to 431d9-e8 and 463a1-b2). To this he adds the claim that role models must be reliable both in their acts and in their words (382e8), unwilling to change or falsify what they really are (380d1-6) in order to make reliable people out of its audience (377c1-5; 378a2-b7; 378c1-3, 378c6-d2, 378d7-e4, 380a2-3, 380b7-c4; 386a1-4). Such an end does not seem to be compatible with an audience of rulers, for, on the one hand, they are allowed to lie as a means to further the good of the whole city (459c9-d3) and, on the other hand, they are the ones harmed by the lies of the ruled (389c1-6). It is above all the ruled who need to be educated as reliable people. In fact, it is a sign of a lack of education in a city if it requires judges to guarantee justice, in order to be just; its citizens must be able to practise justice themselves (405a1-b4).

(b) Temperance

Socrates clearly states that, in producing their stories, poets must be committed to the temperance of the *citizens in general* (see *hos pléthei* at 389d9, 390a2) by avoiding role models engaged in drunkenness, gluttony (389e12-390b4) or urgent sexual appetite (390b4-c8). For temperance,

---

[5] For simulation as incorporation and assimilation of a model in oneself, see Belfiore 1984: 121–46. For simulation as making oneself another 'because there is potentially a place for this other in myself', see Teisserenc 2005: 79. For the object of poetical simulation as human actions, see Moss 2007: 430; for the experience of being someone else, see Nettleship 1922: 78; for the ethical danger of this kind of experience, see Ferrari 1989: 110.

too, *thumos* must be well trained by gymnastics. As Socrates puts it, in a daily routine/'diet', 'variety generates licentiousness, thus generating disease; simplicity, according to *mousikē*, generates temperance in the soul and, according to gymnastics, health in the body' (404e3-5). What is health in the body is temperance in the soul. It is for this reason that, according to the standards just mentioned, gymnastics includes avoiding drunkenness (403e4-6), a nutrition aiming at a good physical condition (403e8-9, 404b11-c10) and not having sex with prostitutes (404d5-6).

In Chapter 10, we referred to an antinomy in Glaucon's city. It is shameful for a doctor (and for a city) to heal certain kinds of disease that originate in 'diet' or lifestyle (405a6-b1). In a good city, health and justice are things that every citizen must care for and exercise *by him/herself* without the prescription of others (405b1-3). By practicing justice, one lives a better life than those who spend their lives in courtrooms (405b5-c5). By practicing a healthy diet, one lives better than those who spend their lives in medical offices (405c7-d5). In support of this view, Socrates makes a strong claim: life is not worth living without this kind of political lifestyle that engages us in an activity directed towards the good of others (407a1-2). The claim comes to the point of his endorsing euthanasia for cases requiring treatment that hinders public activities (407e1-3). Temperance and justice must be virtues of all citizens, that is, popular virtues.

(c) Courage

As I have already argued, political courage is a professional requirement for a government institution (429b1-3). The gymnastic education proper to guardians must therefore make them stronger than a regular person when it comes to resistance to changes in 'diet': they must adapt well to different waters, foods and weather (404b1-3). The *mousikē* by which they are educated must have role models ready to die in battle before defeat and slavery (386b5-6), and who shall not fear death above freedom (387b5-6).

Popular gymnastics is not, however, the specialized training guardians must practice. It is a much more modest hygiene, and one should not fail to notice that most of the account of poetic models for courage revolves around decent men and women (387d4-6; 387e11-388a1) – that is, those which I identified as the standard of a just citizen. By avoiding lamentation in myths, we engender an audience of decent people. Courage of decent people makes them more *autarchai*, more persistent and less dependent on others for their good life (387d11-e2).[6] An agent who is engaged *by himself* in the purpose of his own life does not lose this purpose when he loses a friend, a son or a brother (387d4-e6). Rather, it makes him persevere in preserving his lifestyle when in circumstances of pain. It involves endurance even if, as we have seen, this simply amounts to avoiding a shameful attitude in front of others (see 388d6-7). Courage, which is the integrity of *thumos* in its obedience to rational principles in circumstances of pain and pleasure (442b5-c3), especially when it comes to what is to be feared (429c7-8, 442b10-c2), is present in guardians and in citizens in general *to a different degree*.

---

[6] In Socrates' reasons for a city, we saw that self-sufficiency in producing the goods to supply our basic needs is not our best choice in order to live well. Therefore, it would be strange to suppose that Socrates is now talking about *autarcheia* as a self-sufficiency regarding survival needs, but we do not necessarily need to assume that this is what he does. It is clear by the context that the independence in question relates to the *good* life.

(d) Wisdom

How is the decent person wise? In the previous chapter, we saw that Socrates argues that political wisdom (428b4-429a6) is knowledge possessed by some citizens about the good of the city as a whole (428c11-d3), that is, the expertise of the rulers (428d6-7). On the other hand, he also acknowledges that there are many different species of knowledge in the city (428b10). For instance, there is the knowledge of carpenters (428c2), farmers (428c9) and smiths (428d10). It is undeniable that, in the *Republic,* experts have knowledge and that this knowledge is of the specific forms involved in their activity. Socrates clearly states that the carpenter produces a couch according to its form (596b4-8), and that the flute player knows what a good flute is (601d8-e2).[7] It follows from Socrates' constitutional principle that every citizen must have one species of practical knowledge through which he or she undertakes actions for the good of others.

It is not, however, the education by *mousikē* and gymnastics that provides this kind of expert with their knowledge. In fact, Socrates clearly asserts that *mousikē* educates for a certain harmony rather than for knowledge (522a3-9). Moreover, knowledge of expertise is not knowledge regarding what is good for each part of the soul and for the person – knowledge that both T27 and T31 claim results from the ruling of reasoning. On the other hand, these two texts do not claim that knowledge of what is convenient to each and the three parts of the soul in common is the knowledge of the form of the good. So, what kind of knowledge results from basic public education through *mousikē* and gymnastics?

I begin by rejecting that it is knowledge of the form of the good. Since this is the topic of Chapter 14, I restrict myself here to arguing against a corollary of this thesis that says if knowledge of the form of the good were required for the rule of reasoning, justice would be a *philosophical virtue* or one that only philosophers would possess. In this case, Socrates would be committed to denying citizens the general knowledge of what is good for themselves. As a consequence, he would also be committed to the thesis that citizens in general are unable to be ruled by reason. This assumption leads to the conclusion that they are incapable of temperance, courage, justice and wisdom. As a result, all non-philosophical citizens would be vicious.[8] This is incompatible with the general thesis of T27 and T31, according to which the education by *mousikē* and gymnastics is sufficient to engender virtuous agents. Moreover, rejection of the argument for the excellence of citizens in general leads the interpreter to accuse Socrates of some inconsistencies. For instance, when supposing that all non-philosophical citizens in a just city are vicious, he would still claim that they would do their own. How could one explain that vicious people – those not ruled by reasoning – would do their own in the city? How would they cooperate? And if they do not, what kind of enforcement would a minority of rulers have to use to keep them under control?

There is no need to pay such a high price. Socrates acknowledges that the best part in us is educated either by reason or by character (606a7-8, *a contrario sensu*) and the *Republic* places great emphasis on justice not being dependent on knowledge of the good. Socrates describes the legislative practice – which includes prescribing the education by *mousikē* and gymnastics

---

[7] Interpreters, who assume that non-philosophers are incapable of knowledge, insist on finding these passages nonsensical (see Griswold 1981: 145–6; Bobonich 2002: 62, 68; Schwab 2016: 53). For arguments against this assumption, see Martinez 2011: 332; Vasiliou 2012: 29–30.

[8] For the claim that all non-philosophers are vicious, see Bobonich 2002: 47–8; Rowe 2017: 64. The situation would be such that Socrates would be committed to either an ungovernable city of perverts, or a city of slaves. I note that slaves are those who cannot be ruled by their own reason and must submit themselves to the rule of others (590c8-d6). See 389d9-e2, the analysis of T26 in the previous chapter and Chapter 16 against the slavery option.

– as producing, both in the public and private lives of human beings, temperance, justice and the whole of the *popular virtue* (*demotikē aretē*, 500d5-9).[9] Then, at 518d9-11, he goes on to explain that these are virtues of the soul that are added to it by habit and exercise (*ethesi kai askēsesin*, 518d11), in contrast to the others which are purely intellectual. Justice and temperance are popular virtues, virtues of the *dēmos*, which, with the rulers, form the set of all the citizens (463a1-5).

A textual example of popular virtue is found in the myth of Er at the end of the *Republic*, where, in the fantastical situation of souls choosing their personalities in the absence of a city (617d2-e5), the first of them to choose previously had a virtuous life. However, this soul chooses foolishly and voraciously (619b8-c1) the life of a tyrant. She did not pay attention to the fact that such a life comprised several evils, including eating the flesh of her own children (619b7–c2). The virtue of this soul is described as one who has lived in a well-organized *politeia*, but whose excellence was based on habit without philosophy (619c8–d1). This is someone who possesses the habit of trust and is used to simply picking up a good available to them, with no need to examine (619c1), doubt, analyse or investigate it. She has no experience in making efforts (619d2-3) to investigate beyond appearances. Thus, she makes a mistake in choosing. Nevertheless, this soul does not ignore what is best for her, as immediately after examining her choice, her *thumos* is triggered and she regrets it (619c3-5). She blames her circumstances and the daemons (619c5-6) as she was accustomed to relying on others, in particular regarding the quality of the good she acquires. This point about an environment that promotes excellence is most clear when Socrates describes the purpose of education through *mousikē* and gymnastics (401b1-d2): here he claims that all experts must be able to identify the traces of fairness and good shape so as to produce with fairness themselves:

[T32] But then is it only the poets who need to be overseen, imposing on them to produce images of the good character in the poems, or else not to compose them among us? Or do all other experts need to be overseen as well and be prevented from including such bad character which is unrestrained, subservient and disfigured, whether in the images of living beings, in the construction of houses, or in any other profession? Those who do not do so are not to practice their profession among us, so that the guardians won't be nurtured by images of evil, as if living on a bad pasture, from which, day by day during a long period, they

---

[9] I disagree with Klosko's (1982: 364) basic premise, based on 590c1-d7, that identifies popular virtue with *banausia* and *cheirotechnia*. *Banausia* is clearly linked to the mastery of manual procedures of some expertise, which is not what *mousikē* and gymnastics prepare for (see 522a3-b6, the same parallel between moral formation and manual skill can also be read in 495d4-e2). *Cheirotechnia* also refers to a specific practice of manual skill (547d5-9). When the *cheirotechnēs* has knowledge of the model of what he produces, he is an *dēmiourgos* (597a6); when not, he is a pure *cheirotechnēs* for not associating his manual skill to knowledge of the model of what he manufactures (596b10-d1). The general panorama of these terms in the *Republic* gives a strong reason to consider that, in 590c1-d7, they describe cases in which manual skills are not accompanied by virtuous character or knowledge, and thus are cases of lack of internal government by reasoning. I recall my mentioning in Chapter 10 that the healthy city finds ways for engaging citizens with disabilities in cooperative activities (371d9-e4), and this may well be the point of this passage. A second argument against Klosko is his assumption that the description in 590c1-d7 is compatible with a notion of popular virtue as internal balance and harmony (see Klosko 1982: 376) which assumes the internal government of reasoning. 590c1-d7 is quite clear in saying that the principle that is similar to what rules the best human beings, and which should be transferred to others, is the principle of self-ruling, that these manual workers, typical of democracy, lack. Third, the purpose of the passage is to indicate that democracy fails to promote the flourishing of the *dēmos* precisely because of the lack of laws that would grant them minimal work conditions, including their education as experts. Therefore, it is questionable to take this observation out of its context. Similar readings of this passage are found in Ferrarri [2003] 2005: 45 and Sauvé-Meyer 2005: 238–9.

gradually harvest and nourish themselves, unaware of the fact that they are accumulating a great evil in their soul. On the contrary, we must seek out professionals who are naturally capable of tracking out the nature of fairness and good form, so that the youth can live there as one inhabits a healthy region, obtaining benefit from everything. Whatever aspect of these fair activities that may reach their vision and hearing shall be like a breeze that, coming from good places, brings health, and leads them, unnoticed from childhood on, to resemblance, friendship and harmony with fair reason.

It will be the fairest nutrition.

So, Glaucon, is it not the reason why poetic education is most essential, particularly for making rhythm and harmony penetrate the soul, bringing it into good shape and making it well ordered, if one is educated correctly, and if not, the opposite? Furthermore, he who has been educated as he should will have a much sharper perception of what is missing in something, or what has been badly produced or badly generated, and will correctly reject it, while praising and welcoming what is fair. Accepting it in his soul and being nurtured by it, he becomes fair and good (*kalos k'agathos*). On the other hand, he will avoid the shameful and correctly hate it from a young age, before he is even able to understand the reason and, once the age of reason has arrived, he will welcome it, because he recognizes it as something akin to himself. (401b1-402a4)

The main focus of T32 is on good mores (*ēthoi*). At first, the target is poetry as the vehicle of role models, but it is subsequently widened to include houses and all the goods professionals produce for others. As we know, life in a city is our best choice because, among other things, it allows for the production and acquisition of fair products (369e3-370c7). This principle commits citizens not only to producing the good of others but also to producing them with fairness. For this reason, professionals in general must be prohibited to produce what Socrates calls 'images of evil'. Every citizen has the duty of turning their city into a healthy environment (following the previous model of the healthy city 'of pigs') – that is, one made out of fair goods. In turn, this environment educates the perception of every youth without their noticing, thereby building in them beliefs about what is fair, harmonious and well-done.[10] In being habituated to this environment, the citizens come to associate these beliefs with what really is fair, harmonious and well-done. So, it will not be necessary for them to have to revise their beliefs when they come to the age when they must justify them with reasons.

Socrates' next step is to argue that this environment produced by the work of every professional results from their education in *mousikē*; however, this is not due to the role models it broadcasts, but to the rhythm and the harmony in it (401d4-402a4). Rhythm paces the time of action (400b1-c7); harmony associates a certain emotion to it (398e1-399c6), thereby creating the motivation for the action to be done at its proper time.[11] *Mousikē* thus promotes a certain mode of doing things – with a particular rhythm, emotion and motivation – and develops in its public a more accurate perception of fairness, in particular by means of a capacity to detect flaws and failures, which leads to rejection of what is not well produced. If, on the one hand, experts are qualified by their knowledge of the form of their expertise, on the other, they become fair and good (*kalos k'agathos*) by developing an accurate perception. Such perception is obtained by an aesthetic education which, although it has its basis in *mousikē*, is developed 'environmentally',

---

[10] For these discriminatory skills, see Nettleship 1922: 82, 115. Gill (1996: 271) sees T32 as evidence that a citizen is able to read the manifestation of virtues in the art-works and social forms of a reason-ruled community.

[11] For the effects of the music in the soul, see Brancacci 2005: 99; Schofield 2010: 232.

that is, by living in a city that imprints this fairness in every item, in every detail. The agent of this education is the citizenry: every citizen educates the youth through the fairness they confer to their activities and products.[12]

The youth, in turn, are accustomed to perceiving fairness in things and in interactions, in such a way that, when the moment comes for them to give an account of it, they will do so while regarding it as something akin to them. As I would put it, they know *that* it is good, although they do not know *why*. If this is true, those raised in an environment of citizens who have been educated by *mousikē* begin to recognize, due to the shared mores, that fair things are good to them. We have already established in Chapter 3 that this was the case for decent people, and thus it seems evidence enough to grant that there is excellence without knowledge of the form of the good, and that decent people are virtuous. We must now specify how this knowledge of what is good for oneself is acquired from such mores.

> [T33] For each one of these things, there are three species of expertise: the expertise of use, the expertise of producing and the expertise of simulating, isn't it?
> Yes.
> The excellence, fairness and correctness of each artefact, living being, and action is relative to nothing other than the utility in virtue of which it was produced or naturally aims?
> Indeed.
> It is inevitable then that the user of each thing is the most experienced in it and informs the producer about how his product is good or bad when used for such utility. For instance, the flute-player informs the flute-maker about the flutes – which of them is adequate for playing – and instructs him about which are to be produced. The flute-maker then renders this service.
> Absolutely.
> The knower informs about the useful and the poor flutes; the other trusts him and produces.
> Yes.
> The producer of the artefacts therefore has a correct trust about the fairness and poorness, cooperating with the knower, and inevitably listening to him; the user, in turn, has knowledge.
> Of course. (601d1-602a2)

T33 describes a cooperative interaction typical of a common purpose contract: a flute player hires a flute-maker to make a flute. The premise is that there are three kinds of expertise in this interaction. We, however, shall leave aside the expertise of simulation, the focus of the passage, for we are now interested in the other two. The end of the flute-maker is to produce a good for others, or the flute. The fact that the producer has the correct trust, as opposed to the knowledge of the user, about the fairness and poorness of his product does not entail that the producer has no knowledge. After all, he is an expert and an expertise is a kind of knowledge of the form of what is produced. Socrates' statement is well known: 'Aren't we used to saying that the expert on each artefact produces the couch, the table, or anything else that we use by looking at the form?' (596b4-8). The flute producer knows what a flute is and how to produce it. How did he learn

---

[12] Skemp 1960: 36 argues that the producer's knowledge is not relevant to justice; however, if producing well is producing with fairness, that is, promoting the good of others as well as their own good, it is not possible to disassociate this knowledge from justice.

it? By being instructed by other producers (421e1-2), but also by making inferences himself from positing the form of the flute. As we saw in T12 (533d4-9, Chapter 4), the knowledge of experts consists of positing the forms of what they produce so that they are able to make inferences for practical purposes; a knowledge that is also called thought or discursive reasoning (*dianoia*). When the producer is informed by the player *about what is good for the player*, he is being instructed just as he was by his teachers.

The recipient of this good is the flute player, who has the experience of what his need is and how well the product fulfils it. Note that the product is not a good of the user himself, but qualified as such within his end of producing another good of others – the music of the flute. Therefore the user who judges the excellence of the product does so based neither on his desire nor on his personal flourishing, but for the sake of the utility it has regarding its strict end. In this argument, utility (*chreia*) has a strict meaning, and this is why the user has knowledge: he compares the product with its end, because this end is the object of his expertise, i.e., the good music obtained with the flute. This is also the reason why the producer, who cannot employ the product to its end, must trust the user for the information about what is good and bad about his product. Neither knows the form of the good, but both know the form of their expertise and know that its end is to produce the good of others. What they do is to cooperate to obtain this good.

In detailing the cooperative procedure, we understand that taking the good of others as the end of one's job is to commit oneself to fairness in production. This fairness, as is clear now, includes the dialogue with and the trust in the information provided by the qualified user. This is what I would call the cooperative process to obtain practical knowledge of the good, done through the association of dialogue with discursive reasoning (*dianoia*). I claim this to be the kind of knowledge of the good which experts possess: they know the objects of their expertise, while also trusting others about their good, so that the can produce the good of others. Rigorously speaking, this trust is not a mere belief because it must both be ratified by the expertise of others and work as a hypothesis in the practical inferences of one's own expertise.[13] The average citizen does not need to know the form of the good, but they must trust that the information they receive about the good is true. This is granted by the commitment to the fairness of the other experts.

In my view, this is a case of discursive reasoning because practical inferences are drawn after the positing of the form of a product as a good of others. In order to make inferences of practical import, information from others about the good at which they aim are necessary. On the other hand, this interaction explains the rewards expertise. In evaluating the quality of the flute, the flute player compares the product obtained with the intended purpose because he knows what a good flute is. Here, discursive reasoning operates by postulating the form of music, inferring what a good flute is and receiving information from the producer about which flute can be made. The practical conclusion of this operation qualifies the flute player as a reward expert. None of these citizens has philosophical knowledge, but all of them develop knowledge of a practical sort derived from an environment created by the right education. The laws that set the standards of their education are therefore enough:

> [T34] What about the commercial contracts, by the Gods, I said, those in which an individual engages with others in commerce, if you will, and the contracts with manual workers, reproaches, insults, judicial procedures, pleads to juries, payment and exaction

---

[13] For the claim that citizens in general have know-how obtained by true belief, see Hall 1959: 155, Hoerber 1960: 34; Jeon 2014: 202. As I see it, Socrates offers us a special category of knowledge, discursive thought (*dianoia*), in which to include expertise in general: experts trust what others say is the good they expect; take this as a hypothesis and proceed making inferences about how to produce this good with fairness.

of fees required for commerce or importation, and commercial, urban and harbour regulations in general, as well as everything of this sort, should we dare legislate about these things?

It is not worth it, he said, to make prescriptions to men that are good and fair. They will easily find out by themselves all the things that should be legislated. (425c10-e2)

Well-educated citizens will not require detailed laws as they will engage in their common purpose contracts with fairness. The task of legislation and ruling is therefore significantly reduced, orientated instead primarily towards establishing the education which will engender such citizens. This means they must all possess something like an expertise of rewards, such that they are able to manage their contracts by themselves without the need for regulation.

There is, of course, a circularity involved in any educational proposal of this sort: one needs well-educated people in order to establish the educational principles that will subsequently generate well-educated citizens. Popular virtue is not self-produced. As the lack of ability of the soul in the myth of Er shows, the virtue of these citizens is connected to their environment,[14] for which reason government, as mentioned in Chapter 7, is necessary, even in a city of good and fair citizens. This is the point which leads us to the relation between ruling and philosophy, which is the topic of subsequent chapters.

For now, I would like to conclude that just citizens are decent people who know what is good for them. They cannot give reasons for why this is their good, nor can they make right choices when removed from their healthy environment. This, of course, weakens the concept of 'knowledge' attributed to them. Nonetheless, it is supported by the text and renders us a much more interesting theory of justice, according to which justice is the excellence of a city founded on the excellence of all its citizens in cooperation.

* * *

Finally, I would like to argue that the virtues of the philosophical personality are different in kind from those of the just person we saw in Chapter 11 (see 485a1-2 referring to 484d4-6). It is quite obvious that the philosopher, on account of their obsessive intellectual exercise (485c6-11), is the wisest human being. Their reason, however, does not result from knowing what is better for themselves and their parts of the soul, like the just person (see 441e4-5), rather from a constant process of enquiry and learning of reality that is always the same, which is set in a rational order (*kosmoi . . . kata logon* – 500c5). Learning reality leads the philosopher to try to become similar to it (500b8-c7). Philosophical temperance, in turn, happens due to the channelling of desire that eliminates their interest in riches and appetites – for the so-called bodily pleasures (485d10-e1) – thus reducing their internal conflict (485d6-8, e3-5). Certainly, they must eat and drink, but only due to *anankē* – the pure necessity of survival, since they find no pleasure in it. This also differs from the account of the just person, who was temperate only owing to the belief that their desire should follow the end of reason (see T31, 442b10-d7).

---

[14] Against the evidence of T27, Irwin (1977: 202) claims that, at first, the person educated in *mousikē* and gymnastics has true belief and lack all virtues. He later modifies his view (Irwin 1995: 234–5) to claim that this is a person who does not have genuine virtue (for not having knowledge), and does not choose virtue for its own sake; they pursue it for the sake of being honoured for being virtuous, which is different to choosing virtue for the sake of honour, which would be a case of timocracy. My view has many points in common with this latter position of Irwin, although I do not accept this to be a non-genuine virtue. I claim instead that this is precisely the definition of justice we find in book IV, and this is a popular virtue.

Because the philosopher is not interested in what is of limited extension and duration, their understanding of their own life is singular: they consider themselves as a mortal part of a greater whole (486a8-b2). From the perspective of the laws of nature, it is natural for us to die – and thus the philosophers understand that excessive worry with death and preservation of individual life is a mistake; which results in minimizing the fear (486b1-5). The philosopher is courageous by inference from their knowledge. With their thoughts engaged in contemplating the whole of reality, philosophers are not enslaved to desires or fear, nor submitted to any form of servitude. They are engaged in actions pursuing the good of everything (*tou holou kai pantos aei eporexesthai*, 486a5-6). Therefore, the philosopher is just because they give little importance to the typical concerns of human life (486a8-10), those which are at the basis of the constitutional principle and that allow for human flourishing. They are just not for being cooperative, but for being magnanimous (see *megaloprepeia*, 486a8).[15]

There is a very important reason to differentiate the philosophical virtues from popular virtue: the philosopher offers a singular proof that there are people with the natural tendency for the rule of reason, as opposed to the one only obtained after an education since childhood. Because philosophers may develop virtues on their own, they become the only individuals who have the power to begin the educational proposal for popular virtue (500d5-9), which would otherwise entail circularity. The importance of philosophers in constituting a virtuous cycle is the theme of Chapter 15; before that we must learn more about how popular virtue entails a certain kind of community.

---

[15] For other arguments on how the virtues of the philosophers differ from those of the just person, see Bloom 1991: 395–6.

13

Community

I argued that, for a city to be just, all of its citizens must be cooperative. There must therefore be some kind of public education available to all, wherein citizens are led to develop the virtues of the rule of reasoning. I claimed that, although Socrates' arguments focus on the education of the guardians (because the whole city is jeopardized by their failure), his proposal is not restricted merely to them. Socrates' just city depends on a certain relation between all the citizens – the community of pleasures and pains – and not simply on the character of the rulers and their military auxiliaries. As the community of pleasures and pains is not the only community that Socrates' theory of justice entails, there is much confusion in the tradition about what exactly is shared and by whom. This chapter aims at clarifying Socrates' claims about community.

There are three different communities proposed by Socrates' theory: the community of pleasures and pains, the community of women and children, and the community of property among guardians. We are already familiar with the first of them, introduced in Chapter 9 as the end of the legislator of a just city for its binding of the citizens together (462a2-c1, see T22). I claimed that the community of pleasures and pains was achieved by empathy, that is, by the ability to understand the feelings of others based on reasonable beliefs regularly produced by our cognitive apparatus. When citizens empathize with others, they do not necessarily feel the same emotion. They understand, based on shared beliefs, how the situation justifies the feelings of others. That is a rational motivation for not feeling the opposite, that is, *regarding the same state of affairs*, not to feel pleasure while others are in pain, and not to feel pain while others have pleasure. This community therefore aims at avoiding the presence of opposite feelings regarding the same state of affairs in the city. This, I argued, may only be obtained when citizens believe that other citizens are akin (*oikeia*). These citizens should therefore not be privatizers – the cause of hatred and strife in a city – who believe that others are alien and thus deem it appropriate to hold opposite feelings regarding the same state of affairs. Now that it has been established that justice is the virtue of the citizen aiming at cooperative flourishing and that our own flourishing lies in relating to others as *oikeia*, it is possible to ascertain that injustice comes from believing others to be alien and, therefore, not partners of cooperation.

The community of pleasures and pains indicates that the concept of justice goes beyond simply cooperative partnerships in contracts, to a commitment to relate to other citizens as *oikeia* (463b10-11; 463e1-464d5). This is a more rigorous standard than simply obedience to the laws. It is a prudential attitude in which responsibility for the outcome of action over others – at least when it comes to allowing or hindering the flourishing of others – is imputed to the agent. Actions that are harmful to others are therefore unjust. Although there should be no doubt at this point that this is a community requiring the commitment of all the citizens (see *pantes hoi politai*, 462b5 and the definition of citizens as both rulers and the *dēmos* at 463a1-5), or at least of the greatest number of them (*pleistoi*, 462c6), there are interpreters who, convinced that Socrates does not care for the education of the *dēmos*, assume that it is restricted purely to guardians or rulers. Their textual support for this claim is the following:

> [T35] Can you tell whether the rulers in other cities refer to some of their fellow-rulers as akin and to others as alien?
> Yes, many of them do.
> Isn't it that they consider the akin as their own, and calls them so, and the alien as not their own.
> It is so.
> Then how is it among your guardians? Would they consider one of their fellow-rulers as alien and refer to him as such?
> Not at all, he said. For everyone he may meet he will consider as a brother, or sister, or mother or father, son or daughter, or their descendents or ancestors.
> You speak most fairly, I said, and now tell me this too: will you legislate so that they treat them as akin only in words, or also that they act according to these words in every action? With respect to the fathers, must they be hearkening to progenitors, following the mores relative to fathers regarding reverence and care? If they act in any other manner, wouldn't they accomplish what is neither pious nor just, and fail to become better in relation to the gods and human beings? Do you think that these maxims, and others such as these, will be sung by all the citizens close to the ears of the children, about the parents who produced them, and about the other kin?
> These are indeed the maxims. For it would be ridiculous if they would pronounce these words of kinship only from their mouths without deeds.
> More than in every other city, in this one they will be in tune when saying the words we mentioned: when someone fares well or badly, they will say that 'one of mine fares well' or 'one of mine fares badly'.
> This is very true, he said.
> Didn't we say that the community of pleasures and pains follows from these beliefs and these words?
> And we were correct in saying it.
> Then won't our citizens more than others have the same in common, which they will call 'mine'? And by having it in common, they will have the maximal community of pain and pleasure?
> Very much. (463b9-464a7)

T35 emphasizes that in a just city there is no strife among rulers. Rather, just rulers hold themselves as akin and treat each other accordingly. The text also points out that this kind of relationship is not restricted to rulers; it is an attitude guardians will have towards *everyone* they meet, because children hear from *all the citizens* that this is the correct attitude towards kin people (463d6-7). As I pointed out before, every child in a city will be educated by the same public education and will be submitted to the first tests for guardians. It therefore cannot only be 'guardian children' – if there were such a thing – who would listen to these maxims. Instead, every citizen will learn them. In sum, although the passage talks about rulers in particular, it offers a more general argument about all the citizens who, it concludes, have the same in common, that is, the pleasures and pains regarding a certain state of affairs (464a4-6).

Having clarified this extension of the community, T35 matters to us for spelling out the relationship between one's own and those who are akin – that is, for pointing out that cooperation involves reverence and care to others, as well as hearkening to them (463d1-6). As Glaucon puts it, these are deeds that must follow from the words expressing kinship (463e2-3); therefore, they coincide with an attitude that characterizes doing one's own and not interfering in others doing the same. As we should expect, justice is not only doing something but doing it in a certain way. In other words, it is pursuing one's flourishing while treating others as akin and caring for them, having reverence and hearkening to them. Justice is therefore the attitude that citizens who live in a community of pleasures and pains have towards their fellow citizens. Personalities formed by sharing the beliefs about a certain state of affairs being good or bad do not see others as alien; they understand the feelings of others because of empathy.

In Chapter 9, T22 claimed that the community of pleasures and pains is the end of lawgivers, while T35 states that, were Glaucon the lawgiver of a just city, he would enact laws to establish that citizens should act towards others as *oikeia*. We may now see that these laws aim at educating just citizens who will cooperate with each other. The power device the lawgiver employs to obtain this kind of citizen is, as we saw in the last chapter, the public education in *mousikē* and gymnastics which is given from childhood. Though we are already aware of how this education obtains the virtues of the good citizen, here it is important to emphasize how simulation in *mousikē* exercises our empathy.

In Chapter 3, we saw the case of the spectator of simulative *mousikē*, an individual who associated the pleasure of simulation with compassion for heroes who, on their turn, did not have the best attitude in the circumstances depicted (605c9-d5). This was the basis for Socrates' greatest accusation against the simulative *mousikē* as practised by Homer and the tragedians: they associate pleasure with unreasonable beliefs (see 605c5-608b2). If our reasoning is not well educated to resist such beliefs, either by arguments or by habit, we associate our emotions with the wrong role models (606a3-b5). The active role of reasoning in the reception of simulative *mousikē* is thus the antidote that protects any spectator from the damages it may cause, wherein lies the difference between compassionate and empathic reception. As I have already argued, empathy is the ability to understand the feelings of others *based on true beliefs*. Empathy judges the correctness of the emotion associated with the state of affairs and is able to justify its judgement – hence why it is based on beliefs shared by a community: there may only be a community of pleasures and pains because the judgement of the emotion of others in a certain state of affairs is justifiable.

In Chapter 3, we also saw that simulative *mousikē* is damaging because it chooses vulgar role models and promotes easy emotions. On the other hand, it may also be a powerful educational tool for just citizens both because it can associate its particular pleasure with good role models, and because it has the power to develop the habit of reasoning of its audience. It is true that children are incapable of having an empathic – as opposed to a compassionate – reception of simulative *mousikē* and this is the reason why the lawgiver must be really attentive not only about the role models but also about emotions associated with them by music and rhythm. They must induce the development of a more accurate perception; one in which, for instance, the public becomes more sensitive to the absence of fairness. As they become accustomed to a certain environment, children thus develop judgement on spectacles justified by their rational mores. Through the capacity of simulating themselves as others, they also develop the belief that others are akin to them. I conclude that the community of pleasures and pains is the outcome of a public education of all the citizens from early childhood aiming at their cooperation: interaction with others as akin.

Right after T35, we learn that the cause of this community, called the greatest good, is another community: the one of women and children among the guardians (464a8-9, b5-6). We are now able to understand what this community is. Once it is properly understood, it will become clearer that, while it is said here to hold among guardians (an emphasis repeated at 450c1-2), it is to be extended to all citizens.

The community of women and children is first alluded to in book IV (423e5-424a3) as a custom that would not require positive laws. For, Socrates claims, mores about the possession of women, marriage and the generation of children would easily be deduced by every well-educated person as a corollary of the proverb that recommends 'to make everything to the upmost common among friends' (424a2-3).[1] Although this initially seemed correct to Adeimantus (424a4), after listening to what Polemarchus tells him at the beginning of book V, he worries that it can have a great impact on the *politeia* if not done correctly (449d4-450a2). Subsequently he asks Socrates for an explanation of what kind of community he refers to, as there are many of them (449c7-d4). The variety here refers to different practices in the ancient world regarding the political role of women, marriage and the structure of a nuclear family[2] – important features in a *politeia* for determining how each individual will be educated and what kind of citizen they will be.

The kind of community Socrates has in mind is to be deduced from good education (423e5-7, 451c3-4). I shall argue that the mores about marriage and the structure of the nuclear family are deduced from the political role of women, which is, in turn, deduced from the definition of justice (see 453b1-4). It must be noted again that T26 (433d2) included women in the list of people who would have the parts of their soul doing their own; therefore being just in a just city. Similarly, from the conclusions reached in T27 (that someone in whom the parts of their soul would cooperate would be a cooperative person), we can expect women to be cooperative citizens.[3]

The political role of women, however, is opposed to the contemporary custom in which they practise one single activity, caring for the house (*oikourein*, 451d6). The rationale would be the belief according to which they are incapable of undertaking the same activities as men *because* they bear children and are responsible for raising them (451d7-9). Mores may be changed as long as one understands that other ways of doing things are manifestly better (452d4-5). Of course, one is more likely to reach this conclusion if one can witness these better uses, but this is unlikely to occur when a more is established and justified. Socrates' first challenge thus is to demonstrate that the community of women is better than this more.

---

[1] Plato's scholiast at *Phaedrus* 279c refers the saying to Pythagoras. This seems to be another of the customary Platonic projections onto Pythagoras; see Dawson 1992: 15–18.

[2] Herodotus tells us about different ways in which to have a community of women. The Massagetae and the Nasamones had monogamic marriages, but the women were of 'common use': when a Massagetae man would like to have sex with a woman, he would hang his quiver on her wagon and simply do it. The Nasamones would put their staff in front of the house to indicate they were having sex. The Nasamones also had all the guests having sex with the bride during the wedding night, each of them giving her a gift (see Herodotus, *History*, I, 216, 1–6; IV 172, 7–14). The Ausëes have common sex – every man could have sex with every woman – and none would live in the same house as the other. Three months after a child was born, they would be taken to a meeting of men who would decide to whom they were similar: this man would be their father (Herodotus, *History*, IV, 180, 21–5). The Agathyrsians and the Thracians had a system more similar to Socrates' proposal: common sex with the purpose that 'they will be all brothers of each other and all being akin (*oikēioi*), having neither envy nor hatred towards each other' (Herodotus, *History*, IV, 104, 1–5). Pomeroy (1974: 33–5) suggests that the community of women in the *Republic* would fit the Nasamones' kind, a claim that Fortenbaugh (1975: 1–4) corrected.

[3] The equity of women is deduced neither from the community of pleasures and pains – due to the expansion of the family (as in Barker 1918: 257 and Campese 2000: 259) – nor from the common property of the guardians (as in Vlastos [1989]1995: 21), but from the definition of justice itself. For the claim that the status of women must be deduced from justice, see Smith (1980: 7), who nonetheless thinks that Socrates does not do it. Natali (2005: 200) actually claims that the other two communities are deduced from the defence of the education of women and Forde (1997: 660–1) deduces it from human nature.

There is a second challenge though. Socrates imagines an objector, a practitioner of antilogy, who would charge him with inconsistency because he previously claimed that individuals should do what suits their nature, and women's *nature* is to bear children (453a7-b5). In the presence of such an objection, Socrates suggests a twofold proof in which his proposal is at first shown to be possible (452e3-4) and subsequently shown to be the best (456c10). The first stage aims to prove that the belief regarding the incapacity of women is false; the second aims to prove that it is unreasonable – that is, against our good.

Socrates' argument against the antilogy practitioner is that his technique is not capable of dividing items according to forms (454a5-6); he lacks the power of dialectic (454a8). This is the first mention of a power that (as we will see in Chapter 15) is required for ruling a just city. In the present argument, it is relevant for establishing what the forms of natural difference and sameness are (454b6-7): when it comes to justice, the natural difference that matters for someone to have a different activity is determined by personal talent, which in Greek is denoted by *euphuēs* (see 455b5), that is, having an aptitude. We were introduced to the discussion of this kind of nature in Chapter 11, where T28 distinguished nature not only by possession of the power to accomplish some activity but also by the kind of reward one would expect for producing the good of others (434a3-434c11), thus distinguishing differences of personality.

Such talent is verified by ease in learning, in discovering more by oneself, in keeping everything in memory and in having a body ready to respond to the intellectual demands of a specific activity (455b4-c3). It also refers to the tendency to have a certain personality (such as being a lover or a democratic person). This natural talent, claims Socrates, is equally distributed among men and women (455d8), as both have the aptitude for all the activities (455d9), and no personality is peculiar to one of them (455b1-2). Both may be physicians, cobblers (454d5), educated or uneducated (455e6), gymnastic lovers and haters (456a1-2); both may be war-like or peaceful (456a1-2), be philosophers or haters of wisdom, in possession of a strong or a weak *thumos* (456a4-5).

Natural tendencies for activities and for predominant ends, as the features involved in determining a cooperative person (454d7-9), constitute the form of natural difference that matters for the division according to justice that a dialectician would make within human beings (see 454c7-d3). On the other hand, justice disregards every other difference among human beings, including the power to bear babies (454d10) and the alleged superiority of men over women in every activity they do in common (455c5-7, d3-4). These are differences that do not really divide human beings; they remain collected, despite these differences, under the form of sameness (454e1-2). The conclusion is therefore that, for justice, there is a concept of natural equality of human beings, as well as a concept of natural difference. This same point was present in Socrates' reasons for a city, when he claimed that we were all the same regarding our basic needs – those that come to us due to our species – and different as individuals, that is, each of us has different natural tendencies (see T25, 369c9-370c7). Socrates now defends his concept of justice by including in it this differentiation of the two concepts of human nature.

The argument to the antilogy practitioner is not only a defence of Socrates' consistency but also a proof that it is possible that women have the same political role as men (456c1-9). The latter amounts to arguing that there is no counter-proof that women are incapable of accomplishing these activities (454e6-455a2). As mentioned in Chapter 5, impossibility would be proved only if grounded in the absence of power. Yet Glaucon clearly asserts that 'there are many women that are better in many things than many man' (455d4-5), a proof against the thesis that they might lack these powers. The proposal is therefore feasible, even if against the contemporary custom.

The second part of the proof concerns the proposal being the best option (456c10), which is deduced from Socrates' rhetorical question: 'is there something better for a city than that both the women and the men become excellent?' (456e4-5). Interpreters have read this as evidence of the priority of the good of the city to the detriment of the good of individuals, concluding that Socrates' 'feminism'[4] is therefore nothing but the instrumentalization of women for the sake of the state. If, however, we understand that justice aims at cooperative flourishing, we may regard the statement as claiming that there is nothing to the flourishing of a city but the flourishing of all its citizens. Any non-cooperative interaction between men and women would result in a more unjust city, hence why discussing the community of women matters to justice.

Given the premise that the good of the city is the excellence of all its citizens, the second proof would seem straightforwardly deduced from the first. However, Socrates claims that there remains a point to be clarified: the question of whether, even if they are to accomplish the same activities, the education of men and women should be different (456c12-d1). Again, the concepts of natural sameness and difference guide the conclusion. Glaucon agrees that women and men should have the same education *when* they have the same nature (456d1), but when they have different talents, they should receive different educations accordingly: the most competent individuals of both sexes should have the education they discussed (456d5-11), that is, they should be selected by tests and, if they succeed, move forward to higher education. The best option is thus that *different* educations should be offered according to talent and personality, but each of these different educations should be *the same* for men and women. Once this is established, the proof is simply that the proposal is best because it results in the good of the city.

As mentioned previously, the conclusion of this argument should be extended to all the citizens, and not restricted merely to guardians.[5] Socrates has an undeniable preference for orienting his point towards the capacities of women to become guardians – in particular, their power for military activities (452c1-2, 452e5-452a5), their philosophical and *thumoeidetic* natures (456a4-5), and their education for becoming guardians (456c12-d1) – as each of these are features of what Socrates considers to be a rarer nature. Since his purpose is to make an argument on the equality of women and men, calling attention to their equality on the most uncommon level thus makes a more persuasive point. But the proof is not necessarily restricted to guardians. Quite the opposite, if every activity should be exerted by both sexes, the universality of female education follows. If I am right, Socrates' proposal refers to every citizen in the city, reinforcing the conclusion of the previous chapter, that the education in *mousikē* and gymnastics should be given to all citizens (456e7-457a1). It is therefore not only the best women that should be freed from their enclosure in the household tasks: all should be citizens. If so, this argument concludes more than simply that the political role of women is possible and best: given the concepts of natural sameness and difference, it proves, as Socrates anticipated it would (423e5-424a3), that the equality of men and women for public activities is *deduced* from the concept of justice.

The proof that the political role of women is just does not yet constitute a proof that the community of women and children is good and possible. Rather, it is simply a grounding for

---

[4] In my view, the discussion on whether or not Socrates' proposal is feminist – supposing some specific concept of feminism to which it would correspond – is anachronical. For this discussion, see Annas 1976: 319–21, who also voices the instrumentalization objection. But to my view the question is also misleading because feminism is defined by a claim of rights, and, I submit, once justice is understood as cooperation, it follows that the discussion in the *Republic* concerns forms of life that generate rights, rather than institutions that concede them. For a counterpoint to this claim, see Santas 2010: 114–15.

[5] Smith (1980: 5); Halliwell (1998a: 13) and Campese (2000: 258–9) assume the restriction to guardians; Annas (1976: 311) finds the evidence for the universal extension of the community scanty.

this latter conclusion (457b7-8). For the first part, the connection seems simple, although it is not explicitly spelt out in the text: having women as citizens is a form of having women in common. For in this case, women are not the property of one man who is responsible for their sustenance. On the other hand, the community of children is deduced from the community of women by the premise that performing an activity well entails devoting oneself to only one activity (see *ouk alla prakteon* at 457a8-9). Because every woman will have her own activity to care for, she cannot also devote herself to the activities of caring for the house and raising the children (451d6-9). No double or triple shift is just. The inference is thus that we should have professionals to care for these activities. For example, we would have experts in raising children who would live altogether in a specific part of the city (460c1-3).

Socrates' proposal for the community of children, however, goes far beyond the conclusion of this argument. He claims that 'the children will also be common, the parents should not know their offspring, nor the child his/her parents' (457c10-d3). His postponement of the argument about the possibility of this community (457e7-458b7) (and failure to resume it again) may be indicative of some hesitation on his part in regard to this stronger conclusion, particularly as his proposals are always intercut with clauses such as 'as far as possible' or 'if possible' (see 458e3-4, 459a9-10, 459b2, 460a5, 462b5, 464a6, 464d3-4, 466c9, 469b10). The proposal nevertheless begins addressing reproduction. As we saw in Chapter 10, every healthy city must control its population growth to avoid famine and war (see 372c1-2, 423b10-c4 and 460a3-6) and, given the lack of contraceptive methods in antiquity, this generally implied sex control and child exposure. Here Socrates favours the first (but does not rule out the latter) in proposing a model similar to that of the Athenian institution of sacred marriages (458e3-4),[6] according to which sex during the reproductive ages would become part of a political ritual.

To this model of population control he also adds eugenics, a device that aims at breeding children with better talents and tendencies, which will subsequently lead rulers to tell lies to the ruled (459c9-d3) in order that the city will only raise the children of the best citizens (460d8-e3) exposing children with disabilities and those who are born from base citizens (460c3-5).[7] Reproductive control is an important means to generate cooperation among citizens. The city must not lack the citizens who perform its basic activities, and there cannot be a lack of indispensable goods. Eugenics, however, constitutes an entirely different matter: the improvement of the nature of citizens is no justification for wise rulers to lie to citizens. Period. This is the first reason why Socrates should hesitate.

A further reason for Socrates' hesitation concerns the claim that parents shall not know their offspring and vice versa, a proposal which, given that some taboos must be avoided in this secrecy, thus demands intricate measures to prevent incest (461b8-e3). In my view, Socrates gets entangled in this complication by trying to deduce the community of women and children from the community of pleasures and pains. We have seen that the community of pleasures and pains entails the regard of others as akin, an attitude that T35 compares to considering them as family members (e.g. brother, sister, mother, father). Socrates certainly sees the existence of strong family ties as a motivation against considering others as akin. After all, if family members would be more congenial than those who are not members, one can prove family to be a privatizer factor, prompting individuals to disconnect their flourishing from the flourishing of

---

[6] For the ritual of sacred marriages see Avagianou 1991: 3–18.
[7] For an illuminating approach to Athenian eugenic practices, with particular reference to Plato, *Theaetetus*, 160e2-161a1, see Campese 2000: 272. Maybe it is worth noting that in the twentieth century, eugenics was not a project exclusive to totalitarian regimes, but also pursued by the most important liberal democracies under the name of science and health. For an accurate position on the Platonic eugenic project, see Vegetti 2000: 299.

other citizens (464c6-d4). It is for this reason that Socrates underlines the importance of singing hymns to *every* child about different kinds of kinship (T35, 463d6-e1) – a reference which is most likely to the myth of the metals (414d1-415c8). Socrates deems this myth necessary to persuade every citizen about both their kinship and their differences regarding natural talents and tendencies, so that they will care more for each other and for the city (415d2-3).

The myth of the metals is a foundational myth, that is, it is told to every citizen to explain the origin of the city. The prime function of a foundational myth is to establish a new beginning in history.[8] By associating a population with a particular territory, the myth legitimizes their ownership of the land while rejecting any claim of previous owners. Moreover, it commits the citizens to the collective task of preserving the city and making it flourish. A foundational myth marks the beginning of a *politeia* with its intrinsic justice (which cancels any injustice done in order to found the city), and determines who the citizens of that territory are.

In Socrates' version of it, the myth awakens all the citizens from an early life they spent dreaming.[9] Now ready, they can know the truth. Their mother is the territory, they were all modelled and nurtured beneath the earth (414d1-e5), and thus all those in the city are siblings (415a2) and kin (*suggeneis*, 415a7). This much would persuade them to forget the past history, to take possession of the territory and, by being committed to every other citizen in a joint mission, to become citizens themselves. One detail worth noticing is that, if the traditional role of the foundational myths generally is to erase the violence and injustice of the conquest of the territory, here this role is reversed to the purpose of erasing the previous personal experience of education (414d4-5). Socrates' myth seems therefore to be designed for an already existent city that 're-founds itself' under an educational revolution.

The myth of the metals, however, is more than a foundational myth as it also defends the correspondence of political activities to different talents and tendencies – identified by different earthy metals – to justify different educations.[10] Remarkably, it states that the eugenics will fail, for the talents and tendencies will not necessarily be passed to the offspring (415a7-c7, for the failure of eugenics, see also 546a7-b4), and, as such, all children must be tested to identify the activity for which they are gifted (see also 423c6-d6).

We shall return to the different metals and their purpose; for now, however, I would like to suggest that Socrates' arguments against the nuclear family based on the community of pleasures and pains are not compelling, for the family is not an obstacle to the community of pains and pleasures. If the citizens can be persuaded that their co-citizens are as akin as their family, this would be sufficient for justice. Indeed, Socrates actually suggests a point closer to this one when he states that all the Greeks should be considered akin (*oikeion einai kai suggenes*, 470c2), which would mean an expansion of kinship beyond the city's border. If kinship may be expanded, very likely by the practice of empathy, then family in itself is not a hindrance to justice. On the other hand, the political role of women by itself contributes to the expansion of kinship from family to the city, as, once children do not live in the same house and do not spend time together with

---

[8] For the rhetoric importance of a foundational myth that establishes a 'good beginning' and the continuous occupation of the territory, see Loraux 1996: 25–32. This was considered nothing but an ideological device (see Schofield 2006: 285–6; Wardy 2013: 127–8) as if nothing but false family bonds would count as the reason why citizens live together. The need of such a political lie was seen as totalitarian political propaganda device (see Popper [1945]1966: 138).
[9] Lear (2006: 32) argues that the claim that all previous experience can be understood as a dream is a proto-philosophical belief. For the myth being used for a transition to adult citizenship, see Rowett 2016: 68–70.
[10] Page (1991: 10–12) points out the importance of falsehood for developing resilience necessary for virtue; Rowett (2016 : 85–7) makes the claim that the myth establishes equal opportunity for education.

their parents, they are more prone to holding family members on equal footing with citizens when it comes to kinship.

As long as men and women take part equally in all activities in the city, and that it is from this principle of equality that the best argument about the community of women and children is deduced, we are to understand that the community of women and children extends to all citizens. It is, once again, true that Socrates prioritizes guardians in his argument, for which I already offered a reason: the appeal to the highest level of equity. Now, however, I would like to add that guardians are in an exceptional position relative to women and children because they are the only ones to participate in another community: the one of property. In their case, all items that traditionally would make up a household (*oikos*) – wife, children and estate – are held in common.

The community of property among guardians was also introduced by the myth of the metals, specifically by the thesis that rulers have gold and auxiliaries have silver in their souls (415a4-5). This talent and tendency, plus the special education they shall receive, will not, however, be enough to prevent their use of their superiority in the city to harm the ruled (416b1-c3). Rather, they will have to be told that to have private property is a moral stain (*miainein*, 417a1): having gold and silver in their souls, they are not to have them in their hands. They must therefore have a particular lifestyle regarding property. None shall own anything privately besides what is to supply their basic inevitable needs (416d5-7, 458c9), that is, whatever is necessary for their survival and training as warriors. This excludes travelling and money for small expenses, such as buying gifts for others (420a4-7). In contradistinction to wage earners who own houses, land and money (415e8-9, 417a6-8), they live together in camps open to anyone who wishes to enter and share their meals (416d7-e3, 458c8-9, 464b8-c3) – a lifestyle that allows for the constant surveillance of the other citizens who pay for it.

Ruling must be kept completely apart from wealth and economic interest, financed by public funds, with its expenses open to the scrutiny of all other citizens.[11] As evident in the case of timocracy, Socrates holds that guardians cannot have private property without becoming motivated by *pleonexia*, thereby attacking the public good rather than protecting it, and, subsequently, becoming despots (416a2-6, 417a8-b1). Such a precaution shows that Socrates distrusts the success of education and takes it as necessary to impose laws even upon those who were considered good and fair. His reason for overcaution in these cases is that the outcomes of possible vicious actions of these agents are a dangerous threat to the *politeia*: in Thrasymachus' terms, they do not cause only partial injustice but also bring down the whole city (421a4-8).

Last, but by no means least, it must be noted that Adeimantus objects to the community of property on the grounds that it amounts to forbidding guardians from flourishing by preventing them from taking possession of the goods of the citizens (419a1-5, 465e5-466a2). Socrates' response reinforces the connection between justice and the barring of *pleonexia* in government. He claims that, in order to make an argument about how justice leads to our flourishing (420b8-c1), he is committed to explaining how the *whole* city, not only one kind of people, may flourish (420b4-8; 466a2-6). One should note that he is not claiming that individuals should sacrifice their flourishing to the good of the city as an entity on its own; quite the opposite. Here he has Thrasymachus' assertion that justice (of the citizens) would lead to the exclusive flourishing

---

[11] For the principle of separation between wealth and power see Vegetti 1998: 155. Arruzza (2011: 231) suggests the separation to be in the way of life itself (see Chapter 16).

of the tyrant as a target: Socrates' answer to Adeimantus is that there are more goods than Thrasymachean goods, of which a cooperative political life is one – the guardians flourish more than any Olympic winner (420b4-5; 465d3-4), but they flourish *as* guardians, that is, as the kind of citizen they are, excelling in the activity that is proper to their nature (420d6-e1). The same is true of other experts, who flourish while practising their own activity (420e1-421a3), and who, in living in a just city, do not lack any of their basic needs and have their importance acknowledged by other citizens (421d11-e2; 465d6-e3). Goods are always peculiar to something or someone, and the flourishing of each person refers to their individual way of living within a community – not to a general ownership of stuff (421b5-c5). Even if Socrates is overcautious in demanding the community of property among guardians, he still has a point about material goods not being sufficient for flourishing, and about the higher commitment of guardians to this education, since they obtain their lifestyle as a direct result of public funding and the internal and external protection of the city depends on them.

There remain, however, some gaps in the discussion about justice and the good. For this reason, I hold that Adeimantus' point still stands. These gaps are addressed in the next chapter.

14

The good

Having understood the ways in which different communities are deduced from the definition of justice, we are now in a position to explain why justice is not simply cooperation but also requires the rule of reasoning. An initial insight into this problem is found in Socrates' cooperation argument against Thrasymachus (350d5-352b5), an argument built around the example of a gang of thieves who cooperate in crime, that is, a cooperation for committing injustice. This argument ultimately evidences that the end of cooperative actions may be good for these agents, but not for others who are, by these same actions, deprived of their own good. A similar objection against the understanding of justice as cooperation is found in Adeimantus' speech.

Together, the two brothers, Glaucon and Adeimantus, claim that: (i) the reputation of justice is what gives us rewards (365b5-6 and 361c1-2, see also the connection between 363a3-5 and 362b2-5); (ii) such a reputation can be false, and false reputation can be used towards our flourishing (365c2 and 362a2); (iii) the best path to flourishing is being unjust while maintaining the reputation of justice (362a2-c6 and 366b4-8). Although a great deal of contemporary literature deals with Glaucon's speech as the greatest challenge for Socrates, Adeimantus is very clear that his brother's argument was insufficient and did not make the most relevant point (362d3-5). The mainstream interpretation has it that Adeimantus' contribution to the question of justice is his criticism of poetry as a matrix of education. I would, however, like to argue that Adeimantus' most relevant point, and precisely what Glaucon has left out, is the need for an argument which proves that justice is sufficient for piety.[1] Adeimantus indeed targets poetry as the source of the information we get on the gods, but he also challenges the assumption that justice is simply cooperation.

Adeimantus' criticism of poetry targets the verses of Homer, Hesiod, and Musaeus, according to which (i) just, pious and excellent people are rewarded, and the wicked and unjust are inevitably punished (363a8-d5); but (ii) justice and temperance, however noble, are painful, while licentiousness and injustice are pleasant and easy to practise (364a1-4; 364c7); and finally that (iii) unjust actions are generally more profitable than just ones, and those which unjustly obtain wealth and other forms of power flourish and are worthy of praise (364a4-7, 364b6-7). Honouring the rich and powerful while despising the poor is, according to Adeimantus, typical of the society conveyed by poetry and/or the attitude of the very poets, the gods themselves and finally the very people engaged in a religion that worships these gods. All these agents hold

---

[1] In general, the challenges of the two brothers are presented as one and emphasis is given to Glaucon; see Cross and Woozley 1964: 61; Inwood 1987: 99; Burnyeat 1997: 30; Weiss 2007: 103. Adeimantus' speech is seen as simply introducing the centrality of poets in the matter, see Vegetti 1998: 229; Santas 2010: 52; Lear: 2008 26; O'Connor 2007: 78; Schindler 2008: 170; Burnyeat 1997: 260; Strauss 1964: 91; Rosen 2005: 67. Exceptions in giving more attention to Adeimantus are Diès 1948: xxvi and Stokes 1997: 76. Moors (1981: 84) points out that he is the one to call attention to the problem of piety (see 363a6-8; 612c1-2, see also Adkins 1975: 146–8). Not much on Adeimantus is found in chapters devoted to piety in the *Republic*; see McPherran 2006: 88; Weiss 2012: 129ff.

the same belief. They are not actually deceived by a false reputation of justice; they are flexible, and can become accomplices of injustice should they get a proper share in the goods therewith obtained (364b6–c5).

Despite being a rich source of information about Greek religious practices, Adeimantus' speech is not religious. Rather, he is the spokesman for the most radical atheism found in Plato's pages. In what Vegetti (1998: 222–4) has termed 'Adeimantus' theorem', he presents the three exhaustive hypotheses that together rule out piety as a motivation for action: (i) the gods do not exist (365d8); (ii) gods exist but do not care about humans (365d8-9) or (iii) the gods care for us and we must trust poets and rituals, who describe them as flexible and subject to persuasion (365d9).[2] These theses show that Adeimantus' interest in religion comes from an enlightened point of view, that is, a perspective that requires argumentative consistency to justify such ritual practices. He denounces sacrifices and incantations tailored to acquit crimes as a fraud (364b6–c5), which equally entails a concept of piety compatible with such injustice. His target is the assumption that it is possible to both be unjust and maintain a reputation for justice as long as one shares the goods obtained – a logic that is not exclusive to religion.

Indeed, political associations, such as conspiracies, factions and mobs (365d2-6), follow the same pattern as religious practices. In particular, they take their inspiration from two religious rites: initiation and sacrifice. The first, described by Adeimantus as the most powerful resource (366a8), consists of procedures imposed on individuals willing to join a sect. Sacrifices, in turn, are festive occasions on which the community celebrates its unity and consequently closes itself off to those who are external to it.[3] Through political 'initiation' procedures, factions ensure the secrecy and defence, either by force or by persuasion, of their members against individuals outside the group (365d4–5).[4] Next, they cooperate in order to usurp the goods of the outsiders, in such a way that they are just towards the members of the group and unjust towards others. In this case, the reputation of justice (even if false) is explained by the distribution of the goods that are obtained by injustice among the relevant accomplices. The reputation is false because the outsiders suffer, by means of threats or violence, the effect of their unjust actions. In the end, the illusion of virtue (365c4) is obtained by the association of injustice and cooperation, which together result in what is vulgarly called 'the divine life' (365b7). The cooperative practice of injustice thus enables flourishing understood as the acquisition of Thrasymachean goods (366a3-5), as opposed to the practice of virtue, which is painful (364a4-b2).

Adeimantus defends Thrasymachus' perspective by rejecting Socrates' proof that injustice precludes cooperation (350d5-352b5): the power and money obtained by injustice buy the complicity of others, including the gods. In contradistinction to what Thrasymachus suggests, however, for Adeimantus flourishing entails some correct distribution of the usurped goods among those who practise injustice. Notice that Socrates is very likely caught in this objection when he claims that, although kinship can be expanded among all the Greeks, that is, they may cooperate with each other, it does not occur between Greeks and barbarians (469b8-c2). Without kinship, barbarians are seen as aliens towards whom it is legitimate for the Greeks to practise

---

[2] In these claims, we can see allusions to Gorgias' treatise on non-being (DK 82 B3) and to Protagoras' treatise on the gods (DK 80 B4).

[3] Burkert (1985: 277) emphasizes how initiation rites are used for the cohesion of secret societies, and that the greater the suffering involved in this initiation, the greater the degree of internal solidarity obtained by this group. On the other hand, according to Burkert (1985: 56, 58), as a festive occasion of the community, a sacrifice marks the belonging of human beings to a community: solidarity is obtained when an aggression is carried out communally and guilt is shared. The group thus formed isolates itself from those outside it, and assigns distinct roles to those who integrate it.

[4] On the political associations for injustice, see Vegetti 1998: 161.

injustice. This justifies not only their taking their goods but also enslaving them (469c5-6) – which corresponds almost precisely to what Thrasymachus describes as complete injustice.

When he is about to introduce his account of the parts of soul that would lead to his definition of justice as the cooperative virtue, Socrates mentions that the argumentative path they are pursuing would not give them a rigorous response about the soul having three parts (435c4-d4). This carries implications for the expectation that it would correspond, in its number of parts, to the kinds of human nature that were found in the city (435b4-7). As I understand it, the problem here is that the reason why both a city and a person are just is the form of justice (435b1-2) – a problem that also applies to the other virtues (435b6-7) – and not the number of parts something has. Following the short path helps making it understandable that the cooperation of different people in the city was actually a result of the cooperation of the parts of their soul (obtained by the ruling of reasoning and the moderation of the ends of their desire according to a cooperative model of flourishing), a path which made justice visible for showing how cooperative people may obtain the end of all the parts of their soul. What it did not do, however, was give the reasons that would grant that justice always obtains the good of all, as opposed to injustice which never obtains it. In order to reach such a conclusion, claims Socrates, a longer path is required.

When the longer path is mentioned again in book VI, we learn that it is not a path of argumentation, but a path of learning (504d1) which leads to a different perspective on the matter (504b1-2). For those who go along this path, it is possible to give more rigorous demonstrations (504b3-4), but such demonstrations require a learned audience, while Glaucon and the other interlocutors were already satisfied with the shortcut (435d5-6; 504b5-7).[5] Thus we are introduced to another way of learning what justice is, which does not come from a single conversation, but from a long-term course of studies: in a conversation, we may learn what Socrates proposes as a definition of justice, but we can neither learn how to define things in general, nor how to address more rigorously the problem of what things are (504d6-e2).

The interesting point about this difference of paths is that they do not take people to different places. Rather, we should expect the definition of justice to be the same, though with different ways of accounting for it. The rigorous path entails devoting oneself to this course of learning which leads to knowledge of the form of the good (505a2). This, in turn, allows one to learn the form of justice and thus to give an account of it that does not rely on how many parts a soul has, or how many personalities there are in a city. One can, of course, also take the shortcut and listen to Socrates talking about it as he usually does (505a3), where he insists that it is by learning the form of the good that we can be assured that just things are really beneficial (505a2-4). Socrates undertakes this shortcut explanation of the good, as he did with justice, for the purpose of showing how it is the form of the good (as opposed to someone's good) that accounts for just people being benefitted. One cannot fail to notice that, in doing so, Socrates answers Adeimantus' challenge, to the extent that justice practised according to the form of the good is always beneficial (to everyone).

There are two important features of the good that we must keep in mind when following Socrates' account: the first is that good is basically said of acquired things. Socrates states that

---

[5] A different view claims that the longer path means simply to resort to the form of the good in order to explain why justice is good, and that this is the path Socrates takes in books VI and VII (see Penner 2006: 240, 249; Miller 2007: 310–11). Nonetheless, Socrates insists that his account of the form of the good is not rigorous (506d5-e3), and that the longer path is not a way of arguing for things, but a way of learning things. For the claim that the longer path is mentioned and described, but not taken by Socrates in the Republic; see Rowett 2018: 113, 143–4.

nothing is beneficial to us unless we *acquire* it with the good,⁶ that there is nothing to our acquisitions if they are not good (505a7-b2) and that we even reject the acquisition of things that merely seem to be good without really being so (505d7-8). Acquired goods are items in the world that we turn into our own. They are not necessarily Thrasymachean goods – since, for instance, virtues are a good which is not Thrasymachean. However, they are always a correlative; in other words, they are something that is good for something (or someone). Goods are relative to those who have them; they are, as we saw in T21, connatural, whether regarding individuals, species or kinds. For example, what I call inalienable goods are items required for the flourishing of human beings. These items are good because they allow their owners either to preserve their lives or to flourish. The form of the good, however, is not the peculiar good of someone. It is what is good for every owner, what makes things beneficial to all, according to what each of them naturally is.⁷

The second important feature of Socrates' account is that knowledge of the form of the good is required for our acquisitions to be beneficial to us (505a6-b1). As already discussed, this passage has been called upon to support a mainstream reading that knowledge of the form of the good is required for knowledge of what is good for someone. There is good evidence to suggest that it does not go that far, however. The form of the good is what makes just things beneficial (505a2-4), but not beneficial to only one owner. Rather, they are beneficial to this owner in accordance with what is beneficial to all. This is the difference between knowledge of the form of the good and knowledge of what is good for someone and the parts of their soul. Knowledge of the form of the good allows us to know that the state of affairs obtained by each acquisition of one's good is good to all: it is a knowledge of the all-encompassing and lasting circumstance in which one's acquisition of their particular good is situated. Allow me to explain.

Socrates begins this argument by briefly demonstrating how precarious the common attempts to define the good, which consider it to be either prudence or pleasure, are. It is not a question of denying that prudence is a good (see 357c3), nor that pleasure is a good (see 357b7), but of realizing that neither is coextensive with the good, and that it is not clear what is meant by good in these statements. Prudence is a good for those who have it, but the good is the end of prudent action – the state of affairs it obtains (505b8-10). Pleasure may also be classified as an evil (505c6-8) if, for example, it results in the deterioration of oneself. From these examples, it is evident that, in aiming to acquire these goods, we also aim at the general state of affairs obtained by this acquisition being good for us. If the general state of affairs is good for us, we want it both to be acquired and preserved: to be all-encompassing and lasting are therefore attributes that make our acquisition more truly good – they describe what I would call sustainable goods. The majority of us considers neither whether the general state of affairs that comes about from our actions is good, nor that our actions are interactions with effects on others; in such carelessness, we pursue ends that are not sustainable. Non-sustainable goods, however, fall short of being genuinely good.

Everyone aims at the good (505e1-2).⁸ When we act, we all have the good – a sustainable good that preserves us or makes us flourish – as our end. But in general, we are guessing

---

⁶ For the good as something we acquire and make us good, see Rowe 2007: 131.
⁷ From the fact that the form of the good is what the good really is it does not follow that the good is not the good of a beneficiary (see for instance White 1979: 103; 1986: 43). It is the good of everything taken according to each being. For the defence that the form of the good is the form of benefit, see Wieland 1976: 23; Penner 2007: 31. For a defence of the concept of good as being good *for* something see Adkins 1975: 249–51; Hitchcock 1985: 67; Kraut 2007: 156.
⁸ Some issues about the translation of this sentence were very well addressed by Shorey 1935: 753. On this topic, see Chapter 3, where I argue that, although desire is not based on beliefs, every action that pursues the end determined by desire is based on a belief that its end is good.

(*apomanteuomenē*, 505e2) that something in the world corresponds to this real good. Our soul moves towards what we *believe* to be a good, even when we are following our unreasonable beliefs. This belief may, of course, not correspond to the good that is truly beneficial (505d7-9). Thus though we may trust that our action will provide us sustainable goods, this may fail (505e1-4). It is possible, on the other hand, to have a belief about the good that actually leads us to obtain goods, such as when we follow certain shared beliefs about the good that are true. In this case, we obtain genuinely good things without actually being able to justify why they are good (506c7-9). This is a form of heteronomy, since more complex or extraordinary circumstances cause the agents to be lost in the identification of their good, like the soul of popular virtue in the myth of Er. Beliefs about the good, when they are not grounded in knowledge of the good, make us susceptible to errors; it is only knowledge of the good that makes us capable of always pursuing sustainable goods.

Note that the error described here relates neither to the lack of knowledge of the circumstances of the action, nor to some relevant information that could change the qualification of the object involved in the end of our action. Rather, the error here is the one in which, once the possible courses of action are clear and transparent, we still fail to obtain a good because we do not understand what a good state of affairs to obtain actually is. Thus knowledge of the form of the good is important to identify what we wish to obtain and what our flourishing is in order to avoid this type of error about the end of the action. Knowledge of the form of the good does not, however, prevent errors that are circumstantial to each choice and that concern how objects appear to us (see 516e7-517a4, 517c6-d2). For this, different abilities are required, such as accurate perception, informed judgement of appearances, and other factors involved in the cognition of objects. Should these fail, a bad state of affairs may follow despite knowledge of the good.[9] But this is not the error Socrates is concerned with when dealing with the form of the good. Rather, his concern is about the legislative foundation of political deliberations (506a9-b1) which gives us a natural standard about what is good for each of us, that includes everyone and every good and that determines how to distribute the goods in a sustainable order. The form of the good is relevant to answering Adeimantus' challenge because it is, as I proceed to explain, the natural law about ends.[10]

Socrates' shortcut explanation of the form of the good consists of an analogy that became known as the simile of the sun (507b8-509d5). The argument is based on a singular trait of vision and intellection as powers (507c6-8, 507e5-508a1, b6), which consists in including a third factor (507d1) in addition to the agent and the object, which acts as a link or connection (507e5-508a2). In the case of vision, this factor is light (507d10-508a2), which connects, like a piece of a puzzle, the colour that is always present in eyes (507d11) with the one present in external things (507e1).[11] Vision is chosen as an image of the intellect to the detriment of hearing because (i) it happens by connection (508a1); (ii) something, the sun, responds to this connection (508a4-6); and (iii) the elements for connection are always present in the things connected (507d10-e1). When there is no light, these colours are not visible and we are therefore not able to discern objects by colour

---

[9] About the form of the good not being sufficient for knowledge of particular circumstances, see Rowe 2007: 132; Smith 2010: 97.
[10] On the form of the good and legislation, see Shorey 1895: 239; Wieland 1976: 24–5; Lane 2013: 112.
[11] I disagree with Adam (1902: II, 60) and Delcomminette (2008: 37) that there is something in the simile that corresponds to a distinction between exercise (of vision and intellect) and capacity (of seeing and thinking). I suggest that the powers are activated simply by contact with the third factor. This matters for a better understanding of 518c4-d1 that states that our education depends simply on the *turn* to reality and the good.

contrast. Thus we do not see any*thing* (507e1), although we may still see the colours internal to the eyes. If there is light, however, different colours are perceived and we are able to see objects. If things are illuminated by the glare of the night, they are poorly differentiated; we see unclearly and objects are inadequately identified (508c4-7). Light thus provides us a whole visual field, a connection between the sun, the eyes and the objects themselves in their variety, which makes them distinguishable by contrast according to their own shape and colour. What the third factor does, therefore, is produce a unity out of otherwise discrete entities, and identify what each is within this whole.

Intellect is explained in these same parameters. Here, the thesis is that, like vision in the eyes, intellect is always present within us, even in the lack of 'light' (518b8-c1, d5-6, compare with 507d10-e1): it may turn to nothing, to some poorly differentiated items which come to be and perish, or to the real state of affairs through which we may identify things as what they are (508d3-8).[12] Socrates names this third-factor truth (508d4)[13] which, in the same way as light, provides a whole field wherein all objects of knowledge are connected to each other and to every knower, all of whom previously endowed with 'connectors'. Truth is reality as an interconnected whole; the state of affairs of essences. It is all-encompassing and unperishable. Truth is thus what philosophers strive for in turning their learning towards all intellectual objects.

The object of philosophical knowledge, Socrates has previously remarked (485a10-b8), is all-encompassing in two senses: systematically and temporally. Learning the essence of everything (*pasēs ousias*, 486a9) is not simply a case of assimilating a series of items, but placing each of them within the world as we know it. We grasp reality as an all-encompassing and organized whole (see *tou holou kai pantos*, 486a5) and the end of philosophy is to understand and explain it. Read in a certain way, this statement makes it seem like a task that goes beyond the limits of human life. On the other hand, we learn about the world in an organized way so that, whatever stage of learning we are at, everything we have previously learned forms a unity of interrelations. In this sense, philosophy is seldom about discovering new items in the world, that is, learning something in the strict sense of the word. It is primarily about understanding the connections between things already learned. That is to say, it is about mapping the relations between essences,

---

[12] What is clear in this passage, is that the sun analogy does not consider the visible as the analogue of the object of beliefs – as was supposed in the jargon of Platonism and against which Ferguson (1921, 1922) presented compelling arguments (see also Raven 1953: 23). The simile, of course, treats beliefs as an analogue of blurred vision, an imperfect form of intellection of unclear truth. For the thesis that belief and intellection are the same power turned to different things, see 518c4-d2.

[13] Adam (1902: II, 60) assumes truth as the analogue of light, whereas another line of interpreters, such as Joseph (1948: 16); Ferber (1989: 61); Szaif (1998: 132–51); Vegetti (1998: 89); Ferrari (2003: 302); Baltes (1997: 356–7), claim that there is no analogue of light in intellection, and truth should be considered as equivalent to 'being'. I reject the latter account in favour of Adam's for different reasons: the first is that vision was chosen as the power similar to intellection (in detriment of hearing) because of the third factor (507d1), which is the connecting element, light (508a1-2). When Socrates details the analogy at 507d10-508a3, he emphasizes both light and truth in order to draw inferences at 508e5-509a2 (see also 517c1-3). Truth comes to the scene as that which illuminates (508d3-4). Truth is neither the sun, nor the objects of knowledge, for the whole point was that visible objects needed to be illuminated (507d12-e1), therefore the best reading for 508d3-4 is 'when it fixes itself on what truth illuminates, i.e., being'. I suggest that the notion of a state of affairs that connects forms with the soul according to laws of nature is a more appropriate interpretation of the sense of truth here. For truth as referring to state of affairs and knowledge as a pictorial grasping of it, see Rowett 2018: 34, 36. As for the controversy, I find particularly interesting the opposition between Ferber and Natorp. As Ferber understands the form of the good (instead of truth, as I argued here) as a third between forms and intellect, he criticizes Natorp (1903: 187) for having claimed that the form of the good was the law of pure thinking. Ferber argues that an intermediary third cannot be a law, but only a condition of possibility (Ferber 1989: 61–2, see also Krämer 1969: 122). This kind of priority suggested by Ferber is based on the claim that the form of the good is not an essence, and it belongs to what he calls 'Plato's Metaontology' (Krämer 1969: 69). My reasons for avoiding this position are in note 15 below.

and this justifies why there is always something yet to be explained. This is the exercise of intelligence (*noēsis*, 511d8), also called contemplation (*theōria*, see 486a8).

As to the second characteristic, philosophy aims at understanding this systematic reality from the perspective of a totality of time (486a8-10). To know what something is, its *ousia*, entails knowing what is proper and particular to it at whatever point in time (*ekeinēs tēs ousias tēs aei ousēs*, 485b1-2), past, present or future. This object of knowledge is not subject to change (485b2-3), as it is 'what maintains itself in the same way according to the same things' (484b5). And so, this systematic reality remains the same in respect to all its items and their relation to each other. This establishes what is necessarily true in the world, or what we would today call the laws of nature. The reality the philosopher aims to know is not something that has passed away, exists or will happen, but what is there in all these occasions (see 490a8-b7) – and not something in particular, but everything, the whole of truth (485d3-4). So, truth is neither a single form, nor a property of forms, but the connection of all forms in a complete state of affairs, even if one may also refer to truth as the 'connector' every form has as an item of this whole.

The intriguing thing about the analogy between vision and intellect is that, although it begins by emphasizing that vision and intelligence are special due to their third factor, its focus is not on these elements (on light and truth), rather on a fourth: the sun and the form of the good as the explanatory principles (see *aitios* at 508b9 and *aitia* at 508e2) of the presence of light and truth respectively. There are two different reasons for the fourth factor to be such a principle. One is that it grounds the connective powers of vision and intellect; the other is that it grounds their preservation. In other words, the fourth element explains both the systematic and the temporal inclusiveness of the state of affairs of truth. The first reason is the following:

> [T36] So you are to say that the form of the good provides truth to what is known and gives power to the knower. Being therefore the explanatory principle of knowledge and truth, you should think of it as an object of knowledge,[14] which nonetheless you are to consider as fairer than knowledge and truth, even if they are themselves fair. Just as we correctly take light and vision as solar, even though it is not correct to consider them to be the sun, it is correct to take knowledge and truth as good-like, but not to consider them as the good, for the possession of the good is something to be considered far more valuable. (508d10-509a5)

According to T36, the form of the good explains both the truth of the known object and our power to know. To give truth to an object of knowledge may seem to contradict what I have stated previously about the role of truth; however, this is accounted for by the analogy. If truth is the state of affairs of essences, to give truth to the object of knowledge – the being of these things – is to insert them in such an all-encompassing field. As for our power to know, since it is intrinsic to the soul, we can suppose that it is the good that motivates the soul to know. As indicated in Chapter 4, the intellectual investigation has its origin in a conflict about the real good of the soul in circumstances of perplexity, so that the judgement of what is good for us precedes our acquisition of knowledge. This is how the form of the good grounds knowledge.

T36 also stresses that the form of the good is a form, an object of knowledge with its own unity (see also 507a7-b10, T11 in Chapter 4). The form of the good is not what is good in each

---

[14] Here I follow the reading proposed by Slings (2005: 111–12), based on the best manuscripts, against Adam's modification (1902: II, 61)

case, nor what makes a particular thing good for some other individual. This is important to understand why T21 (Chapter 9) is not about the form of good, but about the good connatural (and therefore relative) to something. Nonetheless, connatural goods explain how essence and good go together: every good either enhances or preserves something *according to its being*. The form of the good itself is the unity of all such peculiar goods, and this is why it is a *sui generis* object of knowledge. It encompasses the relation of everything to everything that allows for the preservation and the flourishing of each of them. The form of the good is the all-encompassing and unchangeable unity of all particular goods.

Moreover T36 claims that, while the form of the good is both an object of knowledge and the explanatory principle of truth and of our knowledge, it should not be mistaken for either one of them. As for knowledge, the argument is simple: the form of the good is not our knowledge for the same reason prudence was not the form of the good: there is a necessary distinction between a power and its objects. As for the distinction from truth, some interpreters have seen a formulation similar to Russel's paradox here: the form of the good is a member of the set of objects of knowledge, but it is also a member of the higher-class set that contains the explanatory principle of objects of knowledge.[15] I think that Plato has something less problematic in mind. If there is a form for everything we know, there are also forms of relations, which, in their turn, also apply to forms. This does not make them another class of forms; rather, they are simply forms that explain relations. This is the case of the form of the good: it is a form on its own, but prior to the others for being the cause of their set. In the simile of the sun, the connection between the four factors is explained by the affinity in kind among them: the eyes, the visible objects, the light and the sun connect to each other because they are all 'solar' (508a9-b11), what I termed their 'connectors'. Such an affinity must occur in the intellectual connection also: they are 'good' because it is the form of the good that explains that this connection can happen. This is why T36 says it is fairer than all the other factors involved in knowledge. I conclude that the form of the good explains the systematic inclusiveness of truth.

As mentioned, there is also a further way in which the form of the good is similar to the sun. This is the text:

> [T37] You will say, I believe, that the sun not only gives things seen the power to be seen, but also their generation, growth and nurture, although it is not itself generation.
> How would it be?
> Therefore, it seems that the good not only makes knowing connected to known things, but it also adds being and essence to them. The being of the good is not essence, but something to the furthermost side of essence, which stands out from it in priority and power. (509b1-9)

The sun promotes life cycles, making it possible for living beings not only to be born but also to grow, nourish themselves and achieve their development. The sun is part of the explanation of how living beings are preserved. This is different from how the sun is part of the explanation of vision, which depends on the difference between the absence and the presence of the sun and

---

[15] For the Russell's paradox, see Ferber 1989: 62; Seel 2007: 109. I see the paradox holds for those who hold that properties of forms are higher-level forms (see Owen 1968; Vlastos 1965: 9–12; Santas [1980]1999: 254–5, Ferrari 2003: 310–12). I think the premise is controversial. As I understand it, forms are postulated as the being of things, and not themselves as things. The properties of forms are simply what they are, grounded on the relation they hold to each other in forming the state of affairs of reality. There cannot be a set of forms which exclude any form, for the only set of forms there is, is reality. This is not to deny that an enquiry may set some forms aside out of its field of knowledge, but this is precisely postulating the principles of a specific knowledge. If I am right 'higher or lower levels' are relations between forms, and not classes of forms.

its light. This temporary absence, nevertheless, does not preclude life, as it does with vision, a feature that, emphasized in the simile, accounts for the second explanatory role of the good: the sun is similar to the form of the good not only for the connection but also for the preservation they both provide.

A good preserves or makes things flourish. The form of the good is thus what explains how beings are preserved and why their flourishing is interconnected – the being of the good is not the essence of things (for each essence is of one thing),[16] but it is something of the essence, the way such essence relates to others so that it is preserved. If the form of the good is a relation between forms, it therefore accounts for the preservation of this all-encompassing interrelation. Reality holds because it is good; it would perish otherwise. The form of the good thus accounts for the idea that there is one true and unchangeable state of affairs of reality, and describes what we would call a law of nature. It is for this reason that it is not something otherworldly, but the connection of essences among themselves, forming a unity that is grounded in what they are.

Though the form of the good accounts for the essence of things (because the good preserves the essence), the good is not itself the essence, but something to the furthermost side of essence,[17] that explains its preservation. This idea of 'something of the essence' is reiterated throughout the dialogue in expressions such as 'the brighter aspect of being' (518c9); 'being in its maximal flourishing' (526e4-5); 'the best among the beings' (532c6-7). I understand that the conclusion of T37 take the form of the good as a grounding principle of an unchanging and all-encompassing reality that holds due to the interrelation of essences. This is an ontological priority to the effect that the state of affairs of reality is such *because* it is good. The good preserves the reality, as the interrelation each form has to each other does not change, neither for the better, nor for the worse. Reality is a good order, and it is good because it is itself grounded in the form of the good.

Interpreters are often puzzled by the fact that Socrates grounds truth in the form of the good, and not something like the form of being. There are two common explanations to account for this choice. The first is that the truth of things is good for us;[18] the second is that the truth of each thing depends on a system.[19] I reject both of these positions. The first of them entails an extrinsic teleology; that is, it states that the reason for the being of something is to be the good of something else. As I understand it, the concept of peculiar goods is committed to the rejection of extrinsic teleology as a peculiar good does not define one's good by the essence of others, but by one's own essence. Moreover, this interpretation mistakes the claim that truth is grounded in

---

[16] In assuming that T37 claims both that the form of the good is not a form and that it is beyond forms, some interpreters claim that Socrates denies that it has a unity and that it is knowable. For the description of the form of the good as a specific arrangement of forms, see Joseph 1948: 18–19; Irwin 1977: 225, 1995: 272; McCabe 1994: 72–3; Fine 1990: 98–9. For the form of the good as being unknowable and object of an intuition, see Cornford 1932: 49; Ferber 1989: 154–60. Baltes (1997: 353–6) gives ten different arguments to demonstrate that the form of the good is an object of knowledge.

[17] The adverb *epekeina*, in my view, has here the same meaning as its nominal form *to ep' ekeina* in the myth of the *Phaedo*. There Socrates describes the surface of the Earth as having different types of craters, some deeper, some not, which form different terrestrial regions. The earth's rivers, says Socrates, all originate from a single opening on this crust and their direction is determined both by the terrain through which they pass, and by the airs and winds in the region: 'For [the air and the winds] accompany it [the flow of water] when it flows to the furthermost side (*eis to ep'ekeina*) or to this side of the Earth' (Plato, *Phaedo*, 112b4-6). What we see here is that *to ep'ekeina* does not denote something beyond the Earth, but something in the Earth, which is situated at the opposite point to some point of reference. If the rivers of the *Phaedo*'s myth still flow on Earth, there is no reason to suppose that the good is anything beyond forms, but a certain 'furthermost side of them', the locative sense being obviously metaphorical. For the form of the good as something of the essence, see Ferrari 2003: 314; Rowe 2007: 149.

[18] Denyer 2007: 307 ascribes an extrinsic teleology to Plato.

[19] Fine 1990: 110, 115 argues that truth depends solely on interrelation.

the form of the good for the claim that truth is good for us, which amounts to taking the form of the good for a particular good.

I would call the second position the 'system's explanatory priority', which supposes the form of the good to be the whole that explains each of the forms. The problem with this interpretation lies in the assumption that forms are explained by the whole – an assumption that goes against Socrates' commitment to the principle that a form explains what something is. If something is only explained by the relation between all the forms, science and expertise, which are all based on specific forms, could not exist. My view therefore differs from this position because I claim that the good grounds the interconnection of essences, and not what each essence is. I do not claim that the essence of things depends on a system; rather, that truth is a system in which the essences of things are interconnected. In this sense, Socrates would be a foundationalist about appearances (they must be explained by forms) and a coherentist about forms (they must be explained by each other). The form of the good grounds the necessity of these interrelations, providing a law of nature.[20]

There is an epistemic version of this interpretation that claims knowledge of the form of the good is required for the knowledge of every other form.[21] Knowledge of the form of the good is, of course, required to give an account of why virtues are beneficial (505a3-4) and to establish that the good one pursues must be a sustainable good (505a6-b2). Nonetheless, one can perfectly know forms without knowing all of them, as in the case of experts who do not have a perspective of the whole of reality but ground their actions on the knowledge of some forms. According to the principle of organization between forms, the form of the good is the object required for a much more restricted knowledge: the one that allows us to give reasons about everything. I would like to claim that one can perfectly know some forms – be an expert about them, be able to give reasons about what concerns them – and that this is not the same as knowledge of the form of the good.

It is time to come back to Adeimantus' objection, which challenged Socrates to demonstrate that justice was sufficient to engender piety. In the formulation I have offered, this amounts to claiming that justice cannot be a cooperative action that usurps the goods from others, and sustains itself through the force of factions. The response to this objection is that cooperation must aim at an all-encompassing and sustainable state of affairs in which the good of all agents obtains; in order to make this feasible, we must pursue ends that are in accordance with the form of the good, that is, all-encompassing, sustainable and real goods. It is not necessary for us to know why they are such qualified goods ourselves; it is acceptable simply to follow guidelines given by someone else who does know the form of the good. This, however, requires legislation.

If legislation intends to promote the flourishing of all citizens, and if the form of the good responds to how beings in general are best related, the knowledge required for legislation is quite simply knowledge of the form of the good. Legislation is therefore an expertise that has the form of the good as its object (see 504c6-d3), that is, the form which explains how the city can be sustainable, as well as how it can flourish cooperatively, without depriving anyone of their proper being. The object of legislation is thus the same object the philosopher pursues in their love of wisdom. This is the theme of the next chapter.

---

[20] For the form of the good as what connects the whole world, see Kosman 2005: 159; Rowe 2007: 130. For it being the relation between forms, see Seel 2007: 182-3. I should add a note about the consequences of Socrates' teleology for his theory of justice. Since the form of the good is both (i) what provides us the good and (ii) what restricts our good; his position can be taken neither as a consequentialist nor as a deontological theory. It is not deontological because good is prior to right; it is not consequentialist because good cannot be maximized in whichever way one decides to. See Annas 1981: 60-4; Santas 1985: 225.

[21] For this claim, see Adam 1902: II, 53; Penner 2007: 33.

15

Philosopher-King

It is clear by now that the form of the good is the object of the expertise of legislation, and that ruling on this basis is what allows for obtaining the right distribution of peculiar goods. Justice is cooperative virtue or excellence (*aretē*), but, for it to obtain cooperative flourishing (*eudaimonia*), its end must be a sustainable good, that is, all-encompassing and lasting. Though the education in *mousikē* and gymnastics is sufficient for teaching us to pursue this good, it is not sufficient for us to know what it is, in which case our flourishing depends on legislation on education grounded in the form of the good, and on ruling that ensures citizens only aim at and obtain sustainable goods. If this kind of legislation and ruling is required for justice (as Adeimantus' challenge pointed out), it is necessary to revise what has previously been said about the rulers (502e2-3, referring to 412b9-417b9 and 428d6-429a4).

Socrates has already argued for specific character features required of rulers: they must be older (412c3), prudent, have the power to obtain their ends, take care of the city and love it (412c13-d3), be able to deliberate well due to their knowledge (428b5-8) and have a knowledge of what is best for the entire city (428c11-d3). Due to these requirements, rulers and auxiliaries must be tested throughout their lives (see 412e4-5, 413e1, 503a5-6) against the pleasures and pains in situations of stress, fear and adversity (503a1-4, 503c8–d1), to ascertain whether they are committed to doing only what is good for the *politeia* (412e6-7); in short, to prove they are lovers of the city (*philopolis*, 503a1). If knowledge of the form of the good is a requirement for such rulers, they must also be philosophers who have undertaken the longer path of education. This has become known as the Philosopher-King thesis.

I would like to propose a distinction between the Philosopher-King and the Kallipolis thesis. Kallipolis is an ordinary city name Socrates uses (527c2) to refer to a political system in which philosophers legislate and rule, which is constitutive of the *Republic*'s theory of justice. This is the theme of the next chapter. The Philosopher-King thesis, however, is a constituent strategy for Kallipolis to occur, which, I emphasize, is not the only means for it. Indeed, although it is the one Socrates favours, it proves to be highly unlikely. This is the theme of this chapter, which begins with one of the most celebrated passages of the *Republic*:

[T38] Unless either philosophers are kings in cities or those now called kings or dynasts philosophize in a genuine and satisfactory way, [unless] these two things, political power and philosophy, coincide in the same bearer, and thus the many natures which now proceed in their activities separately and on their own are prevented by imposition from doing it, there will be no respite of evils, my dear Glaucon, in cities, not even, it seems to me, in humankind. The very *politeia* which we now detail in arguments will not come to be for the first time, not even as far as possible, and will not see the light of the sun. (473c11-e1, my brackets)

An important tradition takes the Philosopher-King thesis as the synthesis of the political project proposed by Socrates in the *Republic*, that would come down to an autocratic political form in which philosophical knowledge would be sufficient to rule over all other citizens. According to these authors, the dialogue would not be concerned with issues such as legitimacy, political participation, citizenship or institutions, under the assumption that philosophers would take it upon themselves to determine all these issues and impose them on the other citizens.[1] From this perspective, what T38 calls 'political power' is total control over means and people, which would therefore strip the citizens of all freedom and responsibility to care for themselves; on this reading, we would do very well to abandon the Platonic political project – especially after the political experiences of the twentieth and twenty-first centuries.

An analysis of the form of T38, however, gives us several reasons not to take this as the last word on the issue. The proposal is formulated as a conditional: *if* X is not done, the just *politeia* will not occur, and evil will not cease. This form shows that X is not the political project, but the way the project can be implemented. Indeed, there are two alternatives for X – either imposing philosophy on kings or dynasts, or imposing kingship on philosophers, both of which are merged together into the 'Philosopher-King' thesis as Socrates' answer to Glaucon's question about the feasibility, the real possibility, of the just *politeia* (471c4-7). In Chapter 5, we saw that explanations of feasibility are based on power: there must be an agent with the power to obtain a certain end in adequate circumstances. Furthermore, we also saw that explanations based on power allow for degrees in obtaining the end as long as one also gives an account about the circumstances that precluded full accomplishment. This leads us to Socrates' methodological observation:

> [T39] But is something to be accomplished just like it is said? Or is nature such that action touches truth less than speech, even if some do not think so? Do you agree or not?
> I agree, he said.
> Then do not force me to show that it [the just *politeia*] will happen in deeds exactly like we have described in argument. Instead if we shall find out how a city can be founded the closest to what was described, we shall say we found what you demanded: that it is feasible [it has the power to happen]. (473a1-b1, my brackets)

There are several interpreters who have assumed that T39 is committed to an incommensurability between being and becoming, that is, for ontological reasons, no historical just city corresponds to what a just city in arguments is. From this perspective, Socrates appears in T38 as taking a compromise position, indicating that concessions must be made in the model of the just *politeia* so that it may become feasible, as justice as such is unattainable.[2] I would like to note that Socrates does not say that justice in deeds is inferior to justice in reason. Rather, he says that action gets less in touch with truth than reason. This may mean, as I shall argue, that it touches it *less often*. If we remember that truth is the real state of affairs preserved by the good, we see that every action aims at truth – the soul always moves towards the good. Actually, this was the argument that granted the form of the good to be the principle of knowledge and truth. However, because most of us only guess at what the good is, in general, actions fail. This is not to say that action

---

[1] For Plato's authoritarian approach in politics, see Arendt 1958: 227; Popper [1945]1966: 22; Bambrough 1962: 103; Leys 1965; Sparshott 1967; Frede 1996: 259-69; Brown 1998: 24; Blössner 2007: 366-72; Annas 2011: 105 ff.; Hitz 2010: 125.
[2] For the claim that justice is unattainable for ontological reasons, see Strauss 1964: 119; Laks 1990: 215-16; Zuolo 2009: 60-4; Fronterotta 2010: 132; Lacroix 2014: 143-4; Smith 2019: 7.

never touches truth, as the aforementioned interpreters claim. It is simply that, because they also involve desire and conflicts, actions do so less often – that is, only when ruled by reasoning.

If we are not to expect that action *always* obtains the real good, we must determine what is the feasibility of the just city, not by simply stating what it is, but by *adding* something to it that ensures that the good state of the city always obtains.[3] With this addition, it will not correspond exactly to what was previously described, but it will be close enough. This interpretation also fits better Socrates' method henceforward. Indeed, there is no evidence of any kind of concession made by Socrates to make his theory of justice feasible by approximation. Rather, here is his proposal:

> [T40] After that, it seems, we shall try to search and demonstrate what is it that is done badly in the cities so that they are not settled accordingly, and what would be the smallest change that would lead a city to this mode of political life (*politeia*), *preferably* a single one; if it is not [sufficient], two; if still not [sufficient], then the smallest number of them and the least regarding power (*tēn dunamin*). (473b4-9, my emphasis, my brackets)

As T40 points out, the first stage of the method is the diagnosis of evil. Having identified the problem, therapy will then be prescribed: philosophers shall become kings or kings philosophers. The change is not applied to the proposal about justice, only to the current state of affairs. Moreover, there are other healing methods, whether through smaller or bigger changes, in which many remedies are necessary. Socrates nevertheless states a preference for minimally invasive treatment or the minimal number of changes that require the least concerning power.[4] This is a pacifist alternative, preferable because, as I shall indicate, it avoids conflicts, seditions or revolutions, and demands a change only in the way people think and behave. As the analysis of the forms of evil in Chapter 9 has shown us, new *politeiai* arise from sedition. Nonetheless, this means to obtain change would be incoherent with a *politeia* committed to the cooperation among its citizens, hence why a pacifist alternative is so important.

This alternative entails a strict concept of 'king'. One obvious restriction, which is also a difference from the Kallipolis project, is that the king must be one in number, so that the change of mindset of only one individual would be enough for a substantial political change. This means

---

[3] For the 'philosopher-king' as an addition required for the feasibility of the city, see Barker 1918: 197; Vegetti 2000b: 336.

[4] What 'power' means here is controversial. One group of interpreters understands that *tēn dunamin* is the power of the aforementioned change and translates it as something like 'its effects' (see for instance Shorey 1930: I,507; Vegetti 2000c: 88; Leroux 2002: 300; Allen 2006: 179; Emlyn-Jones and Preddy 2013: 539). This does not seem to make much sense; after all, in his next statement Socrates says that the change is neither small nor easy (473c3-4). If the change is to be the implementation of a different *politeia*, its effects will certainly be great and not 'the smallest'. A second group reads the *tēn dunamin* as 'what is possible', looking forward to *dunatou* at 473c4, sometimes redoubling its meaning as something like 'the smallest effect as possible' (see Grube 1974: 133; Griffith 2000: 175). From this point of view, change must be the one that is most easily obtained, given the difficulty inherent to the city's feasibility. Although this is compatible with the interpretation I suggest, there is a version of this interpretation that I would like to reject, namely, the one that supposes that being possible entails concessions regarding the previous project. Besides the reasons I already put forward, the difficulty of this interpretation is how to establish a sufficient minimum condition according to which the city is just 'by approximation'. What is the boundary that separates the 'it's almost just but it is still unjust' stage from the 'it's just now' stage? On this problem, see Morrison 2007: 236. The reading I advocate, connects *tēn dunamin* to the political power mentioned in T38, and has the advantage of not having the term *dunamis* change its meaning in such a short interval. As I read it Socrates offers a single change – the smallest in number – which has great effects, preserves the project intact, but is the minimal regarding the political power established in the city where change happens.

that the concentration of political power is what is really at stake in the preference for a king.[5] The change is smaller in a city without opposing parties, and harm is reduced if there is no sedition. Another restriction is that the king must be a ruler acknowledged as good by the ruled. As Socrates will go on to explain, this proposal will work only if the king is someone who takes care of the citizens, in a city in which the citizens listen to him in return (499b6-7); kings cannot be tyrants but must have a government established on the basis of care and hearkening (see 502b3-4).[6] In this circumstance, claims Socrates, when the king proposes a change in the *politeia*, there will be those who protest (501c5-6). But upon receiving arguments about the justice and benefit of the proposals, they will be persuaded. Persuasion about what is best to be done is therefore capable of generating cooperation (501c5–d6) and is the smallest change in regard to political power on account of the city in which it takes place. Peaceful and minimal change arises from a specific *politeia* called a kingdom or dynasty (473c11-d2; 499b7-8; 502a5-6).

Up to this point I have argued that, due to the requirement that they be kings, philosopher-kings as changemakers would only be found in very few cities. I shall now proceed to show that the requirements for a *politeia* in which they will occur are higher still due to the requirement that they also be philosophers, against which there are two major difficulties: first, educating a philosopher to know the form of the good; second, to find a philosopher willing to rule. Let us begin with the first.

Socrates' thesis is that people able to flourish cooperatively are those educated by gymnastics and *mousikē* since childhood (441e7-442a2), an education that must be given to us before we reach the age of reason. The most relevant factor in our flourishing, the habit acquired in childhood, can therefore never be chosen by us. It is necessarily received from others and, in the case of a just *politeia*, received from the city. Notice that this is not a problem for the education of personalities that are not just. As evidenced in Chapter 9, the latter result from an identity conflict when youths reach the age of reason. It is therefore simply coherent that Socrates aims to avoid these kinds of conflict while educating cooperative personalities. A just person is thus the one that grows up in an environment that habituates them to mores based on sustainable goods, so that there will be no conflict when they come of age (see 401b1-402a4, T29 in Chapter 12). If just people depend on a just *politeia* to come to be, they must therefore be preceded by other just people: if a just person cannot come to be in a non-just environment, there exists an infinite regress that will never lead us out of any situation of injustice.

Philosophy is central to Socrates' response to this difficulty. Chapter 6 introduced us to the philosopher as a personality resulting from the channelling of desires and the consequent absence of internal conflict. After an understanding of the concept of natural tendencies furnished by the argument on women in Chapter 13, we may now point out that the channelling

---

[5] Benson (2015: 209) assumes that what Socrates wants to prove is that philosophy is ruling expertise. This would have Socrates begging the question by proving what philosophy is, instead of showing how a just *politeia* is *feasible*. The real difficulty is how a philosopher can prevail over others and, moreover, how power would be conceded to him, that is, having others agreeing with his proposal of pursuing only real good. To put it in terms of the ship–state analogy, it is a given that the philosopher is the best captain, but the challenge is how the sailormen would ever recognize him as such.

[6] It matters that the ruler is a *basileus*, and not simply a *monarchos*, which in the *Republic* refers exclusively to the tyrant (575a2, 576b7). The proposal in the *Republic* therefore differs from the one in the *Laws* (710b4-d5) that states that a prudent tyrant would be the best solution because it is the fastest way to do it (for the approximation between the two texts, see Schofield 1988: 40; Georgini 2009: 126). Kingdoms and dynasties are used interchangeably (473c11-d2; 499b7-8; 502a5-6), for dynasties are simply kingdoms over a succession of generations. Neither enters in the classification of evil forms of ruling (see 544d1-2).

of desire of the philosophical personality is a natural tendency of some individuals. People with this nature learn easily, have good memory and make inferences very quickly – learning is not for them the effort that it is for most people (486c3-d3). In contrast to most human beings, philosophers tend naturally to have an obsession (*eros*) with understanding reality and truth (see T16a, T16b, T17, 474c8-11; 475b8-c5, 485d3-e1, 501d1-2), and the wisdom they desire is not simply knowledge of this or that, like the experts who know some specific form. Rather, their desire is for wisdom as a whole, or, better put, wisdom of all the forms (475b5-9). As we saw in the last chapter, this is an all-encompassing and lasting kind of knowledge: the knowledge of the form of the good.

If a philosopher can be virtuous independently of the *politeia* in which they live, and if they may follow their obsession until they reach the knowledge of the good, the problem of the infinite regress of education is solved. But is it quite this simple? Can a philosopher actually live in a city and practise virtue *in spite of* the city? The question takes on more intense contours if we think of justice: can they really be just without interacting with people around them? Indeed, it is not that simple. The reason for this is that the environment (be it a good *politeia* or a bad one) educates all the children, including those with philosophical tendencies. No one is an island, and dependency is more intense in relation to children and youths.

Natural tendency to philosophy is a double-edged sword for philosophers themselves. Learning is such an important skill that may be employed to many different ends, and the same holds for the philosopher's easiness to learn. It is expected that those around a philosophical youth would encourage them to use it for practical purposes. Corrupted *politeiai* offer occasion for particularly devastating versions of this story that result in the corruption of this promising youth (see 487c4–d5). An extraordinary feature of the *Republic*'s argument is that its corruption is not caused by the sophists (492a5–b4), who are but a symptom of a much more fundamental problem. The real cause of the corruption is the education these youths receive from the citizens in general, that is, what Glaucon terms 'the majority'. The sophists do nothing more than teach certain individuals (who pay them) ways to manage and dominate these people in the public sphere (493a6–c8). The attitude of the people in these circumstances is the real cause of the corruption of others (492b6–c9).

Public opinion, as expressed in assemblies, courts, theatres, armies, etc., comes in the form of praise or reproach of the multitude. When an individual is the target of such manifestation, there is little hope: no individual contradicts the majority (492c4-7), as public opinion conveys the *politeia*'s own criterion of virtue (492c7-9).[7] Against individuals who challenge these shared beliefs, the majority has the power of imposing the greatest *anankē* (492d2-7), also called the *anankē* of Diomedes (493d5-6): political coercion by force. One may recall that, in general, law against constitutional crime prescribes the loss of political participation and property rights, as well as the death penalty. As we saw in the analysis of the political forms of evil, rulers use power devices to obtain their ends, and it is not difficult to deduce how they are employed to make their citizens follow a certain way of life that grants the preservation of such a *politeia*.

It is quite true that this passage on the corruption of the philosophical nature by public opinion describes a democratic setting (specifically, an Athenian setting), about which I would

---

[7] I see here evidence for what Gill calls 'the communal foundation of ethical development': 'it is difficult and perhaps impossible for anyone to develop reasonableness and ethical virtue if she has not been brought up in a community guided by reasonable principles' (Gill 1996: 273).

like to make a brief note. Though it does not need to be the only one, democracy is a good case study for a purpose parallel to the one addressed here. The point is that the institutions of the public sphere (assemblies, courts, theatres, armies, etc.) made Athenians famous for their love of learning, as mentioned in T1. In making this claim about the relation of an individual and a *politeia*, however, Socrates points out that Athenian democracy does not qualify as a genuinely philosophical *politeia*. Rather, what happens in these institutions actually prevents people from pursuing wisdom. They do not allow for the kind of listening and hearkening Socrates thought would be present in a kingdom. Instead, they preclude both the use of the dialogue that aims towards agreement about the good and the philosophical use of reasoning because they encourage decisions that aim at the pleasure of the majority (493c10-d3). They also undertake processes of decision-making that are not useful in moving towards an understanding of what is truly fair and good (493d7–e1). What is lacking in democracy is an institution of dialogue for understanding what the good is.

Leaving the case of Athens aside to return to our point, the general thesis is that other citizens may miseducate the youths of philosophical aptitude in two ways: they make them employ their power of learning before its full development, interrupting the process; and make them employ it not towards knowledge but in acquiring political power (494c1-2; 7-d1). The fact that political power is the object of the love of tyrants (see 565d9-e1) shows how devastating the corruption of a philosophical nature can be.[8] The philosophical nature may develop into the greatest good, but also in the greatest evil for a city (495b3-6). The reason is that it is not enough for a philosopher to be naturally disposed to virtue, they must be educated if not in a fair environment, then at least in isolation from a corruptive one.

As previously mentioned, the requirements for a *politeia* to produce philosophers that are not miseducated are high. Insisting nonetheless that the Philosopher-King proposal is still feasible, Socrates points to two cases of self-educated philosophers. The first is that of Theages (496b6-c3)[9] who, with all the aptitudes for philosophy, managed to avoid his own corruption due to the intense care required by his illness. The alleged reason for Theages' salvation is particularly interesting. In his analysis of public health policies (see Chapter 12), Socrates was emphatic about how lives spent in healthcare (compare *nosotrophia* in 496c2 and 407b1) were harmful to the city for precluding the political participation of the citizen. Claiming now that the constant care of one's health preserves the philosophical nature from the vice of the city sounds like a contradiction. In fact, it is not. This is rather more evidence of the difference between a constituent strategy, such as the Philosopher-King, and a constitutive principle of a just *politeia*. Philosopher-kings are to be obtained if philosophers avoid the education of the corrupted cities they live in, and their isolation from political life contributes to this end. In a just city, on the other hand, every citizen must engage in political life, philosophers shall not be an exception.

This distinction is also found in the second case, which is Socrates himself (496c3-4). There is a disclaimer, though: he does not consider himself worth mentioning because his was not a case of self-education. His way of life results from the extraordinary fact, never or rarely occuring before, of being endowed with a divine signal. He does not explain how his philosophical nature resisted corruption, but situates his case among those who survived by seclusion. Here, the

---

[8] This seems to be a reference for Alcibiades; see Georgini 2009: 114–15; Larivée 2012: 21ff. and Arruzza 2019: 90 ff..

[9] Theages is the son of Demodochus, probably the general mentioned in Thucydides, *History of the Peloponnesian War*, IV, 75, 1. He fits well as Alcibiades' counterpoint in the profile of the young man from a traditional family with a future of political glories ahead, which, in his case, were frustrated by his health issues. See Nails 2002: 278.

formula of 'doing one's own' (*ta hautou prattōn*, 496d6) no longer has the same meaning as 'cooperation' found in the definition of justice. Rather, it refers to the abandoning of political life (496c2-3) that corresponds to one of the opposites of justice as Socrates understands it: *apragmosunē*, or political quietism (see Chapter 11).

Socrates' attitude in Athens, which allegedly involved refraining from politics and engaging only in private actions (496d5-6), would not be permitted for a philosopher in Kallipolis. The recommendation of opposite practices for philosophers, depending on their being in a just or unjust city, gives us an important clue about the role of the *politeia* in personal flourishing: Socrates advises quietism in a *politeia* in which cooperation with fellow citizens aims at obtaining injustice (496d2-3). Nonetheless, this refusal to cooperate puts philosophers in a difficult position as they find no ally who can help them survive judicial prosecution (496c5–d2), likely for constitutional crime. In these circumstances, they are not strong enough to defende themselves and avoid punishment by themselves (496d2-5). Quietism is a personal solution to avoid the destiny that Glaucon attributed, in a graphic description, to the just person with reputation for injustice (361e4-362a2). It is a life that, although virtuous, does not lead to flourishing (see 497a3-7) and that, instead, restricts itself to nourishing some expectation of improvement after death (496e1-3).

It is certainly remarkable that Socrates describes himself as a quietist while, at the same time, he attempts to persuade the guests in Cephalus' house that another *politeia* is possible. In his version of refraining from political activity and engaging in private actions, he advocates for another way of political life, encouraging youths like Glaucon and Adeimantus to simulate the role of its founders and legislators (see 378e7-379a2). As it seems, this sufficed for his being sentenced to death. We now approach our second difficulty regarding the Philosopher-King proposal: even if philosophers manage to educate themselves, they are at great risk if they attempt political engagement in a city that is not just. The *locus classicus* of this discussion is the most famous Platonic image: the allegory of the cave.

The cave, says Socrates, is an image of 'our' nature (514a1-2). This, in my view, refers to the small group of philosophers, including Theages and Socrates himself (see 496b7-c3), and the development of their philosophical education (516b5-6) within a *politeia* identified as promoting miseducation (*apaideusia*, 514a2).[10] The narrative is well known and sounds simple, but dealing with images, as Socrates claims himself, poses the challenge of arguing about a myriad of elements (see 488a4-6): not everything has the same relevance; not everything refers to something in particular. Nonetheless, the story must have some meaning, even if obscure.

The prisoner is freed from miseducation through an unknown agent. Here, we may think about Socrates' divine signal or Theages' congenial love of learning. From the dramatic point of view, this turn is the most strongly emphasized moment of the image, for it aims at explaining why

---

[10] *Apaideusia* is not simply lack of education: it is the accomplishment of a misguided end in educational process, a bad and shameful education leading to unreasonable beliefs, which, for instance, results in citizens who require someone else to force them to be just, generating the proliferation of courts (405a6-b3, see also 552e5-7 and Ferguson 1922: 15–16). I think it is damaging to the understanding of the image of the cave to suppose that its interior stands for perceptual objects while the exterior stands for intelligible objects (see for instance Murphy 1932: 95–7; Malcolm 1962: 40). Beside the claim that the turn of the head is the relevant cognitive turn (518c6–d1), when Socrates states that the upward path is a path towards the intellectual realm (517b4-6), this may simply mean the exercise of dealing with perplexity that already summons the intellect, while not yet knowing all the forms. On the other hand, there has been some controversy about identifying the cave with a *politeia* of misguided education, for Socrates refers to the ruling of philosophers in the just city as a descent to the cave (520c1-3; 539e3-4, see Ferguson 1934: 207 versus Murphy 1934: 211). I think the problem is easily solved in considering that the cave is always the city in which the philosopher lives, that in both cases it refers to those who did not make the ascent. Socrates begins by telling the story of philosophers educated in an unjust city and ends drawing conclusions for philosophers ruling in just cities.

humans always have the cognitive power active in their soul (518b9-c2): they just need to 'turn' it to the right objects. Philosophical education begins when we stop trusting appearances as a reliable source for our beliefs. Trust (*pistis*) is the most elementary way of dealing with the world around us (510a5-6, 511e1), for being based on the belief that perceptual appearances (*eikasia*) are the true state of affairs on which to ground our cognition of the world (see Chapter 4). Realizing that they are not (see 510a8-10) is the beginning of philosophical education.

We summon our intellect when we realize that what we apprehend by perception is the appearance of reality, and our cognition turns away from appearance in the quest for some Archimedean point on which to ground our beliefs. This is what the prisoner does when they turn their head; they leave behind beliefs based on appearances and engage in a journey of *aporia* (515d6), the perplexity caused by lack of trust, with gradual gains in locating some items, until they finally reach the Archimedean point of realizing how the sun, or the form of the good, organizes reality. This educational route suggests that whatever they may posit as real inside the cave falls short of truth, and thus emphasizes the need for persistence in learning.[11] The final view of the sun allows them to understand not only the relation of real items and appearances but how everything along the process relates to each other: shadows, things, stars, the cave and sky (516b8-c2, 517b9-10).

The philosopher who sees the form of the good achieves the end of their education, and thereby fulfils their desire for intellectual activities. They do not, as a result, want to engage in any further human activities for these would entail returning to the cave (516d2-7, 517c6-8) and re-habituating themselves to the miseducating *politeia* (517a1-2, d6-7). In this unjust city, they are liable to face disputes in court or reproach in any of its institutions, and if, on any of these occasions, they were to talk about a conception of justice the majority has never seen, they would be considered ridiculous (516e7-517a4; 517d4-e1). If they insist, attempting to educate their fellow citizens, they would fall victim to Diomedes' *anankē* and be put to death (517a5-6). The cave, which aims at explaining how the philosopher may be self-educated, also shows that philosophical education in an unjust city ultimately results in the philosopher becoming a victim of injustice (517a4-6). The cave therefore points out the tensions between philosophers and the citizens, justifying quietism with a chilling threat.[12]

There has been significant discussion about the vocabulary of *anankē* in the cave, as some interpreters have taken Socrates' proposals to be advocating for a normative, sometimes even authoritarian position about philosophers being educated and subsequently ruling.[13] The reason for this is that Socrates states that the founders of Kallipolis must enact laws that will not permit philosophers to do what they do 'now', that is, they are not to assume that they live on the Isle of

---

[11] I do not see the cave following stages, as suggested by the divided line. This classical approach is found, for instance, in Jackson 1882: 142 and Adam 1902: II, 156–63. As I see it, 517a8-c4 and 532a1-d1 attest that the two similes have in common only three things (1) appearance-based beliefs as the lowest point, provided that the prisoners are to be located in the situation described by the two lower segments of the line; (ii) a hard enquiry (which does not need to be located in the third segment) and (iii) a non-hypothetical end. For a view similar to mine, see Robinson 1953: 192–5.

[12] Some readers believe that not willing to return to the cave means that philosophers do not want to have anything to do with ruling in any circumstances (see Aronson 1972: 394; White 1986: 24; Smith 2010: 96; Brown 2000: 15). This would double the obstacles to Socrates' proposal, for it would not only be hard to find a philosopher, but it would also be difficult to get them to rule. Understanding that the cave may stand for both the just and the unjust *politeia* explains this point, because the philosopher is unwilling to rule in the former (517c6-d2), but glad to do so in the latter (592a7).

[13] For analysis about the presence of the vocabulary of *anankē*, see Wagner 2005: 87; Shields 2007: 21; Barney 2008: 3. See also the note 9 in Chapter 8.

the Blessed (519c5); rather, once they have learned the form of the good, they must take part in political activity (519c8-d7). This is the rationale for such a law:

> [T41] Verify, Glaucon, I said, that we shall not commit an injustice towards those who will become philosophers among us, and that instead we shall tell them just things, imposing on them to care for others and guard them. For we shall tell them that it is reasonable that those who become [philosophers] in the other cities shall not take part in the labours there, for they developed their nature on their own despite the *politeia*. Therefore, it is just that those who were developed on their own, not receiving from anyone the benefit of their upbringing, are not willing to repay the upbringing to anyone: 'As for you, however, we did it for you, both for you and for the rest of the city. We turned you into leaders and kings, like in a beehive. You were better and more completely educated than those others, and have more power to take part in both [activities]. You ought to descend in turns to live with the others and get used to contemplate the obscure things. Once habituated, you shall see countless times better than them and will know what each of the images is and of what, because you have seen what is true about fair, just and good things. Thence, for us and for you, you shall govern the city awake and not dreaming, like many cities today, that are governed by citizens who fight among themselves for shadows and promote strife in order to rule, as if it was a great good. The truth is the following: the city in which those who are least disposed to rule shall rule is necessarily the best and the freest of strife, the city that has the opposite rules is in a condition the opposite to it.' (520a6-d5, my brackets)

The first point to note is that T41 subscribes to the aforementioned standard of 'different *politeia*/different attitude', by claiming that legislation will be just in requiring philosophers to rule *in a city that educates philosophers*, rather than in whichever city. This matches the claim that quietism is a strategy for survival, and not a path to flourishing; philosophers will be required to rule because this is a constitutive principle of an already established just city, not a constituent move for its establishment. The argument in T41 does not address the difficulties of the Philosopher-King thesis regarding the education of the philosopher in the city, but rather the problem of the motivations for a philosopher to rule, even in Kallipolis. Ruling, as well as any other expertise, is not good for the expert, and philosophers in particular are not willing to care for others in exchange for the usual rewards of money and honours (see 347b10-d8, T19 in Chapter 7), as they are not cooperative people. Although they know that their ruling is good for them and for all, they wish to make it clear that they do not undertake it on an ordinary common purpose contract.

The argument offered by the founders of Kallipolis is very interesting: philosophers benefitted from other previous philosophers who gave them the education that led them to flourish in a way they would not obtain in an unjust *politeia*. As such, they must reward the ones who benefitted them. On the other hand, because these previous individuals were also philosophers unwilling to receive rewards, it is therefore just for the present philosophers to reciprocate by taking care of the upbringing of someone else (520b4-5 *a contrario sensu*). Education thereby inserts the philosophers into a system of common contracts among philosophers to maintain their own education system. As this educational system begins in early childhood, selecting children with natural tendencies, the education of philosophers must therefore be part of a more general education of all the citizens. Taking care of the education of philosophers is taking care of the education of all children and youths. Philosophers will rule so as to make sure Kallipolis will always have philosophers to preserve it, and to prevent it from being ruled by someone who does not know the form of the good.

If this is correct, the use of a vocabulary of *anankē* in this and other similar passages expresses the legal enactment of the founders of Kallipolis, which is followed by a justification for why the law is good, since, in Kallipolis, laws must be grounded in the form of the good. *Anankē* is a term used for expressing legislation and does not necessarily mean the Diomedes' *anankē*, the cohersion by force.[14] Interpreters who have understood Socrates as taking an authoritarian position, by placing an imposition on philosophers to abandon a better life, seem to me to be mistaken. There is no Isle of the Blessed for mortals. Philosophers live in cities and, as citizens, they must care for others and preserve the city, which ultimately will prevent their becoming victims of injustice (496d2-5).[15] Demanding that philosophers rule is not depriving them of flourishing (519d8-9). Rather, such a law merely emphasizes that the only option of flourishing available to humans is cooperative (compare 519e1-520a4 to 420b3-421b4). Finally, for the legislation to spell out the terms of the philosophical cooperation, it must make it clear that these philosophers are not undertaking this task for the sake of regular rewards.

On the other hand, it is clear that philosophers will not flourish as quietists (compare 519c4-6 and 496c5-6) as a philosopher cannot be content with being only individually just.[16] If Socrates aimed at simply proving that individual justice suffices for flourishing, all he would be required to do would be to point out the factual examples of Theages and himself. This is not enough. Rather, he aims to prove that justice is politically feasible by showing that, although there are agents with power to make it happen, there is an evil in the present cities that keeps philosophy and political power apart. For this reason, it is not only hard to find a philosopher to become a changemaker; it is also dangerous for a philosopher to attempt to do so. Although Socrates does regard it feasible, he recognizes that it involves a random episode of good luck or the intervention of the gods (499b4-c1, 592a8). The alternative that presents itself as one single change therefore gives us very little hope.

Nevertheless, in his diagnosis of the evils of the city, Socrates opens the path for other therapies. Among these we find, as I would like to argue, another kind of constituent strategy that is not based on individuals but on an institution. I would like to call attention to the following. Notice, first, that Socrates recommends different attitudes for philosophers depending on the city they live in. Also notice that the cave represents an unjust *politeia* in which the philosopher lives and that, being able to escape allows them to conceive another way of living the political life, another *politeia*, outside the cave. This explains why the philosopher is liable for constitutional crimes, for they are an 'outsider'. Finally, this also indicates that all philosophers share the same *politeia*, that is, the one outside the cave.

On the other hand, notice that, in the Philosopher-King proposal, the king represents a *politeia* in which citizens hearken and listen. Furthermore, the damage in the education of youths with philosophical tendencies was caused by the absence of an institution that would

---

[14] Founders of cities are lawgivers, *anankē* is a regular vocabulary for law content, and the law is not against the good when it says something must be done, neither in T41 nor at 500d5-9, 519c8-d2, 520e1-3, 521b7-10, 539e3-540a2, 540a4-b7. Rather, it is a law based on the form of the good; see Shields 2007: 39 and note 9 in Chapter 8. A legislation on philosophers aims simply to spell out the terms of their cooperation, since they are not cooperative people. The fact that a law should be enacted tells us nothing about philosophers not willing to abide, not least about having to rule before they have finished their education (for such positions, see Reeve 1998: 195; Smith 2010: 97–8). I find the claim that philosophers would 'return to the cave' before having learned the form of the good incompatible with the text of the allegory itself as well as with T41, which refers to them as completely educated. More about the philosophical education and the need of legislation in the next chapter.

[15] The claim that philosophers sacrifice themselves in ruling, because they can live a better life by themselves, is found in Aronson 1972: 393; Cooper 1977: 156; Cooper 2000: 19–21. Responses emphasizing that Socrates never considers this better life as a possibility are found in Brickhouse 1981: 8; Mahoney 1992: 269–71.

[16] Menn (2006: 34), for instance, claims that Socrates is glad to prove the feasibility of justice by the existence of a just individual.

grant dialogue in pursuing the good, the same institution that would prevent injustice against the philosopher who returns to the cave. Finally, notice that philosophers in Kallipolis rule both to avoid injustice, preserving the city, and to educate other philosophers. Put all this evidence together, and we can see that philosophical education in Kallipolis is neither casual nor random. Rather, it is an institution in which, generation after generation, philosophers work to educate philosophers and, as a result, all the children of the city. So, I would like to suggest that we may identify an institutional strategy being designed throughout these arguments. This is the topic of the next chapter.

16

Kallipolis

In the last chapter, we saw that the Philosopher-King is a constituent proposal for a political system, the Kallipolis, in which philosophers, who know the form of the good, rule. We also saw that the conclusive assessment of the Philosopher-King proposal was that, although preferable, it depends on good luck or a divine intervention. This is both because an unjust *politeia* would hinder philosophical education and because true philosophers would risk their lives in attempting to rule there. One may notice that the more the Philosopher-King proposal appears impracticable throughout the argument of books VI and VII, the more the argument rests on establishing some laws about the education of philosophers and their cooperation with other citizens. This presence of a lawgiver or city founder has appeared authoritarian to some, for enacting laws that regulate not only the citizens' flourishing but also the education and rule of the philosophers. As it turns out, no citizen, ruler or ruled, would be in such an external authoritative position to enforce these laws in Kallipolis, because they are, as we shall subsequently see, constitutional laws. Indeed, this is what should be expected were we to understand these laws, grounded in the form of the good and aiming at obtaining cooperative flourishing, as 'imposing' that philosophy and political power be brought together (see 473d2-5, T38) Rather, the enforcement-agents of these laws are those who, engaged in a cooperative way of life, merely pursue their own flourishing within the flourishing of all.

In this chapter, I shall argue that, in the absence of a Philosopher-King, the founding of Kallipolis is also feasible by an institutional approach represented by this legislative function. Its role is to bring philosophy and political power together as the cooperation of two different kinds of citizens, with two different kinds of political life. Such an approach consists of installing the institution of philosophical education in addition to the standard institution of *mousikē* and gymnastics. Besides preserving philosophical education and the very life of philosophers, this institution would take upon itself to give reasons, to both philosophers and citizens in general, that justify the mores. It would follow the same standards that qualified the king as a changemaker in the Philosopher-King proposal: to give reasons and to be heard. This was also a feature lacking in the decision-making institutions of the unjust *politeiai*. Let me begin with the end. When the argument about Kallipolis is completed (472e6-544a1), its results are described as follows:

[T42] Well then, now that we've finished all of this, let us remember where we started the digression that brought us here, so that we can start again from the same point.
   It is not difficult, he said. Roughly speaking, the starting point was similar to this one where we are now, because you had gone through the reasons you gave for the city, concluded that a city would be good if it were as you established in your analysis, and that the same was true about the man who was similar to it, even though, as it seems, you had yet to tell about *an even fairer city and man*. (543c4-544a1, my emphasis)

In Glaucon's eyes, their enquiry (i) presented the reasons for a city (369c9-376d8); (ii) described what would be a good city and a good man (376d9-445e2); (iii) introduced a fairer city, the Kallipolis, and a fairer man, the philosopher (472e6-544a1). Some interpreters read this part as dealing with three different cities; however, in my view, this destroys the continuity of the argument in the *Republic*.[1] I would rather suggest that they are three different accounts of a city: why there are cities, why cities are good and how good cities may occur. Why, then, is Kallipolis an even fairer city than the good one? Because, as argued in the previous chapter, something has been added to the just *politeia* in order for it to occur: something that is both a therapy for present evils of the cities and a means to preserve the good in the city. Not only do we know that this addition is philosophy but also the following:

[T43] But what would you say would be a *politeia* convenient [to philosophy]?

None of them, I said, and this is also my complaint: none of the organizations in the cities today are worthy of the philosophical nature. And that is why they pervert and alter it, as native species tend to prevail over a foreign seed, sown in someone else's soil. This is how today's generation does not maintain the power that is their own, and decays into an alien custom. But if they may find the best *politeia*, which is similar to the best character that they have, this would prove how divine they are, while the other ones are human natures with human activities. Having said that, you will of course ask me what *politeia* this would be.

You did not get it right, he said, this is not what I was going to ask, but whether it is the same city we founded in our analyses or whether it is another one.

As for the rest, I said, it is the same one. But it was also said on that occasion that there must always be someone in the city who has the reason for the *politeia*, i.e., there must be the lawgiver there, just like you here have established the laws. (497a8-d2, my brackets)

At the end of this passage, we learn that what is added to 'the city we founded in our analyses', in order to account for its feasibility, is a lawgiver (*nomothetēs*). In antiquity, legislation would always have its roots in the founders of a city, that is, the ancestors. But in times of crisis, a lawgiver was someone who would address the conflicts with new laws that could still be said to be in accordance with founding principles or the *archaia politeia*. In order to do so, the lawgiver should be respected by all and should go into exile after legislating, therefore ensuring no one would be particularly benefitted by the new laws.[2] A *politeia* convenient to philosophy would depend on the addition of a lawgiver to a just *politeia*, as someone who, by giving the citizens the reasons for the *politeia*, would solve the conflicts that may emerge. I understand that the kind of argument found in T41 (the reasons given to philosophers for them to rule, 520a6-d5) fits well with the kind of reasons given by a lawgiver who is constantly present in the city. This kind can also be identified in the arguments exchanged between Socrates and Adeimantus at Cephalus' house, as 'just like you here' in T43 states.[3] Two points are relevant for us not to read here an authoritarian clause. First, the constant presence of a lawgiver cannot possibly refer to the existence of one person who is above the law; it refers instead to an institution that guarantees this presence. Second, if, in the dialogue at Cephalus' house, the interlocutors debated the choices made by individuals and cities, analysed which of these choices promote the good

---

[1] For interpretations that suppose there are three models of cities, see Adam 1902: I, 325; Strauss 1964: 93.
[2] For lawgivers in antiquity, see Gagarin 1989: 57–8; Lewis [2007] 2011: 17,41. For the difference (and occasional overlap) between lawgivers and city founders, see Aristotle, *Politics*, 1273b30-34.
[3] For the role of lawgivers and city founders in the dialogue, see 398b3, 403b4, 409e5, 417b8, 429c1-2, 456c1, 458c6, 463c7.

of the agent and agreed on the principles of an education that would result in their avoiding evil and flourishing, being a lawgiver amounts not only to knowing the reasons of the *politeia* (in particular the principles of education) but also to giving these reasons to others by means of arguments (see also 534d8-10).

We have seen that lawcourts are a sign of injustice in a city (405a6-b3), and that citizens should be just and capable of cooperating with each other based solely on their education. Indeed, Socrates makes it clear that it is by playing lawful games in childhood that children become law-abiding and discover by themselves what is lawful about small things (424e6-425a9). Thus, we are not to expect a lawgiver to be settling these kinds of daily issues (425b7-8). Socrates is emphatic that it is futile to try to regulate mores such as caring for elders (425b1-3), cutting their hair, wearing clothes and shoes (425b3-5), trade contracts and agreements (425c10-e2) (although the law must curb the accumulation of wealth by such contracts; see 556a9-b4). There is no need to legislate about offences, insults (425d1-2), court proceedings or procedures for appointing judges (425d2), nor about import taxes (425d3-5), or other social matters (425d5). Furthermore, it is not part of the lawgiver's function to interfere in religious procedures involving temples, sacrifices, rituals, burials and celebration of the dead, which must be stipulated by the gods and the religious guides (427b6–c5). Laws should form the characters of the citizens; not amend them at every action (425e5-7, 425e8-427a7). Virtuous people are easily able to figure out what to do on each occasion (425d7–e2); attempting to use legislation otherwise is like trying to cut off the many heads of the hydra (426e7).

The agency of justice falls upon the citizens. Lawgivers merely establish the laws necessary for their education and are ready to tell them the reasons why these mores are the best (534d8-10). Within this role, lawgivers are particularly important for bringing philosophy and political power together since, as T43 asserts, the philosophical *politeia* is not identical to the just *politeia*. They differ like the divine as opposed to the human. We are therefore dealing with two different ways of living a political life.

> [T44] [The intelligent person] observes the *politeia* that he has in himself, I said, and guards against disturbing any of his parts by excess or lack of property, and thus commands the acquisition and expenditure of property as far as he can.
> Exactly, he said.
> And also regarding honours he observes the same [*politeia*], and consents to take part and enjoy those that he believes make him better, and avoid those that, whether private or public, loosen his established disposition.
> But if this is what he cares about, he said, he will not be willing to take political action.
> Yes, by the dog!, I said, in that city that is proper to him he will be very willing to do so; but perhaps not in his own homeland, unless some divine chance occurs.
> I understand, he said. You are referring to the city we founded in our talk, the one grounded in reasons, since I assume it does not exist anywhere on Earth.
> But perhaps in the sky, I said, as a model that rests there for whoever wants to see it and thence turn himself into its colony. It does not matter if it does not exist somewhere or that it shall never exist, for such a person will only act according to this [*politeia*] and no other.
> This is reasonable. (591e1-592b5, my brackets)

In the exercise of their intelligence, philosophers understand reality and take it upon themselves to act according to what really is fair, just and good (compare to 484c4-d2). T44 calls this internal standard a *politeia*. As we saw in Chapter 9 while analysing the case of a democratic city, to have a *politeia* in oneself means living a certain kind of political life. In contrast to citizens of a democracy, who choose their *politeia* in the market, the philosophers' own *politeia* is deduced from the reality they love and know. They do not need the democratic freedom of choice, nor do they need to inhabit Kallipolis to become citizens of it. The *politeia* in the soul of philosophers avoids the disturbance caused by desire and honours, so that they maintain their internal serenity. Properties and social recognition are therefore only good if they preserve this disposition, without which they should be avoided. Pursuing only sustainable goods is a mark of the philosophical *politeia*, because, as I shall now argue, their practice of citizenship follows a singular concept of *eleutheria*.

The democratic tradition identified citizens as those among the inhabitants of the city that were free (*eleutheroi*, 557b4, see 562b7-c2 and Chapter 9). The oldest and most common meaning of *eleutheria* is 'freedom' in the sense of those who are not servants or slaves of others.[4] Because in ancient Greece the slaves came from those cities that had lost in war, the opposition between *eleutheros* and slave could also identify the opposition between native and alien (provided that not every alien was a slave). From this meaning, *eleutheria* came to denote the criterion for citizenship by descent (as opposed to both slaves and free foreigners), a sense that I shall term $eleutheros_1$. In Athenian democracy, political rights were given according to citizenship by descent, that is, being a man of age and $eleutheros_1$ was necessary and sufficient for being a citizen. On the other hand, being *eleutheros* additionally came to mean being free of impediment to pursue one's goals, for this was precisely what slaves could not do. We saw how this meaning, which I will call $eleutheros_2$ was at the basis of Socrates' connection of *eleutheria* and *exousia* in democracy as well as of his criticism. As such, I would like to argue that in response to the excess of freedom in democracy, Socrates defends a concept of *eleutheria* for Kallipolis that combines the two meanings (with some change in the meaning of each). According to this concept, citizens are $eleutheroi_1$ – that is, they have a political life, in this case one characterized by the exchange of goods – because they are $eleutheroi_2$ – in the sense that they are free from any impediments to pursuing their true good (though not free to pursue whichever apparent good they might desire). In this sense, citizens are those who follow the mores of the just *politeia*, that is, every citizen is a just citizen.

Textual evidence of this more developed concept of $eleutheria_2$, which is not simply the opposite of slavery, is found in Socrates' description of the tyrannical personality. There, he states that 'never in their whole life had they any friend, they were always masters or slaves of someone else; the tyrannical nature has never tasted true freedom (*eleutheria*) and friendship' (576a4-6). By placing freedom next to friendship, Socrates points out that being free is not comparable to being a master as opposed to a slave, because the subjection of others is not a rational way of pursuing one's good. The reason for this is that, in subjecting others, the tyrant is a slave of his desires (577d1-5) and thus has an internal impediment to obtaining what is truly good for himself. Being free is engaging in cooperative actions, such as those that happen among friends, as opposed to subordinative actions. If being free in this sense is a trait of personality, it also describes the way in which, in the Kallipolis, citizens in general are free ($eleutheroi_1$). Indeed, Socrates states that the ruled are not only free but also friends of the philosopher-rulers, with whom they cooperate by providing for their nutrition (547c1-2, see also 463a10-b2).[5] If

---

[4] For the opposition between *eleutheria* and servitude in a master/slave pattern, see 329c5-6, 344c5-9, 351d8-9, 387b5-6, 433d2, 536d9-e1, 547c1-4, 564a7-8, 567e3-5, 569a1-7, 569b9-c4, 577c4-5, 579a1-3. For the development of the different senses of *eleutheria* see Hansen 2010: 2–9.

[5] For *eleutheria* and citizenship as the rule of reasoning, see Stalley 1998: 145; Schofield 2006: 87–8; Miller Jr. 2018: 10.

democracy in Socrates' eyes merged the freedom of the born citizen with the freedom of doing whatever one desires, the Kallipolis takes the concept of freedom in the sense of having no impediment to pursuing one's true good as the necessary and sufficient condition to be a citizen. Citizenship is therefore not granted by birth but by education:

> [T45] It is clear, I said, that the purpose of the law, which is the ally of everyone in the city, and of the rule about children is to not make them free (*eleutherous*) before we have established the *politeia* in them just like in the city. Only when we have cared for the best in them with what is best in us and installed in them a guardian and ruler similar to our own, will we let them be free (*eleutheron*). (590e1-591a3)

T45 states that children will only have freedom, that is, political participation, when they reach a stage where they possess the *politeia* in themselves, when they become internally free (*eleutheroi$_2$*), so as to obtain the status of citizens (*eleutheroi$_1$*). The criterion for political participation in a just *politeia* is therefore not birth within a given territory but being just. The purpose of the law in Kallipolis is to turn people into citizens by making them just. This means that they must be cared for by those who legislate and rule so as to develop the reasoning which will rule in them. To become a citizen, one needs to learn what is best for oneself and each part of one's soul, that is, to be virtuous, as established in T27 (Chapter 11). T45 refers to it as installing a guardian and ruler in the children. It is also in this sense that the rulers produce the freedom (*eleutheria$_2$*) in the city (395b9-c3), something that can only be accomplished by someone who knows what virtue is (484c4-d2), the philosophers.

Philosophers are also subject to the rule concerning children stated in T45; although they are the rulers and guardians of Kallipolis, their action is primarily described as the preservation of the law by obedience, or by agency according to the law (458c3-4). The philosophers are therefore not above the law. Having said this, the philosophers do practise a different form of citizenship, on account of possessing a different form of *eleutheria*: their freedom rests on having no impediment to pursuing true good (as opposed to *their own* true good) *because they know what true good is*. As we saw in Chapter 12, with their thoughts engaged in contemplating the whole of reality, philosophers are magnanimous no matter where they live. The political life typical of philosophers is, in a very strict sense, a cosmopolitanism (referring to *kosmios* in 486b6).

Returning to T44, there we see evidence of Socrates' standard for different *politeia*/different attitude of philosophers. The passage clearly states that philosophers are willing to rule in a city that welcomes this cosmopolitanism. The last chapter allows us to infer two reasons for this. The first is that philosophers do not flourish in quietism. The second is that the lawgiver provides them with the reasons why they are not to rule in the expectation of receiving the regular cooperative rewards (money and honour), but as a way of preserving the education of philosophers. Their political practice consists of practising philosophy both among philosophers, while they are being educated, and among citizens in general, for, as we shall soon see, the education of philosophers begins with the education of the whole city.

What we have before us is a two-citizenry political model, that is, a coupling of the philosophical citizens with the cooperative citizens by means of introducing an institution that guarantees the constant presence of a lawgiver. This is an institution that brings together philosophers and cooperative citizens with the purpose of knowing and giving reasons why this is the best *politeia*. This institutional solution offers an alternative to the 'Philosopher-King' proposal and, by itself, provides for both the foundation and the maintenance of such a city. The institution that grants the constant presence of lawgivers is the one that establishes laws about education in the city and, within it, the training of philosophers.

Thus far, I have argued that Kallipolis is constituted by two ways of political life: cooperative citizens and philosophers. These constitute two distinct personalities formed by two different educations. Cooperative citizens, however, require the presence of a philosopher-lawgiver to learn the reasons why they practise this kind of political life. For this reason, an institution for philosophical education is necessary in Kallipolis. My next point is therefore about philosophical education. Here, I shall argue that philosophical education must also begin in childhood, and so must be added to *mousikē* and gymnastics as a means to develop the intellectual abilities of every child (see 536d4-7). This addition matters not only to test the philosophical talents of children but also to enhance the intellectual ability of citizens in general – an ability required for their persuasion by philosophers about the laws and what is good for everyone, as well as for the development of their discursive reasoning (with which they may engage in dialogue among themselves and draw inferences about the good). T46 is our first text on this matter:

[T46] Therefore the objects of reasoning, of geometry and all those of the propaedeutics that are required to introduce to dialectic must be presented to children as problems, not in the form of a discipline of compulsory learning.

Why?

Because, I said, free people shall not learn anything through slavish methods. Physical efforts imposed by violence do not make the body worse, but nothing learnt in the soul by violence lasts.

It is true, he said.

So, it is not with violence, I said, my good man, that children shall be educated in these subjects, but through games, so that we also can better observe the natural talents of each one of them.

What you say makes sense, he said. (536d4-537a3)

Children, who are all to be tested for their talents, must be educated in what I would like to call dialectical games. Indeed, this is a controversial claim as the majority of interpreters assumes that the children referred to in T46 have already been selected for having a philosophical nature.[6] This assumption finds no textual support, however. In fact, the evidence stands against it. The text talks about children (see also 527c10) whose talents *are* being assessed. Indeed, how could these be the selective tests if the children have been pre-selected? Moreover, this is an education introduced as one of the first things *everyone* should learn, and which is common to every expertise (522c1-3) – as we are referring to a basic use of rationality, this is important to every citizen, not only for habit-based virtue but also for developing their cognitive powers. No one in Kallipolis should therefore be kept from this learning (527c1-2) as it is valuable for the whole city (528c1-4, e2-3).

Experts in general know, says Socrates, how to count and perform basic mathematical operations (522c5-8), though there has been no previous mention of how children would learn these basic operations. It seems implicit that they are part of their specialized education. A general, for instance, should know how to count soldiers and ships (522d1-7). This type of operation, however, engenders a much more refined procedure, which is identifying and discriminating

---

[6] Interpreters who suppose that only pre-selected children would be exposed to these games are Reeve 19885: 180–1; Dorter 2006: 243; Denyer 2007: 305. See note 4 in Chapter 11.

the individuals that are counted. If I do not know what an individual is, I can neither count them as two or three, nor know how they are added or subtracted. Socrates therefore suggests a distinction between an approach to numbers that summons the intellect and one that does not (523a10-b4). We have already discussed, in Chapter 4, the problem of opposite appearances and how they stimulate reasoning to count, measure and weight, for example, in the case of illusions (compare 523b5-6 with 602d6-7). Now, however, we face a different difficulty in identifying, discriminating and counting – one that is not necessarily connected to our perception organs. This case is that 'we can see the same thing at the same time as one and as an unlimited multitude' (525a5-6). This is not valid only for 'one', but for every number (525a7-8). If the units I count are not units, then what am I counting?

Socrates' proposal is not the inclusion of basic mathematical operations in children's education (this is somehow considered a given). Rather, he wishes to make children in general aware of the difficulty regarding identification and differentiation. He wants to take numbers, geometric figures, motion and harmony as triggers for intellectual problems (530b6-c2, 531c2, 536d6), which, in his words, equals to 'using it for the sake of cognition' (525d2-3, see also 527a10). This is what the cave called the 'turn' of the soul to another type of object (compare 514b2 and 525a1-3, 526e3-9, 527b8-10, 527d7-e1, 529a1-2, 532c4-d1) – the objects that our cognitive apparatus aims to know, that is, what is always the same, the forms and the truth (525c3-6, 527b4). The intellectual access to these objects is done by the 'dialogue (*dialegesthai*) about the numbers themselves' (525d6, compare to 454a4-8, 511b3, c4-6).

Dialectical games are playful ways of introducing children to dialectic, the same subject that philosopher-rulers will have to learn (525b9-c1).[7] While the latter take this practice to its completion in knowing what the numbers are (525b9-c3), others will simply engage with it as a way of developing their cognition through being introduced to formal thought (as well as giving the opportunity for their talents to be tested). This education of the children does not aim to apply numbers to practical purposes; after all, as we saw in the last chapter, the rush to apply the philosophical talents to practical purposes ruins the philosophical education.

We encountered dialectic for the first time in the argument on women, where it was important to establish the form of natural difference and the form of natural sameness (454b6-7) in order to divide and collect human beings, and organize our understanding of them according to the best we can know about them. As a result of this organization, dialectic allows for the giving and receiving of reasons, by referring to the relations things really hold between themselves (531e3-4): dialectical problems aim to develop this power and can emerge from different objects (530b6-c2) such as numbers, geometric figures, stereometric volumes, motion and sound. These, however, are not the objects that answer the problems.

We saw that the dialectical approach to numbers aims at establishing what an individual or a unit is; the problems Socrates is interested in are not those about the intrinsic properties of geometric figures (527a6-10), but those which ground these geometric figures: forms (527b6-7). We may think, for instance, about problems regarding two- and three-dimensional figures, such as: What is a unit in space? Is it relation between points? In approaching astronomy, Socrates says that dialectical interest does not lie in the stars but in objects of intelligence (529a10-b3). When we realize that heavenly motion is relative motion (for there is no fixed point against which we can determine the motion), the problem becomes how to establish relative speed and slowness according to some ratio (see 530a8-b1). A similar and more complex problem of relative forms emerges from harmonics: for dialectical purposes, one should ask what consonance between

---

[7] For dialectical games, see Castelnérac and Marion 2009: 45–7.

ratios is (i.e. a relation between proportions) rather than simply exploring music scales (531c1-8). In this sense, Socrates is not interested properly in numbers, but in the units; not in geometric figures, but in bidimensional and tridimensional space; not in motion, but in the relation that lies behind relative motion; not in harmony, but in the presence and absence of consonance in some proportions.

Although his presentation of these objects follows an order of complexity (see 528d8), Socrates claims that there is no order in which the problems regarding such objects should be learnt (537b8-c1). All the problems point to the same objects (which are different from the objects that they emerged from) – that is, what things really are, the truth about them, how they relate to each other (533a10-b2) and, eventually, how they may relate better (531c2-4). In this sense, all the problems have a common purpose (531c9-d1) that is addressed by the same method: the dialogue on what reality is (532a1-3). Dialectic is therefore a power obtained through the method of considering what each thing is, into which human beliefs and desires do not intervene (533a10–b3). It is not concerned with producing, generating or caring for anything (533b2-5). It differs from the practical use of learning, because it does not take the objects for granted; rather, it questions the assumptions we have about these objects (533b5–c6). Without going through this enquiry and finding some answers, one is not genuinely able to account for what these objects are (534b3-6) precisely because these answers refer to how each of these things relate to others in a kind of mapping of reality. This is the kind of knowledge that dialectic provides us with, a knowledge that grounds the assumptions of the different kinds of expertise, because it is synoptic; that is, it brings all the things together (537c6-7). Understood as a discursive method to identify every item of reality by distinguishing them and relating them to each other, dialectic culminates in the articulation of all these entities in the form of the good (see 526e2, 529c7-d1, 530a6, 532a5-b2, 534b8-d1).

I would like to focus now on the importance of both the early introduction to dialectical games and the philosophical education on dialectical problems. My claim is that together they constitute a single learning to be pursued in a just city from childhood along with *mousikē* and gymnastics – an education which is central to establishing a common purpose contract between just citizens and philosophical rulers. The fact that children are stimulated with problems from childhood does not mean, of course, that they will be finding answers. After all, their reasoning is not ready to do so. But it is from the exposure to these questions about reality that they develop a very important skill for a just citizen: to receive and give reasons, to understand an argument and, even if not interested in pursuing the enquiry further, to be persuaded by it. This is beneficial even for those with less aptitude for intellectual investigation (526b5-9), if only to keep their intellect from being restricted to their expertise (527d8–e2). This use of the intellect is fundamental to reach public agreement about legislation.

In book IV we learn that political temperance is an agreement of all citizens (431e10-432b1) concerning the good of the prevailing end in the city (431b5-7) and those who should rule (431d9-e2). If philosophers are to rule, they must do so among citizens who understand that cooperation is the only available procedure for achieving a rational end in common action. Indeed, an important issue within the city is how these two different kinds of citizens interact – specifically, whether it is possible for the community of pleasures and pains to be extended to both of them and, if so, how to go about it. As we have seen, a basic proposal to accomplish this was to fully publicize the life of philosophers. They are to have no more possessions than the minimum (416d4-417b9; 422d3-4; 457c7-d2), and all citizens have constant access to their dwelling (416d7-8). As such, both the personal life and the public decisions of a philosopher are always under scrutiny. This is essential for the citizens to take them as virtuous people, which, as we saw, is an important character trait of a lawgiver. For real scrutiny, however, citizens must learn how to pose questions, receive reasons and follow a dialogue of formal content. They do not need to become philosophers themselves, but they must understand the reasons for the *politeia* in order for the win-win contract between ruled and ruler to take place. For this, a universal propaedeutic in dialectic is required.

Universal education in dialectical games is therefore an institution that will allow for lawgivers in Kallipolis to give reasons for the *politeia*, bringing about the dialogue that is so important as a qualification of kings in the Philosopher-King project, and which was lacking in the corrupted forms of *politeiai*.[8] Dialectical games in childhood are, however, just the first stage of an institution for philosophical education: children introduced to these problems will subsequently be tested through exams similar to those designed to prevent unreasonable beliefs; those with aptitude will be selected (535a6-7; 537a9-11). After a compulsory period of two to three years of war training (537b1-5), those further selected progress to pursue additional studies. These studies are not, as interpreters generally claim, studies in *mathematics*. Rather, Socrates says that 'the learnings acquired randomly during childhood education must now be brought together into a synoptic approach (*sunopsis*) based on the kinship of these learnings with each other and on the nature of reality' (537b8-c3). This systematic approach forms 'one single discipline of study' (537c4-5) to which students shall devote themselves for ten years, with the aim of bringing together the answers to the problems they began by playing with. Their previous habituation with dialectical games prevents a radical change from childhood to superior education. Although the *Republic* is likely the most important work in the process of unifying all these different subjects as sciences – and the name 'mathematics' most likely sprung from Plato's calling these studies the 'learning subjects' (*ta mathēmata*) – what philosophers must learn is not, however, the deductive sciences that came to be identified with these subjects. Philosophers are to approach what we today call science, not to become scientists, but in order to learn dialectic, as I proceed to argue.[9]

There is sufficient textual evidence to claim that the educational role of these particular objects (units, bidimensional and tridimensional space, relations, proportions, beauty from proportions) lies in summoning our intellect. There remain two further issues still to be addressed in this matter, however. The first is how this education relates to the divided line at the end of book VI. The second is why these are particularly important objects. The divided line establishes four states of the soul relative to its cognitive apparatus. We have seen that belief consists of the apprehension of appearances mediated by judgement that grants us trust that some state of affairs is true. In this sense, the two lower segments of the line explain only what we *believe* objects are, and are not based on truth (510a8-10). By contrast, the two upper segments

---

[8] See Vegetti 2000: 355 and Blössner 2007: 367 for the claim that in Kallipolis philosophers are not kings.
[9] Many are the interpreters who think that the study of mathematics as a science is required for learning the form of the good. Some think that, in doing this, Plato aimed at imparting the scientific basis of mathematics to dialectic (Shorey 1895: 221; Cattanei 2003: 484). However, he rejects the deductive practice as a component of the education for knowing the form of the good (for a similar position see Dixsaut 2005: 227). Another group of interpreters think that Plato was excluding some ways in which mathematics was practised in order to privilege others (White 1976: 96–8; Burnyeat 2000: 17; Payne 2017: 216). However, the text says the curriculum is based on a completely new way of learning (*para ha nun manthanousin*, 529c4). I understand that both interpretations are based on a specific inference from the divided line. It is true that the line suggests that positing formal items are a condition both to deduction from them and to their grounding in principles. But these are two different methods, and a choice must be made. Socrates clearly suggests that deductive methods either aim at practical results or use images to draw inferences, and, in rejecting the practical application of 'mathematics', he rejects this approach all together. The divided line does not offer a continuous method for learning; the two upper segments are different concepts for knowledge, the upper one being knowledge in a more rigorous sense (see Benson 2015: 263–4).

explain truth, knowledge and the forms whose appearances are apprehended by the cognition of the lower segments (510a8-10, 510c5-6; see also 533d4-9, T12 in Chapter 4). I do not think it is controversial that the knowledge required for a lawgiver and a philosopher is represented at the higher segment of the line – that is, a synoptical knowledge which is achieved by dialectic and enables an individual to give reasons about the whole of reality grounded in the interrelation among forms (510b8, c6-d2 *a contrario sensu*, 511b2-c2).

My focus therefore lies in the third section, in which the soul must posit forms (510b4-5). As argued in Chapter 4, I do not see any difference between positing forms here and the method I described in Chapter 3 for dealing with puzzlement that arises when we are faced with opposite appearances: forms are individuals that help us to understand appearances (511a4-5); in the third section of the line they are posited in order to draw conclusions (510b5-6) which may be of two sorts. One is the understanding that appearances are appearances of forms that leads us to conclusions about the appearances that have practical import. In this case an individual may posit forms to solve the puzzlement of opposite appearances that initially forced them to investigate (510d1-3), which is how, as we saw in Chapter 11, experts generally use forms.[10] The other kind of inference regards the properties of specific forms (510d7-e1), an enquiry which is properly theoretical and establishes the field of deductive sciences (mathematics, for instance), the value of which lies in making clear what these specific forms are (511a8-9). Socrates rejects both of these approaches in philosophical education, however; rather, philosophers are to enquire neither about geometrical theorems (527a6-10), nor the irregular motion of celestial bodies (529a10-b3), nor the physical phenomenon of sound (530e5-531a3). Again, there is nothing inherently set against practical expertise or deductive sciences in this claim; it is simply that these kinds of knowledge set the aim of the enquiry somewhere other than the pursuit of an understanding of the interconnection among forms. Dialectic is singular in pursuing a synoptic knowledge which, in turn, grounds every specific field of science and expertise (511b2-c2). The third section of the line describes scientific approaches to forms that are neither dialectic nor propaedeutic to dialectic, and should not be misunderstood as a stage in the longer path to the form of the good.[11]

A more difficult question is why these are the only objects propitious to summon the intellect.[12] As I have tried to show, the objects Socrates is interested in are units, bidimensional and tridimensional space, relations, proportions, and consonance of proportions. These are clearly not the objects specific to arithmetic, geometry, stereometry, astronomy and harmonics

---

[10] As I suggested before, Socrates does ascribe knowledge to experts in general by placing them in the third stage of the line. For interpretations that are inclusive about the objects of knowledge in the third segment, see Nettleship 1920: 249–51; Hackforth 1942: 2; Denyer 2007: 289 (who includes mathematical objects and artefacts).

[11] See Franklin (2012: 504–55) for the 'fictional' status of intermediate objects, and Smith 2019: 165 for the argument that it is always forms that work as summoners of our understanding.

[12] Arguments for the exclusivity of mathematical objects are: (i) Mathematics was the only constituted science back then (Shorey 1895: 221). I would say that, beside the fact that medicine was at least as well consolidated as mathematics, deductive science is not what Socrates is looking for (510d5-511a2). (ii) Mathematics is a good intellectual exercise (Shorey 1895: 221; Cattanei 2003: 524–5). Granted, but this is not enough to exclude other objects (see Burnyeat 2000: 13). (iii) Mathematics leads to the form of the good by means of the concept of proportionality (Sedley 2007: 270). Although I do agree with the thesis, I note that proportionality is not, according to the text, a mathematical object, but one of those others introduced by Socrates. (iv) Mathematics is about objective values – which can only be grasped with the turn of the soul (Burnyeat 2000: 22, 77) – but these values are, again, these other objects introduced by Socrates, not those which are properly mathematical. For the claim that Socrates is introducing new objects, see Miller 2007: 113. Therefore, I do not see how Socrates' proposal precludes other objects, for instance, the analogy between parts of animals, as the one found in Aristotle. I suppose that this enquiry could indeed lead us to understand, for instance, the concept of proportionality.

as scientific fields. I see no reason why these problems cannot emerge from the investigation of other kinds of objects that offer an occasion for opposite appearances, such as living beings or elementary bodies. However, there is a strong reason why some objects are to be avoided in the enquiries of youths. According to the proposed curriculum, individuals are ready to give reasons based on this knowledge, as a *sunoptikos dialektikos* (537c7), at the age of thirty. Socrates thus posits another five years of study (539e3). The argument for the extra time explains why one should begin learning dialectic with these objects, rather than with others.

As we know, in a just *politeia*, children are brought up with certain beliefs about what is just and fair (538c6-8), but they do not know how to give reasons for these beliefs. Facing problems about what things such as numbers, geometric figures, relations and proportions are does not call their own *politeia* into question. This is why these are welcome problems for stimulating the intellect in childhood. On the other hand, the early questioning of the basic principles of the *politeia* as a proper dialectical subject challenges the lawgiver's reasons as well as the beliefs in which these citizens were brought up (538d6-e5). This threatens both that person's flourishing and the cooperation that establishes *politeia*. When young people submit such objects to enquiry, being not able yet to discover truth about them (538e7), they are thrown into nihilism or the lack of any belief about the good (539c1-2). They believe that things are no more fair than shameful, and that there is no difference in being just or unjust, good or evil (538d6-e4). This transforms dialectic into antilogy (539b3) which, as we saw in the argument on women, is not capable of making distinctions according to the nature of things and thus proceeds in refutation of everything (539b4). Employing antilogy towards values leads, Socrates supposes, to transgression or illicit actions (see *paranomos*, 539a3) which, again, engenders a great risk of prompting philosophers to transform into tyrannical personalities. Socrates supposes that older people will avoid this kind of antilogy, because they find the pursuit of truth more valuable than this kind of refutation game (539c5-8), and also because they possess a more stable virtuous character (539d3-6).

The conclusion is that no one is to apply dialectic to the principles of the *politeia* before being tested about their character – not only through the effort of learning dialectic (539d8-9) but also through fifteen years of dealing with war and ruling (539e3-540a2). After the development of their intellectual abilities, this political internship gives them first-hand experience of the importance of grounding values. This is probably an occasion for experiencing evil and injustice in others as something alien (409a1-b9). This, it is plausible to suppose, will prepare them for the next stage. At age fifty, they may finally raise problems about the good and subsequently find reasons to give to others (540a4-9). Having grasped what the good really is, these philosophers will take turns in using their knowledge to organize the city and educate the citizens (540a9-b5) but will also practise philosophy, educate other philosophers (540b1-2) and maintain the presence of the lawgiver in the city.

This is a narrative about the political life of philosophers at Kallipolis. It shows how they are inserted in the cooperative way of life without cooperating with other citizens in precisely the same way, since their own activity does not generate, produce or take care of anything but the preservation of philosophy. Kallipolis is therefore formed by a certain contract between two types of citizens, as opposed to citizens in cooperation, in which philosophers reward with their ruling the livelihood provided by the others. These two types of citizens live different political lives.

Having explained the concept of double citizenry present in Kallipolis, I would now like to draw some conclusions about how the introduction of education in dialectic helps to overcome the difficulties of bringing about a just *politeia*. We have seen that the concept of a just *politeia* implies a circularity insofar as a specific education is required for the rule of reasoning; the solution that Socrates favours is the Philosopher-King proposal, but this proved to be dependent on factors outside human agency. By insisting on the presence of the lawgiver, double citizenry and the institution of philosophical education, I argue that these features allow for another constituent strategy of Kallipolis – one which does not consist of a single change, but gradual development within a virtuous circle, based on changes in children's education:

> [T47] When for once, I said, a *politeia* receives an impulse to the best, it continues growing like a cycle. For if adequate nurture and education are preserved, they produce good natures. In turn, these adequate natures, who receive that education, grow to be even better than the previous ones in many aspects, including in generation, just like it happens with other living beings (...)
> But if [lawlessness] gradually establishes itself, it slowly flows into customs and activities. After that, it increases, extending itself to contracts, and from contracts it passes with great violence to the laws and the *politeia*, Socrates, until it ends up turning everything, the public and the private, upside down.
> Well, I said, is this how it works?
> It seems to me, he said.
> Therefore, as it was said in the beginning, our children are to take part in strictly lawful games, because if they are lawless, so they will become, and it will be impossible for them to grow up into law-abiding and noble men.
> Absolutely, he said.
> But, on the other hand, when children begin by playing lawful games and internalizing the good law through *mousikē*, then the opposite happens; this accompanies them and grows, correcting whatever was previously wrong in the city. (424a5-10; 424d6-425a6, my brackets)

As we know, children's education is the beginning of the necessary civic change, but T47 indicates that it may occur gradually: if education is adequate, the next generation flourishes and educates the following generation even more successfully. We can see the details of this process in Adeimantus' description of the opposite movement: the spread of lawlessness. Lawlessness infiltrates in customs and activities, then introduces corruption in the contracts among citizens, resulting in bad laws and, finally, in a bad *politeia*. This description is very similar to what we saw in Chapter 9 as the peculiar evil of a city: it grows causing degradation and degeneration. If this is possible, then the reverse, Socrates concludes, must also be possible: if we begin by introducing the right children's games, we can foster good character and activities, and thereby improve the relations among the citizens. Indeed, though here Socrates is referring to *mousikē*, it seems fair to suppose that the introduction of dialectical games may gradually change the broader intellectual capacities of the population.

Why does this matter? Because it suggests an alternative to the Philosopher-King solution. Along with the education by *mousikē* and gymnastics, a supplementary intellectual education since childhood is introduced in Kallipolis, the advantage of which being that it is an institutional solution: a school of philosophers must be founded to ensure that all the citizens will be introduced to dialectical games. This institution of dialectical education undertakes two roles at once: it develops the intellectual capacity of children, and it educates philosophers. By making citizens in general more hearkening to arguments, the chances of institutionally educated philosophers ruling the citizens by persuasion are greatly increased. The introduction of dialectical education therefore promotes a virtuous circle in the education of the city, allowing for progressive stages in obtaining justice. It also allows philosophers to live without the constant risk of death, as well as enhances the intellect of the citizens in general, not restricting their horizon of interests purely to the domains of their occupation.

One may regard this as the founding stone of the Platonic Academy.[13] Compared to the information furnished about the Academy from other sources (that are both controversial and fragile), this description of the philosophical *politeia* in the *Republic* is most likely the surest evidence of how it was designed as an institution that would preserve justice in the city in which it was founded, while continuing to dedicate itself to something entirely different: philosophy.

---

[13] See Morrison 1958: 198; Vegetti 2000: 362-4. The relation between the *Republic* and the Academy is widely attested in antiquity, notably by the connection between 527c1-2 – 'Therefore, I said, as far as possible it should be decreed that those who inhabit your Kallipolis may in no way depart from geometry' – and the legendary motto of the Academy – 'Let no one unversed in geometry enter here.' The motto should be included among many anecdotes about Plato and geometry (see Riginos-Swift 1976: 84, 138-47), which in fact express in more popular (and detractive) terms the connection between philosophy and forms (see Cherniss 1962: 67-8). For what we know, the Academy was an institution for dialectical learning and dialogical practice (see Cherniss 1962: 66; Dillon 2003: 10-11; Vegetti 2003: 616-18), much similar to the institution described earlier. In my view the motto expresses the understanding in antiquity that those aiming to join the Academy should learn dialectical games in advance; an important point in defence of early non-academic education for developing intellectual abilities.

17

Flourishing

At the end of the argument about justice – from the building of a personality to the interaction with others and how to become a citizen in Kallipolis – it should be clear that, since justice is the virtue of the citizen who aims at cooperative flourishing, it may only reach this end, and thus its perfection, if shared with others. The excellence of citizens is thence the excellence of the city. Just individuals in an unjust city will not flourish because they are liable to suffer injustice. If we are to obtain this excellence, however, we are to pursue our good *in a certain mode*, that is, cooperatively. Cooperative people are those who act according to rational ends, allowing their desires to be fulfilled only when they are both good for themselves and not harmful to the flourishing of others.

In these people, the *thumos* is trained in such a way that they believe their flourishing entails the flourishing of the city. When all the three parts of the soul are educated thus, this person cooperates with their fellow-citizens in win-win contracts. In order to avoid sedition, such contracts must have as their ends all-encompassing and sustainable goods. This requires mores established by an education designed according to the knowledge of the form of the good. Such knowledge may only be reached after a long period of dialectical education, requiring endurance and love for learning.

Having arrived at these conclusions, the aim of this chapter is to clarify how justice and flourishing go together. The first step is, of course, to let go of naïve conceptions of happiness as individual success. This is, says Socrates, a stupid and childish belief about flourishing that incites individuals to take private possession of everything in the city (466b8-9). Rather, the claim is that the only flourishing available to human beings is cooperative flourishing. The second step is to understand that justice is not altruism. Nor is it a kind of intrinsic good which is not relative to a specific beholder:[1] in adopting natural standards of excellence, it is perfectly legitimate to claim that justice is good for us. In order to show that the justice Socrates defends exhibits these two features, this chapter analyses Glaucon's challenge to Socrates at the beginning of book II as well as Socrates' response to it in book IX.

Glaucon intervenes in the dialogue to demand that Socrates demonstrate one thesis: that it is better in every way to be just than unjust (357b1-2). He assumes that this amounts to comparing the life of the perfectly just agent (who is not reputed just) with that of the perfectly unjust agent (who is not reputed unjust, 361a6-b1), so as to establish which of them flourishes. Convinced neither by Thrasymachus' argument, nor by Socrates's answer, Glaucon is nonetheless unable to refute both interlocutors (358c6-d4), and thus introduces a challenge. Socrates now has the burden of the proof, because two of the points made by Thrasymachus are supported by the

---

[1] For interpreters who claim that justice is necessarily altruism, which rules out the good of the agent, see note 6 in Chapter 8.

majority of people (*hoi polloi*, 358a4), that is, that (i) our *politeiai* require justice from us; and (ii) we have no motivation to be just.

Socrates pointed out Thrasymachus' inconsistency in holding both of these theses; however, Glaucon, in rehearsing the majority's argument, shows that force makes them cohere. The argument has four stages: (i) a classification of goods (357b4-358a9); (ii) the definition and origin of justice and injustice (358b1-359c6); (iii) the narrative on the magic ring, aiming to show that justice is not really a good, but a form of coercion (359c7-360c5); (iv) the description of the behaviour of perfectly just and unjust agents, aiming to prove both that all just actions are performed despite oneself, and that flourishing lies in the unjust life (360d8-361d3). Having discussed the last three points in Chapter 10, we shall now address the classification of the goods, which is where the challenge Socrates faces lies.

The division of the good into three types is cause of controversy in recent literature. I shall begin by remarking that Glaucon presents goods as being pursued by different actions and their correspondent states of the soul; in doing so, he takes Thrasymachus' thesis one step further, for he takes into account how Thrasymachean goods affect us. According to Glaucon, a good is the correlation between the state of affairs obtained in action and our psychological states.[2] Here is the text:

> [T48] Does it seem to you that there is a certain good that we take, not due to some expectation of results, but because we welcome it for its own sake, like delights and pleasures that are both harmless and during which nothing happens[3] except for the enjoyment they promote?
>
> To me, I said, there seems to be a good like that.
>
> Is there a good that we want for its own sake and due to what happens after it, like thinking, seeing and being healthy? For in a certain way we welcome them due to both.
>
> Yes, he said.
>
> Do you see, in addition, a third type of good, he said, to which belong practicing gymnastics, undergoing treatment when sick, practicing medicine and other ways of money-making? For we would say that these are burdensome, but beneficial to us, and we do not take them for the sake of themselves, but due to a reward and other events that happen after them. (357b4-d2)

All these goods are relative to us; they are ends of our actions. The first type is described as what we welcome for its own sake (*hautou heneka*, 357b6), which is exemplified by delights and pleasures that are harmless and do not bring about any other event besides the enjoyment. Some contemporary interpreters argue that Glaucon here mistakes what is desired for its own sake and what promotes immediate satisfaction, claiming that 'for its own sake' must mean that there is something in the object that makes it intrinsically good.[4] I see no reason for this claim, however.

---

[2] For the relation between powers and states, see Reeve 2013: 54-7.

[3] I read *eis ton epeita chronon* not as 'afterwards', but as 'while it lasts', considering that *chronon* entails a definite duration, that of the enjoyment, and this is the duration that follows (*epeita*) the acquisition of this good. So, the idea is that nothing else – either an extra pleasure or a pain – occurs while we are enjoying this good.

[4] This is the first point of controversy. Mabbott, for example, argues that, if what Socrates must prove is that justice is good in itself, then this is a futile task because 'to prove that something is good in itself is to give a reason why it is good, and this is *ipso facto* an admission that this is not good in itself' (Mabbott 1937: 474). Foster is right in correcting him: 'what he means would be better expressed if he said that justice is good in virtue of its proper effect on the soul, apart from its reward' (Foster 1938: 230). Kirwan (1965: 172-3) holds that it is a formal, but not efficient, cause of happiness, and states that 'if praising justice on its own terms then

Glaucon is perfectly entitled to assume that goods are relative to the beholder (a point to which Socrates is also committed, as we have seen in Chapters 9 and 14), since he assumes the premise that goods are ends of our actions.

If this is correct, a good of the first kind is an unmixed pleasure, since, being harmless, there is no pain coming out of it, and no other event, either good or bad, may be added to it while it lasts. This latter clause distinguishes this good from the second kind, which introduces an extra good while the previous one lasts. This feature indicates that Glaucon excludes one alternative from the list of goods: mixed pleasures, that is, those which also generate pain while they last (such as Leontius observing the corpses).

Moving forward, the contrast between the first two and the third types of good brings us more information about the classification: while both of the first goods are distinguished by the presence or the absence of an extra good, the third is defined as a good that obtains after a burdensome action. If this classification may be considered exhaustive, we would be able to infer that the first two kinds cannot be preceded by burdensome tasks (they are effortless),[5] and that events both preceding and succeeding the first kind of good must be included in its description. This is what we can see in Table 2.

Table 2 The Division of Goods in *Republic* II

	T0	T1	T2
Type 1	Neither burden nor good	Good	Neither burden nor good
Type 2	Indifferent	Good	Good + Good
Type 3	Indifferent	Burden	Good

I do not claim that Glaucon has this kind of exhaustive classification in mind, but I do regard these as the terms under which Socrates takes up the challenge. Evidence of this may be found in his final argument to Glaucon in *Republic* IX, in regard to his concept of pure (or unmixed) pleasure exemplified by the smell of a perfume, which is neither preceded nor followed by either pain or pleasure (see 584a12-c2). Pure pleasure plays a key-role in Socrates' defence of justice (a point I shall return to later), and so, in Glaucon's failure to provide one, I shall take the perfume as a good example of the first type of good, welcomed for its own sake.

The second type of good is also welcomed for its own sake, but not as pure pleasure because it is more than that. It is distinguished by the addition of an extra good. Being a good for its own sake is a broader category of which the first two kinds of good are species. On the other hand, since the good for its own sake is the end of an action, and not a means to anything, we must be careful in explaining how, in type two, a good for its own sake relates to the extra good. The second type of good therefore entails two different goods in such a way that, although the second occurs after the first, the first does not constitute a mere means to the latter (see also Adeimantus' emphasis at 367c7-8). If this is correct, the usual translation of *tōn ap'autou gignomenōn* (what

---

includes praising it for the consequence that it makes men happy, Glaucon and Adeimantus must assume a distinction between different kinds of consequences: some must be excluded, others not' (Kirwan 1965: 163). Heinaman insists on the formula of an intrinsic good with the strange definition that 'what is intrinsically good in it is not independent of what we would call its causal consequences' (Heinaman 2002: 311). In the interpretation I propose, the fact that the first kind of good does not have consequences of a certain sort is required by its definition as harmless. Finally, I stand with White that 'we have to take both the proposition that justice generates happiness and the proposition that it generates pleasure as part of Plato's commitment to the thesis that justice is good "by itself"' (White 1984: 403).

[5] Irwin 1999: 174.

happens after it) as 'consequences' is somewhat precarious.⁶ Rather than a sufficient condition, we shall therefore simply suppose something like a necessary condition between the two goods. For similar reasons, our contemporary distinction between intrinsic and extrinsic goods is not helpful with goods of the second type.⁷ First, because both the goods in t1 and in t2 must be good *for the agent*.⁸ Second, because neither is good *for the sake of* something else.

Glaucon's examples for the second type of good may be misleading to a certain extent, for he mentions only the goods in t1: 'to think', 'to see' and 'to be healthy'. One must note, however, that these are actions without previous effort in the sense that they do not imply a movement to supplant a previous lack. What Glaucon has in mind appears to be something like this: I can find an answer to a question while thinking; I can enjoy beauty while seeing; I can experience the perfume while healthy (note that the argument on pure pleasures in book IX is addressed to sick people). If this is correct, we can suppose that, for goods of the second type, the good in t1 is a necessary condition for pure pleasures that are the good in t2. In this case, neither the good in t1, nor the good in t2 coincides with the first type of good, because the latter can neither be preceded by a good (as the good in t2), nor be succeeded by a good (as the good in t1). I conclude that the first two kinds of good correspond to ends that (i) are neither the outcome of anything, nor a necessary condition for anything (the first type of good); and (ii) relate in such a way that one is a necessary condition, but not a means, for the other (the second type of good).⁹

The third type of good is called the painful one (357c8) and is later dismissed as an actual good (see 359b1-2). This is because it is not for its own sake (357c9); that is, it is not an end of our actions. Glaucon (and the majority) supposes that all the ends of our actions are pleasures. It is of key importance to understand that the third kind is a good because it is the end of a burdensome action, coinciding with the relief of this pain, to which a pleasure may be added. Examples of this are physical exercise, medicine (both as the treatment of the sick and as the practice of the doctor) and business in general, that is, work aiming at making money (357c7-8). I shall now proceed to argue that they are neither the end of our actions nor sufficient causes for it.

Neither physical exercise nor medical treatment, both considered physical effort, is sufficient to obtain health. Nor is practising medicine or any other job aiming at money sufficient to obtain a good, for, as we saw, these agents produce the good of others and rely on the reciprocity of the wage experts for obtaining their ends. Goods of the third kind are thus actions pursued under some expectations. They justify the effort, not because the effort is sufficient to obtain goods, but

---

⁶ See Foster 1938: 228; Cross and Woozley 1964: 66–8; White 1984: 395–6, 418; Heinaman 2002: 332.
⁷ White refers to the question as corresponding to the concept of *sunaitia* (White 1984: 395–6); Irwin suggests categories like 'supreme component' (Irwin 1977: 188) or 'dominant component' (Irwin 1999: 174–5); Shields speaks of 'a good partially constitutive of a more comprehensive and ultimate good' (Shields 2006: 70). This means that, according to Irwin, justice being a good of the second kind is a way to ensure that happiness will only come when other goods (provided by social processes or by the favour of the gods) are added to justice – if they are not, there will be no happiness (Irwin 1999: 179). In this sense, being just is not enough for happiness, as other factors are important. But it does not follow from this that 'being just guarantees by itself that just people will be happier than any unjust person, even if they are not happy' (Irwin 1999: 176). As I understand it, the text does not attest that Socrates is committed to degrees of flourishing; rather, it is very clear in stating that philosophers in an unjust city do not flourish, in whichever degree.
⁸ For a critique of this trait as a kind of egoism, see Prichard [1928] 2002: 120; Santas 1985: 227; Brown 2007: 49. Although I can understand that some may hold that there is something as an 'ordinary moral conviction' that the 'moral person's reason for doing just actions is not that to do so is a good to the agents themselves' (Brown 2007: 44), I claim that it is perfectly reasonable to hold that just actions are those performed by agents who, in pursuit of their good, do not harm the flourishing of others, and that there is no reason for considering cooperative actions unjust if they do not harm anyone. See also Penner (2007: 95–101)
⁹ Kirwan (1965: 169) suggests that the distinction in the second type of good is between what is pleasurable and what is beneficial, but this qualitative distinction finds no textual support.

because it is a means that may lead to them.[10] In all cases, obtaining the good is not in the power of the agent; what they can do is an effort to obtain some favourable conditions for it. Other causes must interfere for a good of the third kind to obtain, because the agent is not their own benefactor.[11]

The structure and vocabulary[12] of Glaucon's argument suggest that the same type of condition/event pattern must be found in all types of goods. Nonetheless, we concluded that the causal pattern is very different among them: In the first type, we have pleasures that are not causes of anything. In the second, an action done for its own sake is a necessary condition for other goods to be added to it. In the third type, the action is painful and in expectation of a good that cannot be obtained by the action itself. Therefore, I would like to suggest that the common pattern indicated in the vocabulary is not causal; rather, it is simply temporal, expressing the succession shown in Table 2. On the other hand, by associating this classification with certain psychological states, Glaucon offers us three ways in which we may pursue pleasure. We are motivated by (i) pure pleasure, (ii) pleasure with added pleasure and (iii) pain in expectation of pleasure. I understand this to be a fair portrayal of an account given by the majority, who is not particularly interested in exhaustive classification or logical inferences, and who, on the other hand, assumes pleasure as the end of all their actions.

Given this scenario, Glaucon explains that the majority of people sees justice as a good of the third type (specifically, the type exemplified by the practice of medicine and other ways of making money) in the belief that justice is laborious, difficult and practised only in order to obtain public reputation (358a5). Public reputation, in turn, offers a favourable (neither necessary nor sufficient) condition for others who, believing the agent to be just, would then provide them with goods on a reciprocal basis. A reputation for justice generates trust, and trust is a condition for the expectation of benefits. Agents engage in effort and pain because they trust that this will make others more likely to give them goods that they cannot obtain by their own action. The majority believes that justice is the duty performed by the agent within a system of merit based on reputation, which gives agents some expectation of receiving goods from others. As we have already seen in Glaucon's argument, the majority thus relies on the social contract to be just.

This is an improved development of Thrasymachus' thesis of justice as the good of others. Rather than claiming that the just actions are unreasonable and nonsensical because their end is not a good for the agent, Glaucon shows that they are based on expectations which rely on certain principles of political life: justice is what others expect from us in order to reciprocate us with goods. In this case, we see justice as a duty we have to our community. Yet Glaucon is not satisfied with this account: one cannot know if expectations will be met, and the experience may provide frustration. That justice is a good of the third kind does not give us a cogent argument for practicing it; it is for this reason that Glaucon, the majority, Thrasymachus, Adeimantus, etc. claim that we should leave expectations about others aside and aim at obtaining our ends ourselves. This, of course, entails that we should give up on justice.

Glaucon challenges Socrates to show that justice is a second type good (358a1-3), in particular, the good in t1, which corresponds to the examples of 'thinking', 'seeing' and 'being healthy'. Justice is something we welcome for its own sake to which other unspecified goods may be added. Socrates is excused from arguing for the t2 component of the second kind of good

---

[10] Irwin 1977: 184–5; 325, n. 8; Irwin 1995: 190.
[11] Heinaman (2002: 330), following Kirwan (1965: 163), sees the 'consequences' of the second kind of good as the strongest objection to the general thesis that Glaucon's consequences are all based on reputation.
[12] See *dia tautas gignetai*, 357b8; *tōn ap' autou gignomenōn*, 357c2-3 and *tōn allōn hosa gignetai ap' autōn*, 357d1-2.

(358b6-7), probably because the majority already grants that justice is a condition for benefits from others on the basis of reciprocity.[13] If to demonstrate that justice is a t1 component of the second kind of good amounts to proving that it is something we welcome for its own sake, then the challenge is not to prove that justice is a sufficient cause of flourishing. As a matter of fact, flourishing is not included in the challenge;[14] rather, since there is a t2 component in the second type of good, it is plausible that flourishing may include this additional good (a point suggested by Socrates at 358a1-3). This proves to be the case in book X of the *Republic*, where Socrates clearly states that the goods that come from reciprocating the actions of others are part of human flourishing (613e5-614a3). In Socrates' view, therefore, flourishing is the sum of justice as a good in t1 of the second kind of good plus goods in t2, in which case the latter could be similar to the rewards mentioned in the third kind, though exempted of the prior burden.

On the other hand, undertaking the challenge on these terms does not commit Socrates to the claim of the majority that the mere reputation of justice favours the reciprocation of the actions of others and thus flourishing. Rather, he claims that the gods never reciprocate based on false reputation (612e2-3), and that, as false reputation is always temporary among human beings (613c3-7), in the long run, it is real justice that is necessary for reciprocity. False reputation of justice is a hindrance to flourishing in two stages, for (i) it does not give us the good of justice as a good for its own sake; and (ii) it does not give us a lasting good provided by others.[15] The agent's expectation for reciprocity is properly fulfilled only in the case of the genuinely just person. If Socrates agrees to go along with Glaucon in dispensing with the discussion on rewards, this does not commit him to the assumption that rewards are not necessarily grounded on real justice. His defence is that real and lasting rewards would result only from real justice.[16]

The time factor introduced in Socrates' final conclusion leads to paradoxical positions regarding short-term reciprocity. If a just agent may have a transitory false reputation, as Glaucon suggests, and may also be exposed to torture, violence and even murder, this may not alter the good that their justice provides them with. But it will surely affect their flourishing. Socrates thinks that justice is a good that should not be given up on even under these conditions, and that these are the conditions that would justify actions aiming at lesser evils, rather than goods. Some

---

[13] Perhaps the majority should not assume this, as strictly speaking they consider justice neither necessary nor sufficient for the rewards of others. Rather, I emphasize that, in their view, *reputation* of justice allows for a favourable condition (which is therefore neither necessary nor sufficient) for reciprocity.

[14] Irwin claims that 'the three classes of goods are intended to include all goods that can be considered ways of achieving happiness' (Irwin 1999: 165), and that none of them 'intends to include happiness itself' (1995: 190), in which he is followed by Shields 2006: 67. Some interpreters understand that the argument of the *Republic* is that justice is sufficient for happiness (see Annas 2000: 310). I understand that this approach can offer an adequate reading neither of the second type of good, nor of the argument in book X, nor of Socrates' mention of his own life as a kind of expectation of death (496e1-3). Socrates never states that the just man who is tortured flourishes, nor that the virtuous flourishes in the worst circumstances (as Annas 2011: 112 suggests). Flourishing implies external goods (those I called inalienable goods), for which reason the argument about the *politeia* is central to the dialogue, and not a digression. For better or for worse, the Socrates of the *Republic* is not a Stoic, as suggested by Annas 2000: 311–12.

[15] Pleasure is certainly intrinsic to the definition of justice, not a consequence of being just (see Butler 2008: 237), but I understand, in disagreement with Butler, that reputation is also intrinsic to being just because one cannot be just without acting in a just way, one cannot act with justice without interacting with others, and one cannot perform a just act without obtaining a just state of affairs in that interaction.

[16] Annas (2011: 112) suggests that the argument excludes rewards; instead she reads that the love of the gods will turn external evils into good results, since the just know how to use those evils. It is very difficult to understand how, on this interpretation, the argument amounts to reintroducing reputation in the problem of justice. Moreover, Socrates presents the argument in book X as an extra argument, different from the one given in book IX, and denies that, in the long run, the just can have a reputation for being unjust, because just actions obtain just states of affairs.

of these actions are, as we have seen, quietism in the case of a just person living in an unjust city and ruling in the case of a philosopher living in a just city.

I understand that Glaucon's challenge frames Socrates' account of justice. Glaucon, for instance, considers it a fact that justice is an action performed due to some expectation based on a reciprocity system, which Socrates is thus exempted from proving. Furthermore, Socrates is not required to prove that the duty performed due to expectation is in itself pleasant, for the two categories were clearly distinguished in two different kinds of good; rather, he must show that these efforts of being just are performed as an activity practised for its own sake. I submit that this can be associated with what was addressed, in Chapter 6, as *philoponia*, the transference of pleasure to effort due to a certain psychological state.

Socrates' response to this challenge runs through the entire dialogue, most of which is now clear. At 587d12-e4, however, we find the announcement of a substantive result at the end of a series of three arguments: the best of lives is 729 times more pleasant than the worst. While such a calculus is obviously metaphorical, the conclusion leads us to an objective notion of flourishing that is comparable, quantifiable and demonstrable; moreover, a conclusion in terms of pleasure, just like the challenge. I shall now argue that this notion of flourishing includes three factors that are each mobilized by one of three arguments provided by Socrates for his conclusion:[17] (i) the flourishing by political life; (ii) the flourishing by prudence based on learning and (iii) the flourishing by pure and true pleasures. I shall demonstrate that the first factor presupposes the other two, while the second presupposes the first, and together they configure three types of just life: the ruler's justice, the philosopher's justice and the citizen's justice. My conclusion is that only the combination of the three constitutes the best of lives, the cooperative flourishing found in Kallipolis. If this is true, then the argument in book IX (578c1-588a2) is different from what we find in book IV (435d9-445b8) – which simply argues that justice is the health of the soul – as well as from the argument in book X (612a8-614b1), where rewards are reintegrated into the general motivation for a just life.

In 580b1-c11, Socrates announces that Glaucon agrees with the first demonstration that 'the best, fairest person, who flourishes the most, is the one *who is the best king* and who rules himself as a king; while the worst, most unjust and most decrepit happens to be the one who rules himself in the most tyrannical way, and *who is also a tyrant in the city*' (580c1-5, my emphasis).[18] It is not clear at what point the argument that ends with this conclusion begins, and interpreters differ on this issue.[19] In a certain way, it involves the entire dialogue of the *Republic*, since this finale implies understanding what it means for someone to rule himself 'as a king' or 'in the most tyrannical way'. However, since it is followed by two other arguments that in turn also retrieve previous theses of the *Republic*, it seems more plausible that this is inferred from an argument with a more restricted scope.

I propose that the reference is much more restricted than is generally supposed: the argument refers to the complements emphasized by my italics. In other words, having already defined what the just city, the philosopher, tyranny and the tyrannical personality are, Socrates then concludes what the difference is between the best king (the Philosopher-King) and the

---

[17] In taking this position, I reject the interpretation that only the first argument concerns flourishing, while the other two deal with pleasure (see Murphy 1951: 207; Gosling and Taylor 1982: 100–2; Irwin 1995: 291–2; Kraut 2011: 211). For a position closer to mine, which however disregards the first argument, see Russell 2005: 113.
[18] My italics have gone unnoticed by interpreters in general, who simply state that the first argument compares the lives of the philosopher and the tyrant. For a more attentive interpretation, see Kurihara 2013: 122–3.
[19] Kraut (2011: 209), for example, assumes that the argument starts at 576b10; Butler (1999b: 37) that it begins in 544a5, still in book VIII.

worst tyrant (the one with the tyrannical personality). As we saw in Chapter 9, the fact that such a tyrannical tyrant only occurs due to some misfortune (578c2) indicates that there is nothing in the concept of tyrannical personality which entails that such a person would rule, and nothing in the concept of tyranny which entails that its ruler has such a personality; rather, the case of the tyrannical personality coming to rule a tyranny appears only in 578c1, and thus we should consider the first argument to run from 578c1 to 580c11. By emphasizing the exercise of government as the important feature of the two lives in comparison (578c5-7), this argument deals with what complete justice and complete injustice do to an individual *because* they are the sole ruler of a city.[20]

Socrates begins by comparing the tyrant to a slave master, claiming that they differ only by quantity (578d7): the tyrant enslaves all citizens, while the slave master only those who are his property – a comparison already present in Thrasymachus' speech (344a4-c9). Next, Socrates suggests that if a god were to transport this master, his family and slaves to a wilderness where he did not have the help of other citizens, he would certainly fear being murdered by his slaves, and would be liable to flatter them in an attempt to manage the situation (578e1-579a4). Following this, Socrates projects a further scenario. This time, all members of the *oikos* would be surrounded by neighbours who disapprove of slavery, and who would therefore demand that the master be severely punished (579a5-8). The situation of the tyrannical tyrant thus resembles the situation of the master, because (i) as a flatterer, he is enslaved by his own desires (as the master who cannot be free because his action depends on the action of the slaves); and (ii) as someone who cannot share with others beliefs about his personal flourishing which include the flourishing of others, he is hated by others (as the master that refuses to be equal to his neighbours and is punished).

The tyrannical personality who rules a tyranny is miserable for two connected causes: for not being able to pursue only good pleasures (he lives without satisfaction), and for not being able to cooperate (he lives surrounded by enemies) (579a9-b1). Due to his strong desires, he is forced to live in seclusion for his safety, and, holed up at home in the same way as Greek women (579b7–c1), cannot leave the city or enjoy festivals (579b5-7). In short, he has to deprive himself of the citizen's life (579c1-2). The deprivation of political life is an intrinsic feature, as opposed to an extrinsic reward, of this kind of life, because it is the state of affairs obtained by that person's action. Socrates makes this point well when he says that this condition of misery is true, even if it is hidden from gods and human beings (580c7–8). Thus, Socrates' conclusion is rigorously established within the scope of Glaucon's challenge. He proves that injustice, in this case being a tyrannical personality, is an evil for its own sake – and it is also necessary for obtaining other evils, like becoming a tyrannical tyrant (579c4-d3).

Up to this point, Socrates' description matches Thrasymachus': the tyrant is the complete unjust agent. It is simply a matter of political power that distinguishes the tyrannical tyrant from the tyrannical personality, a detail that increases the harm this person may cause, even to himself, for being a tyrant worsens the life of a tyrannical personality. Though he expects that power will suffice to avoid suffering punishment, the exercise of such a power, in building all these 'walls' to protect him against punishment, only serves to make him more miserable: the tyrannical tyrant thus does great evil unto himself, adopting the life of a slave (compare 579c1-2 to d11). Worse evils

---

[20] This detail about being the sole ruler shows that, for the sake of the argument, which aims at comparing individual lives instead of addressing the feasibility of justice, the Kallipolis proposal was replaced by the Philosopher-King proposal.

may come on the basis of a reciprocity: he must flatter vile people to keep himself alive in his own house and, if others may obtain power to reciprocate, he may suffer punishment at their hands.

What does this first argument tell us about justice? Though it does not say anything explicitly, we are able to infer a great deal since the argument supposes the concept of Philosopher-King. As we have seen, a Philosopher-King cannot, by definition, live in an unjust city, for here philosophers refrain from political life. In claiming that political life is a good required for our flourishing, the present argument confirms our previous inferences that, for a Philosopher-King, to rule is a means by which philosophers flourish. If so, the first argument demonstrates that political life is an inalienable good to any human being, being deprived of which is an evil for its own sake. In addition, the argument demonstrates that the lifestyle of a citizen is required in order to obtain this good. Thus I conclude that political life is an extra good that is added to justice as a good for its own sake, which can be qualified as a good in t2 of the second kind of good. Now I would like to demonstrate how his two following arguments identify justice as a good in t1 of the second kind of good, which is necessary (although not sufficient) for political life. The fact that Socrates needs two arguments corresponds to the fact that he believes both philosophers and just citizens have pleasure in being just.

The second argument (580d2-583b2) takes up the conclusions of the argument regarding the tripartition of the soul in book IV (435e9-441c7) to point out that there are three kinds of pleasure, each peculiar to a specific part of the soul (580d2-7). As we already know, this pleasure occurs when we act in pursuit of an end which is aimed at by such a part: when this kind of action becomes a habit for us, our internal conflicts disappear, as competing ends do not interest us. This allows us to establish a certain character, a certain kind of life. Some lives are structured around one single end, attaching no value to other ends and to the pleasures that are proper to them (581d2-3): we know these as the lovers, among which are three prime kinds of personalities – the lover of money or profit, the lover of victory or honour, and the lover of learning or wisdom (the philosopher). The second argument compares the types of pleasures linked to the structuring ends of these three prime personalities to establish which is the truest among them, or in the terminology I prefer, which of them has the most genuine (*alethēstata*) pleasure (581e5-582a1). I wish to emphasize this pattern of comparison. Just as the first argument compares the just ruler with the unjust, this argument compares the philosopher with the lover of honour and the lover of wealth – and not with other personality types.

The difficulty here is that the pleasures of money and honour are incommensurable with the philosopher's pleasure. It can't be otherwise, since Socrates went to great lengths to show in book IV that they have different sources and different ends. Many interpreters have pointed out Socrates' inconsistency in reducing the parts of the soul to species of pleasure, as well as the folly of attempting to compare incommensurable things, not to mention the arbitrariness of simply concluding that the philosopher's pleasure is superior.[21] Some of these interpreters thus understand the argument as having a relativist premise, amounting to the claim that whoever it is that judges the most pleasant life, will judge their own life as the most pleasant life; which, however, begs the question of Socrates' proof of which is the most pleasant life.

I hold that Socrates is not committed to the relativist premise; rather, his target is to determine what is required in this sort of judgement. The first premise is that someone is a good judge because they either have experience, prudence or arguments (582a3-5). Socrates' next step is to reject that someone can be a good judge of something they ignore. Thus he states that the pleasures of the money-lover, here under the description of nutritive, reproductive and

---

[21] See Bosanquet 1895: 350–1; Nettleship 1922: 321; Cross and Woozley 1964: 264–6.

similar pleasures (see 580e2-581a1), are experienced by everyone from childhood (582b2-3). So, too, are the pleasures of the honour lover, for, in general, when someone accomplishes some achievement, they are honoured by others (582c4-5). The pleasures of learning, Socrates claims, are rarer. This is because they are not simply the pleasures of learning anything whatsoever. They are the pleasures of learning the reality of things (582b4).

Now if the inference were only that the philosopher is a good judge because they have more experience of all kinds of pleasure, it would be invalid. The philosopher does not have other pleasures because these are not ends for their action.[22] This is not the case, however. The argument is simply that others are not good judges of philosophical pleasure because they do not experience it. The pleasure of the philosopher is impossible for anyone else (582c8-9). The argument proceeds on the same standards in addressing prudence and arguments (582d4-14): lives devoted to other ends find no pleasure and no purpose in pursuing prudence or justification for their actions. On the other hand, the end of philosophical life, the pleasure of learning reality, intrinsically provides one with prudence and arguments. The philosophical life is the best judge because it is a life that takes being capable of good judgement as one of the goods at which it aims.

Interpreters have also criticized the argument for its restriction of pleasure to certain activities at the expense of others. Here, they assume that the argument concludes that the most genuine pleasures are only those of philosophical activity, and thus that Socrates appears to be committed to a conception of flourishing that excludes some pleasures proper to the human species.[23] This criticism misses its target, however, for it is important to note that the second argument is restricted to a comparison of the three lovers (excluding other human pleasures) and that it does not compare pleasures, but qualifications for good judgement. The pleasure the philosopher experiences plays a role in the third, rather than in the second, argument and, when we get there, we shall learn that this kind of pleasure, genuine pleasure, is experienced by human beings in general.[24]

Up to now we have two different points: (i) the philosopher governs by gaining the benefit of political life; (ii) the philosopher judges with prudence.[25] Before proceeding, we must note that the second argument makes an implicit critique of Glaucon's challenge. As I pointed out, every good in the challenge was reducible to some pleasure, with their differences accounted for by succession in time and relation to pain. It should not be a surprise that the majority, whom Glaucon represents, would conflate good and pleasure (see 505b5-6), a premise Socrates explicitly rejects in defending that not every pleasure is of the same kind, whilst arguing against the majority on its own terms. Rather than talking about good and bad pleasures, he talks about the most genuine pleasures. I began the analysis of the second argument by stating that there was a problem with comparing incommensurable objects. Now, I can argue that in reducing all objects to pleasure, Socrates may compare them on the same scale and provide the majority with an answer based on some hedonistic calculus.

---

[22] Some interpreters have thought that the philosopher would enjoy wealth (qualifiedly), honour (qualifiedly) and learning. See Reeve 1988: 145–146; Irwin 1995: 293 and Russell 2005: 126.

[23] For interpreters that see Socrates as reducing intrinsically good activities to philosophy, see Gosling and Taylor 1982: 106; Nussbaum 1986: 124.

[24] For interpretations that assume that only philosophers have true pleasure because this concept involves a metaphysics of the degrees of reality set out in books V–VII, see Frede 1985: 160; Scott 2000b: 16; Erginel 2011: 493.

[25] As Kraut (2011: 216) points out, this second argument primarily provides reasons for being a philosopher. It is only indirectly that it gives reasons for being just. As I shall now show, it is the third argument that articulates pleasure, justice and flourishing.

The catch is that, in doing so, he is still able to introduce a qualitative distinction by talking about different degrees of the authenticity of pleasures. This moves Socrates apart from a simple hedonistic position, which claims that justice is pleasure *tout court*. More refined, his answer to the challenge is formulated in the terms he was given while still explaining that being a good for its own sake is not exactly the same as being a pleasure. Notice that, when Glaucon asks Socrates to defend that justice is a good for its own sake, he also assumes that a pure pleasure, whose cessation causes no pain, is a good for its own sake (see 357b6-8). This offers Socrates grounds to show Glaucon what is the relation between a good for its own sake and a pure pleasure. If correct, this argument is an important step in showing that justice leads to a better life by emphasizing that the best life depends on learning that leads to prudence in judgement.

The third argument is heralded as the greatest and most important of the tyrant's downfalls. The thesis that it aims to prove is that there are some pleasures, neither genuine nor pure, that are like chiaroscuro paint. They are made out of their contrast (583b5) and are a case of opposite appearances (584a7-10). Paradoxical as it may sound, this amounts to showing that there is a feeling of pleasure that is not really pleasure. With this claim, Socrates spells out the philosopher's reasons, in the previous argument, for judging some pleasures as more genuine: it is not the feeling of pleasure that counts for the best of lives but the feeling of genuine pleasures. The third argument unfolds in two stages. The first argues that there is serenity (583c1-585a7). The second argues that there are pure and genuine pleasures (585a8-587b11).

We begin with the description of pleasure and pain as activities expressed by the verbs (583c5) 'enjoy' and 'suffer', hereafter characterized as psychic processes or movements of the soul (583e9-10). Next, Socrates introduces his imaginary interlocutors, the sick (583c10-11). Sick people argue that there is nothing as pleasant as being healthy (583c13), although, before getting sick, they were unaware that this was a pleasure (583c13-d1). Thereafter, they present a contradictory account. On the one hand, nothing seems more pleasant to them than the cessation of pain (583d3-5). So, they conclude it is not 'enjoying' that is the most pleasant thing, but serenity – a stage when the movement of the soul ceases (583d6–9). On the other hand, when serenity is reached, pleasure stops and the cessation of pleasure is painful (583e1-2). In sum, serenity is simultaneously the cessation of the pleasure of recovering from pain and the beginning of another pain (583e4-5).[26]

Socrates denounces the account of the sick as absurd for they assume that serenity, which by definition is neither enjoying nor suffering (584a4-5), combines both enjoyment and suffering (583e7-584a3).[27] This is because they think serenity is simply a transition from the pausing of one pain to the beginning of another. The pleasure of pausing pain should, in Socrates' view, be considered a mix of pain and pleasure that also holds true for the pain of pausing the pleasure. These are what he considers to be appearances of pleasure and pain. After all, appearances are the perceptual items that accept the compresence of opposites. If so, the sick do not have a proper

---

[26] The argument only works if it is about the prediction the sick people make about their future states, and the fact that the end of the pleasure they desire will itself be painful (see Butler 1999a: 290–1). Anticipation is a case in which the falsity of a pleasure is much more evident, as it highlights the intentional content – X appears to me as pleasurable – and allows us to analyse it, when it finally happens, as true or false. See Russell 2005: 129; Warren 2011: 129.

[27] I have a different position from Warren, who considers serenity as a 'hedonic state' (Warren 2011: 114), whose evidence would prove the sick people that there can be pleasure without perception of pleasure (idem, 118). I understand that Socrates never considers serenity as a pleasure; it is, by definition, an absence of pleasure, which does not mean that it does not contain well-being. I still agree with Warren that the evidence for serenity is central to the argument.

cognition about pleasure and pain, for they simply judge something that is both as either pain or pleasure (584a7-10).

To differentiate appearances of pleasure and pain from pure pleasure, Socrates introduces the aforementioned example of the latter (584a12-b2): the pleasure of a perfume (584b5) parallel to the pure pain of a bad smell.[28] This is distinct from most of the pleasures we experience, which are mixed with pain (584c3-5). These also include those of anticipation, such as those the sick feel when they think about getting healthier (584c7-9), which, in adding pleasure to our present pain, increase our endurance (as we already noted about the agency of the *thumos*). To argue for the existence of such pure pleasures, Socrates proposes the three-stage scheme: the lower, the intermediate and the higher (584d3-4).

From the perspective of someone who, like the sick, is in the lower stage and has never experienced the upper levels, being transported to the middle stage appears to be the achievement of the upper stage in itself (584d6-7). From this perspective, returning to the lower stage seems to be returning to true pain (584d7-9).[29] Interpreters debate whether, according to the image, pleasure and pain are located in the transition from one stage to another or in the stage itself.[30] A decisive point is that serenity is described, without further justification, as an intermediate stage at 583d7-8. It is thus quite plausible that the three-level image was formulated after this position, allowing us to conclude that the intermediate stage is serenity. On the other hand, the example of the perfume as a pure pleasure seems to be identified with the higher level. It thus seems much more reasonable to consider the transitions between stages as movements of the soul. If this is the case, the lower level coincides with the position of real or pure pain, which is not a cessation of pleasure that is located in the transition from the intermediate to the lower.

The account by the sick of pleasure and pain as motions between the two lower levels is also described by the images of 'emptying' and 'replenishing' (584e8-585a1), which suggest a physiological background. Associated with these descriptions, the transitions between the lower levels become more evidently cyclical: one is constantly in process of emptying or replenishing. At the very moment we become 'full', another emptying movement begins. This means that the sick do not recognize Socrates' stages as levels at which one may remain and so, if there is no permanence, from the perspective of these people, there is no real serenity (the intermediate state) in which there may be rest. Neither is there a pure pain or a pure pleasure in the sense of a feeling that occurs while we remain full. Rather, they understand their life as a constant alternation of filling and emptying (see 586a3).

---

[28] Warren (2011: 126) suggests that there is not actually a pure pain. But it is simple to think that not all aromas are pleasant and that the bad smell would be a perfect candidate for pure pain. I understand that my disagreement with Warren refers to his concept of pure pain as 'a pain whose disappearance does not bring pleasurable relief' (idem, 127). Pure pleasure causes pleasure by being added, and it is strange to think that pure pain does not cause pleasure by being removed. Furthermore, the text is clear in describing pure pain as 'pain that does not come from cessation of pleasure' (584b2). The important criterion for purity is the absence of replenishing or emptying.

[29] Frede (1985: 159) understands this return movement as coming from the 'true upper level to the state of rest'. The text clearly says that the movement starts at the middle stage (584d7). Warren (2011: 132) assumes that while the pleasure of moving up is apparent, the pain of descent is real, but accidental. This is problematic, even more so given his position on the absence of true pain. There is nothing in the text to suggest that the two movements are not analogously apparent – quite the contrary.

[30] For arguments defending pleasure as transition, see Murphy 1951: 216–17; Erginel 2011: 497; Warren 2011: 132. For arguments to the contrary, which defend pleasure as a state, see Butler 1999a: 295. For those who think Plato confuses the two, see Gosling and Taylor 1982: 112–22.

On the other hand, claims Socrates, without serenity, one cannot account for a pleasure like the one of perfume that does not depart from an 'empty' state of pain. When they cease, these pure pleasures do not lead us back into pain. So, their cessation must lead us back to serenity.[31] Pure and genuine pleasures thus depend on the stability of the intermediate level, while their lasting corresponds to the stability of the upper. Because they do not fill a void, and they do not cause a lack when they cease,[32] they are not to be mistaken for serenity, for serenity is their necessary condition of departure and arrival.

The conclusion, then, is that most people confuse pleasure with an appearance of pleasure.[33] Indeed, Socrates goes on to detail how most people's lives never reach true fulfilment, though they constantly revel in the pleasures of food, drink and sex (586a5-8). Their inexperience of pleasures of a different kind relegates them to the lower levels in which all pleasure is a matter of having more of a certain object (*pleonexia*, 586b1). Thus, they require more pleasure in order to avoid the pain of its cessation. Due to the kind of pleasure they seek, however, each time they fulfil a pleasure, they lack more and are confined in an insatiable chain of desire (586b1-4). To claim that there is serenity and pleasures that depart from it is neither to claim that one should not have appearances of pleasure, for this is not even possible, nor that one does not have a pleasant feeling in these experiences. Rather, Socrates' claim is that flourishing comes from genuine and pure pleasure, not from its appearance.[34] This is because appearance promotes the cycles of lack, and *pleonexia* leads us to violence against others (586a8-c6).

The second part of the argument aims to detail two further points:[35] (i) how serenity is achieved; and (ii) how pure pleasures happen. Socrates introduces two examples of replenishment: nutrition (replenishment of bodily emptiness) and learning (replenishment of soul emptiness). He compares them according to the objects we assimilate in each of them, as well as according to the type of repletion they produce. Problematic from a textual point of view, I propose the following translation of the passage:

[T49] Is replenishment more genuine when it is of what is more real or of what is less real?
  Certainly, of what is more real.
  Which of the two types [of object of replenishment] do you consider to take a greater part in pure essence: that which relates to food, drink, spices and nutrition in general, or

[31] Gosling and Taylor (1982: 112) understand that the perfume is a bodily pleasure because it is related to perception. However, it is not the difference of objects that distinguishes true from false pleasure, it is the fact that the former originates in serenity. Erginel (2011: 509) mentions pleasures of honour and pleasures of anticipation (which would have certain opinions as their object) as other impure pleasures whose replenishment would not be done by corporeal objects.
[32] Butler (1999a: 295) assumes that, because the transition between the lower and the intermediate stages is by replenishing and emptying, this would also have to be the case in the transition from the intermediate to the higher stage. This is neither necessary nor compatible with the argument. But to reach this conclusion, one cannot assume stages denote pleasures; one must assume that apparent pleasures and pains are in the transitions, while pure pleasure is the highest stage.
[33] I understand that there is a foreground in which the argument is dialectical to sick people, as defended by Warren (2011: 120), but it also aims the majority of people who does not admit serenity. Having once experienced the absence of health, the majority can understand that serenity is not an illusion of the sick.
[34] I therefore understand that there are not two different criteria for superior pleasure – true pleasure and pure pleasure. I also understand that this is not a philosopher's exclusive pleasure, as it will become clear in what follows. Frede (1985: 159), however, understands that truth and purity are two different criteria for pleasure that end up leading the argument to failure. Her argument for the difference is that the criterion of truth is more restricted than that of purity, as the filling with 'more being' could only be obtained through knowledge, exclusive to the philosopher (idem, 160). The text, however, says that this repletion can very well be done with true belief (see Erginel 2011: 515–16).
[35] There is a gap in the text at 585a8, but there is no doubt that a new argument is introduced here (see Slings 2005: 163).

that which relates to the kind of belief that is true, to knowledge, intelligence and, in sum, to every virtue? Judge as follows: what is always the same, imperishable and true, which both is of such a kind and comes to be in things of this kind, does it seem to you that this is more real than what is never the same, is perishable and which both is of such a kind and comes to be in things of this kind?

What is always the same takes a much greater part in reality.

And then, is there anything that takes a greater part in pure essence than the knowledge of what is always the same?[36]

Not at all. (585b9–c10, my brackets)

This distinction between types of replenishment depends on the duration of the resulting state, which, in turn, depends on objects being more or less lasting. The emphasis is therefore on the durational sense of the verb 'to be',[37] that is, perishable objects are less real than the imperishable ones, the latter belonging to the same kind of being as pure essence, which is always the same. Accordingly, replenishments that last for less time, because their objects are perishable, are less genuine than the long-lasting ones (585d7–9). Replenishments with imperishable objects provide lasting serenity that is found in situations in which knowledge; true belief and intelligence are obtained.[38] Socrates encompasses all these in the general class of virtue or excellence. And so, virtue is serenity achieved by replenishment with lasting objects and such replenishment is the most genuine pleasure (585d11-e5).

One cannot fail to notice that virtue is achieved by true belief and, I argue, by a more general concept of knowledge which is not necessarily the one provided by dialectic.[39] Serenity and virtue are not only achieved by philosophers, but result from learning (a process of replenishment) about stable objects. The important distinction is, I suggest, not between philosophers and non-philosophers, but between those who experience serenity and pure pleasures and those who do not, that is, those who organize their lives around appearances (586a1-b4). The third argument confirms that it is not just philosophers who are just and take pleasure in being so; those who neither possess unreasonable desires nor internal conflicts are of the same condition.

On the other hand, the argument shows that some pleasure of replenishment produces serenity, giving us genuine pleasure by taking us out of the cycle of pleasure and pain and placing us in the serenity 'level'. Now we are to understand that pure pleasures are the pleasures that depart from serenity, whose objects are not used to fill us (not even with lasting replenishment, as in learning). They are enjoyed as an extra good for which serenity is necessary but not sufficient. To have a true belief, to know or to have intelligence is to reach the intermediary level of serenity after which pure pleasure arises. This is also the case for virtue, excellence in general,

---

[36] 585c8 is traditionally considered *locus desperatus* (see Slings 2003: 358). I follow the solution proposed by Ferrari (2000: 304) because I understand that it is the one that grants greater intelligibility to the argument.

[37] For the primacy of the durational sense of the verb to be, see Kahn 2003: 194-8.

[38] Gosling and Taylor (1982: 119–20) object that a philosopher's life would require constant replenishing with more knowledge. As already mentioned, dialectic is not a process of obtaining new learning, but of contemplating the relation between learnt objects. For the philosophical life after learning the form of the good, see 540b1-2 and Erginel 2011: 499.

[39] Mention of true belief is neglected by a number of interpreters who assume that all three arguments are about the philosopher (see Annas 1981: 306–11; Kraut 2011: 211). As a result, these interpreters have considerable difficulty in distinguishing the argument in book IX from what appears in book IV, and in distinguishing the difference in purpose of the three arguments in book IX. Annas understands that the philosopher appears in two distinct ways in the two arguments, but the third argument is not restricted to philosophers. Assuming that all arguments are about the philosopher, Kraut (2011: 221) believes that Socrates' definition of justice is too narrow and too intellectualistic. For the emphasis on true belief, see Erginel 2011: 501.

and justice. Serenity allows us not to act with *pleonexia*, guilt, shame, violence or collusion with injustice, and to approach the good for the genuine pleasure it causes us. Intellectual pure pleasures, for instance, come to us after we have learnt, simply by the inferences we make after what we learn.

This is not an orthodox interpretation of the text. Some interpreters understand that the three proofs lead to the same conclusion[40] (i.e. that the philosopher's life is the best) and do not bother to answer why three arguments, in addition to the other one we find in book IV, are necessary to argue for the connection of justice and flourishing. Other interpreters understand that the conclusions of the arguments are different, but that only the first argument (which in their view is about the philosopher in general) talks about flourishing, the last two being based on pleasure. Thence they either point out Socrates' incoherence of assuming a hedonistic position that he has clear reasons to reject, or minimize the importance of these two arguments, claiming that Glaucon's challenge was not to prove that justice was pleasurable.[41] All these positions contrast startlingly with Socrates' statement that the third argument represents the greatest downfall of the tyrant.[42]

If I am correct, the three arguments are complementary to each other and together form Socrates' final response to Glaucon's challenge. He asserts that justice, as the cooperation of the parts of the soul, promotes serenity as a condition for flourishing (understood as obtaining extra-goods that provide pure pleasure). In this sense, justice is a good of second kind, pursued for its own sake as a kind of health of the soul. This serenity is necessary for pleasures that are not of the replenishment kind. This becomes evident if we understand that the three arguments ground each other in the inverse order of their presentation: First, justice is a form of serenity that frees us from the replenishment cycle of *pleonexia* and thus allows us the pure and genuine pleasures proper to our flourishing. Second, the philosopher is someone whose love is just for one kind of pleasure – the pure pleasure of contemplation and prudence. Third, if the philosopher rules in a just city, they obtain an extra pure pleasure, that is, of living the just political life.

The second argument differs from the third in that it shows which condition must be obtained in order to understand what genuine and pure pleasure is. Understanding what such pleasures are is different from being able to have them. One thing may, of course, lead to the other, but it is the understanding the philosopher has about what pleasure is that qualifies their judgement about the best life. The philosopher's capacity for judgement, presented in the second argument, is certainly a requirement for teaching others, by means of arguments like the third one, about the nature of serenity and justice, as well as how to obtain them. If justice may be obtained by habit, it still depends on philosophical knowledge of the good for the laws and on the mores of a cooperative group to be established: there is no education of just citizens without the ruling of a philosopher. Finally, the first argument demonstrates how government, which was introduced

---

[40] See Gosling and Taylor 1982: 99; Butler 1999b: 40.
[41] The fact that it is an argument on pleasure and that it is considered the most decisive has baffled interpreters who assume that Socrates could not give a hedonistic argument to support virtue (see Murphy 1951: 207; Gosling and Taylor 1982: 100; Kraut 1992: 313; 2011: 216), because he had already rejected hedonism at 505c7-9.
[42] Russell (2005: 120–1) maintains that book IV would have proved that, if the hierarchy of the soul parts is out of order, then one part is not in good condition. But Socrates needs to prove more than that; he needs to prove that the hierarchy of the parts of the soul is in order if and only if all its parts are in good condition. This would then be what he aims to prove in book IX: that, for desire, flourishing is not to be fulfilled, but to be guided by reasoning. I agree that this is a result of the third argument, which is why it differs from the argument in book IV, but this is not sufficient – and Russell avoids the question – to differentiate the third from the previous two.

in book I as a burden no one wishes to bring upon themselves, may promote the philosopher's flourishing by adding to their prudence the pure pleasure of the political life in a just city. In short, the three arguments have different purposes, and are distinct from both the argument in book IV and the later argument in book X, in which rewards by means of someone else's actions are reintroduced. All arguments nevertheless undertake to demonstrate the good that justice accomplishes in an individual's life.

Conclusion

The twentieth-century masterpiece on justice opens by placing justice where we are used to having it: social institutions. According to Rawls, 'justice is the virtue of social institutions, as truth is of systems of thoughts' (Rawls 1971: 3). That a just society must secure the rights of its citizens follows a Roman law tradition, according to which justice is 'to *give* each one its own' (*iustitia est cuique suum tribuere*); thus institutions are the agents that give justice to people. In this book, I have tried to show that Plato places justice on a more fundamental level, that of our interactions, by claiming that justice is to *do* one's own. This is not to deny that justice is also to give each one its own, but to say that the former grounds the latter (see 433e10-434a1). To do one's own is not to mind one's own business, but to act considering others as akin, that is, to cooperate. In order to understand justice as such a virtue it is necessary to move it away from the place we are used to finding it: we must shift it towards our own agency.

Cooperation means to engage oneself in an activity in which one can develop one's natural aptitudes, have leisure and produce goods for others. Its end is a state of affairs in which all agents may, in interaction, obtain their good and so enhance their quality of life by promoting personal improvement through one's own accomplishments and the reciprocity of others. When cooperation reaches its end, human beings flourish (see McIntyre 1981[2007]: 187–91). The challenging point of the understanding of justice as a virtue is that it only obtains its end cooperatively: although a single person may be just, they cannot obtain a state of affairs that promotes the good of others, if others pursue unreasonable ends. Individually, a just agent is thus liable to suffer injustice and to fail to flourish. It was not accidental that we developed institutions we expect to situate every one of us according to our rights and duties. But this does not deny the fact that justice is a cooperative enterprise, since, if they fail to have their grounding in citizen's mores, institutions become either oppressive or ineffective. Justice begins in each of us.

It begins, as does this book, with differentiating reasoning and desire, and learning that our desire does not always point out what is good for us. The good must be learnt, which requires significant effort in the form of endurance and real engagement. The support of others – a community that values and teaches us since childhood that our flourishing depends on learning what is really good for us – definitely makes the path much easier, though it is not impossible to do so on our own. In learning, our internal conflicts become more understandable to us. We learn that the pull we feel towards doing something is our desire, and we collect all that we have learnt to see whether what our desires ask for is good for us. We may still act despite ourselves, trusting an unreasonable belief that judged this thing that appeared to us to be good. When we do so, our *thumos* is triggered. Always having our beliefs on personal flourishing (most of which originated from the values shared with a community) as reference, *thumos* is an emotional judgement of our actions and situations. Each time we are not up to ourselves, it adds pain to our pleasure and is a key factor in setting a standard for subsequent actions or situations: *thumos* helps to stabilize character by default attitudes, which leads us to a personality identifiable with a certain end and a certain mode of acting.

We do what is bad for ourselves; no one would deny that. But we do it, I argue, in the belief that it is good. This may happen merely due to a false belief caused by our ignorance, or due to the more complex case of an unreasonable belief, one that says that our good is the opposite of what we have learnt to be good. Pleasure and pain have the effect of diverting the regular function of our cognitive apparatus, activating our desire, which now points out that 'X is good for desire'. When we, by some sort of bewitchment, let ourselves go, our desire prevails to cause us to believe that 'X is good for me'. In this case our *thumos*, connected to what we have learnt to be our flourishing, reacts and causes us an extra pain for having either pursued an unreasonable pleasure or unreasonably avoided a pain. This can also happen at a deeper level. We may adopt an unreasonable belief about our flourishing, after which *thumos* begins to judge us by criteria that are against our own good. When this happens, we start to develop a vicious personality and become someone who has lost their sense of goodness. One of the ways in which this can happen is by experiencing simulative poetry, and this is the cause of the greatest accusation the *Republic* holds against Homer and the tragedians.

Decent people obtain their good from adopting good mores. They are cooperatively virtuous. When they suffer, such as when they grieve, they find in others the support to recover and resume their good way of living. What happens in a mass event of simulative poetry, such as an Athenian festival, is that, for the sake of the pleasure of simulating other stories, lives, worlds, and so on, this community is exposed to strong emotions by means of compassion. Each of these people identifies themselves with the hero, his situation, his action, or his reaction. They thus feel what he feels: emotions are not simulations. This is the catch. Because this is simply entertainment simulation, temporarily adopting an unreasonable belief seems harmless. But if emotion comes with it, it is for real, and we begin to consider adopting a different set of beliefs. As this is a means which may be used for good or evil, the problem lies with the poets themselves. They aim for glory and popularity, and thus, in order to gratify the masses, they set the bar too low; they choose turbulent characters who exhibit impressive reactions and engage in controversial feats. After all, *c'est avec les bons sentiments qu'on fait de la mauvaise littérature*. If each decent person at a festival begins to consider the tragic hero a standard of flourishing, they shift their shared beliefs and start supporting each other in unreasonable actions. Unreasonable shared beliefs thus destroy the decency in all of them.

The antidote for simulative poetry begins in knowing what it is and what it does to us, but most of all, in resisting, learning truth and avoiding unreasonable beliefs. Our cognitive apparatus is activated by sense perception that allows us to apprehend an appearance. Appearances accept compresence of opposites, which are then judged to be either Φ or non-Φ: supposing what Φ is, we believe that this appearance is a case of Φ, and we trust that 'X is Φ' is true. Because of the assumption on Φ, our beliefs may be false; intrinsic to belief is the power to be otherwise, the power of opposites. This is not the case with knowledge. When we know what Φ is, the opposite is excluded, as knowledge is not a power of opposites, but a case of obtaining (or not) its corelative, the true Φ. Knowledge and belief are therefore different powers *because of what they accomplish with their objects*: if belief believes 'X is Φ', X must allow opposites; if knowledge knows 'X is Φ', Φ must always be true.

Knowledge avoids unreasonable beliefs, but one thesis of this book is that there are two levels of this knowledge: one is typical of philosophers, resulting from life-long enquiry, and consisting of a systematic grasping of truth; the other, which is also called thought or discursive reasoning, posits Φ on the assumption that it is true and proceeds to draw inferences which may be either theoretical or practical. Decent people, I argue, find the antidote to simulative poetry, and unreasonable beliefs in general, by having a discursive reasoning based on inferences deduced from positing what the true good is. These inferences are made by dialogical interaction with others, which allow them to deduce both what is a good for themselves and what is good for others in a cooperative process of obtaining knowledge. Decent people engaged in inferring conclusions about the good are the quintessential embodiment of justice because they pursue the good through cooperation, undertaking an activity in which they find their own good, as well as the good of others. They are committed to learning more about how to provide fairer goods and how to enhance themselves.

People are not naturally just. They must be educated for it through three basic trainments. The first is the traditional simulative poetry (once purged from vulgar role models), whose key function is to develop empathy and identification with others by means of a shared belief that personal flourishing is connected to the flourishing of others. Just people are not cooperative solely by means of their willing to know more about their expertise, thence providing fairer goods to others. They cooperate in different circumstances involving pain or pleasure (just like the support we receive from others when in grief) because they share a specific belief about where their flourishing lies. This is a true belief. Due to the species of living beings we are, there is no flourishing for human beings that operates to the detriment of the flourishing of other human beings. Human flourishing entails serenity as its kernel factor, and it is disturbed when we pursue ends aiming for a state of affairs which causes the pleasure of some and the pain of others. As dissatisfaction of others generates strife, revenge and hatred that destroy any chance of serenity, our best chance to flourish is thus to adopt the true belief of cooperative flourishing by being exposed, from early childhood on, to a poetry that simulates cooperative role models. *Mutatis mutandis*, the best way to ruin this project is to expose people to simulative poetry with non-cooperative role models.

Another important learning is gymnastics, for it gives us discipline and endurance to obtain non-immediate but lasting goods. Gymnastics teaches us to care for our body by putting into practice the virtue of temperance – not only towards our health but towards our goods as a whole. Endurance is key to support pain. Preserving our virtue in adversities and facing the challenges in our path to flourishing is not an easy task. Last but not least, just people must be trained in dialectic, beginning in early childhood, because familiarity with the basic elements of formal reasoning is of utmost importance to our discursive reasoning on the good. Notions of dialectic allow us to engage in dialogue with others so as to understand them and verify the truth of their beliefs. Just people are capable of giving and receiving justification about what is good for them and good for others, which is precisely how they cooperatively obtain their knowledge to practise virtue.

Dialectic is the method that leads to philosophical knowledge. It is an all-encompassing grasping of reality that provides explanations for phenomena based on their real causes, that is, the laws of nature. Dialectical knowledge culminates in the knowledge of the form of the good: the explanatory factor of the interconnection between all items in the world and of their preservation. It is also the truthmaker of the inferences that are drawn by just people in their cooperative engagement to understand what is good for them and what is good for others. Their deductions cannot be true if they depart from a false assumption on what true good is. It is for this reason that they must be assured their inferences depart from a sustainable and all-encompassing notion of good. Though knowledge of the form of the good is a condition for justice, this does not mean that every just person must know it themselves. Rather, they can simply be well informed and trained to pursue sustainable, all-encompassing goods. As such, they need philosophers to give them reasons that guide their own practices and interactions so they may actually obtain their ends.

The rule of philosophers depends on a certain kind of political power incompatible with violence or stealth: philosophers may only rule over citizens who are listening and hearkening, who, instead of creating strife, bring them questions and objections in pursuit of a better way of living. This is a form of ruling undertaken on principles of complete transparency and accessibility to information, but also by the imperative of abandoning unreasonable beliefs and refusing to allow oneself to be bewitched by pleasure and pain. It is a just government for just citizens, because it is a rational government for rational citizens.

A cooperative virtue is collective but not holistic. This, as I said, is the difficulty. One may be just by oneself, by enquiring into what are sustainable and all-encompassing goods, and taking it as a personal maxim only to pursue those. However, within a vicious community, a virtuous individual does not flourish, as they are seen as an outsider and are thus liable to violence. Most of all, in this case the just agent does not succeed in cooperating with the unjust people around them and thus does not find the friendship and support that are available in a community of just persons. Justice is a difficult virtue to achieve because it is collective; all the individuals in the community must share the same believe about flourishing being shareable, so that they may engage in common purpose contracts and activities with each other, and thus receive the reward they expect. If we start from an unjust community, where shall we begin? Who are we going to trust? This is a radical collective change, and the option of a violent revolution does not fit well with the personalities of cooperative individuals.

This is how we arrived at the institutional approach to justice. The institutional approach is, in general, a top-down conception of justice which aims at the virtue of the whole: it distributes rights, it demands duties and it punishes those who do not conform. Virtue does not seem to matter. One may pursue any personal notion of flourishing on the condition that it does not go against rights and duties: therefore we grant people their political freedom. But rights and duties are not formal concepts. They have content and are based on mores. Institutional justice lives off virtue because it lives off of the political life of people, the *politeia*.

Institutional justice is built on a bottom-up approach to justice, whose foremost feature is universal education, which forms citizens out of people. This is not restricted to 'schools'. Rather, it involves ensuring inalienable goods and a system of incentives and rewards for cooperative accomplishments. At its most basic, it is about giving all citizens shared true beliefs. Education for justice is an education for reasonable and shared beliefs about a real, sustainable and all-encompassing good, which our institutions require so as to thrive as institutions. Within an unjust *politeia*, institutions of justice either lose legitimacy or become corrupted. The institutional approach to justice has its roots in the virtue of justice, and thus faces significant challenges – the greatest of which is that it takes a whole village to raise a child. Justice is a virtue of the interaction of citizens, and we must come back to ourselves so as to achieve it – to our reasoning, our desires and the beliefs that trigger our *thumos*. It is for this reason that Plato's *Republic* is never to be a dusty book lost in libraries.

References

Adam, James (1902). *The Republic of Plato*. 2 Vols. Cambridge: Cambridge University Press.
Adkins, Arthur W. H. (1960). *Merit and Responsibility: A Study of Greek Values*. Chicago: Chicago University Press.
Adkins, Arthur W. H. (1976). 'Polupragmosune and "Minding One's Own Business": A Study in Greek Social and Political Values'. *Classical Philology*, 71 (4): 301–27.
Allen, Danielle S. (2000). 'Envisaging the Body of the Condemned: The Power of Platonic Symbols'. *Classical Philology*, 95 (2): 133–50.
Allen, Reginald E. (1960). 'Participation and Predication in Plato's Middle Dialogues'. *The Philosophical Review*, 69: 147–64.
Allen, Reginald E. (2006). *The Republic*. New Haven: Yale University Press.
Anderson, Merrick E. (2016). 'Thrasymachus' Sophistic Account of Justice in Republic I'. *Ancient Philosophy*, 36 (1): 151–72.
Andersson, Torsten J. (1971). *Polis and Psyche: A Motif in Plato's Republic*. Stockholm: Almqvist & Wiksell.
Annas, Julia (1976). 'Plato's "Republic" and Feminism'. *Philosophy*, 51 (197): 307–21.
Annas, Julia (1981). *An Introduction to Plato's Republic*. Oxford: Oxford University Press.
Annas, Julia (1982). 'Plato on the Triviality of Literature'. In J. Moravcsik and P. Temko (ed.), *Plato on Beauty, Wisdom and the Arts*, 1–28. Totowa: Rowman and Littlefield.
Annas, Julia (1997). 'Understanding and the Good: Sun, Line, and Cave'. In Richard Kraut (ed.), *Plato's Republic: Critical Essays*. Lanham: Rowman & Littlefield.
Annas, Julia (2000). 'Politics in Plato's "Republic": His and Ours'. *Apeiron*, 33 (4): 303–26.
Annas, Julia (2011). 'Politics and Ethics in Plato's Republic (Book V 449a–471c)'. In Otfried Höffe (ed.), *Platon: Politeia*, 105–20. Berlin: De Gruyter.
Anscombe, Gertrude E. M. (1958). *Intention*. Cambridge: Harvard University Press
Araújo, Carolina (2017). 'Eros and Communitarianism in Plato's Symposium'. In Luc Brisson and Olivier Renaut (eds), *Érotique et politique chez Platon*, 231–42. Sankt Augustin: Academia.
Arendt, Hannah ([1958] 1998). *The Human Condition*. Chicago: University of Chicago Press.
Aristophanes (2007). *Fabulae*. Ed. N. G. Wilson. Oxford: Oxford University Press.
Aristotle (2008). *Aristotelis politica*. Ed. W. D. Ross. Oxford: Oxford University Press.
Aronson, Simon H. (1972). 'The Happy Philosopher–A Counterexample to Plato's Proof'. *Journal of the History of Philosophy*, 10 (4): 383–98.
Arruzza, Cinzia (2011). 'The Private and the Common in Plato's Republic'. *History of Political Thought*, 31 (2): 215–33.
Arruzza, Cinzia (2019). *A Wolf in the City: Tyranny and the Tyrant in Plato's Republic*. Oxford: Oxford University Press.
Avagianou, Aphrodite (1991). *Sacred Marriage in the Rituals of Greek Religion*. Bern: Peter Lang.
Baltes, Matthias (1997). 'Is the Idea of the Good in Plato's Republic Beyond Being?' In Mark Joyal (ed.), *Studies in Plato and the Platonic Tradition*, 351–71. London: Routledge.
Baltzly, Dirk (1997). 'Knowledge and Belief in Republic V'. *Archiv Für Geschichte Der Philosophie*, 79 (3): 239–72.
Bambrough, Renford (1962). 'Plato's Modern Friends and Enemies'. *Philosophy*, 37 (140): 97–113.
Barker, Ernest (1918). *Greek Political Theory: Plato and His Predecessors*. London: Methuen.
Barker, Ernest (1959). *The Political Thought of Plato and Aristotle*. New York: Dover.
Barnes, Jonathan (2012). 'Justice Writ Large'. *Oxford Studies in Ancient Philosophy*, Supplementary Volume: 31–49.

Barney, Rachel (1992). 'Appearances and Impressions'. *Phronesis*, 37 (3): 283–313.
Barney, Rachel (2006). 'Socrates' Refutation of Thrasymachus'. In Gerasimos Santas (ed.), *The Blackwell Guide to Plato's Republic*, 44–62. Malden: Blackwell.
Barney, Rachel (2008). 'Eros and Necessity in the Ascent from the Cave'. *Ancient Philosophy*, 28 (2): 357–72.
Belfiore, Elizabeth (1983). 'Plato's Greatest Accusation against Poetry'. *Canadian Journal of Philosophy*, 13 (Supplementary Volume 1): 39–62.
Belfiore, Elizabeth (1984). 'A Theory of Imitation in Plato's Republic'. *Transactions of the American Philological Association*, 114: 121–46.
Benardete, Seth (1989). *Socrates' Second Sailing: On Plato's Republic*. Chicago: University of Chicago Press.
Benitez, Eugenio (1996). '"Republic" 476d6-e2: Plato's Dialectical Requirement'. *Review of Metaphysics*, 49 (3): 515–46.
Benson, Hugh (1977). 'Socratic Dynamic Theory: A Sketch'. *Apeiron*, 30 (4): 79–93.
Benson, Hugh (2015). *Clitophon's Challenge: Dialectic in Plato's Meno, Phaedo, and Republic*. Oxford: Oxford University Press.
Benveniste, Émile (1970). 'Deux Modèles Linguistiques de La Cité'. In Jean Pouillon and Pierre Maranda (eds), *Échanges et Communications: Mélanges Offerts à Claude Lévi-Strauss à l'occasion de Son 60ème Anniversaire*, 594–5. The Hague: Mouton.
Benveniste, Émile (1969). *Le Vocabulaire des Institutions Indo-européennes*. 2 v. Paris: Éditions de Minuit.
Bloom, Allan ([1968]1991). *The Republic of Plato*. New York: Basic Books.
Bloom, Paul (2016). *Against Empathy: The Case for Rational Compassion*. New York: Harper Collins.
Blössner, Norbert (1997). *Dialogform und Argument: Studien zu Platons 'Politeia'*. Stuttgart: F. Steiner Verlag.
Blössner, Norbert (2007). 'The City-Soul Analogy'. In G. R. F. Ferrari (ed.), *The Cambridge Companion to Plato's Republic*, 345–87. Cambridge: Cambridge University Press.
Bobonich, Christopher (1994). 'Akrasia and Agency in Plato's Laws and Republic'. *Archiv Für Geschichte Der Philosophie*, 76 (1): 3–36.
Bobonich, Christopher (2002). *Plato's Utopia Recast: His Later Ethics and Politics*. Oxford: Oxford University Press.
Boeri, Marcelo (2010). '¿Por qué el *Thumos* es um 'Aliado' de la Razón en la Batalla contra los Apetitos Irracionales?' *Rivista di Cultura Clássica e Medioevale*, 52 (2): 289–306.
Bordes, Jacqueline (1982). *Politeia dans la Pensée Grecque jusqu'à Aristote*. Paris: Belles Lettres.
Bosanquet, Bernard (1895). *A Companion to Plato's Republic for English Readers*. New York: Macmillan.
Boter, Gerard J. (1986). 'Thrasymachus and πλεονεξία'. *Mnemosyne*, 39: 261–81.
Boter, Gerard J. (1992). 'Parisinus A and the Title of Plato's Republic'. *Rheinisches Museum Für Philologie*, 135 (1): 82–6.
Boyle, Anthony J. (1973). 'Plato's Divided Line: Essay I: The Problem of Dianoia'. *Apeiron*, 7 (2): 1–11.
Brancacci, Aldo (2005). 'Musique et Philosophie en République II-IV'. In Monique Dixsaut (ed.), *Études sur la "République" de Platon: De la Justice, Éducation, Psychologie et Politique*, 89–106. Paris: Vrin.
Brennan, Tad (2005). 'Commentary on Sauvé-Meyer'. *Proceedings of the Boston Area Colloquium in Ancient Philosophy*, 20 (1): 244–63.
Brennan, Tad (2012). 'The Nature of the Spirited Part of the Soul and Its Object'. In Rachel Barney, Tad Brennan, and Charles Brittain (eds), *Plato and the Divided Self*, 102–27. Cambridge: Cambridge University Press.
Brickhouse, Thomas C. (1981). 'The Paradox of the Philosophers' Rule'. *Apeiron*, 15 (1): 1–9.
Brisson, Luc (1982). *Platon: Les Mots et les Mythes*. Paris: François Maspero.
Brown, Eric A. (1997). 'A Defense of Plato's Argument for the Immortality of the Soul at Republic X 608c-611a'. *Apeiron*, 30 (3): 211–38.

Brown, Eric (2000). 'Justice and Compulsion for Plato's Philosopher-Rulers'. *Ancient Philosophy*, 20 (1): 1–17.
Brown, Eric (2004). 'Minding the Gap in Plato's Republic'. *Philosophical Studies*, 117 (1/2): 275–302.
Brown, Eric (2012), 'The Unity of the Soul in Plato's Republic'. In Rachel Barney, Tad Brennan, and Charles Brittain (eds), *Plato and the Divided Self*, 53–73. Cambridge: Cambridge University Press.
Brown, Lesley (1986). 'Being in the Sophist: A Syntactical Enquiry'. *Oxford Studies in Ancient Philosophy*, 4: 49–70.
Brown, Lesley (1998). 'How Totalitarian is Plato's Republic?'. In Erik Nis Ostenfeld (ed.), *Essays on Plato's Republic*, 13–27. Aarhus: Aarhus University Press.
Brown, Lesley (2007). 'Glaucon's Challenge, Rational Egoism and Ordinary Morality'. In Douglas L. Cairns, Fritz-Gregor Herrmann, and Terry Penner (eds), *Pursuing the Good: Ethics and Metaphysics in Plato's Republic*, 42–60. Edinburgh: Edinburgh University Press.
Burkert, Walter (1960). 'Platon oder Pythagoras? Zum Ursprung des Wortes "Philosophie"'. *Hermes*, 88 (2): 159–77.
Burkert, Walter (1985). *Greek Religion*. Cambridge: Harvard University Press.
Burnyeat, Myles (1992). 'Utopia and Fantasy: The Practicability of Plato's Ideally Just City'. In J. Hopkins and A. Saville (eds), *Psychoanalysis, mind and art: Perspectives on Richard Hollheim*, 175–87. London: Blackwell.
Burnyeat, Myles (1997). 'Culture and Society in Plato's Republic'. In *The Tanner Lectures on Human Values*. Cambridge: Harvard University Press.
Burnyeat, Myles (2000). 'Plato on Why Mathematics Is Good for the Soul'. In Timothy Smiley (ed.) *Mathematics and Necessity: Essays in the History of Philosophy*, 1–81. Oxford: Oxford University Press.
Burnyeat, Myles (2006). 'The Truth of Tripartition'. *Proceedings of the Aristotelian Society*, 106 (1): 1–23.
Burnyeat, Myles (2008). 'Utopia and Fantasy: The Practicability of Plato's Ideally Just City'. In Gail Fine (ed.), *Plato 2: Ethics, Politics, Religion and the Soul*, 297–208. Oxford: Oxford University Press.
Bury, Robert G. (1894). 'Δύναμις and Φύσις in Plato'. *The Classical Review*, 8: 297–300.
Butler, James (1999a). 'On Whether Pleasure's Esse Is Percipi: Rethinking Republic 583b–585a'. *Ancient Philosophy*, 19 (2): 285–98.
Butler, James (1999b). 'The Arguments for the Most Pleasant Life in Republic IX: A Note Against the Common Interpretation'. *Apeiron*, 32 (1): 37–48.
Butler, James (2008). 'A Holistic Defense of Justice in the Republic'. *Apeiron*, 41 (4): 229–45.
Cairns, Douglas (2014). 'Ψυχή, Θυμός, and Metaphor in Homer and Plato'. *Études Platoniciennes*, 11: 1–41.
Calvert, Brian (1987). 'Slavery in Plato's Republic'. *Classical Quarterly*, 37 (2): 367–72.
Campese, Silvia (1998). 'Misthotike'. In Mario Vegetti (ed.), *Platone La Repubblica*, vol. I, 257–68. Naples: Bibliopolis.
Campese, Silvia (2000). 'La Seconda Ondata: La Comunanza Di Donne e Figli'. In Mario Vegetti (ed.), *Platone La Repubblica*, vol. IV, 257–94. Naples: Bibliopolis.
Carone, Gabriela R. (2001). 'Akrasia in the Republic: Does Plato Change His Mind?' *Oxford Studies in Ancient Philosophy*, 20: 107–48.
Castelnérac, Benoît and Matthieu, Marion (2009). 'Arguing for Inconsistency: Dialectical Games in the Academy'. In Giuseppe Primiero and Göran Sundholm (eds), *Acts of Knowledge: History, Philosophy and Logic; Essays Dedicated to Göran Sundholm*, 37–76. London: College Publications.
Cattanei, Elisabetta (2003). 'Le Matematiche al Tempo di Platone e la Loro Riforma'. In Mario Vegetti (ed.), *Platone La Repubblica*, vol. V, 473–540. Naples: Bibliopolis.
Chappell, Timothy D. J. (1993). 'The Virtues of Thrasymachus'. *Phronesis*, 38: 1–17.
Chappell, Timothy D. J. (2000). 'Thrasymachus and Definition'. *Oxford Studies in Ancient Philosophy*, 18: 101–7.
Cherniss, Harold (1962). *The Riddle of the Ancient Academy*. New York: Russell & Russell.
Cooper, John M. (1977). 'The Psychology of Justice in Plato'. *American Philosophical Quarterly*, 14 (2): 151–7.

Cooper, John M. (1984). 'Plato's Theory of Human Motivation'. *History of Philosophy Quarterly*, 1 (1): 3–21.
Cooper, John M. (2000). 'Two Theories of Justice'. *Proceedings and Addresses of the American Philosophical Association*, 74 (2): 5–27.
Cooper, Neil (1966). 'The Importance of *Dianoia* in Plato's Theory of Forms', *Classical Quarterly*, 16: 65–9.
Cooper, Neil (1986). 'Between Knowledge and Ignorance'. *Phronesis*, 31: 229–42.
Cornford, Francis M. (1912). 'Psychology and Social Structure in the Republic of Plato'. *The Classical Quarterly*, 6 (4): 246–65.
Cornford, Francis M. (1932). 'Mathematics and Dialectic in the Republic VI.-VII'. *Mind*, 41 (161): 37–52.
Cornford, Francis M. (1945). *The Republic of Plato*. Oxford: Oxford University Press.
Crombie, Ian M. (1962). *An Examination of Plato's Doctrines*. 2 Vols. London: Routlledge & Kegan Paul.
Cross, Robert C., and Anthony D. Woozley (1964). *Plato's Republic*. London: Palgrave Macmillan.
Davidson, Donald (1969). 'How Is Weakness of the Will Possible?'. In Joel Feinberg (ed.), *Moral Concepts*, 93–113. Oxford: Oxford University Press.
Dawson, Doyne (1992). *Cities of the Gods: Communist Utopias in Greek Thought*. New York: Oxford University Press.
Delcomminette, Sylvain (2008). 'Facultés et Parties de l'Âme chez Platon'. *Plato Journal*, 8.
Demos, Raphael (1937). 'Plato's Idea of the Good'. *The Philosophical Review*, 46 (3): 245–75.
Demos, Raphael (1957). 'Paradoxes in Plato's Doctrine of the Ideal State'. *The Classical Quarterly*, 7 (3/4): 164–74.
Demos, Raphael (1964). 'A Fallacy in Plato's Republic?'. *The Philosophical Review*, 73 (3): 395–8.
Denyer, Nicholas (2007). 'Sun and Line: The Role of the Good'. In G. R. F. Ferrari (ed.), *The Cambridge Companion to Plato's Republic*, 284–309. Cambridge: Cambridge University Press.
Destrée, Pierre (2011). 'Poetry, Thumos and Pity in the Republic'. In Pierre Destrée and Fritz-Gregor Hermann (eds), *Plato and the Poets*, 267–82. Leiden: Brill.
Devereux, Daniel (2004). 'The Relationship between Justice and Happiness in Plato's Republic'. *Proceedings of the Boston Area Colloquium of Ancient Philosophy*, 20: 265–305.
Diels, Hermann and Walther Kranz, eds (2004). *Die Fragmente der Vorsokratiker*. Zürich: Weidmann.
Diès, Auguste (2003). 'Introduction'. In Émile Chambry (ed.), *La République*. Paris: Les Belles Lettres.
Dillon, John M. (2003). *The Heirs of Plato: A Study of the Old Academy, 347-274 B.C.* Oxford: Oxford University Press.
Diogenes, Laertius (2013). *Lives of Eminent Philosophers*. Ed. Tiziano Dorandi. Cambridge: Cambridge University Press.
Dixsaut, Monique (2005). 'Encore une Fois le Bien'. In Monique Dixsaut (ed.), *Études sur la "République" de Platon: De la Science, du Bien et des Mythes*, 225–55. Paris: Vrin.
Dominick, Yancy H. (2010). 'Seeing Through Images: The Bottom of Plato's Divided Line'. *Journal of the History of Philosophy*, 48 (1): 1–13.
Donovan, Brian R. (2003). 'The Do-It-Yourselfer in Plato's Republic'. *The American Journal of Philology*, 124: 1–18.
Dorter, Kenneth (1974). 'Socrates' Refutation of Thrasymachus and Treatment of Virtue'. *Philosophy & Rhetoric*, 7 (1): 25–46.
Dorter, Kenneth (2006). *The Transformation of Plato's Republic*. Lanham: Lexington.
Duncombe, Matthew (2015). 'The Role of Relatives in Plato's Partition Argument, Republic IV 436b9- 439c9'. *Oxford Studies in Ancient Philosophy*, 48: 37–60.
Ehrenberg, Victor (1947). 'Polypragmosyne: A Study in Greek Politics'. *The Journal of Hellenic Studies*, 67: 46–67.

Ehrenberg, Victor (1948). 'The Foundation of Thurii'. *The American Journal of Philology*, 69 (2): 149–70.
Else, Gerald F. (1958). '"Imitation" in the Fifth Century'. *Classical Philology*, 53 (2): 73–90.
Emlyn-Jones, Chris J. and William Preddy (2013). *Plato, Republic*. Cambridge: Harvard University Press.
Erginel, Mehmet M. (2011). 'Inconsistency and Ambiguity In *Republic* IX'. *The Classical Quarterly*, 61 (2): 493–520.
Erginel, Mehmet M. (2013). 'How Smart is the Appetitive Part of the Soul?' In Noburu Notomi and Luc Brisson (eds), *Dialogues on Plato's Politeia (Republic): Selected Papers from the Ninth Symposium Platonicum*, 204–8. Sankt Augustin: Academia.
Everson, Stephen (1998). 'The Incoherence of Thrasymachus'. *Oxford Studies in Ancient Philosophy*, 16: 99–131.
Faust, August (1931). *Der Moglichkeitsgedanke: Systemgeschichte Untersuchungen*. Heidelberg: C. Winter.
Ferber, Rafael (1989). *Platos Idee des Guten*. Sankt Augustin: Academia Verlag.
Ferguson, Alexander S. (1921). 'Plato's Simile of Light. Part I. The Similes of the Sun and the Line'. *The Classical Quarterly*, 15 (3/4): 131–52.
Ferguson, Alexander S. (1922). 'Plato's Simile of Light. Part II. The Allegory of the Cave (Continued)'. *The Classical Quarterly*, 16 (1): 15–28.
Ferguson, Alexander S. (1934). 'Plato's Simile of Light Again'. *The Classical Quarterly*, 28 (3/4): 190–210.
Ferrari, Franco (2000a). 'Teoria delle Idee e Ontologia'. In Mario Vegetti (ed.), *Platone La Repubblica*, vol. IV, 365–92. Naples: Bibliopolis.
Ferrari, Franco (2000b). 'Conoscenza e Opinione: il Filosofo e la Città'. In Mario Vegetti (ed.), *Platone La Repubblica*, vol. IV, 393–420. Naples: Bibliopolis.
Ferrari, Franco (2003). 'L'Idea del Bene: Collocazione Ontologica e Funzione Causale'. In Mario Vegetti (ed.), *Platone La Repubblica*, vol. V, 287–326. Naples: Bibliopolis.
Ferrari, Giovanni R. F. (1989). 'Plato and Poetry'. In G. Kennedy (ed.), *The Cambridge History of Literary Criticism*, 94–148. Cambridge: Cambridge University Press.
Ferrari, Giovanni R. F. (2005). *City and Soul in Plato's Republic*. Chicago: University of Chicago Press.
Ferrari, Giovanni R. F. (2007). 'The Three-Part Soul'. In G. R. F. Ferrari (ed.), *The Cambridge Companion to Plato's Republic*, 165–201. Cambridge: Cambridge University Press.
Ferrari, Giovanni R. F. (2009). 'Williams and the City-Soul Analogy (Plato, Republic 435e and 544d)'. *Ancient Philosophy*, 29 (2): 407–13.
Ferrari, Giovanni R. F. (2012). 'The Philosopher's Antidote'. In A. Denhan (ed.), *Plato on Art and Beauty*, 106–24. New York: Palgrave Macmillan.
Fine, Gail (1978). 'Knowledge and Belief in Republic V'. *Archiv Für Geschichte Der Philosophie*, 60 (2): 121–39.
Fine, Gail (1980). 'The One Over Many'. *Philosophical Review*, 89 (2): 197–240.
Fine, Gail (1990). 'Knowledge and Belief in Republic V-VII'. In Stephen Everson (ed.), *Epistemology*, 85–115. Cambridge: Cambridge University Press.
Fissell, Brenner (2009). 'Thrasymachus and the Order of Pleonexia'. *Aporia*, 19: 35–43.
Flew, Antony G. N. (1995). 'Responding to Plato's Thrasymachus'. *Philosophy*, 70: 436–77.
Foley, V. (1974). 'The Division of Labor in Plato and Smith'. *History of Political Economy*, 6 (2): 220–42.
Foot, Philippa (2001). *Natural Goodness*. Oxford: Oxford University Press.
Forde, Steven (1997). 'Gender and Justice in Plato'. *The American Political Science Review*, 91 (3): 657–70.
Fortenbaugh, William W. (1975). 'On Plato's Feminism in Republic V'. *Apeiron*, 9: 1–4.
Foster, Michael B. (1938). 'A Mistake of Plato's in the Republic: A Rejoinder to Mr. Mabbot'. *Mind*, 47 (186): 226–32.

Franklin, Lee (2012). 'Inventing Intermediates: Mathematical Discourse and Its Objects in Republic VII'. *Journal of the History of Philosophy*, 50 (4): 483–506.
Frede, Dorothea (1985). 'Rumpelstiltskin's Pleasures: True and False Pleasures in Plato's Philebus'. *Phronesis*, 30 (2): 151–80.
Frede, Dorothea (1996). 'Plato, Popper, and Historicism'. *Proceedings of the Boston Area Colloquium of Ancient Philosophy*, 12 (1): 247–76.
Frede, Dorothea (2011). 'Die ungerechten Verfassungen und die ihnen entsprechenden Menschen (Buch VIII 543a-IX 576b)'. In Otfried Höffe (ed.), *Politeia*, 193–208. Berlin: Akademie.
Frede, Michael (1980). 'The Original Notion of Cause'. In Malcolm Schofield, Myles Burnyeat, and Jonathan Barnes (eds), *Doubt and Dogmatism: Studies in Hellenistic Epistemology*, 217–49. Oxford: Oxford University Press.
Frère, Jean (2004). *Ardeur et Colère: le "Thumos" Platonicien*. Paris: Kimé.
Fronterotta, Francesco (2010). 'Plato's Republic in the Recent Debate'. *Journal of the History of Philosophy*, 48 (2): 125–51.
Fronterotta, Francesco (2013). 'Plato's Psychology in Republic IV and X: How Many Parts of the Soul'. In Noboru Notomi and Luc Brisson (eds), *Dialogues on Plato's Politeia (Republic): Selected Papers from the Ninth Symposium Platonicum*, 168–78. Sankt Augustin: Academia.
Fronterotta, Francesco (2014). 'Os Sentidos do Verbo Ser no Livro V da República e a sua "Função" Epistemológica na Distinção entre Conhecimento e Opinião'. In Carolina Araújo (ed.), *Verdade e Espetáculo: Platão e a Questão do Ser*, 37–80. Rio de Janeiro: 7 Letras.
Gagarin, Michael (1989). *Early Greek Law*. Berkeley: University of California Press.
Galis, Leon (1974). 'The State-Soul Analogy in Plato's Argument that Justice Pays'. *Journal of the History of Philosophy*, 12: 285–93.
Ganson, Todd (2009). 'The Rational/Non-Rational Distinction in Plato's Republic'. *Oxford Studies in Ancient Philosophy*, 36: 179–97.
Gavrielides, Era (2010). 'What is Wrong with Degenerate Souls in the "Republic"'. *Phronesis*, 55 (3): 203–27.
Georgini, Giovanni (2009). 'Plato and the Ailing Soul of the Tyrant'. In Silvia Gastaldi and Jean-François Pradeau (eds), *Le Philosophe, le Roi, le Tyran*, 113–30. Sankt Augustin: Academia.
Gill, Christopher (1985). 'Plato and the Education of Character'. *Archiv für Geschichte der Philosophie*, 67 (1): 1–26.
Gill, Christopher (1996). 'Ethical Reflection and the Shaping of Character: Plato's Republic and Stoicism'. *Proceedings of the Boston Area Colloquium of Ancient Philosophy*, 12 (1): 193–225.
Gill, Christopher (1998). *Personality in Greek Epic, Tragedy, and Philosophy: The Self in Dialogue*. Oxford: Clarendon Press.
Gonzalez, Francisco J. (1996). 'Propositions or Objects? A Critique of Gail Fine on Knowledge and Belief in "Republic" V'. *Phronesis*, 41 (3): 245–75.
Gosling, Justin C. (1960). '"Republic": Book V: τὰ πολλὰ καλά'. *Phronesis*, 5 (2): 116–28.
Gosling, Justin C. (1968). 'Δόξα and Δύναμις in Plato's "Republic"'. *Phronesis*, 13 (2): 119–30.
Gosling, Justin C. and Christopher, C. W. Taylor (1982). *The Greeks on Pleasure*. Oxford: Oxford University Press.
Graeser, Andreas (1975). 'Die platonischen Ideen als Gegenstände sprachlicher Referenz'. *Zeitschrift für Philosophische Forschung*, 29 (2): 218–34.
Griffith, Tom (2000). *The Republic*. Cambridge: Cambridge University Press.
Griswold, Charles L. (1981). 'The Ideas and the Criticism of Poetry in Plato's Republic, Book 10'. *Journal of the History of Philosophy*, 19 (2): 135–50.
Grube, George M. A. (1974). *Plato's Republic*. Indianapolis: Hackett.
Guthrie, William K. C. (1975). *A History of Greek Philosophy, Volume IV: Plato, the Man and His Dialogues, Earlier Period*. Cambridge: Cambridge University Pres.
Gutierrez, Raul (2017). *El Arte de la Conversion: un Estudio sobre la República de Platón*. Lima: Pontifícia Universidad Católica del Peru.

Hackforth, Reginald (1942). 'Plato's Divided Line and Dialectic'. *The Classical Quarterly*, 36 (1/2): 1–9.
Hadgopoulos, Demetrius J. (1973). 'Thrasymachus and legalism'. *Phronesis*, 18: 204–8.
Hall, Dale (1980). 'Interpreting Plato's Cave as an Allegory of the Human Condition'. *Apeiron*, 14 (2): 74–86.
Hall, Robert W. (1959). 'Justice and the Individual in the "Republic"'. *Phronesis*, 4 (2): 149–58.
Hall, Robert W. (1974). 'Plato's Political Analogy: Fallacy or Analogy?'. *Journal of the History of Philosophy*, 12 (4): 419–35.
Halliwell, Stephen (1988a). *Republic 5*. 2nd ed. Warminster: Aris & Phillips.
Halliwell, Stephen (1988b). *Republic 10*. Warminster: Aris & Phillips.
Halliwell, Stephen (2011). 'Antidotes and Incantations: Is There a Cure for Poetry in Plato "Republic"?'. In Pierre Destrée and Fritz-Gregor Hermann (eds), *Plato and the Poets*, 241–66. Leiden: Brill.
Halperin, David M. (1985). 'Platonic Eros and What Men Call Love'. *Ancient Philosophy*, 5 (2): 161–204.
Halperin, David M. (1989). 'Plato and the Metaphysics Of Desire'. *Proceedings of the Boston Area Colloquium of Ancient Philosophy*, 5 (1): 27–52.
Hamlyn David W. (1958). 'Eikasia in Plato's Republic'. *Philosophical Quarterly*, 8 (30): 14–23.
Hansen, Mogens Herman (2010). 'Democratic Freedom and the Concept of Freedom in Plato and Aristotle'. *Greek, Roman and Byzantine Studies*, 50: 1–27.
Harlap, Shmuel (1979). 'Thrasymachus' Justice'. *Political Theory*, 7: 347–70.
Harrison, E. L. (1967). 'Plato's Manipulation of Thrasymachus'. *Phoenix*, 21 (1): 27.
Harte, Verity (2007). 'Language in the Cave'. In Dominic Scott (ed.), *Maieusis: Essays in Ancient Philosophy in Honour of Myles Burnyeat*, 195–215. Oxford: Oxford University Press.
Harte, Verity (2010). 'Republic 10 and the Role of the Audience in Art'. *Oxford Studies in Ancient Philosophy*, 38: 69–96.
Harte, Verity (2018). 'Knowing and Believing in Republic 5'. In Verity Harte and Raphael Woolf (eds), *Rereading Ancient Philosophy: Old Chestnuts and Sacred Cows*, 141–62. Cambridge: Cambridge University Press.
Havelock, Eric Alfred (1978). *The Greek Concept of Justice: From Its Shadow in Homer to Its Substance in Plato*. Cambridge: Harvard University Press.
Heinaman, Robert (2002). 'Plato's Division of Goods in the Republic'. *Phronesis*, 47 (4): 309–35.
Hellwig, Dorothee (1980). *Adikia in Platons "Politeia": Interpretationen zu den Büchern VIII Und IX*. Amsterdam: Grüner.
Helmer, Étienne (2005). 'Histoire, Politique et Pratique aux Livres VIII-IX de la République'. In Monique Dixsaut (ed.), *Études sur la "République" de Platon: De la Justice, Éducation, Psychologie et Politique*, 149–68. Paris: Vrin.
Helmer, Étienne (2010). *La Partie du Bronze: Platon et l'Économie*. Paris: Vrin.
Henderson, Toliver Y. (1970). 'In Defense of Thrasymachus'. *American Philosophical Quarterly*, 7: 218–28.
Herodotus (2015). *Historiae*. Ed. N. G. Wilson. Oxford: Oxford University Press.
Hesiod (1990). *Theogonia Opera et Dies*. Ed. Friedrich Solmsen. Oxford: Oxford University Press.
Hintikka, Jaako (1973). 'Knowledge and Its Objects in Plato'. In J. M. E. Moravcsik (ed.), *Patterns in Plato's Thought*, 1–30. Dordrecht: Reidel.
Hitchcock, David (1985). 'The Good in Plato's Republic'. *Apeiron*, 19 (2): 65–92.
Hitz, Zena (2010). 'Degenerate Regimes in Plato's Republic'. In Mark L. McPherran (ed.), *Plato's Republic: A Critical Guide*, 103–31. Cambridge: Cambridge University Press.
Hobbs, Angela (2000). *Plato and the Hero: Courage, Manliness, and the Impersonal Good*. Cambridge: Cambridge University Press.
Hoerber, Robert G. (1960). 'More on Justice in the "Republic"'. *Phronesis*, 5 (1): 32–34.

Hoernlé, Alfred (1938). 'Would Plato Have Approved of the National-Socialist State?'. *Philosophy*, 13 (50): 166–82.
Hourani, George F. (1949). 'The Education of the Third Class in Plato's Republic'. *Classical Quarterly*, 43: 58–60.
Hourani, George F. (1962). 'Thrasymachus' Definition of Justice in Plato's "Republic"'. *Phronesis*, 7 (2): 110–20.
Hourani, George F. (1971). 'Thrasymachus... or Plato?'. *Phronesis*, 16 (2): 142–63.
Hume, David (1888). *A Treatise of Human Nature*. Ed. Lewis A. Selby-Bigge. Oxford: Clarendon Press.
Inwood, Brad (1987). 'Professor Stokes on Adeimantus in the Republic'. In Spiro Panagiotou (ed.), *Justice, Law, and Method in Plato and Aristotle*, 97–103. Edmonton: Academic Printing.
Irwin, Terence (1977). *Plato's Moral Theory: The Early and Middle Dialogues*. Oxford: Oxford University Press.
Irwin, Terence (1991). 'Aristippus Against Happiness'. *The Monist*, 74 (1): 55–82.
Irwin, Terence (1995). *Plato's Ethics*. Oxford: Oxford University Press.
Irwin, Terence H. (1999). 'Republic 2: Questions about Justice'. In Gail Fine (ed.), *Plato 2: Ethics, Politics, Religion and the Soul*, 164–85. Oxford: Oxford University Press.
Irwin, Terence H. (2011). 'The Parts of the Soul and the Cardinal Virtues (Book IV 427d–448e)'. In Otfried Höffe (ed.), *Platon: Politeia*, 89–104. Berlin: Akademie Verlag
Isocrate (1938). *Discours*. Ed. George Mathieu and E. Brémond. Paris: Belles Lettres.
Jackson, Henry (1882). 'On Plato's Republic VI, 509D sqq'. *The Journal of Philosophy*, 10: 132–50.
Jaeger, Werner ([1946]1960). 'A New Greek Word in Plato's Republic'. In *Scripta Minora II*, 309–16. Roma: Edizioni di Storia e Letteratura.
Janaway, Christopher (1995). *Images of Excellence: Plato's Critique of the Arts*. Oxford: Clarendon.
Jang, In H. (1997). 'Socrates' Refutation of Thrasymachus'. *History of Political Thought*, 18: 189–206.
Jeon, Haewon (2014). 'The Interaction Between the Just City and Its Citizens in Plato's Republic: From the Producers' Point of View'. *Journal of the History of Philosophy*, 52 (2): 183–203.
Johnstone, Mark (2011). 'Changing Rulers in the Soul: Psychological Transitions in Republic 8-9'. *Oxford Studies in Ancient Philosophy*, 41: 139–67.
Johnstone, Mark (2013). 'Anarchic Souls: Plato's Depiction of the "Democratic Man"'. *Phronesis*, 58 (2): 139–59.
Johnstone, Mark (2015). 'Tyrannized Souls: Plato's Depiction of the "Tyrannical Man"'. *British Journal for the History of Philosophy*, 23 (3): 423–37.
Jonas, Mark E., Yoshiaki M. Nakazawa, and James Braun (2012a). 'Appetite, Reason, and Education in Socrates' "City of Pigs"'. *Phronesis*, 57 (4): 332–57.
Joseph, Horace W. B. (1948). *Knowledge and the Good in Plato's Republic*. Oxford: Oxford University Press.
Jütte, Robert (2008). *Contraception: A History*. Cambridge: Polity.
Kahn, Charles H. (1972). 'The Meaning of "Justice" and the Theory of Forms'. *The Journal of Philosophy*, 69 (18): 567–79.
Kahn, Charles H. (1981). 'The Origins of Social Contract Theory'. In George B. Kerferd (ed.), *The Sophists and Their Legacy*, 92–108. Wiesbaden: Steiner.
Kahn, Charles H. (1987). 'Plato's Theory of Desire'. *Review of Metaphysics*, 41 (1): 77–103.
Kahn, Charles H. (1993). 'Proleptic Composition in the Republic, or Why Book 1 Was Never a Separate Dialogue'. *The Classical Quarterly*, 43 (1): 131–42.
Kahn, Charles. ([1973]2003). *The Verb "Be" in Ancient Greek*. Indianapolis: Hackett.
Kamtekar, Rachana (1998). 'Imperfect Virtue'. *Ancient Philosophy*, 18(2): 315–39.
Kamtekar, Rachana (2001). 'Social Justice and Happiness in the "Republic": Plato's Two Principles'. *History of Political Thought*, 22 (2): 189–220.
Kamtekar, Rachana (2004). 'What's the Good of Agreeing? Homonoia in Platonic Politics'. *Oxford Studies in Ancient Philosophy*, 26: 131–70.

Kamtekar, Rachana (2006). 'Speaking with the Same Voice as Reason: Personification in Plato's Psychology'. *Oxford Studies in Ancient Philosophy*, 31: 167–202.
Kamtekar, Rachana (2009). 'The Powers of Plato's Tripartite Psychology'. *Proceedings of the Boston Area Colloquium in Ancient Philosophy*, 24 (1): 127–62.
Kamtekar, Rachana (2010). 'Ethics and Politics in Socrates' Defense of Justice'. In Mark L. McPherran (ed.), *Plato's Republic: A Critical Guide*, 65–82. Cambridge: Cambridge University Press.
Kamtekar, Rachana (2017). *Plato's Moral Psychology: Intellectualism, the Divided Soul, and the Desire for Good*. Oxford: Oxford University Press.
Kerferd, George B. ([1947]1976). 'The Doctrine of Thrasymachus in Plato's "Republic"'. In Carl Joachim Classen (ed.), *Sophistik*, 545–63. Darmstadt: Wissenschaftliche Buchgesellschaft.
Kerferd, George B. (1964). 'Thrasymachus and Justice: A Reply'. *Phronesis*, 9 (1): 12–16.
Keyt, David (2006). 'Plato on Justice'. In Hugh Benson (ed.), *A Companion to Plato*, 341–55. Malden: Blackwell.
Kirwan, Christopher (1965). 'Glaucon's Challenge'. *Phronesis*, 10 (2): 162–73.
Klosko, George (1982). '"Demotike Arete" in the "Republic"'. *History of Political Thought*, 3 (3): 363–81.
Klosko, George (1984). 'Thrasymachos' Eristikos: The Agon Logon in Republic I'. *Polity*, 17: 5–29.
Klosko, George (1988). 'The "Rule" of Reason in Plato's Psychology'. *History of Philosophy Quarterly*, 5 (4): 341–56.
Klosko, George (2006). *The Development of Plato's Political Theory*. Oxford: Oxford University Press.
Kosman, Aryeh (2005). 'The Faces of Justice. Difference, Equality, and Integrity in Plato's Republic'. *Proceedings of the Boston Area Colloquium of Ancient Philosophy*, 20 (1): 153–75.
Krämer, Hans J. (1969). 'Epekeina tes Ousias: Zu Platon, Politeia 509b'. *Archiv für Geschichte der Philosophie*, 51: 1–30.
Kraut, Richard (1973a). 'Egoism, Love, and Political Office in Plato'. *Philosophical Review*, 82: 330–44.
Kraut, Richard (1973b). 'Reason and Justice in Plato's Republic'. *Phronesis*, Supplementary Volume, 207–24.
Kraut, Richard (1992). 'The Defense of Justice in Plato's Republic'. In Richard Kraut (ed.), *The Cambridge Companion to Plato*, 311–37. Cambridge: Cambridge University Press.
Kraut, Richard (2007). 'Flourishing: The Central Concept of Practical Thought'. In Douglas L. Cairns, Fritz-Gregor Herrmann, and Terry Penner (eds), *Pursuing the Good: Ethics and Metaphysics in Plato's Republic*, 154–67. Edinburgh: Edinburgh University Press.
Kraut, Richard (2011). 'Plato's Comparison of Just and Unjust Lives (Book IX 576b-592b)'. In Otfried Höffe (ed.), *Platon: Politeia*, 209–23, Berlin: Akademia.
Kurihara, Yuri (2013). 'Plato's "True" Tyrant in *Republic* Book 9'. In Noboru Notomi and Luc Brisson (eds), *Dialogues on Plato's Politeia (Republic): Selected Papers from the Ninth Symposium Platonicum*, 115–25. Sankt Augustin: Academia.
Lacroix, Jean-Yves (2014). *Platon et l'Utopie: L'Être et l'Existence*. Paris: Vrin.
Lafrance, Yvon ([1981]2015). *La Théorie Platonicienne de la Doxa*. 2nd éd. Paris: Les Belles lettres.
Laks, André (1990). 'Legislation and Demiurgy: On the Relationship between Plato's "Republic" and "Laws"'. *Classical Antiquity*, 9 (2): 209–29.
Lampe, Kurt (2015). *The Birth of Hedonism: The Cyrenaic Philosophers and Pleasure as a Way of Life*. Princeton: Princeton University Press.
Lane, Melissa (2007). 'Virtue as the Love of Knowledge'. In Dominic Scott (ed.), *Maieusis: Essays in Ancient Philosophy in Honour of Myles Burnyeat*, 44–67. Oxford: Oxford University Press.
Lane, Melissa (2013). 'Founding as Legislating: The Figure of the Lawgiver in Plato's Republic'. In Noboru Nōtomi and Luc Brisson (eds), *Dialogues on Plato's Politeia (Republic): Selected Papers from the Ninth Symposium Platonicum*, 104–14. Sankt Augustin: Academia.
Lane, Melissa (2021). 'Technē and Archē in Plato's Republic Book 1'. *Oxford Studies in Ancient Philosophy*, 57: 1–24.

Larivée, Annie (2005). 'Malaise dans la Cité: Eros et Tyrannie au Livre IX de la République'. In Monique Dixsaut (ed.), *Études sur la République de Platon: De la Justice, Éducation, Psychologie et Politique*, 169–97. Paris: Vrin.

Larivée, Annie (2012). 'Eros Tyrannos: Alcibiades as the Model of the Tyrant in Book IX of the Republic'. *The International Journal of the Platonic Tradition*, 6: 1–26.

Larivée, Annie (2013). 'Alcibiades as the Model of the Tyrant in Book IX of the Republic'. In Noburu Notomi and Luc Brisson (eds), *Dialogues on Plato's Politeia (Republic): Selected Papers from the Ninth Symposium Platonicum*, 152–60. Sankt Augustin: Academia.

Lear, Jonathan (1992). 'Inside and Outside the "Republic"'. *Phronesis*, 37 (2): 184–215.

Lear, Jonathan (2006). 'Allegory and Myth in Plato's Republic'. In Gerasimos Santas (ed.), *The Blackwell Guides to Plato's Republic*, 25–43. Malden: Blackwell.

Lee, Edward N. (1989). 'Plato's Theory of Social Justice in Republic 2–4'. In J. Anton and A. Preus (eds), *Essays in Ancient Greek Philosophy 3*, 117–40. Albany: SUNY.

Lefebvre, David (2018). *Dynamis: Sens et Genèse de la Notion Aristotélicienne de Puissance*. Paris: Vrin.

Leroux, George (2016). *La République*. Paris: Flammarion.

Lewis, Hywel D. (1939). 'Plato and the Social Contract'. *Mind*, 48 (189): 78–81.

Lewis, John David ([2007]2011). *Early Greek Lawgivers*. London: Bristol Classical Press.

Leys, Wayne A. R. (1965). 'Was Plato Non-Political?'. *Ethics*, 75 (4): 272–6.

Liddell, Henry G., Robert Scott and Henry S. Jones (1996). *A Greek-English Lexicon*. Oxford: Clarendon Press.

Liebert, Rana S. (2013). 'Pity and Disgust in Plato's *Republic*: The Case of Leontius'. *Classical Philology*, 108 (3): 179–201.

Loraux, Nicole (1996). *Né de La Terre: Mythe et Politique à Athènes*. Paris: Seuil.

Lorenz, Hendrik (2004). 'Desire and Reason in Plato's Republic'. *Oxford Studies in Ancient Philosophy*, 27: 83–116.

Lorenz, Hendrik (2006a). *The Brute within: Appetitive Desire in Plato and Aristotle*. Oxford: Oxford University Press.

Lorenz, Hendrik (2006b). 'The Analysis of the Soul in Plato's Republic'. In Gerasimos Santas (ed.), *The Blackwell Guides to Plato's Republic*, 146–65. Malden: Blackwell

Ludwig, Paul (2007). 'Eros in the Republic'. In Giovanni R. F. Ferrari (ed.), *The Cambridge Companion to Plato's Republic*, 202–31. Cambridge: Cambridge University Press.

Mabbott, John D. (1937). 'Is Plato's Republic Utilitarian?'. *Mind*, 46 (184): 468–74.

Macé, Arnaud (2006). *Platon, Philosophie de l'Agir et du Pâtir*. Sankt Augustin: Academia Verlag.

Maguire, Joseph P. (1971). 'Thasymachus… or Plato?'. *Phronesis*, 16: 142–63.

Mahoney, Timothy A. (1992). 'Do Plato's Philosopher-Rulers Sacrifice Self-Interest to Justice?' *Phronesis*, 37 (3): 265–82.

Malcolm, John (1962). 'The Line and the Cave', *Phronesis*, 7 (1): 38–45.

Martinez, Joel A. (2011). 'Rethinking Plato's Conception of Knowledge: The Non-Philosopher and the Forms'. *Apeiron*, 44 (4): 326–34.

McCabe, Mary-Margaret (1994). *Plato's Individuals*. Princeton: Princeton University Press.

McKeen, Catherine (2004). 'Swillsburg City Limits (The "City of Pigs": Republic 370C–372D)'. *Polis*, 21 (1–2): 70–92.

McLaren, Angus (1992). *A History of Contraception: From Antiquity to the Present*. Oxford: Blackwell.

McPherran, Mark (2006). 'The Gods and Piety in Plato's Republic'. In Gerasimos Santas (ed.), *The Blackwell Guide to Plato's Republic*, 84–103. Malden: Blackwell.

Meinwald, Constance (1991). *Plato's Parmenides*. Oxford: Oxford University Press.

Menn, Stephen (1994). 'The Origins of Aristotle's Concept of Ἐνέργεια: Ἐνέργεια and Δύναμις'. *Ancient Philosophy*, 14 (1): 73–114.

Menn, Stephen (2006). 'On Plato's Πολιτεία'. In John J. Cleary and Gary M. Gurtler (eds), *Proceedings of the Boston Area Colloquium in Ancient Philosophy*, vol. XXI, 1–55. Leiden: Brill.

Miller Jr, Fred (2018). *Platonic Freedom*. Oxford: Oxford University Press.

Miller, Mitchell (2007). 'Beginning the "Longer Way"'. In Giovanni R. F. Ferrari (ed.), *The Cambridge Companion to Plato's Republic*, 310–44. Cambridge: Cambridge University Press.
Moline, Jon (1978). 'Plato on the Complexity of the Psyche'. *Archiv Für Geschichte Der Philosophie*, 60 (1): 1–26.
Moore, Christopher (2020). *Calling Philosophers Names: On the Origin of a Discipline*. Princeton: Princeton University Press.
Moors, Kent F. (1981). *Glaucon and Adeimantus on Justice: The Structure of Argument in Book 2 of Plato's Republic*. Washington: University Press of America.
Moraes-Augusto, Maria das Graças (2012/2013). 'Politeia e Utopia: o Caso Platônico'. *Kléos*, 16/17: 103–51.
Morrison, Donald R. (2007). 'The Utopian Character of Plato's Ideal City'. In Giovanni R. F. Ferrari (ed.), *The Cambridge Companion to Plato's Republic*, 232–55. Cambridge: Cambridge University Press.
Morrison, John S. (1958). 'The Origins of Plato's Philosopher Statesman'. *Classical Quarterly*, 8 (3–4): 193–218.
Moss, Jessica (2005). 'Shame, Pleasure, and the Divided Soul'. *Oxford Studies in Ancient Philosophy*, 29: 137–70.
Moss, Jessica (2007). 'What is Imitative Poetry and Why is it Bad?'. In Giovanni R. F. Ferrari (ed.), *The Cambridge Companion to Plato's Republic*, 415–44. Cambridge: Cambridge University Press.
Moss, Jessica (2008). 'Appearances and Calculations: Plato's Division of the Soul'. *Oxford Studies in Ancient Philosophy*, 34: 35–68.
Moss, Jessica (2014). 'Plato's Appearance-Assent Account of Belief'. *Proceedings of the Aristotelian Society*, 114: 213–38.
Moss, Jessica (2021). *Plato's Epistemology: Being and Seeming*. Oxford: Oxford University Press.
Murphy, Neville R. (1932). 'The "Simile of Light" in Plato's Republic'. *The Classical Quarterly*, 26 (2): 93–102.
Murphy, Neville R. (1934). 'Back to the Cave'. *Classical Quarterly* 28 (3/4): 211–13.
Murphy, Neville R. (1951). *The Interpretation of Plato's Republic*. Oxford: Clarendon Press.
Murray, Penelope (1996). *Plato on Poetry*. Cambridge: Cambridge University Press.
Naddaff, Ramona (2002). *Exiling the Poets: The Production of Censorship in Plato's Republic*. Chicago: University of Chicago Press.
Nails, Debra (1998). 'The Dramatic Date of Plato's Republic'. *The Classical Journal*, 93 (4): 383–96.
Nails, Debra (2002). *The People of Plato: A Prosopography of Plato and Other Socratics*. Indianapolis: Hackett.
Narcy, Michel (1997). 'Dictature, Absolutisme et Totalitarisme: Le Cas de Platon'. *Revue Française d'Histoire des Idées Politiques*, 6: 233–43.
Natorp, Paul (1903). *Platons Ideenlehre: Einführung in den Idealismus*. Leipzig: Dürr'sche.
Natali, Carlo (2005). 'L'Élision de l'Oikos dans la République de Platon'. In Monique Dixsaut (ed.), *Études sur la République de Platon: De la Justice, Éducation, Psychologie et Politique*, 199–226. Paris: Vrin.
Nawar, Tamer (2018). 'Thrasymachus' Unerring Skill and the Arguments of Republic 1'. *Phronesis*, 63 (4): 359–91.
Nehamas, Alexander (1982). 'Plato on Imitation and Poetry in Republic 10'. In Julius Moravcsik and P. Temko (eds), *Plato on Beauty, Wisdom and the Arts*, 47–78. Totowa: Rowman and Littlefield.
Nettleship, Richard Lewis (1906). *The Theory of Education in the Republic of Plato*. Chicago: University of Chicago Press.
Nettleship, Richard Lewis (1922). *Lectures on the Republic of Plato*. Philadelphia: R. West.
Neu, Jerome (1971). 'Plato's Analogy of State and Individual: *The Republic* and the Organic Theory of the State'. *Philosophy*, 46 (177): 238–54.
Nicholson, Peter P. (1974). 'Unravelling Thrasymachus' Arguments in the Republic'. *Phronesis*, 19: 210–32.
Nussbaum, Martha (1986). *The Fragility of the Goodness: Luck and Ethics in Greek Tragedy and Philosophy*. Cambridge: Cambridge University Press.

Nussbaum, Martha (2013). *Political Emotions: Why Love Matters for Justice*. Cambridge: Harvard University Press.
O'Connor, David K. (2007). 'Rewriting the Poets in Plato's Characters'. In G. R. F. Ferrari (ed.), *The Cambridge Companion to Plato's Republic*, 55–89. Cambridge: Cambridge University Press.
Obdrzalek, Suzanne (2013). 'Eros Tyrannos: Philosophical Passion and Psychic Ordering in the Republic'. In Noburu Notomi and Luc Brisson (eds), *Dialogues on Plato's Politeia (Republic): Selected Papers from the Ninth Symposium Platonicum*, 215–22. Sankt Augustin: Academia.
Ostenfeld, Erik Nis (1998). 'Eudaimonia in Plato's Republic'. In Erik Nis Ostenfeld (ed.), *Essays on Plato's Republic*, 73–84 Aarhus: Aarhus University Press.
Owen, Gwilym E. L. (1957). 'A Proof in the ΠΕΡΙ ΙΔΕΩΝ'. *The Journal of Hellenic Studies*, 77 (1): 103–11.
Owen, Gwilym E. L. (1968). 'Dialectic and Eristic in the Treatment of Forms'. In G. E. L. Owen (ed.), *Aristotle on Dialectic: The Topics*, 103–25. Oxford: Clarendon.
Page, Carl (1991). 'The Truth about Lies in Plato's Republic'. *Ancient Philosophy*, 11 (1): 1–13.
Palumbo, Lidia (2009). *Mimesis: Rappresentazione, Teatro e Mondo nei Dialoghi di Platone e nella Poetica di Aristotele*. Napoli: Loffredo.
Parry, Richard (2007). 'The Unhappy Tyrant and the Craft of Inner Rule'. In G. R. F. Ferrari (ed.), *The Cambridge Companion to Plato's Republic*, 386–414. Cambridge: Cambridge University Press.
Paton, Herbert J. (1921–22). 'Plato's Theory of Eikasia'. *Proceedings of the Aristotelian Society*, 22: 69–104.
Payne, Andrew (2011). 'The Division of Goods and Praising Justice for Itself in Republic II'. *Phronesis*, 56 (1): 58–78.
Payne, Andrew (2017). *The Teleology of Action in Plato's Republic*. Oxford: Oxford University Press.
Penner, Terry (1971). 'Thought and Desire in Plato'. In Gregory Vlastos (ed.), *Plato*, vol. II, 96–118. New York: Anchor.
Penner, Terry (1990). 'Plato and Davidson: Parts of the Soul and Weakness of Will'. *Canadian Journal of Philosophy*, 20 (Supplementary Volume 1): 35–74.
Penner, Terry (2005a). 'La Forme du Bien et le Bien de l'Homme: Quelque Problèmes d'Interpretation du Passage 504–509 de la République'. In Monique Dixsaut (ed.), *Études sur la "République" de Platon: De la Science, du Bien et des Mythes*, 177–207. Paris: Vrin.
Penner, Terry (2005b). 'Platonic Justice and What We Mean by "Justice"'. *Plato Journal*, 5: 1–76.
Penner, Terry (2006). 'The Forms in the Republic'. In Gerasimos Santas (ed.), *The Blackwell Guides to Plato's Republic*, 234–62. Malden: Blackwell.
Penner, Terry (2007a). 'What is the Form of the Good Form of?'. In Douglas L. Cairns, Fritz-Gregor Herrmann, and Terry Penner (eds), *Pursuing the Good: Ethics and Metaphysics in Plato's Republic*, 1–14. Edinburgh: Edinburgh University Press.
Penner, Terry (2007b). 'The Good, Advantage, Happiness and the Form of the Good: How Continuous with Socratic Ethics is Platonic Ethics'. In Douglas L. Cairns, Fritz-Gregor Herrmann and Terry Penner (eds), *Pursuing the Good: Ethics and Metaphysics in Plato's Republic*, 93–123. Edinburgh: Edinburgh University Press.
Penner, Terry (2009). 'Thrasymachus and the ὡς ἀληθῶς Ruler'. *Skepsis*, 20: 199–215.
Pomeroy, Sarah (1974). 'Feminism in Book V of Plato's Republic'. *Apeiron*, 8: 33–35.
Popper, Karl (1945[1966]). *The Open Society and its Enemies*. 5th ed, 2 vols. London: Routledge.
Prauscello, Lucia (2014). *Performing Citizenship in Plato's Laws*. Cambridge: Cambridge University Press.
Price, Anthony W. (1995). *Mental Conflict*. London: Routledge.
Price, Anthony W. (2009). 'Are Plato's Soul-Parts Psychological Subjects?'. *Ancient Philosophy*, 29 (1): 1–15.
Prichard, Harold A. (1928[2002]). 'Duty and Interest'. In Jim MacAdam (ed.), *Moral Writings*, 21–49. Oxford: Oxford University Press.
Prince, Brian D. (2014). 'How to Individuate the Powers of Knowledge and Opinion in Plato's Republic V'. *Journal of Ancient Philosophy*, 8 (2): 92.
Proclus (1965). *Procli Diadochi in Platonis Rem Publicam Commentarii*. 2 Vols. Ed. Guilemus Kroll. Leipzig: Teubner.

Raven, John E. (1953). 'Sun, Divided Line, and Cave'. *The Classical Quarterly*, 3 (1/2): 22–32.
Rawls, John (1971). *A Theory of Justice*. Cambridge: Belknap.
Reeve, Charles D. C. (1985). 'Socrates Meets Thrasymachus'. *Archiv Für Geschichte der Philosophie*, 67 (3): 246–65.
Reeve, Charles D. C. (1988). *Philosopher-Kings: The Argument of Plato's Republic*. Indianapolis: Hackett.
Reeve, Charles D. C. (2013). *Blindness and Reorientation: Problems in Plato's Republic*. Oxford: Oxford University Press.
Reeve, Charles D. C and George M. A. Grube (2004). *Republic*. Indianapolis: Hackett.
Renaut, Olivier (2006). 'Le Role de la Partie Intermediaire (Thumos) dans la Tripartition de l'Âme'. *Plato*, 6: 1–10.
Renaut, Olivier (2014). *Platon: la Médiation des Émotions: l'Éducation du Thymos dans les Dialogues*. Paris: Vrin.
Rickert, Gail Ann (1989). *Hekón and Akón in Early Greek Thought*. Atlanta: Scholars Press.
Riginos-Swift, Alice (1976). *Platonica: The Anecdotes Concerning the Life and Writings of Plato*. Leiden: Brill.
Robinson, Richard (1941). *Plato's Early Dialectics*. Ithaca: Cornell University Press.
Robinson, Richard (1951). 'Dr. Popper's Defense of Democracy'. *The Philosophical Review*, 60 (4): 487–507.
Robinson, Richard (1971). 'Plato's Separation of Reason from Desire'. *Phronesis*, 16 (1): 38–48.
Romilly, Jacqueline (1959). 'Le Classement des Constitutions d'Hérodote à Aristote'. *Revue des Études Grecques*, 72 (339): 81–99.
Rosen, Stanley (2005). *Plato's Republic: A Study*. New Haven: Yale University Press.
Rothschild, Nathan (2017). 'On Why Thumos Will Rule by Force'. *History of Philosophy and Logical Analysis*, 20 (1): 120–38.
Rowe, Christopher (2007). 'The Form of the Good and the Good in Plato's Republic'. In Douglas L. Cairns, Fritz-Gregor Herrmann and Terry Penner (eds), *Pursuing the Good: Ethics and Metaphysics in Plato's Republic*, 124–53. Edinburgh: Edinburgh University Press.
Rowe, Christopher (2017). 'The City of Pigs: A Key Passage in Plato's Republic'. *Philosophie Antique*, 17: 55–71.
Rowett, Catherine (2016). 'Why the Philosopher Kings Will Believe the Noble Lie'. *Oxford Studies in Ancient Philosophy*, 50: 67–100.
Rowett, Catherine (2018). *Discovering What Justice Is in Plato's Republic*. Oxford: Oxford University Press.
Russell, Bertrand (1947). *Philosophy and Politics*. Cambridge: Cambridge University Press.
Russell, Daniel C. (2005). *Plato on Pleasure and the Good Life*. Oxford: Oxford University Press.
Ryle, Gilbert (1947). 'Review of K. R. Popper, The Open Society and Its Enemies'. *Mind*, 57: 167–72.
Sachs, David (1963). 'A Fallacy in Plato's Republic'. *The Philosophical Review*, 72 (2): 141–58.
Santa-Cruz, María Isabel (2013). 'Qualité et Relatifs dans République IV'. In Noboru Notomi and Luc Brisson (eds), *Dialogues on Plato's Politeia (Republic): Selected Papers from the Ninth Symposium Platonicum*, 71–5. Sankt Augustin: Academia.
Santas, Gerasimos (1973). 'Hintikka on Knowledge and Its Objects in Plato'. In J. M. E. Moravcsik (ed.), *Patterns in Plato's Thought*, 31–51. Dordrecht: Reidel.
Santas, Gerasimos ([1980]1999). 'The Form of the Good in Plato's Republic'. *Philosophical Inquiry*, 2 (1): 374–403.
Santas, Gerasimos (1985). 'Two Theories of the Good in Plato's Republic'. *Archiv für Geschichte der Philosophie*, 67: 223–45.
Santas, Gerasimos (2006). 'Methods of Reasoning about Justice in Plato's Republic'. In Gerasimos Santas (ed.), *The Blackwell Guides to Plato's Republic*, 125–45. Malden: Blackwell.
Santas, Gerasimos (2007). 'Plato's Criticisms of Democracy in the *Republic*'. *Social Philosophy and Policy*, 24 (2): 70–89.
Santas, Gerasimos (2010). *Understanding Plato's Republic*. Chichester: Wiley-Blackwell.

Sauvé-Meyer, Susan (2005). 'Class Assignment and the Principle of Specialization in Plato's Republic'. *Proceedings of the Boston Area Colloquium in Ancient Philosophy*, 20 (1): 229–44.
Schindler, David C. (2008). *Plato's Critique of Impure Reason: On Goodness and Truth in the Republic*. Washington: Catholic University of America Press.
Schofield, Malcolm (1993). 'Plato on the Economy'. In M. H. Hansen (ed.), *The Ancient Greek City-State*, 183–96. Copenhagen: The Royal Danish Academy.
Schofield, Malcolm (1999). *Saving the City: Philosopher-Kings and Other Classical Paradigms*. London: Routledge.
Schofield, Malcolm (2006). *Plato: Political Philosophy*. Oxford: Oxford University Press.
Schofield, Malcolm (2007a). 'The Noble Lie'. In G. R. F. Ferrari (ed.), *The Cambridge Companion to Plato's Republic*, 138–64. Cambridge: Cambridge University Press.
Schofield, Malcolm (2007b). 'Language in the Cave'. In Dominic Scott (ed.), *Maieusis: Essays in Ancient Philosophy in Honour of Myles Burnyeat*, 216–31. Oxford: Oxford University Press.
Schofield, Malcolm (2010). 'Music All Pow'rful'. In Mark L. McPherran (ed.), *Plato's Republic: A Critical Guide*, 229–48. Cambridge: Cambridge University Press.
Schriefl, Anna (2013). *Platons Kritik an Geld und Reichtum*. Berlin: Gruyter.
Schwab, Whitney (2016). 'Understanding Episteme in Plato's Republic'. *Oxford Studies in Ancient Philosophy*, 51: 41–85.
Scott, Dominic (2000a). 'Plato's Critique of the Democratic Character'. *Phronesis*, 1 (1): 19–37.
Scott, Dominic (2000b). 'Metaphysics and the Defence of Justice in the *Republic*'. *Proceedings of the Boston Area Colloquium of Ancient Philosophy*, 16 (1): 1–20.
Scott, Dominic (2007). 'Eros, Philosophy and Tyranny'. In Dominic Scott (ed.), *Maieusis: Essays in Ancient Philosophy in Honour of Myles Burnyeat*, 136–53. Oxford: Oxford University Press.
Sedley, David (1998). 'Platonic Causes'. *Phronesis*, 43 (2): 114–32.
Sedley, David (2007). 'Philosophy, the Forms, and the Art of Ruling'. In Giovanni R. F. Ferrari (ed.), *The Cambridge Companion to Plato's Republic*, 256–83. Cambridge: Cambridge University Press.
Seel, Gerhard (2007). 'Is Plato's Conception of the Form of the Good Contradictory'. In Douglas L. Cairns, Fritz-Gregor Herrmann and Terry Penner (eds), *Pursuing the Good: Ethics and Metaphysics in Plato's Republic*, 168–96. Edinburgh: Edinburgh University Press.
Shellens, Max S. (1953). 'Der Gerechtigkeitsbegriff des Thrasymachus'. *Zeitschrift für Philosophishe Forschung*, 7: 481–92.
Shields, Christopher (2001). 'Simple Souls'. In Ellen Wagner (ed.), *Essays on Plato's Psychology*, 137–56. Lanham: Rowan and Littlefield.
Shields, Christopher (2006). 'Plato's Challenge: The Case against Justice in Republic II'. In Gerasimos Santas (ed.), *The Blackwell Guides to Plato's Republic*, 63–83. Malden: Blackwell.
Shields, Christopher (2007). 'Forcing Goodness in Plato's Republic'. *Social Philosophy and Policy*, 24 (2): 21–39.
Shields, Christopher (2010). 'Plato's Divided Soul'. In Mark L. McPherran (ed.), *Plato's Republic: A Critical Guide*, 147–70. Cambridge: Cambridge University Press.
Shields, Christopher (2011). 'Surpassing in Dignity and Power: The Metaphysics of Goodness in Plato's Republic'. In Georgios Anagnostopoulos (ed.), *Socratic, Platonic and Aristotelian Studies: Essays in Honor of Gerasimos Santas*, 281–96. Dordrecht: Springer.
Shipley, Graham (2005). 'Little Boxes on the Hillside: Greek Twon Planning, Hippodamos and Polis Ideology'. In Mogens Herman Hansen (ed.), *The Imaginary Polis: Symposium*, 335–403. Copenhagen: The Royal Danish Academy of Sciences and Letters.
Shorey, Paul (1895). 'The Idea of Good in Plato's Republic: A Study in the Logic of Speculative Ethics'. *Studies in Classical Philology*, 1: 188–239.
Shorey, Paul (1930). *The Republic*. 2 Vols. Cambridge: Harvard University Press.
Sidgwick, Henry (1869). 'A Passage in Plato, Republic'. *The Journal of Philology*, 2 (3): 96–103.
Silverman, Allan (1991). 'Plato on "Phantasia"'. *Classical Antiquity*, 10 (1): 123–47.

Singpurwalla, Rachel (2006a). 'Are There Two Theories of Goodness in the Republic? A Response to Santas'. *Apeiron*, 39 (4): 319–29.
Singpurwalla, Rachel (2006b). 'Plato's Defense of Justice in the Republic'. In Gerasimos Santas (ed.), *The Blackwell Guide to Plato's Republic*, 263–82. Malden: Blackwell.
Singpurwalla, Rachel (2011). 'Soul Division and Mimesis in Republic X'. In Pierre Destrée and Fritz-Gregor Hermann (eds), *Plato and the Poets*, 283–98. Leiden: Brill.
Singpurwalla, Rachel (2013). 'Why Spirit is the Natural Ally of Reason: Spirit, Reason, and the Fine in Plato's Republic'. *Oxford Studies in Ancient Philosophy*, 44: 41–65.
Skemp, Joseph B. (1960). 'Comment on Communal and Individual Justice in the Republic'. *Phronesis*, 5: 35–8.
Slings, Simon R. (2003). *Platonis Rempublicam*. Oxford: Oxford University Press.
Slings, Simon R., Gerard Boter, and Jan M. van Ophuijsen (2005). *Critical Notes on Plato's Politeia*. Leiden: Brill.
Smith, Adam ([1776] 1977). *An Inquiry into the Nature and Causes of the Wealth of Nations*. Chicago: University of Chicago Press.
Smith, Nicholas D. (1976). 'Republic 476e–480a: Intensionality in Plato's Epistemology?'. *Philosophical Studies*, 30 (6): 427–9.
Smith, Nicholas D. (1979). 'Knowledge by Acquaintance and "Knowing What" in Plato's Republic'. *Dialogue*, 18 (3): 281–8.
Smith, Nicholas (1980). 'The Logic of Plato's Feminism'. *Journal of Social Philosophy*, 11 (3): 5–11.
Smith, Nicholas D. (1996). 'Plato's Divided Line'. *Ancient Philosophy*, 16: 25–46.
Smith, Nicholas D. (1997). 'How the Prisoners in Plato's Cave Are "Like Us"'. *Proceedings of the Boston Area Colloquium of Ancient Philosophy*, 13: 187–204.
Smith, Nicholas D. (2000). 'Plato on Knowledge as a Power'. *Journal of the History of Philosophy*, 38 (2): 145–68.
Smith, Nicholas D. (2010). 'Return to the Cave'. In Mark L. McPherran (ed.), *Plato's Republic: A Critical Guide*, 83–102. Cambridge: Cambridge University Press.
Smith, Nicholas D. (2012). 'Plato on The Power of Ignorance'. In Rachana Kamtekar (ed.), *Virtue and Happiness*, 51–73. Oxford: Oxford University Press.
Smith, Nicholas D. (2019). *Summoning Knowledge in Plato's Republic*. Oxford: Oxford University Press.
Solomon J. H. M. (1967). 'Exousia in Plato'. *Platon*, 19: 189–97.
Souilhé, Joseph (1919). *Étude sur le Terme δύναμις dans les Dialogues de Platon*. Paris: Félix Alcan.
Sparshott, Francis E. (1966). 'Socrates and Thrasymachus'. *The Monist*, 50 (3): 421–59.
Sparshott, Francis E. (1967). 'Plato as Anti-Political Thinker'. *Ethics*, 77: 214–19.
Stalley, Richard F. (1975). 'Plato's Argument for the Division of the Reasoning and Appetitive Elements within the Soul'. *Phronesis*, 20 (2): 110–28.
Stalley, Richard F. (1998). 'Plato's Doctrine of Freedom'. *Proceedings of the Aristotelian Society*, 9: 145–58.
Stocks, J. L. (1911). 'The Divided Line of Plato Rep. VI'. *The Classical Quarterly*, 5 (2): 73–88.
Stokes, M. C. (1987). 'Adeimantus in the Republic'. In Spiro Panagiotou (ed.), *Justice, Law, and Method in Plato and Aristotle*, 97–103. Edmonton: Academic Printing.
Stokes, M. C. (1992). 'Plato and the Sightlovers of the "Republic"'. *Apeiron*, 25: 103–2.
Storey, Damien (2014). 'Appearance, Perception, and Non-Rational Belief: Republic 602c–603a'. *Oxford Studies in Ancient Philosophy*, 47: 81–118.
Storey, Damien (2020). 'What Is Eikasia?'. *Oxford Studies in Ancient Philosophy*, 58: 19–57.
Strauss, Leo (1964). *The City and Man*. Chicago: University of Chicago Press.
Szaif, Jan (1998). *Platons Begriff der Wahrheit*. Freiburg: Alber.
Szaif, Jan (2007). 'Doxa and Episteme as Modes of Acquaintance in Republic V'. *Études Platoniciennes*, 4: 253–72.
Tarrant, Harold (2012). 'Plato's Republics'. *Plato*, 12: 1–13.

Taylor, Alfred E. (1939). 'The Decline and Fall of the State in *Republic*, VIII'. *Mind*, 48 (189): 23-38.
Taylor, Christopher C. W. (1997). 'Plato's Totalitarianism'. In Richard Kraut (ed.), *Plato's Republic: Critical Essays*, 31-48. Lanham: Rowman & Littlefield Publishers
Teisserenc, Fulcran (2005). 'Mimesis, Narrative et Formation du Caractère'. In Monique Dixsaut (ed.), *Études sur la "République" de Platon: De la Justice, Éducation, Psychologie et Politique*, 65-88. Paris: Vrin.
Thesleff, Holger (1982). *Studies in Platonic Chronology*. Commentationes Humanarum Litterarum, 70. Helsinki: Societas Scientiarum Fennica.
Thucydides (1942). *Historiae*. Ed. Stuart Jones. Oxford: Oxford University Press.
Turnbull, Robert G. (1988). 'Becoming and Intelligibility'. *Oxford Studies in Ancient Philosophy*, Supplementary Volume: 1-14.
Vallejo Campos, Álvaro (2013). 'The Theory of Conflict in Plato's Republic'. In Noburu Notomi and Luc Brisson (eds), *Dialogues on Plato's Politeia (Republic): Selected Papers from the Ninth Symposium Platonicum*, 192-8. Sankt Augustin: Academia.
Vallejo Campos, Álvaro (2018). *Adonde nos Lleve el Logos: Para Leer la República de Platón*. Madrid: Trotta.
Vasiliou, Iakovos (2012). 'From the *Phaedo* to the *Republic*: Plato's Tripartite Soul and the Possibility of Non-Philosophical Virtue'. In Rachel Barney, Tad Brennan, and Charles Brittain (eds), *Plato and the Divided Self*, 9-32. Cambridge: Cambridge University Press.
Vegetti, Mario (1998a). 'Trasimaco'. In Mario Vegetti (ed.), *Platone La Repubblica*, vol. I, 233-56. Naples: Bibliopolis.
Vegetti, Mario (1998b). 'Ricchezza/Povertá e l'Unità della Polis'. In Mario Vegetti (ed.), *La Repubblica*, vol. III, 151-8. Naples: Bibliopolis.
Vegetti, Mario (1998c). 'Adimanto'. In Mario Vegetti (ed.), *La Repubblica*, vol. II, 221-32. Naples: Bibliopolis.
Vegetti, Mario (1999). *Guida alla Lettura della Repubblica di Platone*. Roma: Laterza.
Vegetti, Mario (2000a). 'La "Razza Pura"'. In Mario Vegetti (ed.), *La Repubblica*, vol. IV, 295-300. Naples: Bibliopolis.
Vegetti, Mario (2000b). 'Il Regno Filosofico'. In Mario Vegetti (ed.), *La Repubblica*, vol. IV, 355-64. Naples: Bibliopolis.
Vegetti, Mario (2000c). *La Repubblica*. Naples: Bibliopolis.
Vegetti, Mario (2003). 'Megiston Mathema: L'Idea del 'Buono' e le sue Funzione'. In Mario Vegetti (ed.), *Platone La Repubblica*, vol. V, 253-86. Naples: Bibliopolis.
Vegetti, Mario (2005). 'Il Tempo, la Storia, l'Utopia'. In Mario Vegetti (ed.), *La Repubblica*, vol. VI, 137-68. Naples: Bibliopolis.
Vegetti, Mario (2013). 'How and Why Did the Republic Become Unpolitical?'. In Noburu Notomi and Luc Brisson (ed.), *Dialogues on Plato's Politeia (Republic): Selected Papers from the Ninth Symposium Platonicum*, 3-15. Sankt Augustin: Academia.
Vernant, Jean-Pierre and Pierre Vidal-Naquet (2005). *Mythe et Tragédie en Grèce Ancienne*. Paris: La Découverte.
Vlastos, Gregory (1965). 'Degrees of Reality'. In Renford Bambrough (ed.), *New Essays in Plato and Aristotle*, 1-19. London: Routledge & Kegan Paul.
Vlastos, Gregory (1968). 'The Argument in the Republic That "Justice Pays"'. *The Journal of Philosophy*, 65 (21): 665-74.
Vlastos, Gregory (1969a). 'Reasons and Causes in the Phaedo'. *The Philosophical Review*, 78 (3): 291-325.
Vlastos, Gregory (1969b). 'Justice and Psychic Harmony in the Republic'. *The Journal of Philosophy*, 66 (16): 505-21.
Vlastos, Gregory ([1971]1978). 'Justice and Happiness in the Republic'. In Gregory Vlastos (ed.), *Plato: A Collection of Critical Essays. 2: Ethics, Politics, and Philosophy of Art and Religion*, 66-95. New York: Anchor.
Vlastos, Gregory (1977). 'The Theory of Social Justice in the Polis in Plato's Republic'. In Helen North (ed.), *Interpretations of Plato*, 1-40. Leiden: Brill.

Vlastos, Gregory (1981). 'The Individual as Object of Love in Plato'. In *Platonic Studies*, 31–42. Princeton: Princeton University Press.
Vlastos, Gregory ([1989]1995). 'Was Plato a Feminist?'. In Daniel W. Grahan (ed.), *Studies in Greek Philosophy*, 133–46. Princeton: Princeton University Press.
Vogt, Katja Maria (2009). 'Belief and Investigation in Plato's Republic'. *Plato*, 9:1–24.
Vogt, Katja Maria (2012). *Belief and Truth: A Skeptic Reading of Plato*. Oxford: Oxford University Press.
Wagner, Ellen (2005). 'Compulsion Again in the Republic'. *Apeiron*, 38 (3): 87–101.
Wardy, Robert (2013). 'The Platonic Manufacture of Ideology, or How to Assemble Awkward Truth and Wholesome Falsehood'. In: Verity Harte and Melissa Lane (eds), *Politeia in Greek and Roman Philosophy*, 119–38. Cambridge: Cambridge University Press.
Warren, James (2011). 'Socrates and the Patients: Republic IX, 583c-585a'. *Phronesis*, 56 (2): 113–37.
Waterfield, Robin (1998). *Plato Republic*. Oxford: Oxford University Press.
Wedberg, Anders (1955). *Plato's Philosophy of Mathematics*. Westport: Greenwood Press.
Wedgwood, Ralph (2017). 'The Coherence of Thrasymachus'. *Oxford Studies in Ancient Philosophy*, 53, 33–63.
Weiss, Roslyn (2007). 'Wise Guys and Smart Alecks in Rep. 1 and 2'. In Giovanni R. F. Ferrari (ed.), *Cambridge Companion to Plato's 'Republic'*, 90–115. Cambridge: Cambridge University Press.
Weiss, Roslyn (2012). *Philosophers in the Republic: Plato's Two Paradigms*. Ithaca: Cornell University Press.
Westerink, Leendert G. (1981). 'The Title of Plato's Republic'. *Illinois Classical Studies*, 6 (1): 112–15.
White, Frances C. (1978). 'J. Gosling on τὰ πολλὰ καλά'. *Phronesis*, 23 (2): 127–32.
White, Nicholas P. (1976). *Plato on Knowledge and Reality*. Indianapolis: Hackett.
White, Nicholas P. (1979). *A Companion to Plato's Republic*. Indianapolis: Hackett.
White, Nicholas P. (1984). 'The Classification of Goods in Plato's Republic'. *Journal of the History of Philosophy*, 22 (4): 393–421.
White, Nicholas P. (1986). 'The Rulers' Choice'. *Archiv für Geschichte der Philosophie*, 68 (1): 22–46.
White, Stephen A. (1995). 'Thrasymachus the Diplomat'. *Classical Philology*, 90: 307–27.
Wieland, Wolfgang (1976). 'Platon und der Nutzen der Idee: Zur Funktion der Idee des Guten'. *Allgemeine Zeitschrift Für Philosophie*, 1: 19–33.
Wieland, Wolfgang ([1982]1999). *Platon und die Formen des Wissens*. Göttingen: Vandenhoeck & Ruprecht.
Wilberding, James (2004). 'Prisoners and Puppeteers in the Cave'. *Oxford Studies in Ancient Philosophy*, 27: 117–39.
Wilburn, Josh (2015). 'Courage and the Spirited Part of the Soul in Plato's Republic'. *Philosophers Imprint*, 15 (26): 1–21.
Williams, Bernard (1973). 'The Analogy of City and Soul in Plato's Republic'. In Edward N. Lee, Alexander P. D. Mourelatos and Richard M. Rorty (eds), *Exegesis and Argument*, 196–206. Assen: Van Gorcum.
Wolff, Francis (2004). 'Polis; Politeia'. In Barbara Cassin (ed.), *Vocabulaire Européen des Philosophies: Dictionnaire des Intraduisibles*, 961–3. Paris: Seuil.
Woodruff, Paul (2012). 'Justice as a Virtue of the Soul'. *Oxford Studies in Ancient Philosophy*, Supplementary Volume, 89–101.
Woods, Michael (1987). 'Plato's Division of the Soul'. *Proceedings of the British Academy*, 73: 23–47.
Zuolo, Federico (2009). *Platone e L'Efficacia: Realizzabilità della Teoria Normativa*. Sankt Augustin: Academia.

Index nominorum

Academy 186
action
   (un)consented actions 42, 46
   features of 12
   intentional 35–6
   interactive theory of 13, 19–29
   painful actions 190–1
   and power 14, 61–6
   principles of 5, 11–12, 19, 37
   self-commitment to 42
activity 112–14, 120–4
Adam, James 19 n.1, 20 n.4, 31 n.2, 57 nn.20, 22, 83 n.9, 157 n.11, 158 n.13, 159 n.14, 162 n.21, 170 n.11, 175 n.1
Adeimantus 15, 49, 64–5, 113, 127, 146, 151–5, 162–3, 185
Adkins, Arthur W. H. 27 n.24, 42 n.12, 89 n.1, 107 n.23, 124 n.12, 153 n.1, 156 n.7
adunaton/adunata 66
aitia 5–6, 21, 23, 159
aition 6 n.10
akousiōs 41–2
Allen, Danielle S. 31 n.3
Allen, Reginald E. 19 n.1, 50 nn.4–5, 51 n.6, 165 n.4
analogy
   'analogy of meaning' 11
   of the divided line 54–7, 182–3
   simile of the sun 157–61
anankē 167, 170–2
anarchy 74 n.10, 75
Anderson, Merrick E. 8 n.20, 80 n.2, 84 n.11, 86 n.14
anger 30–1, 33–6
animals, aggressiveness of 31–2, 35
Annas, Julia 4 n.7, 8 n.18, 21 n.6, 28 n.29, 41 n.8, 50 n.5, 53 n.12, 81 n.5, 87 n.16, 94 n.12, 101 n.4, 104 n.10, 107 n.21, 126 n.17, 148 nn.4–5, 162 n.20, 164 n.1, 192 nn.14–16, 200 n.39
Anscombe, Gertrude E. M. 1 n.2
antilogy 147, 184
aporia. See puzzlement
appearance 37–41, 43–4, 48–52, 57, 61, 68, 79, 180, 182–4, 204

appetite 26 n.18, 28, 145
   conflict between reason and 30–3
   and desire distinguished 72 n.6
apragmosunē 123–4, 169
Araújo, Carolina 72 n.7
Arendt, Hannah 107 n.22, 164 n.1
aristocracy 80
Aristotle 2, 3
Aronson, Simon H. 7 n.13, 8 n.19, 122 n.9, 170 n.12, 172 n.15
Arruzza, Cinzia 75 n.12, 103 n.8, 108 n.24, 151 n.11, 168 n.8
autocracy 86, 164
Avagianou, Aphrodite 149 n.6
avarice 70–1

Baltes, Matthias 158 n.13, 161 n.16
Baltzly, Dirk 50 n.5, 53 n.15
Bambrough, Renford 7 n.14, 164 n.1
banausia 137 n.9
Barker, Ernest 2 n.4, 11 n.24, 86 n.14, 146 n.3, 165 n.3
Barnes, Jonathan 5 n.9, 6 n.12, 11 n.22, 12 n.25, 121 n.8, 126 n.17
Barney, Rachel 38 n.1, 39 n.4, 75 n.12, 83 n.9, 87 n.16, 90 n.2, 93 n.9, 94 n.12, 96 n.14, 170 n.13
being (verb 'to be') 49–51, 200
Belfiore, Elizabeth 47 n.18, 134 n.5
belief (and judgement) 13, 24, 33
   and apprehension of appearance distinguished 53
   conflict of 40
   good judgement 16
   half-belief 41 n.11
   and knowledge distinguished 54–8, 64
   on personal flourishing 203–4
   as power 59–61
   second-order conflict of 46, 105
belief-based desires 24–5
Benardete, Seth 7 n.13, 8 n.16, 10 n.21, 91 n.4
Benitez, Eugenio 53 n.15
Benson, Hugh 62 n.13, 166 n.5, 182 n.9
Benveniste, Émile 1 n.1, 26

Index Nominorum

Bloom, Allan 8 n.16, 31 n.4, 82 n.7, 91 n.4, 106 n.16, 107 n.21, 142 n.15
Bloom, Paul 103 n.9
Blössner, Norbert 1 n.1, 8 n.20, 26 n.23, 70 n.2, 75 n.12, 104 n.11, 105 n.15, 122 n.9, 127 n.18, 164 n.1, 182 n.8
Bobonich, Christopher 5 n.9, 7 n.15, 19 n.1, 20 nn.2, 4, 21 n.6, 22 n.10–11, 24 n.13, 26 n.23, 28 n.29, 133 n.3, 136 nn.7–8
body
  'bodily' 24
  care of 73, 205
  and gymnastics 134–5, 205
  harm to 28
  and soul 101, 102
Bordes, Jacqueline 1 n.1, 2 n.3
Bosanquet, Bernard 57 n.22
Boter, Gerard J. 1 n.1, 5 n.8, 81 n.5, 83 n.10, 84 n.12
Boyle, Anthony J. 57 n.20
Brancacci, Aldo 138 n.11
Brennan, Tad 35 n.10, 119 n.4, 133 n.3
Brickhouse, Thomas C. 172 n.15
Brisson, Luc 133 n.4
Brown, Eric A. 19 n.1, 27 n.24, 100 n.2, 101 n.4, 133 n.3, 170 n.12
Brown, Lesley 7 n.14, 8 n.18, 164 n.1, 190 n.8
Burkert, Walter 71 n.4, 154 n.3
Burnyeat, Myles 11 n.24, 21 n.6, 24 n.13, 32 n.6, 74 n.10, 84 n.12, 153 n.1, 182 n.9, 183 n.12
Bury, Robert G. 59 nn.2–3, 63 n.19
Butler, James 97 n.16, 192 n.15, 193 n.19, 198 n.30, 199 n.32, 201 n.40

Cairns, Douglas L. 30 n.1
Calvert, Brian 121 n.7
Campese, Silvia 91 n.3, 146 n.3
care 89–92, 98, 131, 144–5
Carone, Gabriela R. 25 n.15, 28 n.29, 31 n.4, 42 n.13
Castelnérac, Benoît 180 n.7
Cattanei, Elisabetta 182 n.9, 183 n.12
causation 66–7
cave 169–72, 180
Cephalus 61, 64, 68, 126–7, 169, 175–6
Chappell, Timothy D. J. 80 n.2, 81 n.5, 83 n.10, 86 n.13, 87 n.16, 93 n.11
cheirotechnia 137 n.9
Cherniss, Harold 186 n.13
children/childhood 126, 127
  aggressiveness of 31–2, 35
  community of children 149
  dialectical games 179–86
  education of 15, 144, 166
  and justice 121
  and *mousikē* 133–4
  political participation of 178
Cicero 1
citizen/citizenship. *See also politeia*
  character and reputation of 5–7
  by descent 177, 178
  "doing one's own" 120–4, 168–9
  double citizenry model 15, 174, 178–86
  education for 131–7
  in extreme poverty 106 n.19
  good life of 4
  holistic and distributive sense of 1–2
  and justice 85
  Socrates's notion of 5 n.9
  types of 13
  virtues of 132–4
city
  accounts of 174–5
  concept of 11–13
  good and evil for 102–4
  good city 115–17, 148, 175
  good city, virtues of 118–22
  just city 4, 7, 12, 15, 125–6, 143–4
  life in 137–8
  origin of 3, 14, 112–15, 118, 120–1, 131, 150–1
  and soul compared 9–10
  'soul' of the 3, 5–6
  and soul relationship 84–5
Cleitophon 82
cognition/cognitive apparatus 13, 37, 180, 204
  functioning of 48–54
  misfunctions of 43
  powers of 58–61
common action 89, 95–7. *See also* cooperation
common purpose 85, 91–5, 115, 116, 127, 139–41
community
  of pleasures and pains 102–4, 119, 143–4, 149–50, 181
  of property among guardians 143, 151–2
  of women and children 15, 143, 145–51, 203
compassion 44–7, 103, 134, 145

compresence of opposites   20–1, 39–40, 44,
    51–2, 204
conflict (internal conflict)   23–6, 28, 30, 40
    and acquisition of unreasonable belief   48
    between appetite and reason   32–5
    decrease of   72–4
connatural good and evil   14, 100–2, 126,
    160
    justice as connatural good   121–2
(un)consented actions   42, 46
constitutional principle   14, 136
    and education   118
    and justice distinguished   120–1, 125–6
contraception   115
contract   85. *See also* social contract
    and expertise   91–2
cooperation   14, 15, 28, 33, 95–8, 131–2,
    143–5
    cooperative citizens   177–9, 187
    and "doing one's own"   120–4, 168–9
    empathy-based notion of   103–4
    and injustice   154–5
    justice as   126–8, 131–2, 155–6, 203
Cooper, John M.   8 nn.17–18, 12 n.25, 21 n.6,
    25 n.16, 26 nn.20, 23, 27 n.27, 32 n.6,
    35 n.8, 111 n.2, 114 n.7, 125 n.14,
    126 n.17, 132 n.1, 172 n.15
Cooper, Neil   50 n.5, 52 n.7, 55 n.19
Cornford, Francis M.   32 n.6, 35 n.9, 109 n.1,
    123 n.11, 161 n.16
correlative   24–6
    of cognition   49, 54, 60 n.9
    of knowledge   60–1
corruption   167–9
courage   118, 119, 123, 135
crime   85–7
Crombie, Ian M.   20 n.3, 59 n.5, 60 n.6
Cross, Robert C.   5 n.9, 7 n.13, 22 n.11,
    24 n.13, 50 n.4–5, 55 n.18, 57 n.20,
    80 n.2, 86 n.13, 87 n.16, 90 n.2, 97 n.17,
    109 n.1, 114 n.5, 115 n.11, 119 n.5,
    122 n.9, 132 n.1, 133 n.3, 153 n.1,
    190 n.6
customs (*ēthē*)   5–6

daily routine. *See diaitē* ('diet')
Davidson, Donald   35
Dawson, Doyne   1 n.1, 146 n.1
death   101, 142
decent man/people   44–7, 68–9, 137–9, 204–5
deductive sciences   182–3

Delcomminette, Sylvian   22 n.9, 24 n.13,
    31 n.5, 48 n.1, 53 n.13, 60 n.7, 157 n.11
democracy   74, 75, 80, 105, 137 n.9, 176–8
    Athenian   107 n.20, 167–8, 177
    as evil   107, 110
dēmos   80, 124, 137, 143–4
Demos, Raphael   7 n.13, 8 n.20, 104 n.10,
    114 n.6, 122 n.9, 125 n.14
Denyer, Nicholas   161 n.18, 179 n.6, 183 n.10
desire   13, 19–20, 203
    channelling of   72–4, 132–3, 141
    concept of   30
    cooperation between reasoning and   25,
        26 n.20, 28, 68–9
    dispute between reasoning and   40–3
    excellence of   123
    and fairness   116–17
    and internal conflict   24–6, 31–3
    and lovers   70–2
    and unreasonable beliefs   46
Destreè, Pierre   45 n.16
diaitē ('diet')   114–18, 135
diachronical appearance of opposites   37–9
dialectical knowledge   56
dialectical games/dialectic   15, 147, 179–86,
    200, 205
dialogue   2–3
dianoia (discursive reasoning)   38–40, 56–7,
    140
Diès, Auguste   153 n.1
Dillon, John M.   186 n.13
distribution   84–5, 94, 105, 109–10, 154
division of labour   113 n.3, 114
Dixsaut, Monique   52 n.8, 182 n.9
Dodds, Eric R.   157 n.11
"doing one's own"   120–4, 168–9
Dominick, Yancy H.   55 n.19
Dorter, Kenneth   91 n.4, 96 n.14, 179 n.6
Duncombe, Matthew   25 n.17, 101 n.3
dunamis   14, 62–4, 67, 105 n.14, 165
dunasthai   61–2. *See also* power
dunaton/dunata   63, 66. *See also* power

education   35 n.8, 117–18, 166, 205
    and citizenship   177–8
    for courage   135
    for justice   134
    miseducation (*apaideusia*)   47, 48, 168–70
    philosophical   15, 168–71, 174, 179–86
    purpose of   137–40
    for temperance   134–5

universal   131–3, 143–4, 148, 182, 206
  for wisdom   136–7
  of women   148
efficiency   114–15
Ehrenberg, Victor   2 n.3, 124 n.13
eleutheria. *See* freedom
Else, Gerald F.   44 n.14
Emlyn-Jones, Chris J.   165 n.4
emotion, and *thumos*   30–1
empathy   103, 145, 205
emptying   198–9
endurance   13, 33–5, 44–7, 68–9, 205
equality/equal   113–14, 119 n.3
Erginel, Mehmet M.   28 n.29, 196 n.24, 198 n.30, 199 nn.31, 34, 200 nn.38–9
essence (*ousia*)   53–4, 57, 159–61
eugenics   149
Everson, Stephen   80 n.2, 81 n.5, 82 n.7, 83 n.10, 87 n.16
evil/peculiar evil
  for a city   102–4
  diagnosis of   165
  for a person   14, 100–2
  personalities and *politeia*   104–7, 131
  Socrates account of   14, 99–100
excellence (virtue)   14–15, 89, 91–3, 97–8, 148, 187
  environment for promotion of   137–40
  of *thumos*   123
excluded third, principle of   20 n.4, 21, 41, 53
existence   50
exousia   107, 110–11, 177
expertise/expert   56, 82–3, 136
  and fairness in production   137–40
  in good city   118–19
  and good of others   89–91, 94–5, 98
  kinds of   139–41
  and power   65–6
external relations   22–3

fairness   51–4, 61, 113–19, 126, 137–40
Faust, August   66 n.26
fear   3, 14, 31–2, 46, 116–17
feasibility   15, 66–7, 164–5, 175
feminism   148
Ferber, Rafael   158 n.13, 160 n.15, 161 n.16
Ferguson, Alexander S.   55 nn.18–19, 158 n.12, 169 n.10
Ferrari, Franco   12 n.25, 34 n.7, 50 n.5, 104 n.12, 115 n.11, 133 n.3, 158 n.13, 160 n.15, 161 n.17, 200 n.36

Ferrari, Giovanni R. F.   8 n.20, 11 n.22, 24 n.13, 36 n.11, 45 n.16, 46 n.17, 47 n.18, 73 n.8, 104 n.11, 107 n.21, 124 n.12, 134 n.5
Fine, Gail   50 n.5, 51 n.6, 52 n.8, 53 n.15, 55 n.18, 59 n.5, 161 nn.16, 19
Fissell, Brenner   84 n.12
Flew, Antony G. N.   86 n.13
Flourishing (*eudaimonia*)
  achievement of   15–16
  achievement of, by *thumos*   33–5
  and citizenship   1–2
  of guardians   151–2
  and injustice   93–4
  and justice   187–8, 201
  by political life   193–5
  by prudence   193–7
  by pure and true pleasure   193, 197–201
  Thrasymachus's understanding of   86–7
  and *thumos*-like person   71
  unreasonable belief about   105–6
Foley, Vernard   114 n.5
Foot, Philippa   1 n.2
force/strength   26–7, 35
Forde, Steven   146 n.3
forgetfulness   43
forms, appearance of   51–3, 55–7, 68, 139–40, 183
Fortenbaugh, William W.   146 n.2
Foster, Michael B.   8 n.19, 188 n.4, 190 n.6
Franklin, Lee   53 n.11, 183 n.11
Frede, Dorothea   106 n.16, 196 n.24, 198 n.29, 199 n.34
Frede, Michael   6 n.10
freedom (*eleutheria*)   106–7, 116, 126, 164, 177–8
Frère, Jean   30 n.1
friendship   134
Fronterotta, Francesco   50 n.5, 101 n.5, 164 n.2
functional teleology   12

Gagarin, Michael   2 n.4, 175 n.2
Galis, Leon   127 n.18
Gastaldi, Silvia   148 n.5, 149 n.7
Georgini, Giovanni   166 n.6, 168 n.8
Gill, Christopher   25 n.15, 24 n.27, 32 n.6, 40 n.7, 105 n.14, 138 n.10, 167 n.7
Glaucon
  account of social contract   14, 109–12, 127
  classification of goods   188–92

critique of   196
on education   148
on justice and flourishing   15–16, 187–8
on kinship   145
on opposition of political law and human nature   116–17
on perfect cognition   53–4
on power   62
on reputation of justice   13
Gonzalez, Francisco J.   50 nn.4–5, 51 n.6, 53 n.14
good   4, 37
for city   102–4
classification of   188–92
false beliefs about   37, 41–3, 48
features of   155–6
for its own sake   191–2, 197–201
form of the good   15, 97 n.17, 133, 155–61, 170–2
functional theory of   97
good of others   14, 83–4, 86–7, 89–91, 94–5, 139–41, 191
peculiar goods   161–2
reduction of   30
unalienable good   113–16, 156
Gosling, Justin C. B.   50 n.5, 52 n.9, 53 n.15, 59 nn.3, 5, 193 n.17, 196 n.23, 198 n.30, 199 n.31, 200 n.38, 201 nn.40–1
government   81, 86, 93 n.10, 141, 201–2
Graeser, Andreas   53 n.11
Griffith, Tom   165 n.4
Griswold, Charles L.   136 n.7
Grube, George M. A.   102 n.7, 165 n.4
guardians   43–4, 116–17, 119
education of   135
flourishing of   151–2
philosophical and personal virtues of   132–3
women as   148
guess   53–4, 56–7
Guthrie, William K. C.   8 n.18
Gutierrez, Raul   55 n.18
Gyges of Lydia   110–11
gymnastics   9, 13, 32, 73, 122, 132–3, 137–8, 145, 166, 185, 205

habit   14, 28 n.29, 46, 56, 68, 73–4, 137
Hackforth, Reginald   57 n.22, 183 n.10
Hadgopoulos, Demetrius J.   82 n.7
haecceity, denial of   72
Hall, Dale   55 n.18

Halliwell, Stephen   47 nn.18–19, 148 n.4
Hall, Robert W.   132 n.1, 140 n.13
Halperin, David M.   71 n.4, 72 n.6
Hamlyn, David W.   55 n.18
happiness   1 n.2, 97 n.17, 128, 187, 188 n.4, 189 n.4, 190 n.7, 192 n.14
Harlap, Shmuel   80 n.2, 83 n.10, 86 n.15
harmony   136, 137 n.9, 138
Harrison, E. L.   80 n.2, 83 n.9
Harte, Verity   59 n.4, 60 nn.7, 10, 65 n.25
Havelock, Eric A.   64 n.20
health/sickness   24, 28, 65, 100, 101, 135, 168, 190, 197–8
healthy city   115–16, 118, 137 n.9, 138, 149
Heinaman, Robert   189 n.4, 190 n.6, 191 n.11
hekousiōs   41–2
Hellwig, Dorothee   106 nn.16–17
Helmer, Étienne   106 nn.16–17, 114 n.5
Henderson, Toliver Y.   80 n.2, 82 n.8, 84 n.12, 87 n.16
Herodotus   2–3
Hesiod   128, 153
Hintikka, Jaakko   60 n.9
Hipodammus of Miletus   2, 3, 4
Hitchcock, David   156 n.7
Hitz, Zena   8 n.18, 75 n.12, 106 n.17, 164 n.1
Hobbs, Angela   30 n.1, 32 n.6
Hoerber, Robert G.   140 n.13
Hoernlé, Reinhold F. A.   7 n.14
Homer   45, 145, 153
honour   124, 195–6, 199 n.31
Hourani, George F.   80 n.2, 81 n.5, 82 nn.5–7, 133 n.3
human nature   110–17
effect of education on   169–71
Hume, David   27 n.25
hypothesis (positing)   38–9
forms   51–3, 55–7, 139–40, 183

identity conflicts   166
and *thumos*   35–7
ignorance   43, 49, 53–4
individual/individuation   5, 9, 20–3, 40
concept of   30
and denial of compresence of opposites   51–2
and emotional self-assessment   35–6
inequality   84, 85, 96–7, 113
inevitability/inevitable   28, 92–3, 110, 114, 141
infallibility   54
inferences   56, 65, 140, 204–5

initiation 154
injustice
  complete injustice 86–7, 89, 96, 111–12, 155, 193–4
  and cooperation 154–5
  as *pleonexia* 84–6, 91, 93–5
  power of 64–5, 95–7
institutions
  Athenian 168
  and citizenship 1
  for philosophical education 179–86
  and power of citizens 12–13
  preservation of 119–23
  stability of 13
instrumental powers 59, 62, 64, 90
intellect 157–60, 170, 179, 183–4
intentional action 35–6
intentional teleology 12
interaction 2–3, 11–12, 14, 19–28, 41 n.9, 112
  between cities 118 n.1
  and justice 79–82
  and power 61–3, 65–6
  and *thumos* 36
interference 124–6
internal relations 22–3
Inwood, Brad 153 n.1
Irwin, Terence H. 7 n.13, 8 nn.17, 20, 20 n.4, 21 n.6, 25 n.15, 26 n.20, 55 n.18, 74 n.11, 105 n.14, 114 n.8, 122 n.9, 126 n.17, 132 n.1, 141 n.14, 161 n.16, 189 n.5, 190 n.7, 191 n.10, 192 n.14, 193 n.17
Isocrates 3

Jackson, Henry 55 n.18, 170 n.11
Jaeger, Werner 30 n.1
Janaway, Christopher 47 n.19
Jang, In H. 87 n.16, 91 nn.4, 6
Jeon, Haewon 133 n.3, 140 n.13
Johnstone, Mark 70 n.2, 74 n.10, 75 n.12, 105 n.14, 107 n.21
Jones, Henry S. 1 n.1
Joseph, Horace W. B. 11 n.24, 21 n.6, 28 n.28, 84 n.12, 158 n.13, 161 n.16
justice
  according to majority 109–12, 187–8, 191–2
  analogical interpretation of/'both wholes at once' thesis 8–11
  as attribute of certain actions 68
  in a city 120–2, 125–6
  as cooperation 126–8, 131–2, 155–6, 203

education for 134
and flourishing 15–16, 151–2, 187–8, 201
Glaucon's notion of 114 n.8
as a good for its own sake 191–2, 197–201
as good of others 83–4
holistic psychological interpretation of 7–8
holistic top-down concept of 6–7, 9–10
institutional approach to 174, 178–84, 206
instrumental role of 96–7
as interactive concept 79–82
and *politeia* 2 n.3
power of 64–5
in soul 122–4

Kahn, Charles H. 11 n.22, 32 n.6, 49, 72–3, 109 n.1, 122 n.9, 126 n.17, 200 n.37
Kallipolis 15, 163–6
  freedom in 177–8
  institutional approach 174, 178–84
  laws 170–2
Kamtekar, Rachana 6 n.11, 19 n.1, 20 n.2, 21 n.6, 24 n.13, 25 n.15, 26 n.23, 31 n.4, 32 n.6, 38 n.1, 41 n.9, 102 n.7, 114 n.7, 128 n.19
Kerferd, George 80 n.2, 81 n.5, 82 n.6–7, 83 n.10
Keyt, David 8 n.20, 68 n.1, 104 n.10, 119 n.3
kinship (akin) 124–6, 143–5, 146 n.2, 149–51
Kirwan, Christopher 188 n.4, 190 n.9, 191 n.11
Klosko, George 70 n.2, 83 n.9, 91 n.6, 137 n.9
knowledge
  acquisition of 48–50
  and belief distinguished 13–14, 54–8, 64
  of form of the good 15, 136, 156–7, 162
  and good city 118–19
  levels of 204–5
  as perfect cognition 53–4
  and *pleonexia* 89, 93–5
  as power 59–61, 65–6
  Thrasymachus's views on 82–3
Kosman, Aryeh 113 n.4, 120 n.6, 162 n.20
Krämer, Hans J. 158 n.13
Kraut, Richard 1 n.1, 70 n.2, 126 n.17, 156 n.7, 193 nn.17, 19, 196 n.25, 200 n.39, 201 n.41

Lacroix, Jean-Yves 164 n.2
Lafrance, Yvon 55 n.18, 57 nn.21–2
Laks, André 164 n.2

Lampe, Kurt 74 n.11
Lane, Melissa 3 n.6, 73 n.8132 n.1, 157 n.10
Larivée, Annie 75 n.12, 108 n.24, 168 n.8
lawgiver 103, 119, 174–6, 178
laws/legislation 81, 82, 103, 136–7, 140–1, 145, 151, 174
  and form of the good 157, 170–2
  purpose in *Kallipolis* 178
Lear, Jonathan 12 n.25, 104 n.12, 150 n.9, 153 n.1
Lefebvre, David 26 n.22, 59 n.1, 63 n.18, 107 n.20
leisure 114, 203
Leontius 31–3, 35–6, 43
Lewis, John D. 175 n.2
Leys, Wayne A. R. 164 n.1
Liddell, Henry G. 1 n.1
Liebert, Rana S. 31 n.3, 45 n.16
Lorenz, Hendrik 19 n.1, 20 nn.2, 4, 22 nn.8–9, 11, 24 n.13, 26 nn.18, 20, 28 n.29, 36 n.12, 38 n.1–2, 44 n.15, 71 n.3
lover 69, 79, 132–3
  and channelling of desire 72–4
  multiplicity of 70–2
  and philosopher compared 195–6
  spectacle-lover 54, 58, 60, 70
Ludwig, Paul 72 n.7

Mabbott, John D. 188 n.4
McCabe, Mary-Margaret 20–1, 161 n.16
Macé, Arnaud 21 n.7, 63 n.17, 190 n.6
McKeen, Catherine 115 n.9
McLaren, Angus 115 n.10
McPherran, Mark L. 153 n.1
Maguire, Joseph P. 80 n.2, 82 n.7, 83 n.9, 86 n.15, 87 n.16
Mahoney, Timothy A. 172 n.15
majority 109–12, 116, 167–8, 187–8, 191–2
Malcolm, John 169 n.10
Marion, Mathieu 180 n.7
marriage 146
Martinez, Joel A. 136 n.7
mathematics 179–83
means-end reasoning 28 n.29, 70 n.3
Meinwald, Constance 27
Menn, Stephen 1 n.1, 2 n.3, 3 n.6, 4 n.7, 8 n.18, 66 n.26, 172 n.16
Miller Jr, Fred 177 n.5
Miller, Mitchell 155 n.5, 183 n.12
mimēsis. See simulation
mistakes 60–1, 82–3, 157

modal possibility 66
Molière's regress 64, 90
Moline, Jon 21 n.6
money 28 n.29, 91–2, 115
  'the money-lover' 70–1, 195
Moore, Christopher 71 n.4
Moraes-Augusto, Maria das Graças 1 n.1
morality 8
Morrison, Donald R. 165 n.4
Morrison, John S. 186 n.13
Moss, Jessica 25 n.15, 32 n.6, 38 n.1, 44 nn.14–15, 49 n.2, 54 n.16, 55 n.18, 60 n.6, 60 n.10, 134 n.5
motivation
  for care expertise 90–3
  for expertise 94–5
  and justice 80–1, 84–6
  for philosophers to rule 171
  piety as 154
mousikē 32, 37, 43, 122, 132–42, 145, 166, 185
Murphy, Neville R. 41 n.11, 57 n.21, 169 n.10, 193 n.17, 198 n.30, 201 n.41
Musaeus 153
myth of the metals 150–1

Naddaf, Ramona 45 n.16
Nails, Debra 4 n.7, 31 n.2, 168 n.9
Narcy 8 n.18
Natali, Carlo 146 n.3
Natorp, Paul 158 n.13
natural good 97 n.17
natural tendency 142, 147–8
  to philosophy 166–8
nature, and power 66
Nawar, Tamer 82 n.8, 91 n.4, 96 n.14
Nehamas, Alexander 38 n.1, 41 nn.8, 11, 44 n.14
Nettleship, Richard L. 2 n.4, 8 n.18, 20 n.4, 55 n.18, 57 nn.21–2, 134 n.5, 138 n.10, 183 n.10
Neu, Jerome 8 n.20
Nicholson, Peter P. 80 n.2, 81 n.5, 82 n.7, 83 n.9, 87 n.16
nobility 33–4
noēsis 57 n.23
nomos 2 n.3
non-contradiction 20 n.4
non-interference 120–1, 123–4
nuclear family 146–51
Nussbaum, Martha 72 n.7, 103 n.9, 196 n.23
nutrition 19, 20, 23–6, 28, 199–201

Obdrzalek, Suzanne   73 n.8, 75 n.12, 133 n.2
object of knowledge argument   53
O'Connor, David K.   153 n.1
Odysseus   34, 124
oikeion   104, 124–5, 143–5, 146 n.2
oikeiopragia   125–6
oikos   15
oligarchy   33, 70, 105–7, 124
Ophuijsen, Johannes M. van   5 n.8
opposite appearance   37–41, 43–4, 48–51, 54, 61, 180, 182–4
optical illusion   37–41, 54
Ostenfeld, Erik N.   1 n.1
Owen, Gwilym E. L.   160 n.15

Page   150 n.10
pain   14, 33–5, 43, 46, 204
   community of   102–4
   painful actions   190–1
   and personality formation   73–5
   pleasure mixed with   189, 198
Palumbo, Lidia   44 n.14
Parry, Richard   71 n.3, 72 n.6, 75 n.12, 105 n.14
partial existence   50
partial injustice   85–6
'part-like' people   69–70, 132–3
Paton, Herbert J.   55 n.18
Payne, Andrew   12, 60 n.7, 64 n.22, 65 n.24, 92 n.7, 182 n.9
Penner, Terry   5 n.9, 8 nn.17–18, 11 n.22, 27 n.24, 35 nn.9–10, 53 n.11, 80 n.3, 82 n.8, 93 n.10, 94 n.12, 121 n.8, 126 n.17, 132 n.1, 155 n.5, 156 n.7, 162 n.21, 190 n.8
perception   37
   and appearances   79
   and judgement   39–40
perfect injustice   86, 97
personal flourishing   1, 15, 127–8, 194, 203–5
   of decent man   45–6
   and justice   110
   role of *politeia* in   169
   and *thumos*   32–3
   unreasonable beliefs about   104–6
personality   14
   of city   5–6
   diversity of   19–20
   evil   104–6, 131
   formation of   37, 69–70, 73–5
   freedom as a trait of   177–8

and pleasure   195–6
and *politeia*   102–4
schematic personality   68
Socrates's concept of   6
stable personality   68
vicious personality   46, 105, 136
personal responsibility   27 n.24
persuasion   3–5, 14
philoponia (lover of the effort)   73–4, 193
philosopher-king   15, 163–5, 174, 195
   alternative to   174, 178–84
   dialectic for   180–1
   and *politeia*   166–7, 172–3
philosophers   7–8, 11 n.23, 166–7
   capacity for judgement   195–7, 201
   freedom of   178
   and lovers compared   195–6
   pleasures of   195–7
   self-education   168–71
   virtues of   132–3, 136, 141–2
   the wisdom-lover   71–3
philosophy   47 n.18, 158–9
   relation between ruling and   141
   separation from politics   7–8
piety   151–2, 154, 162
pleasure   14, 204
   'bodily' pleasures   24, 28, 199 n.31
   and channelling of desire   73–5
   community of   102–4
   as evil   156
   flourishing in terms of   193, 197–201
   genuine pleasure   195–7, 199
   mixed pleasure   189, 198
   pure pleasure   189–91, 193, 197–201
   shift between pain   33–5
   and unreasonable beliefs   43–4, 46, 145
pleonexia   84–7, 91, 93–4, 109, 110, 117, 124 n.13, 199
poetry
   criticism of   153–4
   as simulation   44–7, 68–9, 205
   as vehicle of role models   137–8
Polemarchus   62, 91–2, 94, 96, 127, 146
politeia. See also citizen/citizenship
   and citizens' powers   84–5
   classical understanding of   3
   concept of   1–2, 19, 81, 109
   diversity of   5–6
   and flourishing   86–7, 169
   and justice   80–1, 121
   as a literary genre   2–3

as pamphlet literature 3–4
and personality 102–4
and philosopher-king 166–7, 172–3
philosophical 175–7
and principles of action 11–12
vicious *politeia* approach 105–7
Politeia of the Athenians 2, 4
political evil 105–7
political justice 7–10, 13–15, 121–2, 125 n.14
political participation 15, 178
political power 67, 97, 164–6, 168, 205–6
flourishing by 193–5
and philosophy 174, 176
political propaganda 3–4, 13 n.26
politics
organic and holistic view of 102–3
separation of philosophy from 7–8
polupragmosunē 124–5
Pomeroy, Sarah 146 n.2
Popper, Karl 7 n.14, 102 n.7, 106 n.16, 107 n.22–3, 113 n.3, 150 n.8, 164 n.1
popular virtue 15, 132, 134–7
and philosophical virtue differentiated 141–2
positive law 2 n.4, 82 n.6, 146
power 11–14
belief and knowledge as 59–61
and city-soul relationship 84–5
concept of 58–9, 165
and evil 100
expertise as 90, 94–5
and identity conflicts 36
interaction of 67
phrasal variations of 61–4
restrictive expression of 63, 65
self-transmitting powers 64 n.22
power device 66, 85–8, 106 n.16, 145
power struggle 85–6, 106
practical knowledge 56–7, 136, 140
Prauscello, Lucia 13 n.26
Preddy, William 165 n.4
predication 27
predominance (and prevailing) 12
of desire over reasoning 37–40
as interactive concept 26–7
modes of 13, 27–8
and power distinguished 67, 86
"prevailing over oneself" 42–3
and ruling 69–70
of unreasonable desire 31–3, 46
preservation 119–23, 159, 161, 178

Price, Anthony W. 19 n.1, 20 n.2, 20 nn.4–5, 21 n.6, 22 nn.10–11, 24 n.13, 25 n.15, 26 nn.20–1, 23, 28 nn.28–9, 41 n.11
Prichard, Harold A. 8 n.18
Prince, Brian D. 60 n.7
privatization/privatizer 14, 104–6, 143, 151
Protagoras of Abdera 2, 3
prudence 156, 193, 195–7
psychological justice 7, 14–15, 121–2
public opinion 167–8
punishment 14, 31, 33–5
avoidance of 85–7
and enforcement of law 81
and motivation 92–3
puzzlement (*aporia*) 40, 79
learning through 51–2

quietism 169, 172, 178, 193

rationality 4–5, 105 n.14
rational motivation 90–3
Raven, John E. 158 n.12
Rawls, John 203
reasoning 21 n.6, 37
conflict between appetite and 32–5
conflict between desire and 24–5
and cooperation 127–8
cooperation between desire and 25, 26 n.20, 28, 68–9, 132–3
discursive reasoning 38–40, 56–7, 140
and "doing one's own" 122–3
function of 13
of money-lover 70–1
and power 66
prevailing of 27–8, 40–3
reciprocity 192–5, 203
Reeve, Charles D. C. 41 n.9, 75 n.12, 86 n.14, 91 n.4, 102 n.7, 104 n.10, 114 n.8, 133 n.3, 172 n.14, 179 n.6, 188 n.2, 195 n.21
religion 153–4
Renaut, Olivier 22 n.8, 26 n.19, 30 n.1, 31 nn.4–5
replenishment 198–201
reproduction 115, 149
Republic
date controversy 4 n.7
as pamphlet literature 9, 13 n.26
purpose of the 4–5
reputation 111, 127, 153–4, 191, 192
revenge 33–5

rewards 15–16, 89, 91–3, 153
Rickert, Gail A. 42 n.12, 92 n.9
Robinson, Richard 7 nn.13–14, 19 n.1, 20 nn.3–4, 52 nn.7, 10, 57 n.20, 170 n.11
Romilly, Jacqueline 2 n.5, 80 n.1
Rosen, Stanley 8 n.16, 10 n.21, 20 n.4, 80 n.3, 153 n.1
Rothschild, Nathan 35 n.10
Rowe, Christopher 115 n.9, 120 n.6, 136 n.8, 156 n.6, 157 n.9, 161 n.17, 162 n.20
Rowett, Catherine 53 n.11, 54 n.16, 91 n.6, 119 n.4, 133 n.3, 150 nn.9–10, 155 n.5, 158 n.13
ruling 69–70, 80–3, 85–6, 92–3, 98, 119, 151, 163
Russel, Bertrand 7 n.14
    Russel's paradox 160
Russell, Daniel C. 193 n.17, 197 n.26, 201 n.42
Ryle, Gilbert 7 n.14

Sachs, David 8 n.19, 126–7
sacrifice 154
Santa-Cruz, María Isabel 24 n.14
Santas, Gerasimos 60 n.7, 74 n.9, 80 n.2, 97 n.17, 101 n.6, 104 n.10, 113 n.4, 132 n.1, 148 n.4, 153 n.1, 160 n.15, 162 n.20, 190 n.8
Sauvé-Meyer, Susan 5 n.9, 7 n.15, 119 n.4, 133 n.3, 137 n.9
schematic personality 68
Schindler, David C. 153 n.1
Schofield 1 n.1, 2 n.3, 3 n.6, 4 n.7
Schwab, Whitney 49 n.2, 54 n.16, 60 n.10, 136 n.7
Scott, Dominic 72–3, 74 nn.9–10, 75 n.12, 196 n.24
Scott, Robert 1 n.1
Sedley, David 6 n.10, 183 n.12
Seel, Gerhard 160 n.15, 162 n.20
self-censorship 31–3
self-education 168–71
self-harm 83, 87–8, 90–1
self-sufficiency 135 n.6
serenity 16, 44–5, 197–201, 205
shame 44–6, 133, 135
Shellens, Max S. 81 n.5, 86 n.14
Shields, Christopher 20 n.5, 23 n.11, 25 n.17, 36 n.12, 93 n.9, 101 n.5, 170 n.13, 172 n.14, 190 n.7, 192 n.14
Shipley, Graham 2 n.3

Shorey, Paul 28 n.28, 55 n.18, 156 n.8, 157 n.10, 165 n.4, 182 n.9, 183 n.12
Sidgwick, Henry 55 n.18
Silverman, Allan 41 n.10
simulation (*mimēsis*) 37–40, 44–7, 133–4, 145, 205
Singpurwalla, Rachel 25 n.15, 31 n.4, 32 n.6, 34 n.7, 41 n.11, 97 n.17, 103 n.9, 126 n.17, 133 n.2
Skemp, Joseph B. 139 n.12
slavery/slave 33, 83, 95, 108, 121, 194
Slings, Simon R. 5 n.8, 38 n.2, 159 n.14, 199 n.35, 200 n.36
Smith, Adam 114
Smith, Nicholas 39 n.5, 50 n.4–5, 51 n.6, 53 nn.12, 14, 55 n.18, 57 nn.20, 22, 60 n.8, 146 n.3, 148 n.5, 157 n.9, 164 n.2, 170 n.12, 172 n.14, 183 n.11
social contract 14
    Glaucon's account of 109–12
    Socrates's account of 112–14
Socrates
    analogy of the divided line 54–7, 182–3
    communitarian proposals of 15
    critique of Thrasymachus's conception of justice 81–2, 89–92, 131
    critique of Thrasymachus's conception of injustice 93–7
    the decent man case 44–7, 68–9
    on flourishing 193–7
    on good and evil 14, 99–100
    interactive theory of action of 13, 19–23
    on knowledge as perfect cognition 53–4
    on learning process 48–50
    on multiplicity of forms 52
    notion of city 5 n.9
    notion of justice 8, 14–15, 189, 191–3
    notion of personality 6
    notion of *politeia* 109
    on pure pleasure 197–201
    on social contract 14, 112–14
    on stable institution 13
    on 'three prime kinds of human beings' 69–70
    on *thumos* 31–3
    on true and false beliefs 41–3
    on tyrant 193–5
    on women as guardians 148
Souilhé, Joseph 63 n.19, 64 n.20, 66 n.28
soul
    of city 3

and city relationship 84–5
cooperation of parts of 127–8
excellence of 97–8
immortality of 101
interactionist concept of 13, 19–29, 36,
    41 n.9, 101, 155, 187, 195
justice in the soul 122–3
sovereignty, and justice 80–1, 83, 86–7
Sparshott, Francis E. 81 nn.4–5, 86 n.13–15,
    87 n.16, 92 n.7, 97 n.15, 164 n.1
specialization 113, 118–19
Stalley, Richard F. 20 n.4, 22 n.11, 177 n.5
Stocks, John L. 55 n.18, 57 n.20
Stokes, Michael C. 50 nn.4–5, 59 n.5, 153 n.1
Storey, Damien 38 n.1, 39 n.4, 40 n.6,
    55 n.18–19
Strauss, Leo 8 n.16, 11 n.24, 82 n.7, 96 n.13,
    106 n.16, 153 n.1, 164 n.2, 175 n.1
strife 96–7, 105–6, 144
suffering
    as means of flourishing 33–5
    and simulative poetry 44–7, 68–9
sun (simile) 157–61
survival 31–2
sustainability/sustainable 156–7, 162, 206
Szaif, Jan 59 n.5, 60 n.6, 158 n.13
synchronic opposite appearance 39–40
system's explanatory priority 162

talent 147
Tarrant, Harold 1 n.1
Taylor, Alfred E. 106 n.16
Taylor, Christopher C. W. 6 n.11, 7 n.14,
    193 n.17, 196 n.23, 198 n.30, 199 n.31,
    200 n.38, 201 nn.40–1
Teisserenc, Fulcran 134 n.5
teleology (telos, end) 11–14, 25–8, 30, 44–5,
    97 n.17, 161–2
temperance 42–3, 118, 134–5, 141, 153, 181,
    205
Theages 168, 169
Thesleff, Holger 4 n.7
thirst 23–6
thought 40
    and knowledge 56–7
    and simulative poetry 44–7
Thrasymachean good 82–4, 87–8, 107, 110,
    152, 154, 188
    and connatural good compared 101
Thrasymachus 27
    conception of flourishing 86–7

conception of power 14, 61, 64, 66
first conception of justice 80–3, 97, 187–8
on *pleonexia* 109
on power struggle 85–6
second conception of justice 83–4, 87
Socrates's critique of 81–2, 89–97, 131
thumos 13
    and achievement of flourishing 33–5
    and desire distinguished 30–3
    excellence of 123
    and gymnastics 134–5
    vis-à-vis prevailing and ruling 70
time/temporality 159
    and reciprocity 192–3
    relevance in manifestation of *thumos* 34
    restriction on 22
timocracy 105–7, 151
tolerance 107
totalitarianism 7
trust 137, 140
truth 61, 68, 158–62
Turnbull, Robert G. 39 n.5
two-world theory 50–1
tyranny/tyrannical personality 74–5, 86, 91,
    97, 106–8, 137, 177, 193–5, 201
    and crime distinguished 87

unreasonable belief 13, 37, 41–4, 48, 79, 157
    about flourishing 105–6, 204
    and simulative poetry 44–7
unreasonable desires. *See* appetite
unrelenting desire 71–2
user 64, 110–11, 139–40

Vallejo Campos, Álvaro 20 n.4
Vasiliou, Iakovos 136 n.7
Vegetti, Mario 91 n.4, 106 n.16, 133 n.3,
    149 n.7, 151 n.11, 153 n.1, 154, 158 n.13,
    165 nn.3–4, 182 n.8, 186 n.13
Vernant, Jean-Pierre 42 n.12
Vidal-Naquet, Pierre 42 n.12
violence 43
virtue 162, 200–1
    of citizens 132–4
    and good city 118
    peculiar virtue 89
vision 59, 157–61
Vlastos, Gregory 6 nn.10–11, 7 n.13, 8 n.18,
    50 nn.4–5, 72 n.7, 114 n.7, 120 n.6,
    121 nn.7–8, 122 n.9, 125 n.14, 127 n.18,
    133 n.3, 146 n.3, 160 n.15

Vogt, Katja Maria 50 n.5, 53 n.15, 60 n.10
vulgar justice 126–7

Wagner, Ellen 170 n.13
Wardy, Robert 150 n.8
Warren, James 197 nn.26–7, 198 nn.28–30, 199 n.33
Waterfield, Robin 8 n.18
Wedberg, Anders 57 n.22
Wedgwood, Ralph 80 n.2
Weiss, Roslyn 91 n.6, 93 n.9, 123 n.11, 153 n.1
Westerink, Leendert G. 1 n.1
White, Frances C. 51 n.6, 52 nn.7, 9
White, Nicholas P. 91 n.6, 104 n.10, 126 n.17, 156 n.7, 170 n.12, 182 n.9, 189 n.4, 190 nn.6–7
White, Stephen A. 80 n.2, 86 nn.13–14
whole-part rule 6–7
Wieland, Wolfgang 53 n.11, 55 n.19, 57 n.21, 156 n.7, 157 n.10
Wilberding, James 55 n.18
Wilburn, Josh 42 n.13
will 26–7, 42
    weakness of 35–6

Williams, Bernard 6, 7 n.13, 107 n.21, 118 n.2, 122 n.9
    'analogy of meaning' 11
    'predominant character rule' 12
wisdom 71–3, 118–19, 136–7
Wolff, Francis 1 n.1
women 126
    instrumentalization of 148
    and justice 120
    nature of 66
    political role of 15, 146–51
Woodruff, Paul 6 nn.11–12, 8 n.18, 114 n.7, 132 n.1
Woods, Michael 20 n.4, 21 n.6, 22 n.11, 24 n.13
Woozley, Anthony D. 5 n.9, 7 n.13, 22 n.11, 24 n.13, 50 n.4–5, 55 n.18, 57 n.20, 80 n.3, 86 n.13, 87 n.16, 90 n.2, 97 n.17, 109 n.1, 114 n.5, 115 n.11, 119 n.5, 122 n.9, 132 n.1, 133 n.3, 153 n.1, 190 n.6

Xenophon 2

Zuolo, Federico 164 n.2

Index locorum

Aristophanes
Birds
1406   31 n.2

Aristotle
Politics
1261a6   1 n.1
1266a39-b5   2 n.3
1266b31-8   2 n.3
1267b22-1268a15   2 n.3
1267b29-30   2 n.3
1273b30-4   175 n.2
1289a15-18   3, 3 n.6
1289a16-18   3
1295a40-b1   3, 3 n.6

Diogenes Laertius
Lives of eminent philosophers
III, 37, 420-1   2 n.3
IX, 50, 3-4   2 n.3
IX, 55, 60   2 n.3

Herodotus
History
I, 216, 1-6   146 n.2
III, 80-2 1299-1370   2
III, 83, 1371-2   2 n.5
IV 172, 7-14   146 n.2
IV, 104, 1-5   146 n.2
IV, 180, 21-5   146 n.2
IX, 34, 536   1

Homer
Odyssey
XX, 17   34

Isocrates
Areopagiticus
14, 1-2   3 n.6
Panatenaicus
138, 9   3 n.6

Plato
Phaedo
99c6-105c6   6 n.10

112b4-6   161 n.17
Gorgias
503b7   5 n.10
Parmenides
137e3-138a1   23 n.11
Republic
327c12   61 n.11, 62
328c7   64
329c5-6   177 n.4
329e6-330a1   3
331c2-3   68
331c4-5   68
331c5-8   68
332a7-10   96
332c1-3   127
332d4-6   127
332d7-8   91
332d7-333d2   91
332d10-11   63
332d10-e10   91
332e3-4   63
333a11-15   127
333a11-c3   92
333a14   91
333b1-6   91, 94
333b4-5   91
334c1-2   53
334c5   96
335c9   59
335c10   66
335d2   66 n.27
336a6-7   61
336c3-6   81
336e9-337a1   61 n.11
338b7   61 n.11, 63, 63 n.18
338c2-3   80
338c7-d1   27
338d6-7   80
338d9   80, 81, 81 n.4
338d9-339a4 [T18]   80
338e1-4   81
338e2-5   81
338e4-6   81
338e6-339a3   81, 81 n.4
339b9-10   81, 83

Index Locorum

339c1-2 82
339c3 82, 89
339d1-3 82
339d7 82
339e3 82
340b6-8 82
340b7-8 82
340c3-4 53
340c6-7 82
340d2-341a4 82, 89
340d2-6 82, 94
340d3 82
340d6-e3 82
340d8-9 90
340e1 82
340e2-3 111
340e2-7 82, 94
340e3 82
341a9-b2 59 n.2
341b6-7 81, 83
341b8-9 62
341c5-342e6 83, 89
341c6 91 n.3
341c6-8 90
341c7 90
341c10-d10 90
341d11-12 90
341d12 90
341e2 90
341e3 90
341e4-7 90
341e5 90
342a3 90
342a4-5 90
342a6-b2 90, 91, 91 n.4
342b2-6 90
342c1-6 90
342c4-5 90
342c10-d2 90
343a7-8 90
343b1-4 90
343b1-c1 90
343b1-d1 97
343b4-c1 90
343c1-d1 83
343c3-4 83
343c3-5 90, 123 n.10
343c4-6 87, 90
343c5 83
343c5-d1 86
343c7-d1 83
343d2-6 127

343d3 84–5
343d3-6 91
343d4 85
343d5 85
343d6 85
343d7-e1 85
343d8 85
343e1-7 85
343e3-4 85
343e4 85
343e5-6 85
344a1-2 63, 85
344a4 86
344a4-c9 93, 194
344a7 83
344a7-8 83, 86
344a7-c3 95
344a8-b1 83
344b1 85
344b2 86
344b3-4 85
344b5 85
344b6 83
344b6-7 83, 86
344b7 86
344b7-c1 86
344c5-9 177 n.4
345a5-6 59 n.2
345b8-347e6 89
345d1 91 n.3
345e5-6 91
346a1-b6 [T14] 65
346b1 91
346b8-12 91 n.5
346c5-7 91 n.5
346c9-11 92
346d5-6 92
346e8 92
347a3-5 92
347b2-4 92
347b7-10 92
347b10-c2 93 n.9
347b10-d8 [T19] 92, 126, 171
347d2-6 93 n.9
347d8-e4 93
348a4 59 n.2
348b8-c4 97
348b8-349a4 93
348b9-10 93
348c1-350c11 89
348d2-6 93, 94
348d3-350c11 93

348d5-6   63
348e1-3   93 n.11
349b2-3   93
349b2-350c11   93
349b8-9   94
349b10   61 n.11
349c7-9   93
349c11-d1   94
349d4-5   94
350a6-9   94
350a8-9   94
350b7-c5   94, 98
350c12-d2   94
350d5-352b5   89, 95, 153, 154
350d8-9   94
350d9-10   94
351a2-3   63, 95
351b1-5   95
351b7-8   64
351b7-9   95
351c7-352a10 [T20]   95
351c7-9   95
351c8-9   62, 95–6
351d3-4   96
351d3-352a10   99
351d4-5   13, 133
351d8   96
351d8-9   177 n.4
351e1-2   63, 96
351e5   96
351e7-8   64, 64 n.21, 96
351e9   96
351e10-352a2   64
351e10-352a10   96
352a1-3   96
352a2-3   96
352a7-8   63 n.17
352a9   96
352b7-9   63
352c4-d1   97
352c7-d1   96
352d1   63 n.17
352d2-354a11   89, 97
352e3-4   97
353a9-11   97
353c5-7   97, 101
353d4-7   97
353d4-10   113
353d9   11
353d9-10   97
353e1-2   97

353e1-3   66 n.27
353e7-8   98
353e10   97
354a1   97
354a1-2   97
354b1-9   93
357b1-2   187
357b4-d2 [T48]   188
357b4-358a9   188
357b6   188
357b6-8   197
357b7   156
357b8   191 n.12
357c2-3   191 n.12
357c3   156
357c7-8   190
357c8   190
357c9   190
357d1-2   191 n.12
358a1-3   191–2
358a4   188
358a4-6   109
358a5   191
358b1-359c6   188
358b4-6   64
358b4-7   110, 111
358b6-7   192
358c2-5   110
358c3   110
358c3-4   110
358c6-d4   187
358e2-359a7   114 n.8
358e4   110
358e4-6   110
358e6-359a2   109
358e7-359a1   63 n.17
359a2-3   109
359a2-5   109, 127
359a5-6   109
359a7   63 n.17
359a7-b2   109
359b1-2   190
359b2-3   63 n.15, 110
359b2-4   111
359b2-5   110
359b7-8   110
359b7-9   110
359b8   63 n.17
359b9-c1   110
359c4   110
359c7-360c5   188

Index Locorum

359d1-2   64
359e5-360a2   110
360a5-6   64
360b4-c5   110, 111
360c6-7   110
360c6-8   111
360d4-7   111, 111 n.2
360d8-e5   111
360d8-361d3   188
360e5-361a1   66, 111
361a1   111
361a1-2   111
361a2-5   111
361a6-b1   111, 187
361b2   63 n.15, 111
361b3-4   111
361b4   111
361c1-2   153
361d7   61 n.11
361e4-362a2   169
362a2   153
362a2-c6   153
362b2-5   127, 153
362d3-5   153
362d8-9   63 n.17
363a3-5   153
363a6-8   153 n.1
363a8-d5   153
364a1-4   153
364a4-7   153
364a4-b2   154
364a6   63
364b6-7   153
364b6-c5   64 n.21, 154
364c7   153
365b5-6   153
365b7   154
365c2   153
365c4   154
365d2-6   154
365d4-5   154
365d7   67
365d8   49, 154
365d8-9   154
365d9   154
366a3-5   154
366a8   62 n.12, 154
366b4-8   153
366c1-2   64 n.21
366d2-3   63 n.17
366d3-4   63 n.18

366e5-6   65
367a8-9   64
367b2-3   63 n.18
367c7-8   189
368a6-7   63 n.15
368b4-5   63 n.17
368c2-3   63 n.15
368c3-4   63 n.18
368c8-369a4 [T2]   9–11
369c1-4   11
369c2-4   102
369c9-370c7 [T25]   112–13, 147
369c9-376d8   4, 175
369d1-9   113
369d11   113
369d11-e1   113
369e3-6   113
369e3-370c7   138
369e6-370a4   113
370a4   120
370b1-2   113
370b1-3   113
370b9   114
370b11-c2   114 n.6
370b5-371e10   125
370c1   114
370c1-2   114
370c8-9   13
370e5-8   66 n.27
370e5-371b11   115
370e12-371a2   115
371d9-e4   115, 137 n.9
371e8-9   115
371e8-12   118
371e11-12   115
372a1-2   115
372a3-5   115, 118
372a5-b7   115
372b7-8   115
372b7-c2   115
372c1-2   115, 149
372d8-e1   116
372e3   115
372e6-7   115
372e8   116
373a2-d3   116
373a4-5   116
373d7-e4   115, 116
374a5-6   116
374a6   66 n.27
374a7   116

374b6-c3   116
374c1-3   114 n.6
374c3   59 n.4
374c8-d6   116
374e1-3   133
374e2   114
374e4   116
374e12   63 n.18
375a9-b3   32
375b11   13
375c10-d1   66 n.27
375e5   66
376c8-d3   117, 133
376d9-427e8   4
376d9-445e2   175
377c1-5   134
377c4-6   134
377e6-378a3   134
378a2-b7   134
378b2   134
378b8-c6   134
378c1-3   134
378c4-8   134
378c6   134
378c6-d2   13, 134
378d2-6   134
378d7-e4   134
378e7-379a2   169
379b3   134
379b5-10   134
379b11-16   134
379b16   134
379e3   134
380a1   134
380a2-3   134
380a9-b6   134
380b1   134
380b5-6   134
380b7-c1-3   134
380d1-6   134
381c1   134
381c2-5   42
381c2-8   66 n.27
381c7   63 n.18
381e6   59 n.4
382b1-4   43
382e8   134
386a1-4   134
386a2-4   134
386b5-6   135
387b5-6   135, 177 n.4

387d4-6   45, 135
387d4-e6   135
387d11-e2   135
387e10-388a3   45
387e11-388a1   45, 135
388d2-8   45
388d6-7   135
389b9   13
389c1-6   134
389d9   134
389d9-e2   136 n.8
389e12-390b4   134
390a2   134
390b4-c8   134
390d1-5   34, 35 n.8
390d1-6   32
391a7-8   64 n.21
391e1-2   66 n.27
392a10   66 n.27
392e1   63 n.17
393c5-6   133
394e8-9   63 n.16
395a3-6   62 n.13
395b4-7   66 n.28
395b5-6   63 n.17
395b9-c3   178
395c1   116
397d9-e9   125
398a1-2   63 n.16
398b3   175 n.3
398c1-5   133
398e1-399c6   138
399b1-3   32
399b3-4   42
400b1-c7   138
400c8-10   62 n.13
401b1-402a4 [T32]   137–8, 138 n.10, 166
401b1-d2   137
401c3-5   63 n.16
401d4-402a4   138
402a2-3   63 n.16
402a3   32
402a7-c8 [T3]   10–11
402d4   63 n.15
403b4   175 n.3
403e4-6   135
403e8-9   135
404b1-3   135
404b11-c10   135
404d5-6   135
404e3-5   135

405a1-b4   134
405a6-b1   135
405a6-b3   169 n.10, 176
405b1-3   135
405b5-c5   135
405c7-d5   117, 135
407a1-2   135
407b1   168
407d2-e3   117
407e1-2   63 n.16
407e1-3   135
408d8-9   117
408e2-3   117
409a1-2   117
409a1-b9   184
409e5   175 n.3
411a5-b4   32
411c4-8   32
412b9-417b9   163
412c3   163
412c10-d8   43
412c13   63
412c13-d3   163
412d2   73
412d4-7   73
412d9-e2   119
412e4-5   163
412e4-7   43
412e6-7   163
412e9-413c4 [T8]   41–3
413d3-4   43
413d9-e1   43
413e1   163
413e1-5   43
414d1-415c8   150
414d1-e5   150
414d4-5   150
415a2   150
415a4-5   151
415a7   150
415a7-c7   150
415c7-d1   110
415d2-3   150
415e8-9   151
416a2-6   151
416b1-c3   151
416b2   13
416d1   13
416d4-417b9   181
416d5-7   151
416d7-8   181

416d7-e3   151
417a1   151
417a6-8   151
417a8-b1   151
417b1   13
417b8   175 n.3
419a1-5   151
420a4-7   151
420b3-421b4   172
420b4-5   152
420b4-8   128 n.19, 151
420b8-c1   151
420d6-e1   152
420d7   59 n.4
420e1-421a3   152
421a4-8   151
421b5-c5   152
421d11-e2   152
421e1-2   140
422d3-4   181
423a3-4   63 n.14
423b10-c4   149
423c6-d6   150
423d3   13
423d3-4   121
423e5-7   146
423e5-424a3   146, 148
424a2-3   146
424a4   146
424a5-10 [T47]   185
424d6-425a6 [T47]   185
424e6-425a1   66 n.29
424e6-425a9   176
425b1-3   176
425b3-5   176
425b7-8   176
425c10-e2, [T34]   140–1, 176
425d1-2   176
425d2   176
425d3-5   176
425d5   176
425d7-e2   176
425e5-7   176
426e7   176
425e8-427a7   176
427b6-c5   176
427e1-2   63 n.18
427e6-10   118
427e7   116
427e9   118
427e9-472e5   4

428a10   118
428b4-429a6   136
428b5-8   163
428b7-8   118
428b10   136
428b12-e10   118
428c2   136
428c9   136
428c11-d3   118, 136, 163
428d3   118
428d6-7   136
428d6-429a4   163
428d10   136
428e7-429a3   118
429b1-3   135
429b2-3   119
429b5-7   119, 126
429b8-9   64
429b8-d2   119
429c1-2   175 n.3
429c7-8   135
429e2-3   62, 62 n.13
429e7   63 n.18
430b3-5   64
430e1-3   119
430e5-6   42
430e6   42
430e9   42
431a3-7   41–2
431a5-7   28 n.28
431b4-7   119
431b5-7   181
431d9-e2   119, 134, 181
431e4-5   13
431e5   119
431e10-432b1   181
432a7   119
432c4   63 n.15
433a1-b1   123
433a1-d9 [T26]   120–5, 127, 133, 146
433a3   120
433a8-9   124
433a8-b1   120
433b8-9   64 n.21
433c5   59 n.4
433d1-4   121
433d2   146, 177 n.4
433d3-4   123–4
433d7-8   64
433e10-434a1   126, 128, 203
434a3-434c11, [T29]   125, 133, 147, 166

434b6   123
434e1-2   63 n.18
435b1-2   155
435b4-7   155
435b6-7   155
435b7   21 n.5
435c1   21 n.5
435c4-d4   155
435c5   21 n.5
435d5-6   155
435d9-436a4 [T1]   5–8, 10–11, 19–20, 24 n.13, 40, 104, 168
435d9-441c7   195
435e1   21 n.5
435e9-445b8   193
436a8-c2 [T4a]   19, 24–5, 28, 122
436a9   25
436a10-b2   24, 123
436b3   24 n.13
436b9   22, 22 n.11
436b10   22
436c3-4   24
436c6   22, 22 n.11
436c6-7   66 n.27
436c9-d2   22
436d4-e5   22
436d8   22 n.11
436e8-437a1 [T4b]   19, 40
437b1   37
437b1-4   24 n.13, 35
437b8   21 n.5
437b8-c2   24
437c3   37
437d7-e6   24
437e7-8   24
438a7-b2   24
438b4-d8   24
438d9-e1   24
438e1-10   24
439a9-b1   24 n.13, 25
439b3-7   23
439b8-c1   23
439c3-d9 [T5]   25–6, 69
439d1-2   28
439d7   28
440a2-4   35
440a2   31
440a6   30, 31
440a9-d4 [T6]   28, 32–4
440b1   31
440b4   33

440b9   34
440c1   30
440c2   61 n.11
440c6   34
440c7   30, 34
440d1   40
441a3   33
441a5-b3   31
441b3-c2   34
441b6   34
441c1-2   34
441c2   35
441c6   21 n.5
441d7-442a2   9
441d8   21 n.5
441d11-12   123
441d11-442b4 [T27]   122–3, 128, 132, 136, 141 n.14, 146, 178
441e3-4   122–3
441e4-5   123, 141
441e7-8   133
441e7-442a2   166
442a4-b2   123
442a5   123
442a6-7   123
442a7-8   123
442b5-c3   135
442b10-c2   123, 135
442b10-d7 [T31]   132–3, 136
442c4-7   123
442c9-d2   21 n.6
442e1   126
442e6-443a11   126
443b4-5   10, 64 n.21, 128
443c4-444a2 [T28]   124, 132, 147
443d1-5   123–4
443d3   21 n.5
443d5   132
443d7-e1   36
444b2   123–4
445c4-7   12
445c6   104
449c7-d4   146
449d4-450a2   146
450c1-2   146
450c7-8   66
450c8   63 n.18
451a5-6   42
451c3-4   146
451d6   146
451d6-9   149

451d7   63
451d7-9   146
452c1-2   148
452d4-5   146
452e3-4   147
452e3-453a5   66
452e5-453a5   148
453a7-b5   147
453b1-4   146
454a1-2   65 n.24
454a4-8   180
454a5-6   147
454a8   147
454b6-7   147, 180
454c7-d3   147
454d5   147
454d7-9   147
454d10   147
454e1-2   147
454e6-455a2   147
455b1-2   147
455b4-c3   147
455b5   147
455b5-8   73
455b8-c1   73
455c5-7   147
455d3-4   147
455d4-5   147
455d8   147
455d9   147
455e6   147
456a1-2   147
456a1-5   73
456a4   72, 72 n.5
456a4-5   147–8
456c1   66 n.29, 175 n.3
456c1-9   147
456c10   147–8
456c12-d1   148
456d1   148
456d5-11   148
456e1-2   13
456e4-5   148
456e7-457a1   148
457a1   59 n.4
457a8-9   149
457b7-8   149
457c7-d2   181
457c10-d3   149
457e7-458b7   149
458a1-b1   65

458c3-4   178
458c6   175 n.3
458c8-9   151
458c9   151
458e3-4   63 n.18, 149
459a9-10   149
459b2   149
459c9-d3   134, 149
460a3-6   149
460a5   63 n.18, 149
460c1-3   149
460c3-5   149
460d8-e3   149
461b8-e3   149
462a2-c1 [T22]   102–3, 143, 145
462b4-464a7   13
462b5   143, 149
462b8   104
462c3-4   104
462c4   104
462c6   143
462c9   102
462c9-10   102
462c10-11   102, 102 n.7
462c11   102
462c11-d1   102
462d1-2   102
462d2   102
462d7   104
463a1-5   137
463a1-b2   134
463a10-b2   177
463b10-11   143
463b9-464a7 [T35]   144–5, 149–50
463c7   175 n.3
463d1-6   145
463d6-7   144
463d6-e1   150
463e1-464d5   143
463e2-3   145
464a4-6   144
464a6   149
464a8-9   145
464b5-6   145
464b8-c3   151
464c6   59 n.4
464c6-d4   150
464d3-4   63 n.18, 149
465d3-4   152
465d6-e3   152
465e5-466a2   151

466a2-6   151
466a5   128
466b4-c2 [T30]   128, 128 n.19
466b8-9   187
466c7   13
466c9   63 n.18, 128, 149
466d7   63 n.18
467b5-6   66 n.27
469b8-c2   154
469b10   63 n.18 149
469c5-6   154
470b6-8   125
470c1-3   125
470c2   150
470d4-5   104
470d5-9   104
471c4-7   164
472d9-10   116
472e6-544a1   4, 175
472e7-8   63
473a1-b1 [T39]   164
473b4-9 [T40]   165
473c3-4   165 n.4
473c4   165 n.4
473c11-d2   166, 166 n.6
473c11-e1 [T38]   163–4, 174
473c11-e3   50
473d2-5   174
473d3   67
473d7-e1   4
474a6-7   62
474a7-8   62 n.12
474c8-10   24
474c8-11 [T16a]   71, 167
474d1-2   72
474d3   70
475a5   70
475b5   72
475b5-9   167
475b8-c5 [T16b]   71, 167
475c2-4   72
475c4   70
475c6-8   72
475d2   70
475d4-6   61
475e4   72 n.5
476a1-8 [T10]   51–2, 56, 61, 68
476a1-9   23 n.12
476a7   56
476a10-d3   50
476b4-7   53

476b6-7   63 n.17
476b9-10   63 n.16
476c2-3   63 n.15
476c7   53
476c7-8   63 n.16
476d4   49
476e7   49
476e7-477b3 [T9]   48–51, 53, 60
476e10   49
477a2-4   53
477a3   60
477a10   54
477a10-11   53
477b1   60
477b6   64
477b6-7   58
477b6-9   59
477b6-10   60
477b8-13   54
477b11   58
477b11-12   53, 60
477c1-2   59
477c1-d5 [T13]   58, 59 n.4, 62
477c3   59
477c7   57 n.21
477d2   59
477e1   60
477e3   54, 60
477e7   54
477e7-8   58, 60–1
478a7   60
478a9   60
477a10   53
478a14   60
478b1-2   54, 61
478b9   52 n.7, 61
478b11   49
478c3   49, 53
478d5   61
478d5-6   50, 61
478e1-2   61
479a3   52
479a5-6   49, 61
479a5-7   54
479a9-b1   61
479b2-3   54
479b8-9   23 n.12, 54 n.7
479b10-c5   54
479c3-5   63 n.16
479c7   54
479d7   60

479d10-e4   63 n.16
484b4-5   63 n.16
484b5   159
484b9-10   63 n.16
484c4-d2   176, 178
484c6-d2   63 n.16
484d4-6   141
485a1-2   141
485a10-b8   158
485b1-2   159
485b2-3   159
485c6-11   141
485c6-e1 [T17]   72–3, 167
485c12-d1   72 n.5
485d3-4   159
485d3-e1   167
485d6-8   141
485d10-e1   141
485d10-e5   133
485d11-12   24
485e3-5   141
486a4-b13   178
486a5   158
486a5-6   142
486a8   142, 159
486a8-10   142, 159
486a8-b2   142
486a9   158
486b1-5   142
486c3-d3   167
486c7   62 n.13
487c4-d5   167
488a4-6   169
489c1-2   63 n.15
490a8-b7   159
490b1-3   54 n.16
492a5-b4   167
492b6-c9   167
492c4-7   167
492c7-9   167
492d2-7   167
493a6-c8   167
493c6   63 n.15
493c10-d3   168
493d5-6   167
493d7-e1   168
494c1-2   168
494c2   64 n.21
494c7-d1   168
495b3-6   168
495d4-e2   137 n.9

496b6-c3   168
496b7-c3   169
496c2   168
496c2-3   169
496c3-4   168
496c5-6   172
496c5-d2   169
496d2-3   169
496d2-5   169, 172
496d5-6   169
496d6   169
496e1-3   169, 192 n.14
497a3-7   169
497a8-d2 [T43]   175–6
499b4-c1   172
499b6-7   166
499b7-8   166, 166 n.6
500a5-501c3   11 n.23
500b8-c7   141
500c5   141
500d2   63 n.18
500d5-9   137, 142, 172 n.14
500d6   11 n.23
500d7-9   11 n.23
501c5-6   166
501c5-d6   166
501c6-7   11 n.23
501d1-2   167
501d2   72 n.5
501e3   4
501e6-502a2   13
502a5-6   166, 166 n.6
502b3-4   166
502e2-3   163
503a1-2   43
503a1   163
503a1-4   63 n.16, 163
503a5-6   163
503c8-d1   163
504b1   63 n.18
504b1-2   155
504b3-4   155
504b5-7   155
504c6-d3   162
504d1   155
504d6-e2   155
505a2   155
505a2-4   155, 156
505a2-b1   133
505a3   155
505a3-4   162

505a6-b1   156
505a6-b2   162
505a7-b2   156
505b5-6   196
505b8-10   156
505c6-8   156
505c7-9   200 n.41
505d7-8   156
505d7-9   157
505e1-2   156
505e1-4   157
505e2   157
506a6   53
506a9-b1   157
506c7-9   157
506d5-e3   155 n.5
507a1   62 n.13
507a6   63 n.18
507a7-9   52
507a7-b10 [T11]   52, 159
507b5   52 n.10
507b6   52 n.10
507b8-509d5   157
507c6-8   64, 157
507d1   157, 158 n.13
507d10-e1   157–8
507d10-508a2   157
507d10-508a3   158 n.13
507d11   157
507d12-e1   158 n.13
507e1   157–8
507e5-508a1   157
507e5-508a2   157
508a1   157
508a1-2   158 n.13
508a4-6   157
508a9-b11   160
508b6-7   64 n.21
508b6   157
508b9   159
508c4-7   158
508d3-4   158 n.13
508d3-8   158
508d4   158
508d10-509a5 [T36]   159–60
508d10-e2   64 n.21
508e2   159
508e5-509a2   158 n.13
509b1-3   64 n.21
509b1-9 [T37]   160–1
509c9-10   63 n.18

Index Locorum

509d4   57 n.23
509d6-511e5   54
509d10   55
510a1   55
510a5-6   170
510a8-10   170, 182–3
510a9   55
510b2   57 n.23
510b4-5   56, 183
510b5   56
510b5-6   56, 183
510b6-7   56
510b7-8   57
510b8   56, 183
510c2   57
510c3   57
510c5-6   183
510c6-7   56
510c6-8   57
510c6-d2   183
510d1   56
510d1-3   56, 183
510d2   57
510d5-511a2   183 n.2
510d7-e1   56, 183
511a4-5   183
511a5-7   63 n.16
511a8-9   56, 183
511b1   57
511b2-c2   183
511b3   56, 57, 180
511b3-5   56
511c1   57
511c2   57
511c4-6   180
511c6   57
511c7-8   57
511d7   55, 59
511d8   56, 57 n.23, 159
511e1   55, 55 n.18, 170
511e2   55
514a1-2   169
514a2   169
514b2   180
514b2-3   63 n.17
515c5-6   169
515c8-d1   63 n.17
515d6   170
516a2-3   62 n.13
516b5-6   62 n.13
516b8-c2   170

516d1-2   63
516d2-7   170
516e7-517a4   157, 170
517a1-2   170
517a4-6   170
517a5-6   62 n.13, 170
517a8-c4   170 n.11
517b4-6   169 n.10
517b9-10   170
517c1-3   158 n.13
517c5   61 n.11
517c6-8   170
517c6-d2   157, 170 n.12
517d6-7   170
517d4-e1   170
518a5   63 n.17
518b8-c1   158
518b9-c2   170
518c4-d1   157 n.11
518c4-d2   158 n.12
518c6-d1   169 n.10
518c9   161
518d5-6   158
518d9-11   137
518d11   137
518e2   64 n.21
519c4-6   171–2
519c8-d2   172 n.14
519c8-d7   171
519d8-9   172
519d9   63 n.15
519e1-520a4   63 n.16, 128 n.19, 172
519e4-520a2   63 n.16
520a6-d5 [T41]   171, 172 n.14, 175
520b4-5   171
520b8-c1   63
520c1-3   169 n.10
520e1-3   172 n.14
521b7-10   172 n.14
521d1-2   64 n.22
522a3-9   136
522a3-b6   137 n.9
522c1-3   179
522c5-8   179
522c6-8   57 n.21
522d1-7   179
522e1-2   64 n.22
522e1-523a3   57 n.21
522e2   61 n.11
523a10   39
523a10-b4   180

523a10-524d5   40
523b1-2   39
523b3-4   39
523b5-6   180
523b5-7   39
523c4-d6   39
523e3-524a3   39
524a1-3   39, 54
524a5-9   40
524b3-5   40
524b4   40
524c10-14   40
524d2   40
525a1-3   180
525a5-6   180
525a7-8   180
525b1-c6   57 n.21
525b9-c1   180
525b9-c3   180
525c3-6   180
525d2-3   180
525d6   180
526b5-9   181
526c11-d5   57 n.21
526e2   181
526e3-9   180
526e4-5   161
527a1-4   57 n.21
527a6-10   180, 183
527a10   180
527b4   180
527b6-7   180
527b8-10   180
527c1-2   179, 186 n.13
527c2   163
527c10   179
527d7-e1   180
527d8-e2   181
528a3   62 n.13
528c1-4   179
528d8   181
528e2-3   179
529a1-2   180
529a10-b3   180, 183
529b3-4   62 n.13
529c4   182 n.4
529c7-d1   181
530a6   181
530a8-b1   180
530b6-c2   180
530e5-531a3   183

531c1-8   181
531c2   180
531c2-4   181
531c9-d1   181
531e3-4   63 n.16, 180
532a1-3   181
532a1-d1   170 n.11
532a2-3   64
532a5-b2   181
532c4-d1   65 n.24, 180
532c6-7   161
533a10-b2   181
533a10-b3   181
533b2-5   181
533b5-c6   181
533c2   63 n.17
533c3   63 n.16
533d4-534a1   57 n.23
533d4-9 [T12]   56, 99, 140, 183
534a1-2   57
534a4-5   57
534b1   63 n.18
534b3-6   181
534b8-d1   181
534d8-10   176
535a6-7   182
535a11-b1   63 n.18
535d1-7   73
535d3-4   73
535d4-6   73
535e3-4   43
536d1   63 n.15
536d4-7   179
536d4-537a3 [T46]   179
536d6   180
536d9-e1   177 n.4
537a9-11   182
537b1-5   182
537b3   63 n.17
537b8-c1   181
537b8-c3   182
537c4-5   182
537c6-7   181
537c7   184
538c6-8   184
538d6-e4   184
538d6-e5   184
538e7   184
539a3   184
539b3   184
539b4   184

539c1-2   184
539c5-8   184
539d3-6   184
539d8-9   184
539e3   184
539e3-4   169 n.10
539e3-540a2   172 n.14, 184
540a4-9   184
540a4-b7   172 n.14
540a9-b5   184
540b1-2   184, 200 n.38
543c4-544a1 [T42]   174
544a5   193 n.19
544c1-3   4 n.7
544c2-3   106 n.17
544d1-2   166 n.6
544d1-3   104 n.13
544d5-e2 [T23]   104
545a2   40
545a3   40
545a3-547c8   4 n.7
545b6-7   40
546a7-b4   150
546d4-5   64 n.21
547a5-6   104
547c1-2   134, 177
547c1-4   177 n.4
547d5-9   137 n.9
548a5-b2   105
548a6   70
548c5-7   105
548c8-d4   69, 105
548d3-4   104
549a4   40
550b6-7   105
550e1-6   105
551a7-10   105
551d9-10   63 n.17
551e4   124 n.13
552a7-b2   106 n.19
552b5-6   102, 106 n.19
552c2-4   106 n.19
552d4-7   106 n.19
552e5-7   169 n.10
553b7-c1   70
553b7-c7   21 n.6
553b7-c8   105
553d1-2   33
553d1-7   33, 70
554a5-8   71
554c11-d3   21 n.6, 71

554d9-e2   26 n.18
555a1-6   71
555c1-5   106 n.19
555c7-d1   66 n.27
555c8   13
556a9-b4   176
556b1   42
557b4   106, 177
557d2-7 [T24]   107
558a10   107
558d4-5   71
558d8-559c2   28
558d11-e3   28
559a11-b6   28
559b3-4   63 n.16
559b8-c2   28
559b9-10   63 n.16
559d7-8   63 n.16
559e9-560a2   26 n.18
560b1   74
560d7   74
560d9-561a4   74
561a6-7   74
561b1   74
561b1-2   74
561b3-4   74
561b4-5   74
561b4-6   74
561b8-c4   74, 106
561c6   74
561c6-e2   74
562b7-c2   106, 177
563d6-7   107
564a7-8   177 n.4
565a1-3   124
565a6-7   63 n.18
565b2-3   61 n.11
566a12-b2   66 n.27
566d9-e1   168
567a6-7   106
567b1-2   64
567d5-7   106
567e3-5   106, 177 n.4
567e7-568a2   108
568d1   63 n.17
568d6-e1   107
569a1-7   177 n.4
569b4-6   106
569b9-c4   177 n.4
571d3   31 n.2
573a8   75

573a8-b4   74
573b1   75
573b6-7   74
573b9   75
573c4-5   63 n.15
573c9   75
573d4-5   74
573e8-574a1   63 n.16
574b4   61 n.11
575a1-2   75
575a2   166 n.6
575b9   63 n.15
575d2   108
575d2-e1   108
575e4-576a3   108
576a4-6   177
576b6-8   108
576b7   166 n.6
576b10   193 n.19
577a2   62 n.13
577a6   63 n.15
577b6-7   63 n.15
577c4-5   177 n.4
577d1-5   177
577d13-e2   75
577e1   75
578b11-c4   108
578c1   194
578c1-588a2   193
578c2   108, 194
578c5-7   194
578d7   194
578e1-579a4   194
579a1-3   177 n.4
579a5-8   194
579a9-b1   194
579b5-7   194
579b7-c1   194
579c1-2   194
579c4-d3   194
579d11   194
579e2-4   75
580b1-c11   193
580c1-5   193
580c7-8   194
580c11   194
580d2-7   195
580d2-583b2   195
580d6-7   24 n.13
580d6-581a1   21 n.6

580e2-581a1   28 n.29, 196
580e2-581c6 [T15]   69–71, 71 n.3
581a2-581b11   72 n.5
581b1   71
581c1-2   69
581d2-3   195
581e5-582a1   195
582a3-5   195
582b2-3   196
582b4   196
582c4-5   196
582c7-9   66 n.27
582c8-9   196
582d4-14   196
583b5   197
583c1-585a7   197
583c5   197
583c10-11   197
583c13   197
583c13-d1   197
583d3-5   197
583d6-9   197
583d7-8   198
583e1-2   197
583e4-5   197
583e7   66 n.29
583e7-584a3   197
583e9-10   197
584a4-5   197
584a7-10   197–8
584a12-b2   198
584a12-c2   189
584b2   198 n.28
584b5   198
584c3-5   198
584c7-9   73, 198
584d3-4   198
584d6-7   198
584d7   198 .29
584d7-9   198
584e8-585a1   198
585a8   199 n.35
585a8-587b11   197
585b9-c10 [T45]   199–200
585c8   200 n.36
585d7-9   200
585d11-e5   200
586a1-b4   200
586a3   198
586a5-8   199

586a8–c6   199
586b1   199
586b1-4   199
587a1-2   63 n.18
587d12-e4   69, 193
588b6-8   64
590c1-d7   137 n.9
590c3-5   61 n.11
590c8-d6   136 n.8
590d5-6   63 n.18
590e1-591a3 [T45]   178
591a7-8   63 n.14, 64 n.21
591e1-592b5 [T44]   176, 178
592a7   170 n.12
592a8   172
595b5-6   47
595b6-7   47, 47 n.18
596b4-8   56, 136, 139
596b10-d1   137 n.9
597a6   137 n.9
598b8-601b8   47 n.19
599a7-8   62 n.13
601b9-602b11   47 n.19
601d1-602a2 [T33]   139
601d8-e2   136
602c1-605c4   47 n.19
602c4-5   65
602c4-603a8, [T7]   37–41, 41 n.9, 43–4, 48, 55–6, 65
602c7-8   38
602d1-2   38
602d6-7   180
602d6-9   38
602e4-603a8   21 n.6
602e8-9   41
603a1-7   41
603a9-b3   44
603b10-c1   44
603c5-8   44
603c5-9   46
603c11-d6   45
603d5-6   36
603e4-6   44
603e8-604a2   44
604a9   44
604a9-10   44
604b7-8   45
604b7-c3   45
604c5-d1   45
604e1-6   45

605a4   45
605a7-c3   46
605a9-b5   46
605b7   44
605c5-6   45
605c5-606d7   47, 47 n.19
605c5-608b2   145
605c9   46 n.17
605c9-d5   45, 145
605d3-4   44
605d4   45
605d7-9   45
606a3-b5   145
606a4   44
606a7   44
606a7-8   47, 136
606b1-3   46
606b2   45
606b3   45
606b4   44
606b5-7   47
606b5-8   45
606b8   45
606b8-9   45
606c5   45
606d4-7   47
607a1-2   63 n.18
608d2-612a7   101
608d11-609b3 [T21]   99–101, 156, 160
609b9-d3   101
609d4-8   101
609d6-7   101
609e5-6   101
610c5-d4   101
610e10-611a2   102
611a10-b8   11
611d2-5   101
612a8-614b1   193
612c1-2   153 n.1
612c8-9   67
612e2-3   192
613b1   63 n.18
613c3-7   192
613e5-614a3   192
617d2-e5   137
618c2-3   64 n.21
618c4-5   66
619a7   63 n.18
619b7-c2   137
619b8-c1   137

619c1   137
619c3-5   137
619c5-6   137
619c8-d1   137
619d2-3   137
620b7   61 n.11
620c2-d2   124
621c3-4   66 n.28
Theaetetus
160e2-161a1   149 n.7
169a5   5 n.10
Timaeus
17c1-3   1 n.1
Laws
710b4-d5   166 n.6

Proclus
Commentary on Plato's Republic
I, 11.5ss   2 n.4
I, 12.16-19   11 n.22
I, 207.14-211.3   27 n.26
I, 207.28-207.2   125 n.16
I, 209.1-6   125 n.16
I, 225.3-227.27   26 n.18
I, 291.21-5   57 n.20

Thucydides
History of the Peloponesian War
II, 40, 2   124 n.12
IV, 75, 1   168 n.9

www.ingramcontent.com/pod-product-compliance
Lightning Source LLC
Chambersburg PA
CBHW080935300426
44115CB00017B/2829